CHARMING SMALL HOTEL GUIDES

ITALY

CHARMING SMALL HOTEL GUIDES

ITALY

EDITED BY

Fiona Duncan, Leonie Glass & Nicky Swallow

DUNCAN PETERSEN

This new expanded and redesigned 2004 edition
conceived, designed and produced by
Duncan Petersen Publishing Ltd,
31 Ceylon Road, London W14 0PY

17th edition

Copyright © Duncan Petersen Publishing Ltd 2004, 2003, 2001, 2000, 1999,
1998, 1997, 1996, 1995, 1994, 1993, 1992, 1991, 1990, 1989, 1988, 1986

All rights reserved. No reproduction, copy or transmission of this
publication may be made without written permission. No paragraph of this
publication may be reproduced, copied or transmitted save with written
permission or in accordance with the provisions of the Copyright Act 1956
(as amended). Any person who does any unauthorized act in relation to
this publication may be liable to criminal prosecution and civil claims for
damages.

Editorial Director Andrew Duncan
Editors Fiona Duncan, Leonie Glass and Nicky Swallow
Contributors Diana Johnson and Lucia Labouchère
Production Editor Sophie Page
Designer Tony Chung
Maps Map Creation Ltd

This edition published 2004 by
Duncan Petersen Publishing Ltd,
31 Ceylon Road, London W14 0PY

Sales representation and distribution in the U.K. and Ireland by
Portfolio Books Limited
Unit 5, Perivale Industrial Park
Horsenden Lane South
Greenford, UB6 7RL
Tel: 0208 997 9000 Fax: 0208 997 9097
E-mail: sales@portfoliobooks.com

A CIP catalogue record for this book is available
from the British Library

ISBN 1-903301-36-X

DTP by Duncan Petersen Publishing Ltd
Printed by E.G. Zure, Spain

CONTENTS

INTRODUCTION

IN THIS INTRODUCTORY SECTION

Welcome to this 2004 edition of *Charming Small Hotel Guides Italy*. Recently, we introduced some big changes which have made the guide more popular than ever with our readers.

• *Almost every hotel was given a colour photograph and a full page of its own. A few, on half pages, also have colour photographs.*

• *The maps were upgraded.*

• *The layout was changed in order to take you more quickly to essential booking information.*

We believe that these have proved to be real improvements, rather than change for its own sake. In all other respects, the guide remains true to the values and qualities that make it unique (see opposite), and which have won it so many devoted readers. This is its seventeenth new edition (including the first edition) since it was first published in 1986. It has sold hundreds of thousands of copies in the U.K., U.S.A. and in five European languages.

WHY ARE WE UNIQUE?

This is the only independently-inspected (no hotel pays for an entry) UK-originated accommodation guide that:

- has colour photographs for every entry;

- concentrates on places that have real charm and character;

- is highly selective;

- is particularly fussy about size. Most hotels have fewer

than 20 bedrooms; if there are more, the hotel must have the feel of a much smaller place. We have found that a genuinely warm welcome is much more likely to be found in a small hotel;

- gives proper emphasis to the description, and doesn't use irritating symbols;

- is produced by a small, non-bureaucratic company with a dedicated team of like-minded

So what exactly do we look for? –
Our selection criteria

• A peaceful, attractive setting. Obviously, if the entry is in an urban area, we make allowances.

• A building that is handsome, interesting or historic; or at least with real character.

• Adequate space, but on a human scale. We don't go for places that rely too much on grandeur, or with pretensions that could be intimidating.

• Good taste and imagination in the interior decoration. We reject standardized, chain hotel fixtures, fittings and decorations.

• Bedrooms that look like real bedrooms, not hotel rooms, individually decorated.

• Furnishings and other facilities that are comfortable and well maintained. We like to see interesting antique furniture that is there to be used, not simply revered.

• Proprietors and staff who are dedicated and thoughtful, offering a personal welcome, but who aren't intrusive or overly effusive. *The guest needs to feel like an individual.*

• Interesting food. In Italy, it's increasingly the norm for food to be above average. There are few entries in this guide where the food is not of a high standard.

• A sympathetic atmosphere; an absence of loud people showing off their money; or the 'corporate feel'.

Palazzo Ravizza, Siena

A FATTER GUIDE, BUT JUST AS SELECTIVE

In order to accommodate most entries with a whole-page description and colour photograph, we've had to print more pages. *But we have maintained our integrity by keeping the selection to around 300 entries.*

Over the years, the number of charming small hotels in Italy has increased steadily – not dramatically. We don't believe that there are presently many more than about 350 truly charming small hotels in Italy, and that, if we included more, we would undermine what we're trying to do: produce a guide which is all about places that are more than just a bed for the night. Every time we consider a new hotel, we ask ourselves whether it has that extra special something, regardless of category and facilities, that makes it worth seeking out.

TYPES OF ACCOMMODATION IN THIS GUIDE

Despite its title, the guide does not confine itself to places called hotels or places that behave like hotels. On the contrary, we actively look for places that offer a home-from-home (see page 10). We include small- and medium-sized hotels; plenty of traditional Italian guesthouses (*pensioni*) – some offering just bed and breakfast, some offering food at other times of day, too; restaurants with rooms; *agriturismi*, which are usually bed-and-breakfasts on farms or working rural estates; and some self-catering apartments, in town and country houses, provided they offer something special.

NO FEAR OR FAVOUR

To us, taking a payment for appearing in a guide seems to defeat the object of producing a guide. If money has changed hands, you can't write the whole truth about a hotel, and the selection cannot be nearly so interesting. This self-evident truth seems to us to be proved at least in part by the fact that pay guides are so keen to present the illusion of independence: few admit on the cover that they take payments for an entry, only doing so in small print on the inside.

Not many people realize that on the shelves of British bookshops there are many more hotel guides that accept payments for entries than there are independent guides. This guide is one of the few that do not accept any money for an entry.

Albergo Pietrasanta, Pietrasanta, Lucca

HOME FROM HOME

Perhaps the most beguiling characteristic of the best places to stay in this guide is the feeling they give of being in a private home – but without the everyday cares and chores of running one. To get this formula right requires a special sort of professionalism: the proprietor has to strike the balance between being relaxed and giving attentive service. Those who experience this 'feel' often turn their backs on all other forms of accommodation – however luxurious.

THE ITALIAN HOTEL SCENE

Our latest survey of Italian hotels for this new edition of the guide has left us in little doubt about just how much we like them, and how much we enjoy to stay in them. Quite apart from the fact that many of them are in wonderful buildings and beautiful locations, their standards of welcome, ambience, cleanliness, attention to detail and food are – on the whole – above average. Perhaps the main quality that sets them apart from other European hotels is the genuinely relaxed, informal yet sophisticated, atmosphere that you find in even the smartest places. It's easy to feel at ease; there's much less talking in hushed tones in sepulchral public rooms than elsewhere, and staff are, by and large, warm and friendly. They won't snigger (as the French might) at a guest's attempt to speak their language, however botched, although many Italian hoteliers and their staff have several languages. Standards, once set, tend to be maintained: there's much less fluctuation than in, say, English hotels, since the majority remain in the family for generations, even these days. Yet despite this reassuringly old-fashioned characteristic, Italian hoteliers have been quick to take up new technology and the vast majority, even very simple ones, have e-mail and their own excellent websites.

The food is another bonus of Italian hotels. While you won't find many dining rooms presenting culinary fireworks, you will find it hard not to eat at least adequately and at best extremely well in all the hotels included in this guide. You will come across little international food on the menu: the emphasis is on regional, seasonal dishes using fresh local ingredients.

Impressed though we remain with the warmth of welcome of most hotels in this guide, we can't pretend that there isn't a marked fall in temperature, as in most other European countries, in the cities. Florence isn't too bad, Venice is not great, but Rome is the worst; indeed two strong canditates for inclusion in this edition had to be discounted purely because the receptionists were so rude. But these are quibbles; by and large, we are delighted with this selection of Italian hotels. When we have finished an inspection trip, all we want to do is return.

CHECK THE PRICE FIRST
In this guide we have adopted the system of price bands, rather than giving actual prices as we did in previous editions. This is because prices were often subject to change after we went to press. The price bands refer to the approximate price of a standard double room (high season rates) with breakfast for two people. They are as follows:

€	under 110 Euros
€€	110-180 Euros
€€€	180-260 Euros
€€€€	260-350 Euros
€€€€€	more than 350 Euros

To avoid unpleasant surprises, always check what is included in the price (for example, VAT and service, breakfast, afternoon tea) when making the booking.

HOW TO FIND AN ENTRY
In this guide, the entries are arranged in geographical groups. First, the whole of Italy is divided into three major sections; the book starts with Northern Italy, then proceeds to Central Italy and lastly Southern Italy. Within these sections, the entries are grouped by regions. Some of these regions correspond to the administrative regions of the country (Tuscany and Emiglia Romana, for example). Some are combinations of these regions (Lazio and Abruzzo, for example). Some are broader – the North-West or the North-East, for example.

Within each regional section the entries follow a set sequence: first comes an

Area Introduction – an overview of the accommodation scene in that region, together with extra addresses of places which didn't quite deserve a full entry, or of places which we have heard good things about but have not yet been able to inspect and which might be useful if our main choices are booked up. Next come the full entries themselves, arranged alphabetically by city, town or nearest village. If several occur in or near one town, entries are arranged in alpha order by name of hotel.

To find a hotel in a particular area, use the maps following this introduction to locate the appropriate pages.

To locate a specific hotel, whose name you know, or a hotel in a place you know, use the indexes at the back, which list entries both by name and by nearest place name.

HOW TO READ AN ENTRY

TUSCANY

ARTIMINO

PAGGERIA MEDICEA
~ COUNTRY HOTEL ~

Viale Papa Giovanni XXIII, 59015 Artimino, Firenze
TEL 055 8718081 **FAX** 055 8751470
E-MAIL artimino@tin.it **WEBSITE** www.artimino.com

ARTIMINO IS A VILLAGE of some distinction, drawing visitors to see its museum and nearby Etruscan tombs. It also has a number of imposing buildings, one being a grand villa built by Ferdinand I of Medici in the 16th century, who was struck by the beauty of the surroundings. Now the outbuildings and servants' quarters of this villa have been converted into an elegant and peaceful hotel.

As befits its aristocratic pedigree, the atmosphere is classy, but unshowy. Furnishings are a stylish, unpretentious mix of new and old, and original features such as sloping rafters, chimneys and ceilings have, where possible, been retained both in bedrooms and in public areas.

A short walk across manicured lawns brings you to the restaurant Biagio Pignatta (named after a celebrated Medici chef). Its specialities are Tuscan dishes 'with a Renaissance flavour' (*pappardelle sul coniglio*, for instance – broad noodles with rabbit sauce), served on a terrace overlooking hillsides of vines and olives. The estate produces its own wine, which is reverently decanted at your table.

~

NEARBY Prato (15 km); Florence (24 km); Etruscan museum.
LOCATION 24 km NW of Florence; car parking
FOOD breakfast, lunch, dinner
PRICE ©©
ROOMS 37; 36 double and twin with bath or shower, 1 single with shower; all rooms have phone, TV, air conditioning, minibar; 44 apartments in village with own pool
FACILITIES sitting room, breakfast room, TV room, restaurant, garden, swimming pool, tennis
CREDIT CARDS AE, DC, MC, V
DISABLED ground floor rooms
PETS accepted
CLOSED 10 days Christmas-New Year
MANAGER Alessandro Gualtieri

Name of hotel

Type of establishment

Description – never vetted by the hotel

Places of interest within reach of the hotel

This sets the hotel in its geographical context and should not be taken as precise instructions as to how to get there; always ask the hotel for directions.

Rooms described as having a bath usually also have a shower; rooms described as having a shower only have a shower.

Essential booking information.

This information is only an indication for wheelchair users and the infirm. Always check on suitability with the hotel.

City, town or village, and region, in which the hotel is located.

Some or all the public rooms and bedrooms in an increasing number of hotels are now non-smoking. Smokers should check the hotel's policy when booking.

Telephoning Italy from abroad
To call Italy from the U.K., dial 00, then the international dialling code 39, then dial the number, including the initial 0. From the U.S., dial 001 39.

Postal address and other key information.

Children are almost always accepted, usually welcomed, in Italian hotels. There are often special facilities, such as cots, high chairs, baby listening and early supper. Check first if they may join parents in the dining room.

Breakfast, is normally included in the price of the room. We have not quoted prices for lunch and dinner. Other meals, such as afternoon tea, may also be available. 'Room service' refers to food and drink, either snacks or full meals, which can be served in the room.

We list the following credit cards:
AE   American Express
DC   Diners Club
MC   Mastercard
V   Visa

Always let the hotel know in advance if you want to bring a pet. Even where pets are accepted, certain restrictions may apply, and a small charge may be levied.

In this guide we have used price bands rather than quoting actual prices. They refer to a standard double room (high season rates, if applicable) with breakfast for two people. Other rates – for other room categories, times of the year, weekend breaks, long stays and so on – may well be available. In some hotels, usually out-of-the-way places or restaurants-with-rooms – half-board is obligatory. Always check when booking. The price bands are as follows:

€	under 110 Euros
€€	110-180 Euros
€€€	180-260 Euros
€€€€	260-350 Euros
€€€€€	more than 350 Euros

Tipping
Italian waiters do not rely on tips in the same way as in some other European countries (if lucky, they will get a share of the profits). However, Italians usually round up the bill if pleased with service.

REPORTING TO THE GUIDE

Please write and tell us about your experiences of small hotels, guest houses and inns, whether good or bad, whether listed in this edition or not. As well as hotels in Italy, we are interested in hotels in France, Spain, Austria, Germany, Switzerland and the U.S.A. We assume that reporters have no objections to our publishing their views unpaid.

Readers whose reports prove particularly helpful may be invited to join our Travellers' Panel. Members give us notice of their own travel plans; we suggest hotels that they might inspect, and help with the cost of accommodation.

The address to write to us is:

Editor, *Charming Small Hotel Guides*,
Duncan Petersen Publishing Limited,
31 Ceylon Road,
London W14 0PY.

Checklist
Please use a separate sheet of paper for each report; include your name, address and telephone number on each report.

Your reports will be received with particular pleasure if they are typed, and if they are organized under the following headings:

Name of establishment
Town or village it is in, or nearest
Full address, including postcode
Telephone number
Time and duration of visit
The building and setting
The public rooms
The bedrooms and bathrooms
Physical comfort (chairs, beds, heat, light, hot water)
Standards of maintenance and housekeeping
Atmosphere, welcome and service
Food
Value for money

We assume that in writing you have no objections to your views being published unpaid, either verbatim or in an edited version. Names of major outside contributors are acknowledged, at the editor's discretion, in the guide.

HOTEL LOCATION MAPS

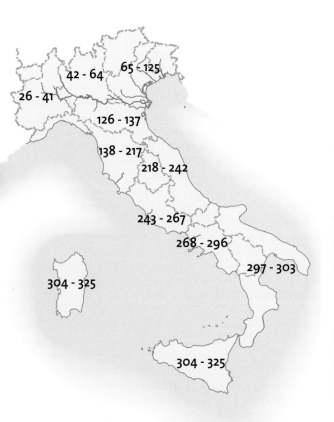

26 - 41

42 - 64

65 - 125

126 - 137

138 - 217

218 - 242

243 - 267

268 - 296

297 - 303

304 - 325

304 - 325

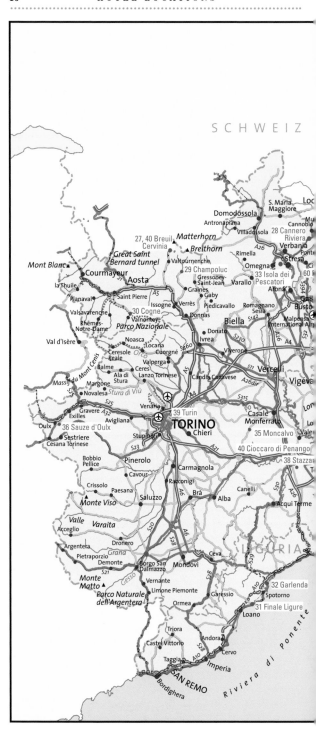

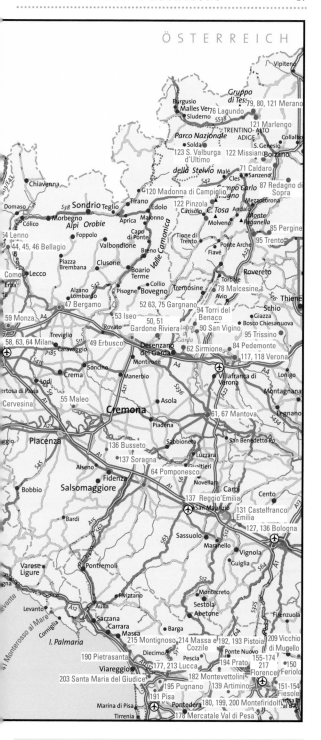

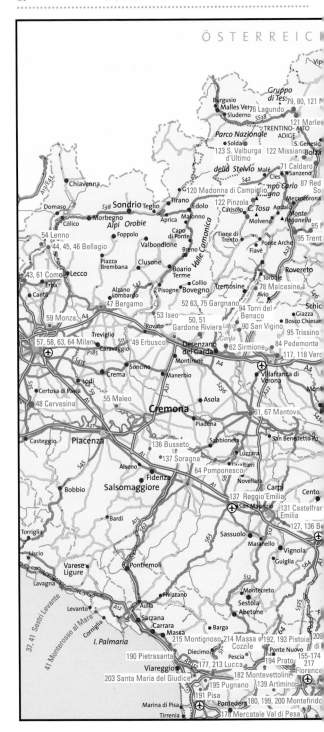

ÖSTERREICH

rpass/
del Brennerio
Campo Tures
Brunico
Dobbiaco
ovacella
S. Candido
70 Bressanone
iano
Carbonin
Misurina
Comelico
Superiore
83 Ortisei
119 Cortina
Sto Stefano
Comeglians
Tarvisio
an Osvaldo
d'Ampezzo
di Cadore
A23
usi allo Sciliar
Forni di
Ampezzo
Tolmezzo
allo Sciliar
Caprile
Borca di
Pieve di
Sopra
S346
Cadore
Cadore
Sella Nevea
Cencenighe
Forni di
Falcade
Agordo
Sotto
Venzone
tino di
Longarone
Gemona di Friuli
rozza
Fiera di Primiero
86 Pieve d'Alpago
SP13
Belluno
Feltre
Spilimbergo
Cividale del Friuli
Vittorio
FRIULI-VENEZIA
74, 120 Follina
Veneto
Udine
88 San Floriano del Collio
Pordenone
GIULIA
91 Solighetto
Palmanova
68 Bannio di Fiume Verlato
M
Conegliano
SS14
Monfalcone
66, 67 Asolo
Oderzo
Latisana
Aquileia
Sistiana
Bassano
Portegruaro
SS14
del Grappa
77 Levada
Grado
Trieste
Castelfranco
Treviso
Golfo
Cittadella
SS47
Veneto
SS53
Golfo
92 Scorze
82 Zerman
Bibione
di Trieste
nza
Jesolo
Caorle
rbarano
Mestre
106 Torcello
Lido di Jesolo
ino
81 Mira
Murano
Cavallino
lo
Porto di Lido
Padua
96-116, 123-125 Venice
Brenta
Laguna
Golfo di
nale
Chioggia
ste
Monsélice
Sottomarina
Venezia
Te
A13
Rovigo
Adria
Taglio
di Po
33 Ferrara
Delta
Gorino
Comacchio
Porto Garibaldi
Argenta
132 Castel Guelfo
Marina di Ravenna
a
Ravenna
Faenza
A14
Cervia
0 Brisighella
Cesenatico
Marradi
Dovadola
SS9
Cesena
SS16
Rimini
E45
Santa Sofia
Verucchio
San Piero
S. Marino
236, 241 Pesaro
Pelago
in Bagno
Novafeltria
Fano
Pennabilli
Stia
Bagno di
Macerata Feltria
A14
Romagna
SS16
Poppi
215 Pieve Sto.
Urbino
134 Montegridolfo
Senigallia
Reggello
Stefano
Borgo Pace
Urbania
Ancona
Acqualagna
Ostra

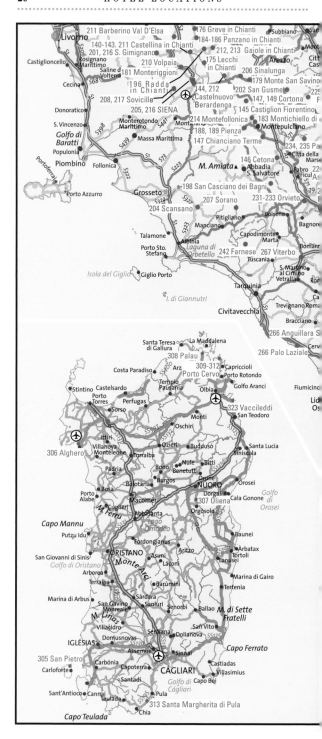

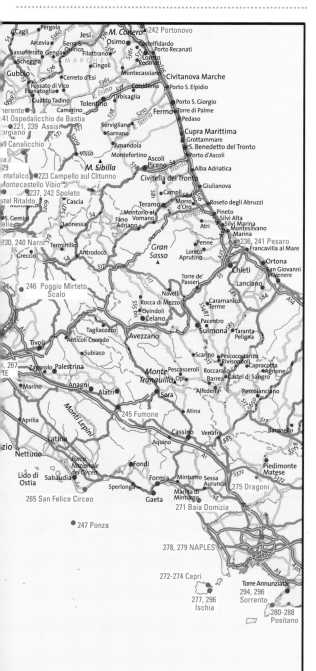

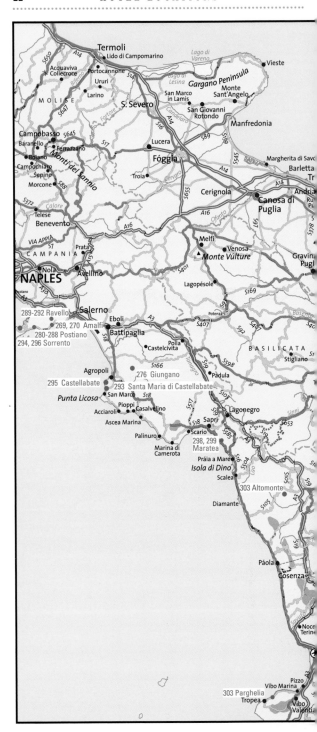

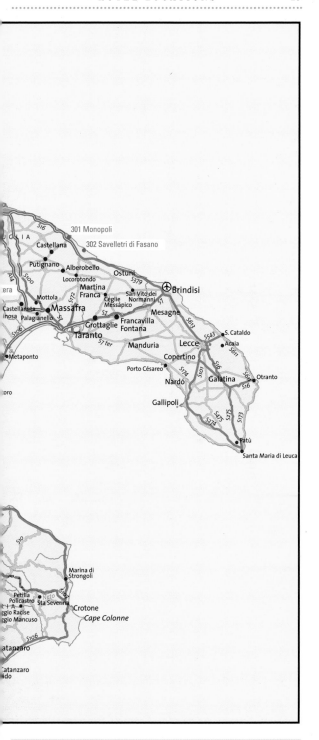

I. Strómboli

I. Panarea

udi

I. Salina

olian Islands

Milazzo

Golfo di Patti

Messina

Naso · S. Biagio

Oliveri

Barcellona

Ciampilieri

Villa S. Giovanni
· Gambarie

Acquedolci
· S. Fratello

Floresta

Castiglione di Sicilia

Francavilla
di Sicilia

Roccalumera
Sta. Teresa di Riva

REGGIO DI
CALABRIA

· Troina

Randazzo

Piedimonte

Bronte   Etneo

Monte

Etna

Fiumefreddo di Sicilia

320-322 Taormina

Adrano

Giarre

gira   Biancavilla   Nicolosi

Catenanuova

314 Carruba

Paternò

Acireale

Misterbianco

Aci Catena

Aci Castello

CATANIA

Golfo
di
Catania

Palagonia   Lentini

Grammichele

Carlentini

Augusta

Vizzini

Golfo
di
Augusta

Buccheri

Palazzolo
Acréide   Canicattini

318, 319, 325 Siracusa

Cómiso

Lido Aranella
Ognina
Fontane Bianche

317 Ragusa

Noto

Avola

amarina

324 Modica

Calabernardo
Lido di Noto

Golfo
di
Noto

· Scicli

Ispica

Marzamemi

rina di
gusa

Donnalucata

Sampieri   Pozzallo

Pachino

Páola

Cosenza

Lake
Arvo

Villaggio
Racise

Villaggio
Mancuso

Nocera
Terinese

Maida

Tropea

Vibo
Valentia

Palmi

Scilla

Gerace

Roccella
Iónica

Locri

THE NORTH-WEST

HOTELS IN THE NORTH-WEST

NORTH-WEST ITALY OFFERS three contrasting regions: the land 'at the foot of the mountains', Piedmont; the mountainous Valle d'Aosta; and the coastal Liguria.

Piedmont (Piemonte) does, no doubt, have its attractions, but they do not impress themselves on many foreign visitors, who tend to hurry across this large region on their way to the recognized glories of Italy to the east and south. To the traveller, as to the resident, the region is dominated by the city lying at its heart – Turin. Here is certainly no shortage of swish, large impersonal hotels right in the heart of things but we have at last found one of our sort: **La Maddalena** (see p 39). Of the swish hotels, the most attractive (and not quite the most expensive) is the **Jolly Hotel Ligure** (tel 011 55641). Of the more modest places, the **Genio** (tel 011 6505771) and the stylish **Victoria** (tel 011 5611909) are smartly modern, of moderate size and central, the former particularly handy for the station.

A little further away from the middle is the cheaper **Piedmontese** (tel 011 6698101). Within easy reach of Turin, we can recommend the **Salzea** (tel 011 6497809) at Trofarello, the **Panoramica** (tel 0125 8549) at Loranze, and the **Locanda del Sant' Uffizio**, featured on page 40. New to the guide this year is **Cascina Orsolin** (page 35), and **La Traversina** (page 38). In addition, readers recommend two places, **Locanda del Pilone** (tel 0173 366616) at Madonna di Como near Alba, and **Tra Arte e Querce** (tel 0173 792156) at Monchiero, south of Barolo – a 'fantastic' family-run restaurant-with-rooms 'in the middle of nowhere' specialising in truffles. In the region of the Italian Lakes, **Hotel Cannero** at Cannero Riviera on Lake Maggiore is a great favourite (p 28), as well as the **Verbano** on Isola dei Pescatori (see p 33).

To the north of Turin is the mainly French-speaking Valle d'Aosta, a steep-sided valley surrounded by some of the highest peaks in the Alps, and best known for its mountain scenery and winter sports facilities. It borders France to the west, where Monte Bianco (Mont Blanc) is the highest peak in Europe, and Switzerland to the north, where the Cervino (the Matterhorn) and Monte Rosa also tower well above 4,000 m. In this area we have chalet-style hotels to recommend in Champoluc (p 29) and Breuil-Cervinia (p 27).We can also recommend a new boutique hotel in Entreves near Courmayeur, **Auberge de la Maison** (tel 0165 86.98.11), an adjuct of the highly regarded restaurant, **La Maison de Filippo**.

To the south is Italy's highest mountain, Gran Paradiso, surrounded by a stunning national park named after it. In the middle of the park, in Cogne, we have another recommendation, **Le Bellevue** (p 30).

The third region is Liguria, a thin strip of mountainous coastline dominated by the Italian Riviera, for which we offer several recommendations. On the Riviera di Levante, south-east of Genoa, we include one hotel in Sestri Levante, one in Levanto, and one in the Cinque Terre village of Monterosso al Mare. We have not yet had the opportunity to visit a new bed-and-breakfast establishment, **Castello di Monleone** in Moneglia (tel 0185 49291) on the same stretch of coast, but it looks lovely, as does **Hotel Villa Edera**, in the grounds of which the Castello stands (tel 0185 49291). We can also recommend an old favourite, **Ca' Peo** at Leivi in the hills, family run with excellent food served in a charming dining room and very simple, dated bedrooms which don't suit everyone (tel 0185 319696).On the Riviera di Ponente, west of Genoa, we feature the **Punta Est** at Finale Ligure and, just inland at Garlenda, **La Meridiana**.

THE NORTH-WEST

BREUIL-CERVINIA

HERMITAGE
∽ MOUNTAIN CHALET ∽

11021 Breuil-Cervinia, Aosta
TEL 0166 948998 **FAX** 0166 949032
E-MAIL info@hotelhermitage.com **WEBSITE** www.hotelhermitage.com

WAKE UP TO A SPECTACULAR view of Monte Cervino (better known as the Matterhorn) through your bedroom window, then relax after a hard day's skiing with a massage, a mud bath or a book in front of a crackling log fire. This glossy Relais & Château hotel comes with all the trimmings: a health and beauty centre, small indoor pool, a sitting room furnished with vast deep sofas and chairs, and an elegant dining room, candlelit by night. It even boasts liveried porters and a heated garage. A low modern chalet built in traditional style, it has been done up with country-house furnishings and an appropriately Alpine flavour. Wood floors and walls, antique furniture and oak beams abound. There are as many suites as bedrooms, and all succeed in being cosy as well as luxurious, with pretty wallpaper, well-placed lamps, knick-knacks, mirrors and prints and some particularly handsome pieces of furniture. Our favourite rooms are the ones in the attic, which have sloping beamed ceilings and the most character.

The dining room, whose picture windows frame a blue larch forest, prides itself on a menu of simple local dishes accompanied by excellent regional wines. The hotel only accepts children over eight.

∽

NEARBY golf (500 m); Aosta (50 km).
LOCATION just NE of Breuil-Cervinia; garage
FOOD breakfast, lunch, dinner
PRICE €€€€
ROOMS 36; 18 double and twin, 18 suites, all with bath; all rooms have phone, TV, air conditioning, minibar, hairdrier, safe
FACILITIES sitting room, dining room, meeting room, health and beauty centre, swimming pool, lift, terrace
CREDIT CARDS AE, DC, MC, V
DISABLED access difficult
PETS not accepted
CLOSED May-Jul, Sept-Dec
PROPRIETORS Neyroz family

THE NORTH-WEST

CANNERO RIVIERA

CANNERO

~ LAKESIDE HOTEL ~

Lungo Lago 2, 28821 Cannero Riviera, Verbania
TEL 0323 788046/788113 (winter) **FAX** 0323 788048
E-MAIL info@hotelcannero.com **WEBSITE** www.hotelcannero.com

CANNERO IS ONE OF THE quietest resorts on Lake Maggiore and its most desirable hotels lie right on the shore. Only the ferry landing-stage and a dead-end road separate the Cannero from the waters of Maggiore.

The building was once a monastery, though only an old stone column, a couple of vaulted passageways, a quiet courtyard and a beautifully preserved 17thC well suggest it is anything other than a modern hotel. The emphasis is on comfort and relaxation, and the atmosphere is very friendly, thanks largely to the attention of Signora Gallinotto and her family. Downstairs, big windows and terraces make the most of the setting. The restaurant focuses on the lake, with an outdoor terrace running alongside. Bedrooms are light and well cared for with adequate bathrooms, and the restoration of a next-door house provides an additional 15 rooms plus some new apartments. There are gorgeous views of lake and mountains from front rooms, all with balconies, though many guests are happy overlooking the pool at the back – which, if anything, is quieter. By day this provides a delightful spot to take a dip or hang out under the yellow parasols. Readers' plaudits are legion: 'please be sure to rate it A+++!'; 'clean as a whistle, exceptional value, wonderful'; 'family and staff the most friendly and helpful imaginable'.

~

NEARBY Borromean Islands; Ascona (21 km), Locarno (25 km).
LOCATION in resort, overlooking lake; car parking
FOOD breakfast, lunch, dinner; poolside snacks
PRICE €
ROOMS 55 double and twin and single, all with bath or shower; all rooms have phone, air conditioning; 10 self-catering apartments
FACILITIES sitting room, piano bar, dining room, library, lift, 2 lakeside terraces, garden, swimming pool, tennis, rowing boat, bicycles **CREDIT CARDS** AE, DC, MC, V
DISABLED 10 rooms accessible **PETS** accepted by arrangement
CLOSED Nov to mid-Mar
PROPRIETORS Signora Gallinotto and sons

THE NORTH-WEST

CHAMPOLUC

VILLA ANNA MARIA
~ MOUNTAIN CHALET ~

Via Croues 5, 11020 Champoluc, Monte Rosa, Aosta
TEL 0125 307128 **FAX** 0125 307984
E-MAIL hotelannamaria@tiscali.it **WEBSITE** www.hotelvillaannamaria.com

IN A QUIET WOODED HILLSIDE setting close to the village of Champoluc, the main community in a steep-sided valley beneath the mighty Monte Rosa, this traditional shuttered chalet is as charming in summer, surrounded by mountain flowers as it is deep in winter snow. Its charm lies in the fact that hardly anything seems to have changed since the house was built in 1940 by the eponymous mother and grandmother of the present owners. In the rustic dining room, for example, polished wood covers the floor, ceiling and walls, bright copper pots gleam from shelves, and red-and-white gingham curtains frame the windows. Guests sit at tables with crisp white cloths, and are served simple but delicious country fare including *fonduta* with *fontina*, the local cheese fondue.

The cosy bedrooms also have panelled walls and, whether they look up at the mountain or down the valley, benefit from utter peace and quiet, spared from traffic noise as cars are not allowed up to the hotel. Guests must park in the private car park 50 metres or so down the hill, and then walk up to the chalet through romantic pine woods, while kind staff collect their luggage. The father and son owners extend a warm welcome.

~

NEARBY Verrès (27 km); Valtournenche and Gressoney valleys.
LOCATION off lane to right at end of village, signposted to hotel; car parking
FOOD breakfast, lunch, dinner
PRICE ©© (half board only in high season)
ROOMS 20 double and twin, family, 14 with bath or shower; all rooms have phone, TV
FACILITIES sitting room, dining room, terrace, garden
CREDIT CARDS MC, V
DISABLED access difficult
PETS not accepted
CLOSED never
PROPRIETOR Aldo Aquarone

THE NORTH-WEST

COGNE

BELLEVUE

～ MOUNTAIN CHALET ～

Rue Grand Paradis 22, 11012 Cogne, Aosta
TEL 0165 74825 **FAX** 0165 749192
E-MAIL bellevue@relaischateaux.com **WEBSITE** www.hotelbellevue.it

THIS HOTEL IS APTLY NAMED, nestled in the heart of a national park on the flat grassy floor of a valley dominated by Gran Paradiso and other peaks. Its 'beautiful view' stretches across meadows filled with wildflowers to the snow-capped peaks and most of the public rooms and balconied bedrooms reap the benefit. The Bellevue has been owned and run by the same family, with tradition as the keynote, since it was built in the 1920s. The simple decoration combines pale colours with the glow of wood, local artworks and antiques, lace and fresh alpine flowers. Open fires blaze in every grate. Home-baked bread is served with the imaginative regional meals by a cheerful staff, who speak French and wear national costume. In addition to the hotel dining room you can eat at the new Bar à Fromage, Restaurant de Montagne and Jeantet-Roullets' village Brasserie du Bon Bec. Start the day with the generous buffet breakfast to set you up for ski-ing or hiking. On your return, in the renovated health centre, La Valheureusa, you can try a hay bath or 'peeling on the hot stone'.

The neat comfortable bedrooms and suites, with cosy sitting rooms and fireplaces, have ultra-modern bathrooms, some with Jacuzzis. The three chalets – sadly minus the view – are ideal for families.

～

NEARBY Valnontey Alpine Garden (3 km); Saint Pierre (20 km).
LOCATION in centre of Cogne facing the Glacier; car parking and garage
FOOD breakfast, lunch, dinner
PRICE €€€
ROOMS 41; 31 double and twin, 7 suites, 3 chalets, all with bath or shower,suites with Jacuzzi, some with sauna; all rooms have phone, TV, minibar, hairdrier
FACILITIES sitting room, TV room, playroom, dining rooms, bars, indoor swimming pool, health centre, lift, terrace, garden
CREDIT CARDS AE, DC, MC, V
DISABLED 2 specially adapted rooms **PETS** accepted by arrangement
CLOSED early Oct to mid-Dec
PROPRIETORS Jeantet-Roullet family

THE NORTH-WEST

FINALE LIGURE

PUNTA EST
~ SEASIDE VILLA ~

Via Aurelia 1, 17024 Finale Ligure, Savona
TEL 019 600612 **FAX** 019 600611
E-MAIL info@puntaest.com **WEBSITE** www.puntaest.com

THE ITALIAN RIVIERA west of Genoa is for the most part disappointing: most of its resorts are dreary, and most of its hotels mediocre. Happily, both the Punta Est and Finale Ligure are exceptions. The hotel is converted from a splendid 18thC villa which stands high and proudly pink above the buzz of the main coastal road, overlooking the sea. Signor Podestà, who used to be a sculptor, has acted as resident architect since the hotel was first created in the late 1960s, and with great success. By preserving the original features of the house and adding to it in a sympathetic style, he has managed to preserve the atmosphere of a private villa. The interior is cool and elegant – all dark-wood antiques, fine stone arches, fireplaces and tiled floors. But with such an impressive setting, the focus is on the outdoor terraces, pool and gardens, with their lovely views.

Breakfast is taken (off Staffordshire china) in a sort of canopied greenhouse – a lovely sunny spot, surrounded by greenery. Other meals are served in a dining room in the annexe, where stone arches and beams create a vaguely medieval setting. You can choose between international and Ligurian dishes, including bass cooked with strong aromatic local herbs. The beach is only a couple of minutes' walk down the hillside.

~

NEARBY Finale Borgo (3 km); Alássio (26 km).
LOCATION E of the historic town; car parking
FOOD breakfast, lunch, dinner
PRICE €€€€
ROOMS 40; 30 double, 4 single, 6 suites, all with bath; all rooms have phone, minibar; some rooms have TV, air conditioning
FACILITIES sitting room, bar, TV room, meeting room, piano bar, terrace, garden, swimming pool
CREDIT CARDS AE, DC, MC, V
DISABLED access difficult **PETS** not accepted
CLOSED mid-Oct to late Apr
PROPRIETORS Podestà family

THE NORTH-WEST

LA MERIDIANA
~ COUNTRY HOUSE HOTEL ~

Via ai Castelli 11, 17033 Garlenda, Savona
TEL 0182 580271 **FAX** 0182 580150
E-MAIL meridiana@relaischateaux.com **WEBSITE** www.relaischateaux.com/meridiana

IF YOU'RE A SERIOUS GOLFER or keen to improve your handicap, La Meridiana might be the place for you – it has an 18-hole course in the grounds. Not that this gorgeous place appeals to golfers alone. Set in the Garlenda valley, but with acres of vineyards and lush gardens shielding it from the outside world, it is a rare breed: a chic Relais et Châteaux hotel without a whiff of formality. The owners and staff are caring and courteous. The rooms are in a rambling mixture of old buildings and new extensions, tastefully furnished with antiques, downy sofas, bright chintzes and checks. All the bedrooms and suites are fresh-looking and light with balconies on to the gardens.

Gourmets and gourmands alike queue up to sample the exquisite seafood and contemporary versions of traditional Ligurian dishes from the hotel's renowned kitchen, where only fresh, natural ingredients are used. The restaurant prides itself on a well-stocked and wide-ranging cellar.

For the energetic, there is riding and tennis at a nearby country club, and with a car you are in striking distance of the Italian Riviera.

~

NEARBY Albenga (10 km); Alássio (17 km).
LOCATION 10 km SW of Albenga, off A10; car parking
FOOD breakfast, dinner; lunch at pool Jun-Sep
PRICE €€€
ROOMS 30; 14 double and twin, 16 suites, all with bath; all rooms have phone, TV, air conditioning, minibar, hairdrier, safe
FACILITIES sitting room, TV room, dining room, bars, meeting room, sauna, lift, terrace, garden, swimming pool, golf, bicycles, mountain bikes, helipad
CREDIT CARDS AE, DC, MC, V
DISABLED access possible
PETS accepted
CLOSED Nov to Apr
PROPRIETORS Segre family

THE NORTH-WEST

VERBANO
~ LAKESIDE GUESTHOUSE ~

Via Ugo Ara 2, Isola dei Pescatori, 28049 Stresa, Novara
TEL 0323 30408/32534 **FAX** 0323 33129
E-MAIL hotelverbano@tin.it **WEBSITE** www.hotelverbano.it

THE ISOLA DEI PESCATORI may not have the *palazzo* or gardens of neigh-bouring Isola Bella (unlike the other islands, it has never belonged to the wealthy Borromeo family), but it is just as charming in its own way. The cafés and the slightly shabby, painted fishermen's houses along the front are, perhaps, reminiscent of a Greek island – though not an undis-covered one.

The Verbano is a large russet-coloured villa occupying one end of the island, its garden and terraces looking across Lake Maggiore to Isola Bella. It does not pretend to be luxurious, but it does offer plenty of char-acter and local colour. There are beautiful views from the bedrooms, and 11 of the 12 have balconies. Each room is named after a flower; most are prettily and appropriately furnished in old-fashioned style, with painted furniture; those which were a little tired-looking have been refurbished, and more refurbishment has been undertaken since a change of owner-ship. The quietest bedrooms are those away from the terrace.

But the emphasis is really on the restaurant, with home-made pastas a speciality. If weather prevents eating on the terrace, you can still enjoy the views through the big windows of the dining room. 'Excellent food, friendly staff,' says a visitor. Reports welcome.

~

NEARBY Isola Bella; Stresa; Pallanza; Baveno.
LOCATION on tiny island in Lake Maggiore; regular boats from Stresa, where there is ample car parking space
FOOD breakfast, lunch, dinner
PRICE €€
ROOMS 12 double and twin, 8 with bath, 4 with shower; all rooms have phone, hairdrier
FACILITIES sitting room, dining room, bar, terrace **CREDIT CARDS** AE, DC, MC, V
DISABLED no special facilities **PETS** accepted
CLOSED mid-Jan to mid-Feb
MANAGER Signor Gafforini

THE NORTH-WEST

AGRITURISMO VILLANOVA
～ COUNTRY BED-AND-BREAKFAST ～

Loc. Villanova, 19015 Levanto, Spezia
TEL 0187 802517 **FAX** 0187 803519
E-MAIL massola@iol.it **WEBSITE** www.agriturismovillanova.it

THE LOVELY OLD red and cream Villa Villanova is where Barone Giancoarlo Massola's ancestors spent their summers in the 18th century. Set in a sunny clearing at the end of a long drive, the property is surrounded by vines, fruit and olive trees, from which the family produces olive oil, wine and homemade jams. 'We so enjoyed our visit that we plan to return' a satisfied guest wrote to tell us. And so they did, enthusing on both occasions about their charming and rustic-elegant room with comfortable bed dressed in embroidered cotton sheets and small but stylish, well-designed bathroom. 'The buffet breakfast was delicious, including homemade fruit compote, preserves and bread as well as ham and cheese. There were lovely views from our room and the atmosphere was one of comfort and peace. The staff could not have been more helpful.'

Barone Massola has converted his villa and the small farmhouse behind to include eight bedrooms and suites and three self-catering apartments, each with its own entrance and terrace. There are no public rooms, but a communal terrace for breakfast and an indoor breakfast room for use during inclement weather. The position is perfect: close to the unspoilt seaside town of Levanto and near the Cinque Terre.

～

NEARBY Levanto (1 km); Cinque Terre.
LOCATION on private estate about 1 km outside Levanto; car parking
FOOD breakfast
PRICE €
ROOMS 11; 3 double, 3 triple, 2 suites, 3 self-catering apartments, all with bath or shower; all rooms have phone, TV, minibar, hairdrier
FACILITIES breakfast room, terrace, garden,
CREDIT CARDS AE, MC, V
DISABLED access possible
PETS not accepted
CLOSED Nov to Feb
PROPRIETOR Barone Giancarlo Massola

THE NORTH-WEST

CASCINA ORSOLINA
~ COUNTRY GUESTHOUSE ~

Via Caminata 28, 14036 Moncalvo, Asti
TEL 0141 921180 **FAX** 0141 917124
E-MAIL cabalcet@tin.it **WEBSITE** www.cascinaorsolina.com

IN SPITE OF THE INCREASE in tourism in this gentle part of Piemonte, there is still a dearth of nice places to stay, so it was a real pleasure to stumble on this delightful guest house. Around here, a *cascina* is a large, L-shaped rural building surrounded by its own vineyards; Daniela Cortassa's family has produced wine for several generations, but she only opened her house to guests in 2002.

Situated in rolling countryside just outside the small town of Moncalvo d'Asti, the origins of the building can still be seen in the two floors of tall arched windows which once housed the granary but which today allow sunlight to come flooding in. Inside, a tasteful, up-market country style predominates, starting with gorgeous blond wood floors. The huge ground floor living room has a big stone fireplace at one end and comfortable sofas and armchairs grouped around low tables; the breakfast room also has a open fire for cool weather. The bedrooms are beautifully and individually furnished with antiques, pretty fabrics and personal objets. Soft lighting gives everything a warm glow while Mexican wall hangings and oriental carpets add colour.

A well-furnished terrace, overlooking the pretty garden and lily pond, offers a peaceful spot for outdoor relaxation.

~

NEARBY Asti (21 km); vineyards.
LOCATION one km SW of Moncalvo, in own grounds; car parking
FOOD breakfast
PRICE €€€
ROOMS 9 double and twin, all with bath or shower; all rooms have TV, hairdrier
FACILITIES sitting rooms, breakfast room, terrace, garden, swimming pool, sauna, Turkish bath, small gym
CREDIT CARDS AE, DC, MC, V
DISABLED one specially adapted room **PETS** accepted
CLOSED Jan
PROPRIETOR Daniela Cortassa

THE NORTH-WEST

SAUZE D'OULX

IL CAPRICORNO
~ MOUNTAIN CHALET ~

Case Sparse 21, Le Clotes, 10050 Sauze d'Oulx, Torino
TEL 0122 850273 **FAX** 0122 850055
WEBSITE www.chaletilcapricorno.it

THIS TYPICAL WOODEN CHALET has a fairytale setting surrounded by pine trees on the slopes above the busy ski resort of Sauze d'Oulx and can only be reached by a steep, winding dirt track. In summer you can drive right up to the hotel, but in winter, you must park in town and be collected by snowmobile. Inside, it is as spick-and-span and cosy as a chalet should be: the snug rooms, brightened by fresh flowers, log fires and traditional wooden furniture, mostly handmade by Carlo himself. The dining room, beyond a tiny bar, is especially cheerful with its burnished copper pots and kettles, neat pile of logs beside the hearth and pretty blue-and-white tablecloths. The seven spotless bedrooms and bathrooms have recently been updated, and there are balconies for a select few.

In winter you can ski down the hill from the front door; in summer there are mountain hikes that beckon in all directions. Because they have so few guests (there are only seven rooms), the Sacchis go to great lengths to indulge them, not least with the delicious meals that Mariarosa produces every day.

After a long day's skiing or walking, this is the perfect place to return to. And as more people are beginning to realize this, you must book early.

~

NEARBY Susa (28 km); Briançon, France (28 km).
LOCATION above and 2 km E of town; car parking in summer
FOOD breakfast, lunch, dinner
PRICE €€
ROOMS 7 double and twin with bath; all rooms have phone, TV, hairdrier
FACILITIES bar, dining room, terrace
CREDIT CARDS MC, V
DISABLED access difficult
PETS not accepted
CLOSED May to mid-Jun, mid-Sep to Dec
PROPRIETORS Carlo and Mariarosa Sacchi

THE NORTH-WEST

SESTRI LEVANTE

HELVETIA
~ SEASIDE HOTEL ~

Via Cappuccini 43, 16039 Sestri Levante, Genova
TEL 0185 43048/41175 **FAX** 0185 457216
E-MAIL helvetia@rainbownet.it **WEBSITE** www.hotelhelvetia.it

THE HELVETIA'S CLAIM that it has 'the quietest and most enchanting position of Sestri Levante' is no exaggeration: it stands at one end of the appropriately named Baia del Silenzio. The hotel is distinguished by its spotless white façade, and the yellow and white canopies that shade its balconies and terrace.

Lorenzo Pernigotti devotes himself wholeheartedly to his guests and provides the sort of extras – including 15 gleaming yellow bikes – that you might expect to find in a four-star hotel; but the Helvetia remains small and personal; one satisfied guest says he 'felt just like part of the family'. (the hotel was opened by Signor Pernigotti's parents in what was their own seaside villa.) Another was delighted by the sophisticated key system which controls the lights and music in the bedrooms. The sitting room/bar has the air of a private home – antiques, coffee-table books, newspapers, potted plants – and the breakfast room is lovely, with views of the bay. Bedrooms are light and airy, overlooking either the bay or the gardens. The day starts on the terrace, with an unusually liberal help-yourself breakfast. Luxuriant gardens climb up the hillside, with tables in the shade of palm trees. Serious sunbathers can take to sunbeds. And there is a tiny pebble beach just across the road.

~

NEARBY Portofino (28 km); Genoa (50 km).
LOCATION at end of small 'Bay of Silence' beach; limited car parking and garage
FOOD breakfast
PRICE €€€
ROOMS 21 double and twin with shower; all rooms have phone, TV, video, minibar, hairdrier, safe
FACILITIES sitting room, TV/video room, dining room, bar, lift, terrace, garden, table tennis **CREDIT CARDS** AE, MC, V
DISABLED no special facilities **PETS** not accepted
CLOSED Nov to Feb
PROPRIETOR Lorenzo Pernigotti

THE NORTH-WEST

STAZZANO

AGRITURISMO LA TRAVERSINA

~ COUNTRY BED-AND-BREAKFAST ~

Cascina La Traversina 109, 15060 Stazzano, Alessandria
TEL 0143 61377 **FAX** 0143 61377
E-MAIL latraversina@latraversina.com **WEBSITE** www.latraversina.com

WHAT A LOVELY PLACE. You can hardly make out a building behind the great swathe of creepers, climbers, roses and geraniums that smother this delightful old farmhouse, set on a thickly wooded hillside, that has belonged to Rosanna Varese's family for 300 years or so. Shuttered windows peak out through the foliage and look down on rows of potted plants, cats sleeping in the sun, and flowers everywhere. In the garden there is a small, inviting swimming pool, surrounded by more trees, flowering shrubs and roses (180 varieties , plus 50 varieties of irises and 70 of hostas). In the lovely garden, best in late May, there are plenty of spots to find some shade and relax with a book.

Rosanna (formerly an architect) and Domenico warn visitors what to expect on their website, so no one is left in any doubt. Do you love dogs and cats? Do you mind not smoking in the bedrooms? Do you mind no television in the bedrooms (there are plenty of books and magazines)? And last, but not least, would you enjoy eating together with us and other guests in the evening? If the answers are yes, then La Traversina is for you. The hosts are warm and welcoming, bedrooms are homely and attractive, and Rosanna's home cooking, eaten on the terrace or in the conservatory, is superb.

~

NEARBY Marengo; Asti; Albugnano; Milan-Genoa autostrade.
LOCATION on hillside 2 km from Stazzano; in Stazzano follow sign for 2 km on unpaved road; in own grounds; car parking
FOOD breakfast, dinner
PRICE €
ROOMS 6; one double, one family, 4 apartments, all with bath or shower
FACILITIES breakfast room, conservatory, terrace, garden, swimming pool
CREDIT CARDS MC, V
DISABLED not suitable **PETS** accepted
CLOSED never
PROPRIETORS Rosanna and Domenico Varese

THE NORTH-WEST

TURIN

LA MADDALENA
~ CITY BED-AND-BREAKFAST ~

Via San Secondo 31, 10128 Torino
TEL 011 591267 **FAX** 011 591267
E-MAIL mv@iam-maddalena.com **WEBSITE** www.iam-maddalena.com

MANY SMALL GUEST HOUSES IN ITALY call themselves 'B&Bs' these days, but few really understand the concept. Maddalena Vitale's small but perfectly formed house is an exception, a true home-from-home in the heart of the city. Mirto, the small, friendly house dog, greets guests as they arrive at the elegant apartment on the third floor of a *palazzo* dating from the early 1900s, only five minutes walk from the main train station. The place has a very lived-in feel to it with framed family photographs, books, pictures, scented candles, ornaments, plants and flowers all over the place. There is a sitting area in the hall and a pretty breakfast room with cabinets stuffed full of pretty china and a big antique table where a generous, home made breakfast is served.

The bedrooms are all decorated and furnished as they might be in a private house with family antiques and attractive fabrics. One has hard wood floors and a four poster hung with filmy white curtains. Each room has at least one comfy arm chair and lots of individual touches such as Maddalena's embroidered linens and cushions. The bathrooms are as individual as the bedrooms with fluffy towels piled in the closets and Crabtree and Evelyn bath goodies.

~

NEARBY Piazza San Carlo; Egyptian Museum; Museo Nazionale del Risorgimento.
LOCATION 5 minutes walk SW of the Porta Nuova station; on third floor with lift; garage parking nearby
FOOD breakfast
PRICE €
ROOMS 3; one double, 2 twins, all with bath or shower, only one is en suite; all rooms have phone, TV, hairdrier
FACILITIES sitting rooms, breakfast room
CREDIT CARDS MC, V
DISABLED no special facilities **PETS** not accepted
CLOSED never
PROPRIETOR Maddalena Vitale

THE NORTH-WEST

BREUIL-CERVINIA

NEIGES D'ANTAN
MOUNTAIN CHALET

*Frazione Cret-Perrères, 11021
Breuil-Cervinia, Aosta*

TEL 0166 948775 **FAX** 0166 948852
E-MAIL info@lesneigesdantan.it
WEBSITE www.lesneigesdantan.it
FOOD breakfast, lunch, dinner
PRICE €€ **CLOSED** early May to
late Jun, Oct-Nov or mid-Sep to
Dec **PROPRIETORS** Bich family

I T IS THE WARMTH and generosity of the hands-on owners, the Bich family, that make this simple hotel in the shadow of Monte Cervino (the Matterhorn) a great place for a holiday. From the outside, you couldn't call the large chalet, with its pebbled-dash and timber façade, beautiful. But the simple rustic interior is welcoming. Signora Bich is the chef, expert at reviving old family recipes and robust traditional Mediterranean dishes. Her son is the *sommelier*: in addition to a carefully-chosen cellar, he oversees an impressive range of *grappa* on offer in the snug wood-panelled and rough-stone bar. The hotel is ideal for families, and excellent value for money.

CIOCCARO DI PENANGO

LOCANDA DEL SANT' UFFIZIO
CONVERTED MONASTERY

14030 Cioccaro di Penango, Asti

TEL 0141 916292 **FAX** 0141 916068
E-MAIL santuffizio@thi.it
WEBSITE www.thi.it
FOOD breakfast, lunch, dinner
PRICE €€€
CLOSED Jan, Feb
MANAGER Vito Adresini

S ET IN A GLORIOUS landscape of vineyards and hills, the *locanda* impresses from the moment you catch sight of its mellow-brick exterior and, when you step through the door, the interior does the same. Original features, including frescoed ceilings, have been preserved, and furnishings are a blend of antique and chic modern. Try to secure one of the bedrooms in the old cloisters. These have a small terrace or balcony overlooking the inviting pool and mature garden. Readers have in the past been impressed by the food, although a recent guest reports slipped standards in the kitchen (it no longer has a Michelin star) as well as housekeeping, since the Firato family sold to Turin Hotels International. Reports please.

THE NORTH-WEST

PORTO ROCA
SEASIDE HOTEL

Via Corone 1, 19016 Monterrosso al Mare, La Spezia

TEL 0187 817502 **FAX** 0187 817692
E-MAIL portoroca@cinqueterre.it
WEBSITE www.portoroca.it
FOOD breakfast, lunch, dinner
PRICE €€€
CLOSED Nov-Mar
PROPRIETORS Jacazzi family

PERCHED ABOVE A SPECTACULAR, almost inaccessible stretch of coastline, Monterrosso is the largest of the charming, relatively undiscovered Cinque Terre villages. This, their best hotel clings precariously to a rocky headland. It's a steep climb up from the beach, but the location is all-important here, with sweeping views of the rugged coast and clear sea. When you book, be sure to ask for a room with a sea view. The ones at the back are desperately disappointing. Inside, the furnishings are dated but comforting. The bedrooms (at least the ones at the front) are fresher and brighter, most with balconies, and their decoration has received attention in the last year or so.

GRAND HOTEL DEI CASTELLI
CONVERTED CASTLE

Via Penisola 26, 16039 Sestri Levante, Genova

TEL 0185 487220 **FAX** 0185 44767
E-MAIL info@hoteldeicastelli.com
WEBSITE www.hoteldeicastelli.com
FOOD breakfast, lunch, dinner
PRICE €€€
CLOSED mid-Oct to late Apr
MANAGER Anselmo Maurizio

WITH A SPLENDID LOCATION high up on Sestri Levante's wooded peninsula, this castle hotel has been highly recommended to us by a recent visitor. 'From arrival at the gate onwards, there were no disappointments. The whole complex has been beautifully restored to a very high standard. The gardens and wooded areas are most attractive and beautifully kept with extensive views of the town and coastline. The staff were welcoming and helpful, especially in the restaurant... The food was excellent and good value, and the breakfast terrace had superb views.' Two lifts take guests down to the private beach.

LOMBARDIA

HOTELS IN LOMBARDIA

LOMBARDY IS AN ENORMOUS REGION, stretching from the high Alps bordering Switzerland almost as far as the Adriatic and Ligurian seas. It contains Lake Como, with Lakes Maggiore and Garda forming its boundary in the west and east respectively, and has at its heart the glossy economic and industrial centre of Italy: Milan. Despite Milan's considerable heritage – notably a marvellous cathedral, important art collections and the world's most famous opera house – Milan's hotels are business-oriented and as big and glossy as the city itself. Surprisingly though, we have been able to find a clutch of excellent small hotels and in addition to these we can recommend **Antica Locanda Solferino** (tel 02 6570129).

Our main lakeside recommendations concentrate on Lake Como and Lake Garda. Bellagio is the main resort on Lake Como and the location of most of our hotels, with Menaggio a close second. As we don't have any recommendations here, try the **Bellavista** (tel 0344 32136) in Menaggio itself, or the **Loveno** (tel 0344 32110) in the village of Loveno 2 km away – a 13-room hotel with a garden and views of the lakes and mountains. In Argegno is **Villa Belvedere**, now run on bed and breakfast lines by the Cappelletti family, with wonderful views (tel 031 821116). At Varenna we have heard good reports of the little **Milano**, with just eight rooms (tel 0341 830298). Midway between Lakes Como and Maggiore at Cantello a reader recommends **Hotel Madonnina** (tel 0131 556 0764) as 'charming, good food, good value for money'.

On Lake Lugano, try the **Stella d'Italia** at San Mamete Valsolda (tel 0344 68139) and on tranquil Lake Orta the exotic 1879 **Villa Crespi**, now a beautifully restored luxurious hotel with health spa (tel 0322 911902). On tiny Lake Mergozzo, an extension of Lake Maggiore, **La Quartina** is a simple hotel with good food (tel 0323 80118).

As for Lake Garda, the main resort for the southern end is Sirmione, beautifully situated, with the massive Castle of the Scaligers, Roman remains and lovely gardens to visit, but also very conveniently placed for the main Milan-Venice motorway and therefore very busy during the day with trippers trying to 'see' Lake Garda, Verona and Venice in a day. (For our recommendations on the eastern shore of the lake, see our North-East section.) In Sirmione, you'll find the **Grifone**, a modestly-priced stalwart of the guide. Further north, on the lakes's western shore, there are more recommendations at Gardone Riviera and Gargnano. The latter has seen the opening of one of the most lavish new hotels in Italy, **Villa Feltrinella**, with a peerless waterside location and a wonderful Belle Epoque interior (tel 0365 798000). At Riva del Garda, surrounded by vineyards, is **Albergo al Maso**, a reader's recommendation (tel 0464 521514). On the smaller neighbouring Lake Iseo is another stalwart of the guide, **I Due Roccoli**, while a smart new hotel, **Relais Mirabella at Clusane sul lago** (tel 030 9898051) may also be worth investigating.

In Mantua, south of Garda, we have one recommendation, the **San Lorenzo**, and south of that **Il Leone** at Pomponesco. In Bergamo we also have one entry, **Il Gourmet**, and in addition can recommend **Il Sole**, a restaurant-with-rooms in the walled upper town (tel 035 218238); and not far away in Capriate San Gervasio, **Il Vigneto** (tel 02 90939351). In countryside north-west of Bergamo is a new 10-room eco-friendly hotel, **Casa Clelia**, with much rustic character (tel 035 799133). Last but not least, **Villa San Pietro** (tel 030 961232), an elegant private home in Montichiari south of Garda, sounds really lovely - we will report in the next edition.

LOMBARDIA

ALZATE BRIANZA

VILLA ODESCALCHI
~ COUNTRY VILLA ~

Via Anzani 12, 22040 Alzate Brianza, Como
TEL 031 630822 **FAX** 031 632079
E-MAIL info@villaodescalchi.it **WEBSITE** www.villaodescalchi.it

THE ODESCALCHI FAMILY built the splendid villa at the heart of this complex in Brianza at the beginning of the 17th century. Later Pope
Innocent XI took such a fancy to its relaxing atmosphere – or perhaps to
its private chapel – that he settled in himself. Set in 30 hectares of
grounds, the fine formal gardens are now shared (like all the hotel's facilities) with 32 apartments. The villa, complete with a mezzanine gallery in
its immense hall, has kept its period presence but has been extended to
add all the usual features of a modern hotel: floodlit tennis courts, swimming pools indoors and out, gym, Jacuzzi and Turkish bath, conference
rooms and most of the fairly standard bedrooms.

The attractive barrel-vaulted restaurant is housed in the original villa
where it offers a competent mixture of international and local dishes.
Highest marks here go to the presentation, excellent service and wine list.
Breakfast includes a splendid assortment of cheeses and cold cuts, fruit
and yoghurt. Como and Lecco are each 20 minutes away and it's a 40-
minute drive to Milan.

~

NEARBY Lakes Como and Lecco; Milan (50 km).
LOCATION 10 km SE of Como; garage
FOOD breakfast, lunch, dinner
PRICE €€
ROOMS 44; 39 double and twin, 5 single, 37 with bath, 7 with shower; all rooms
have phone, TV, minibar, hairdrier; some rooms have air-conditioning, safe
FACILITIES restaurant, bar, conference rooms, gym, health centre, indoor and
outdoor swimming pools, terrace, garden, tennis
CREDIT CARDS AE, DC, MC, V
DISABLED 2 specially adapted rooms
PETS small dogs accepted
CLOSED early Dec to mid-Jan
MANAGER Pierre Taillandier

LOMBARDIA

FLORENCE
～ LAKESIDE HOTEL ～

Piazza Mazzini, 22021 Bellagio, Como
TEL 031 950342 **FAX** 031 951722
E-MAIL hotflore@tin.it **WEBSITE** www.bellagio.co.nz

BELLAGIO IS THE PEARL OF LAKE COMO. It stands on a promontory at the point where the lake divides into two branches, and the views from its houses, villas and gardens are superb. The Florence is a handsome 18thC building occupying a prime position at one end of the main *piazza*, overlooking the lake. A terrace under arcades, where drinks and snacks are served, provides a welcoming entry to the hotel and the interior is no less appealing. Whitewashed walls, high vaulted ceilings and beams create a cool, attractive foyer; to one side, elegant and slightly faded seats cluster round an old stone fireplace.

Bedrooms have the same old-fashioned charm as the public rooms, furnished with cherry-wood antiques and attractive fabrics; the most sought after, naturally, are those with balconies and views over the lake. Meals can be taken on a delightful terrace under shady trees across the street from the hotel, watching the various craft ply across the lake. The hotel has been in the same family for 150 years, and is now in the hands of brother and sister, Ronald and Roberta Ketzlar; they both speak good English, and have created a gourmet restaurant and two new suites. A recent visitor was thoroughly enchanted.

～

NEARBY Villa Serbelloni; Madonna del Ghisallo (37 km).
LOCATION on main *piazza* overlooking lake; garage
FOOD breakfast, lunch, dinner
PRICE ⓔⓔ
ROOMS 34; 32 double and twin, 2 suites, all with bath; all rooms have phone, TV, minibar, hairdrier, safe
FACILITIES dining room, bar, reading/TV room, terrace
CREDIT CARDS AE, MC, V
DISABLED not suitable **PETS** accepted
CLOSED late Oct to mid-Apr
PROPRIETORS Ketzlar family

LOMBARDIA

BELLAGIO

HOTEL DU LAC
～ LAKESIDE HOTEL ～

Piazza Mazzini 32, 22021 Bellagio, Como
TEL 031 950320 **FAX** 031 951624
E-MAIL dulac@tin.it **WEBSITE** www.bellagiohoteldulac.com

SMACK IN THE MIDDLE of Bellagio's waterfront, the Hotel du Lac's stunning view of Como is matched by the Leoni family's pretty faultless performance in all departments. If you want to be picky you might say that one or two of the rooms are on the small side, or that the decoration in some of the bathrooms is a little dated, but there your list would have to stop. The smart marble-floored reception hall runs off an arcade where the café's wicker chairs offer a comfy spot from which to keep an eye on Bellagio's pavement society. The bright and inviting bar is also on the ground floor but the staff will bring you a drink (they have an impressive selection of cocktails) anywhere in the hotel.

On the first floor the windows in the unfussy restaurant run the width of the building to make the most of the panoramic view and the inventive menu offers a broad choice of excellent dishes – with cheeses and wines to match. The impeccably maintained bedrooms are simply decorated, the beds comfortable and, it ought to go without saying, the best have views of the lake. The rooftop terrace offers another vantage point, with deckchairs for sunbathing and awnings for those who prefer some shade. Staff are friendly, professional and helpful.

～

NEARBY Villa Serbelloni; Madonna del Ghisallo (37 km).
LOCATION on main piazza overlooking lake; car parking
FOOD breakfast, lunch, dinner
PRICE €€€
ROOMS 48; 41 double and twin, 7 single, all with bath or shower; all rooms have phone, TV, air conditioning, minibar, hairdrier
FACILITIES restaurant, bar, terrace
CREDIT CARDS MC, V
DISABLED not suitable
PETS accepted
CLOSED Nov to mid-Mar; restaurant Tue
PROPRIETORS Leoni family

LOMBARDIA

BELLAGIO

LA PERGOLA
~ RESTAURANT WITH ROOMS ~

Via San Vigilio 1, 24100 Bergamo
TEL and **FAX** 035 4373004
E-MAIL info@lapergolabellagio.it **WEBSITE** www.lapergolabellagio.it

L A PERGOLA IS RELAXED and informal, and very much a family affair. Don't come here looking for up-to-the-minute decoration, or even for clues on how they did it many years ago. But, set as it is on a little bay to the south-west of Bellagio, this simple hotel is away from the tourist bustle and there is a fishing village feel to the area. The hotel takes its name from the pergola that shelters diners at its enchanting lakeside restaurant, the focal point of the entire establishment. Really only a matter of centimetres from the water, this proximity is not just romantic: it is also reflected in the restaurant's enticing menu which features dishes based on fish from the lake, alongside a selection of non-fishy regional alternatives with wines to match.

A long passage, attractively flagged with black stone and housing a love-seat and a few pieces of furniture, connects the small reception with the restaurant's terrace. The bedrooms are reached by a large staircase which rises from the passage. The good sized room are simple and clean, and most have large windows with glorious views of the lake, and the best have balconies. There's no air conditioning, but each room has a serious-looking ceiling fan. It's only a few minutes walk to Bellagio.

~

NEARBY Villa Serbelloni; Madonna del Ghisallo (37 km).
LOCATION in village of Pescallo just SW of Bellagio, overlooking lake; public car parking
FOOD breakfast, lunch, dinner
PRICE ©©
ROOMS 11; 5 double, 4 twin, 2 with bath, 7 with shower, 2 single with shower; all rooms have phone, TV, safe
FACILITIES restaurant, terrace
CREDIT CARDS AE, DC, MC, V
DISABLED no special facilities **PETS** accepted
CLOSED Nov to Mar
PROPRIETOR Mazzoni family

LOMBARDIA

BERGAMO

GOURMET

RESTAURANT WITH ROOMS

Via San Vigilio 1, 24100 Bergamo
TEL and **FAX** 035 4373004
E-MAIL il.gourmet@tiscali.it **WEBSITE** www.gourmet-bg.it

BERGAMO IS QUITE A FAVOURITE with the foodies and, given the pretty stiff competition downtown, it must have taken a certain amount of confidence to hang out a shingle in the High Town with 'gourmet' on it. Although the emphasis here is obviously on food, the rooms are not to be sniffed at. They are all of a good size, extremely well maintained and, although modern in decoration, there are plenty of wood fittings and pieces of furniture to soften them.

The entrance to Ristorante Gourmet is airy and spacious, with a pale tiled floor and a small seating area. This is not a seasonal business: there is as much dining space indoors as there is outside on the large (covered) but uncrowded terrace. The atmosphere is gently civilized and unforced, with pleasant staff taking their cue from the charming owner. The menu is a refined document, wide-ranging and creative with a broad selection of regional specialities, with an extensive wine list. The whole place is dotted with lush, well-cared-for plants, and guests have the use of a lovely private garden when they feel the need for some real peace and quiet. A reader tells us he enjoyed his stay: 'room large, airy and well appointed, though somewhat marred by the view of the felt roof below; dinner excellent, served by waiters who breathed the spirit of the Commedia dell'Arte'.

NEARBY Brescia (48 km); Milan (50 km); Lakes Como, Lecco and Iseo.
LOCATION in Città Alta (High Town); car parking
FOOD breakfast, lunch, dinner; room service
PRICE €
ROOMS 11; 2 double, 7 twin, 3 with bath, 6 with shower, 1 single with shower, 1 suite with bath; all rooms have phone, TV, air conditioning, minibar, hairdrier
FACILITIES restaurant, bar, garden
CREDIT CARDS AE, DC, MC, V
DISABLED no special facilities **PETS** not accepted
CLOSED late Dec to early Jan
PROPRIETOR Aldo Battista Beretta

LOMBARDIA

CASTELLO DI SAN GAUDENZIO

~ CONVERTED CASTLE ~

Loc. San Gaudenzio, 27050 Cervesina, Pavia
TEL 0383 3331 **FAX** 0383 333409
E-MAIL info@castellosangaudenzio.com **WEBSITE** www.castellosangaudenzio.com

SET IN FORMAL GARDENS less than 60 km from Milan, this spacious and elegant 15thC *castello* has been owned over the years by a succession of smart Italian families and has the ivy, walls, towers, gateways, statuary and other embellishments to prove it. Times have changed: the horses are now gone from the stables and have been replaced by an indoor swimming pool and solarium, and a spectacular barrel vault has been turned into a conference room. Period furniture is watched over by ancestral portraits, and red and black marble fireplaces remind you that wood-burning can be done in considerable style.

Most of the bedrooms are brand new, with handsome bathrooms to match, but their pale striped wallpapers and hangings, polished parquet or stone floors, panelled and frescoed ceilings and light, elegant furniture have successfully integrated them with the well-restored older portions of the castle. Almost all look out over the garden. There are three suites, the most baronial (and expensive) of which occupies two stories of a tower.

The restaurant offers Italian and international dishes and the wines on their list include some specially bottled for the *castello*. The staff are professional and helpful.

~

NEARBY Voghera (6 km); Pavia (25 km); Milan (56 km).
LOCATION 6 km NW of Voghera, exit Casei Gerola from the 'Autostrada dei Fiori'; car parking
FOOD breakfast, lunch, dinner
PRICE €€€
ROOMS 45; 35 double and twin, 7 single, 3 suites, all with bath or shower; all rooms have phone, TV, minibar, safe, hairdrier; some rooms have air conditioning
FACILITIES sitting rooms, dining room, conference rooms, bar, indoor swimming pool, solarium, lift, garden **CREDIT CARDS** AE, MC, V
DISABLED 2 specially adapted rooms **PETS** not accepted
CLOSED restaurant Tue
MANAGER Pierangelo Bergaglio

LOMBARDIA

ERBUSCO

L'ALBERETA

~ COUNTRY VILLA ~

Via Vittorio Emanuele 11, 25030 Erbusco, Brescia
TEL 030 7760550 **FAX** 030 7760573
E-MAIL albereta@albereta.it **WEBSITE** www.terramoretti.it

IN THE MIDDLE OF THE famous vineyards of Francioforta, L'Albereta is an ancient manor which has had a very elegant and upmarket new life breathed into it. Home of the Moretti family, who still own it, this (Relais & Châteaux) villa is so smart that, unless they have met you at the station or airport, you might just consider nipping through a car-wash before driving up to the front door. But you needn't bother, because the staff here are very professional though not in the least precious. You will also find muted marble, arches, parquet, wrought iron, chintz, beams, flowers and vineyards as far as the eye can see. Virtually everything has been put here to please you and this includes Gualtiero Marchesi's double-starred restaurant which is as much of a draw as the stunning modern bedrooms. His kitchen is a symphony of stainless steel, copper and starched white chefs' uniforms. If you feel an urgent need to work off the effects of a particularly good dinner, you can either play tennis or get your exercise flitting between the Jacuzzi, the sauna and the solarium. Last but not least, just in case you are thinking of arriving by helicopter, L'Albereta helpfully publishes its GPS co-ordinates so that your navigation system can deliver you with pinpoint precision.

~

NEARBY Brescia (20 km); Bergamo (30 km).
LOCATION 3 km N of A4 Milan-Venice motorway (Rovato exit); car parking
FOOD breakfast, lunch, dinner; room service
PRICE €€€€
ROOMS 41; 25 double, 10 twin, 32 with bath, 3 with shower, 3 single with shower, 3 suites with bath; all rooms have phone, TV, air conditioning, minibar, hairdrier, safe
FACILITIES sitting rooms, billiard room, restaurant, bars, meeting rooms, health and fitness centre, indoor swimming pool, garden, tennis, helipad
CREDIT CARDS AE, DC, MC, V
DISABLED not suitable **PETS** not accepted
CLOSED never
PROPRIETORS Moretti family

LOMBARDIA

GARDONE RIVIERA

VILLA FIORDALISO
∼ LAKESIDE RESTAURANTS WITH ROOMS ∼

Corso Zanardelli 132, 25083 Gardone Riviera, Brescia
TEL 0365 20158 **FAX** 0365 290011
E-MAIL info@villafiordaliso.it **WEBSITE** villafiordaliso.it

MICHELIN-STARRED VILLA FIORDALISO has been well known as one of the best restaurants in Northern Italy for some years, but it is also a chic and romantic small hotel. Built in 1902, the pale pink and white lakeside villa was home to Gabriele d'Annunzio, and later to Claretta Petacci, Mussolini's mistress. Inside, the intricately carved wood and marble work on walls, floors and doorways and the splendid gold and frescoed ceilings are the perfectly preserved remnants of another age. A magnificent Venetian-style marble staircase, with columns and delicate wrought iron-work leads from the reception hall at garden level to the intimate first-floor restaurant and up to the seven luxurious bedrooms. Three of these have been left with their original furniture and decoration. The Claretta suite, a room of impressive dimensions with terrace and lake view, has a stunning marble bathroom. Other rooms are lighter in style with fresh wallpapers and fabrics.

The shady garden, bordering the lake (and, unfortunately, the main road), is a wonderful setting for the elegant summer restaurant, immaculately decked out in a terracotta and white colour scheme.

∼

NEARBY Brescia (40 km); Sirmione (35 km).
LOCATION on SS572, 3 km NE of Salò; ample car parking
FOOD breakfast, lunch, dinner
PRICE €€€€
ROOMS 7; 6 double, one suite, all with bath or shower; all rooms have phone, TV, air conditioning, minibar
FACILITIES sitting room, dining room, tower with bar, terraces, garden
CREDIT CARDS AE, DC, MC, V
DISABLED no special facilities
PETS not accepted
CLOSED mid-Nov to Feb; restaurant Mon, Tues lunch
PROPRIETORS Tosetti family

LOMBARDIA

GARDONE RIVIERA

VILLA DEL SOGNO
~ LAKESIDE VILLA ~

Via Zanardelli 107, 25083 Gardone Riviera, Brescia
TEL 0365 290181 **FAX** 0365 290230
E-MAIL info@villadelsogno.it **WEBSITE** www.villadelsogno.it

BUILT IN 1904 AS THE HOLIDAY HOME of an Austrian silk industrialist, this imposing villa became a hotel in 1938. Like so many of the hotels around Lake Garda, it has an amazing position, above the lake but near enough to feel part of the lakeside scene. It is approached by a long winding drive and cradled in exotic gardens, where we stumbled upon two little neoclassical temples. An extension added in the 1980s contains some rather ordinary rooms, including the reception (disappointing when you first arrive). But go through to the wood-panelled hall and staircase and you'll find much more character. The huge wooden fireplace and painted ceramic tiles reveal the villa's Austrian heritage, only slightly at odds with the stone arches, Grecian urns, and other neoclassical flourishes.

Armchairs in cheerful floral prints and a bar at one end make the sitting room especially congenial. There is also a refined restaurant in two rooms, where the parquet floor gleams almost as much as the silver candlesticks. Upstairs, there are several enormous suites, furnished traditionally. Rooms in the new wing are lighter with their own terraces. Prices are steep; reports please.

~

NEARBY beach (300 m); Brescia (50 km).
LOCATION 2 km N of Gardone, off SS45; car parking
FOOD breakfast, lunch, dinner
PRICE €€€€
ROOMS 32; 25 double and twin, 20 with bath, 5 with shower, 7 suites with bath; all rooms have phone, TV, air conditioning, hairdrier
FACILITIES sitting room/bar, dining room, health centre, lift, terrace, garden, swimming pool, tennis
CREDIT CARDS AE, DC, MC, V
DISABLED no special facilities
PETS accepted
CLOSED mid-Oct to end Mar (or Easter if earlier)
PROPRIETORS Calderan family

LOMBARDIA

GARGNANO

VILLA GIULIA

~LAKESIDE HOTEL ~

Viale Rimembranza 20, 25084 Gargnano, Lago di Garda, Brescia
TEL 0365 71022/71289 **FAX** 0365 72774
E-MAIL info@villagiulia.it **WEBSITE** www.villagiulia.it

ONCE A SIMPLE PENSIONE, Villa Giulia is a beautiful, spacious house, built over a hundred years ago in Victorian style with Gothic touches. The Bombardelli family has been here for fifty years, and have gradually upgraded their hotel to become one of the most delightful places to stay on Lake Garda.

For a start, it has a wonderful location, with gardens and terraces running practically on the water's edge. Inside, light and airy rooms lead off handsome corridors – a beautiful dining room with Murano chandeliers, gold walls and elegant seats; a civilized sitting room with Victorian armchairs; and bedrooms which range from light and modern to large rooms with timbered ceilings, antiques and balconies overlooking the garden and lake. The rooms in the rear annexe are less appealing, lacking view and air conditioning; other rooms are in three garden chalets. At garden level a second, simpler dining room opens out on to a terrace with ample space and gorgeous views. At any time of day, it is a lovely spot to linger among the palm trees and watch the boats plying the blue waters of Garda. The beautiful swimming pool is an added bonus.

~

NEARBY ferry services to villages and towns around Lake Garda.
LOCATION 150 m from middle of resort, with garden and terrace down to lake; car parking
FOOD breakfast, lunch, dinner
PRICE ©©©
ROOMS 22 double and twin, one single, all with bath or shower; all rooms have phone, TV, minibar, safe, hairdrier; most have air conditioning
FACILITIES dining room, veranda taverna, sitting room, TV room, terrace, beach, swimming pool, sauna
CREDIT CARDS AE, DC, MC, V
DISABLED access possible **PETS** accepted
CLOSED mid-Oct to Apr
PROPRIETORS Bombardelli family

LOMBARDIA

ISEO

I DUE ROCCOLI
~ MOUNTAIN INN ~

Via Silvio Bonomelli, 25049 Iseo, Brescia
TEL 030 9822977 **FAX** 030 9822980
E-MAIL relais@idueroccoli.com **WEBSITE** www.idueroccoli.com

L AKE ISEO IS IN THE MISTY, southernmost foothills of the Alps. Sixty miles one way would take you into Switzerland and it is not much further in another to reach Austria. The lake's principal island, Monteisola, is the largest on any European lake and home to about 2,000 people. Between the southern tip of the lake and the *autostrada* connecting Milan with Venice lies the Franciacorta, a region highly respected for the quality of its wines. Up a winding mountain road to the south-east of the lake, elegant and tranquil in its carefully tended park, lies I Due Roccoli. Built of stone, and beautifully decorated inside, here is a place to rest and recharge batteries. Simply to praise the views is selling the place short because even the swimming pool has one, and from the moment you spot the vases of fresh roses on each of the tables on the fabulous terrace you just know that you have come to the right place.

Fish from the lake, organically-grown produce from their own gardens and home-cured ham all feature on the short but well-balanced menu and you will dine by candlelight. The spacious and spotless rooms are decorated in modern style with fine prints hanging on the walls. The staff are every bit as charming as their hotel. Our readers concur: 'maybe the best view anywhere I have ever been'; 'an amazing bargain'; 'great food'.

~

NEARBY Brescia (20 km); Lakes Idro and Garda.
LOCATION 4 km SE of Iseo up a mountain road; car parking
FOOD breakfast, lunch, dinner
PRICE €€
ROOMS 19; 15 double and twin, one single, 3 suites, all with bath; all rooms have phone, TV, minibar, hairdrier, safe
FACILITIES sitting room, bar, dining room, garden, swimming pool, tennis
CREDIT CARDS AE, DC, MC, V
DISABLED access possible **PETS** accepted
CLOSED Nov to mid-Mar
PROPRIETOR Guido Anessi

LOMBARDIA

LENNO

SAN GIORGIO

~ LAKESIDE HOTEL ~

Via Regina 81, Lenno, 22019 Tremezzo Como
TEL 0344 40415 **FAX** 0344 41591

THIS LARGE WHITE 1920s VILLA on the shores of Lake Como stands out against a backdrop of wooded hills and immaculate gardens running right down to the shore. A path lined with potted plants leads down through neatly tended lawns to the lakeside terrace and the low-lying stone wall which is all that divides the gardens from the pebble beach and the lake. There are palm trees, arbours and stone urns where geraniums flourish. For a trip on the lake the ferry landing-stage lies close by.

The interior is no disappointment. The public rooms are large and spacious, leading off handsome halls. There are antiques wherever you go, and attractive touches such as pretty ceramic pots and copper pots brimming with flowers. The restaurant is a lovely light room with breathtaking views and the salon is equally inviting, with its ornate mirrors, fireplace and slightly faded antiques. Even the ping-pong room has some interesting antique pieces. Bedrooms are large and pleasantly old-fashioned. Antiques and beautiful views are the main features, but there is nothing grand or luxurious about them – hence the reasonable prices. One of our reporters rates this his favourite hotel – 'sensational view, friendly reception, firm bed, great towels'.

~

NEARBY Tremezzo, Cadenabbia, Villa Carlotta (2-4 km); Bellagio.
LOCATION on lakefront; car parking and garage
FOOD breakfast, lunch, dinner
PRICE ©©
ROOMS 29; 26 double, 20 with bath, 6 with shower, 3 single; all rooms have phone, hairdrier, safe
FACILITIES dining room, reading room, table tennis, terrace, tennis
CREDIT CARDS MC, V
DISABLED access difficult
PETS not accepted
CLOSED Oct-Apr
PROPRIETOR Margherita Cappelletti

LOMBARDIA

MALEO

SOLE

~ RESTAURANT WITH ROOMS ~

Via Trabattoni 22, 26847 Maleo, Milano
TEL 0377 58142 **FAX** 0377 458058

THE EXTERIOR OF THIS 15THC coaching inn is marked solely by a gilt wrought-iron sun. Inside, the walls are whitewashed, the ceilings timbered and the arched chambers carefully scattered with antique furniture, copper pots and ceramics. There are three dining areas: the old kitchen, with its long table, open fire and old gas hobs where on occasion dishes are finished in front of the guests; a smaller dining room, with individual tables; and the stone-arched portico which looks out on to the idyllic garden.

The late Franco Colombani had brought his own distinctive personality to the regional cuisine – dark, tasty stews, roast meats and fish, accompanied by vegetables from the kitchen garden and fine wines from the unfathomable cellars. Now his son and daughter are continuing with the tradition that has helped rate the Sole as among Italy's finest restaurants.

The three traditionally styled, air-conditioned bedrooms above the restaurant all have individual high points, and good bathrooms, and make great places in which to collapse after a delicious dinner.

~

NEARBY Piacenza; Cremona (22 km).
LOCATION behind church, off main piazza in village, 20 km NE of Piacenza; car parking
FOOD breakfast, lunch, dinner
PRICE €€
ROOMS 3; 2 double, one single with bath; all rooms have phone, TV, air conditioning, minibar; one apartment
FACILITIES sitting room, 3 dining rooms, garden
CREDIT CARDS MC, V
DISABLED no special facilities
PETS accepted
CLOSED Jan, Aug, restaurant Sun eve, Mon
PROPRIETORS Mario and Francesca Colombani

LOMBARDIA

MANTUA

SAN LORENZO
~ TOWN HOTEL ~

Piazza Concordia 14, 46100 Mantova
TEL 0376 220500 **FAX** 0376 327194
E-MAIL hotel@hotelsanlorenzo.it **WEBSITE** www.hotelsanlorenzo.it

SAN LORENZO IS SMART, CONSERVATIVE, technologically up-to-date and as central as it could possibly be. It is literally surrounded by pearls of Mantua's historic architecture. Even if you are only there for a satellite-connected conference, skip past the registration desk, go straight up to the roof terrace, look around you, and marvel at how easy it is to slip back a few centuries (some rooms have terraces overlooking the monuments).

Inside is a hotel where all the 'i's have been dotted and the 't's crossed. It is the sort of place where you just know, as you step across the threshold, that there are no spiders lurking behind the plentiful antiques. The public rooms are quiet and well dressed with fresh flowers, elegant furnishings and furniture, some fine paintings, porcelain and a fascinating collection of 16thC brass offertory plates.

The staff are friendly and professional and can provide you with a potted history of Mantua and a suggested walking tour with some very helpful notes on the places and buildings you will see along the way. The bedrooms are spacious and bright ('I hated the lighting in mine', comments our inspector) each with its own complement of things ancient and modern; and the individual bathrooms, at least the ones she saw, were immaculate. Overall, a well-run, brilliantly located, if slightly characterless base.

NEARBY Piazza dell'Erbe; Basilica di Sant'Andrea; Palazzo Ducale.
LOCATION in city centre; garage
FOOD breakfast
PRICE €€€
ROOMS 32; 23 double and twin, 9 suites, 25 with bath, 7 with shower; all rooms have phone, TV, air conditioning, minibar, hairdrier
FACILITIES sitting room, meeting rooms, bar, terrace
CREDIT CARDS AE, DC, MC, V
DISABLED 2 specially adapted rooms **PETS** not accepted
CLOSED never
PROPRIETORS Giuseppe and Ottorino Tosi

LOMBARDIA

MILAN

ANTICA LOCANDA LEONARDO
~ TOWN HOTEL ~

Corso Magenta 78, 20123 Milano
TEL 02 463317 **FAX** 02 48019012
E-MAIL desk@leoloc.com **WEBSITE** www.leoloc.com

A SCANT 30 SECONDS AWAY FROM the tourist-powered mayhem that radiates outwards from Santa Maria delle Grazie, home of Leonardo's Cenacolo, Antica Locanda Leonardo presents a rather drab and faintly inauspicious exterior to the outside world. But don't be dismayed: as you cross the threshold of the front door on the courtyard, you enter a different world. The light, bright entrance hall has a cool pale grey mosaic floor with an attractive stone staircase rising gently to the first floor. Beyond the hall is a pale yellow living room which in turn gives on to a small, peaceful and tree-shaded private terrace with a white-painted wrought-iron table, chairs and a love seat.

Upstairs are the small reception, the breakfast room and all the bedrooms. With the sensible exception of the corridor passing the bedrooms, all the floors are polished wood and the furniture and beds made of rose or cherry wood. The breakfast room manages to be cheerful and elegant at the same time, its two large windows flooding it with light. Breakfast itself is continental – including cereals, fruit and yoghurt – all very fresh and of high quality. The spotless bedrooms are of modest size, but not cramped. Some have little terraces looking over the internal courtyard. Bathrooms are modern, functional, immaculate and graced with good towels.

~

NEARBY Palazzo delle Stelline; Teatro alla Scala; duomo.
LOCATION in city centre, W of duomo; car parking outside
FOOD breakfast
PRICE ⓔⓔ
ROOMS 23 double and twin, 11 with bath, 12 with shower; all rooms have phone, TV, air conditioning, hairdrier, safe
FACILITIES sitting room, breakfast room, garden
CREDIT CARDS AE, DC, MC, V
DISABLED not suitable **PETS** not accepted
CLOSED 3 weeks in Aug, late Dec to early Jan
PROPRIETOR Mario Frefel

LOMBARDIA

MILAN

SPADARI AL DUOMO
~ TOWN HOTEL ~

Via Spadari 11, 20123 Milano
TEL 02 72002371 **FAX** 02 861184
E-MAIL reservation@spadarihotel.com **WEBSITE** www.spadarihotel.com

'HOTEL' MAY BE A SLIGHT MISNOMER for this chic, unusual establishment, just steps away from the Duomo. While it's true that you can stay here (very comfortably, too), you also share the space with the owners' family passion: contemporary art and design. This is not mere decoration but a substantial collection of works by both known and up-and-coming artists and sculptors. The blue-themed decoration has been chosen to show the pieces to their best advantage and even the design of the striking furniture was specially commissioned from Ugo La Pietra.

Downstairs the reception and sitting room, with the American Bar beyond it, introduce the collection. The focal point is the fireplace with a sculpture by Gio Pomodoro above it. Yet in the midst of all this elegant form there is also excellent function. Although the bedrooms are not large they are well laid out, fresh looking and in tip-top condition; each is recharged daily with fresh fruit and flowers. The top-quality carpets, curtains and bedspreads complement the pictures and eye-catching furniture, and the beautiful bathrooms, all done in blue and white, are immaculate. There is no restaurant but the friendly staff will whip you up a snack if your feet won't carry you another step that day.

~

NEARBY Galleria Vittorio Emanuele; *duomo.*
LOCATION in city centre, just SW of *duomo*; private garage
FOOD breakfast; snacks
PRICE €€€
ROOMS 39; 25 double, 10 twin, 3 single, 1 suite, 27 with bath, 12 with shower; all rooms have phone, TV, air conditioning, minibar, hairdrier, safe
FACILITIES sitting room, bar
CREDIT CARDS AE, DC, MC, V
DISABLED not suitable
PETS not accepted
CLOSED Christmas
PROPRIETOR Marida Martegani

LOMBARDIA

MONZA

HOTEL DE LA VILLE
~ TOWN HOTEL ~

Viale Regina Margherita 15, 20052 Monza, Milano
TEL 039 382581 **FAX** 039 367647
E-MAIL info@hoteldelaville.com **WEBSITE** www.hoteldelaville.com

WHEN YOU ARRIVE AT THE SLIGHTLY dreary exterior of this hotel (facing Villa Reale, the former summer house of Savoy's royal family) your first thought may be that you have made a ghastly mistake. Actually you have done the opposite, because you are in for a delightful surprise. The atmosphere inside is one of opulent but understated elegance: vases of fresh flowers highlight the superb decoration, and throughout the hotel there is a never-ending succession of rare objects collected by Tany Nardi, the owner, for whom perfection is obviously a passion. The corridors are dotted with things like silver trays of little crystal glasses or pieces of perfectly preserved antique luggage, as well as collections of porcelain, glass, clocks,walking sticks and more. Good Persian rugs, antique furniture, pots, plants, gilt-framed pictures and polished marble are lit subtly and gently to persuade you to leave the cares of the world at the front door.

The immaculate bedrooms are beautifully furnished, decorated and appointed, the bathrooms perfect. Here too is the elegant yet cosy wood-panelled restaurant where food is superb. Adjacent to this building is a further surprise: a turn-of-the-century villa superbly restored to create seven luxurious rooms and suites decorated with antiques, gorgeous fabrics and every possible modern gadget artfully hidden in various ways .

~

NEARBY Villa Reale; *duomo*; Milan (15 km).
LOCATION in city centre, in front of Villa Reale; car parking
FOOD breakfast, lunch, dinner
PRICE €€€€
ROOMS 62; 21 double and twin, 8 with bath, 13 with shower, 39 single, 2 suites, all with shower; all rooms have phone, TV, air conditioning, minibar, hairdrier, safe
FACILITIES restaurant, bar, meeting rooms; billiards, sauna, gym (for annexe only)
CREDIT CARDS AE, DC, MC, V
DISABLED one specially adapted room **PETS** not accepted
CLOSED Aug, Christmas
PROPRIETORS Nardi family

LOMBARDIA

RANCO

SOLE

~ RESTAURANT WITH ROOMS ~

Piazza Venezia 5, 21020 Ranco, Varese
TEL 0331 976507 **FAX** 0331 976620
E-MAIL ivanett@tin.it **WEBSITE** www.ilsolediranco.it

A S YOU ENTER THE SOLE'S LIGHT AND AIRY FOYER, you can't be sure whether you'll be met by the fifth or the sixth generation of the Brovelli family: Carlo and his son Davide run the restaurant and Andrea, Davide's younger brother, now looks after the hotel in this long-lived family business overlooking Lake Maggiore. Either way you will instantly realize that they have avoided the demon of self-importance which so often follows in the trail of culinary honours (currently one Michelin star and accolades for the superb wine cellar). This is an inviting, friendly place where they have combined a superb restaurant, a splendid view of the lake and truly delightful rooms to stay in; and now, a new pool.

To add to the expectations aroused by the star (there used to be two, and may well be again) you should know that ,despite the sophistication of their menu, the Brovellis are loyal to their region and feature many local delicacies. Except in poor weather, when tables retreat into the charming dining room, they are set on the lovely terrace beneath a pergola. The bedrooms, recently renovated, are a treat, decorated in sophisticated country style with ankle-deep pile carpets and colour co-ordinated curtains, bedspreads and paintwork. The bathrooms are sparkling white with big tubs, bigger towels and stacked with high-quality 'freebies'.

~

NEARBY Lakes Lugano and Como; Milan (67 km).
LOCATION on E side of Lake Maggiore, N of Angera; car parking
FOOD breakfast, lunch, dinner
PRICE €€€
ROOMS 15; 3 double, 4 junior suites, 8 suites, one single, all with bath; all rooms have phone, TV, air-conditioning, minibar, hairdrier, safe
FACILITIES restaurant, breakfast room, garden,
CREDIT CARDS AE, DC, MC, V
DISABLED one specially adapted room **PETS** small dogs accepted
CLOSED Jan to mid-Feb
PROPRIETORS Brovelli family

LOMBARDIA

SAN FEDELE D'INTELVI

VILLA SIMPLICITAS
~ COUNTRY VILLA ~

22010 San Fedele d'Intelvi, Como
TEL 031 831132 **FAX** 031 830455
EMAIL info@villasimplicitas.it **WEBSITE** www.villasimplicitas.it

AS YOU GET FURTHER FROM THE A9 two things happen: the roads get small-er and a delicious sense of peace begins to creep over you. The final 2 km to Simplicitas are up a roughish mountain road, but when you finally reach this utterly unpretentious 19thC villa , just switch off your engine, open the door and listen to the glorious sound of absolutely nothing at all. This is a much-loved, lived-in house, oozing charm and character and filled with 19thC antiques and objects (and a magnificent billiard table) and an air of rustic gentility. Meals, taken on the terrace in fine weather, usually feature produce from the surrounding 80-hectare farm. 'Very vari-able, with very limited choice amongst the five courses and the wines,' has been a negative comment; other recent visitors have been happier.

The bedrooms (some small), most with lovely views, are like comfort-able guest rooms in a private house, with a liberal scattering of knick-knacks. Shower rooms are simple. Six further rooms have recently been renovated and added, but overall, with the exception of electric lights, the 20th century hasn't made much impression on the villa. Standards of housekeeping have been criticized by a couple of readers. Once your energy levels are restored, you can walk, ride, play tennis or golf nearby. 'Gorgeous building in a wonderful setting' - so ends the latest report .

NEARBY Lakes Como, Lugano and Maggiore; Como 20 km.
LOCATION 2 km up mountain from San Fedele d'Intelvi; car parking
FOOD breakfast, lunch, dinner
PRICE €€
ROOMS 16 double and twin, all with shower; all rooms have phone
FACILITIES dining room, sitting room, billiard room, garden, table tennis
CREDIT CARDS AE, DC, MC, V
DISABLED not suitable
PETS accepted
CLOSED mid-Oct to Mar
PROPRIETOR Ulla Wagner

LOMBARDIA

SIRMIONE

GRIFONE

~ LAKESIDE RESTAURANT WITH ROOMS ~

Vicolo Bisse (Via Bocchio) 5, 25019 Sirmione, Brescia
TEL 030 916014 **FAX** 030 916548

ALTHOUGH THE GRIFONE IS ONE of the cheapest and simplest hotels in this guide, it also has one of the loveliest locations, and makes a great place to stay for a night or two. Essentially it is a restaurant specializing in fish ('the waiter removed the bone with the air of a man cleaning his spectacles, a routine gesture, performed with aplomb' writes a correspondent) with a mouth-watering selection of *antipasto* to start. It has an enticing tree-filled terrace overlooking both Lake Garda and the ramparts of Sirmione's castle; also a tiny sandy beach.

The entrance to the hotel is found off a narrow street just inside the city walls. A small sitting room equipped with television and cheerful bamboo furniture leads to a little patio where breakfast is served (though our reader was directed to the baker's shop to buy it himself) and, if the water beckons, on to the scrap of beach. Upstairs, rooms are simple, furniture is basic, the fans noisy, but everything is spotless. Some rooms look right over the castle walls, and the five balconies are full of flowers. Those on the top floor enjoy the best views: rooftops, mountains, and of course the lake. There is no traffic noise in this pedestrian zone, but you may be woken by church bells. The younger generation of the Marcolini family – brother and sister – who now run the Grifone are friendly and helpful.

~

NEARBY Lake Garda; Brescia (39 km); Verona (35 km).
LOCATION just inside city walls, next to castle, on lake; car parking (50 m)
FOOD breakfast, lunch, dinner
PRICE €
ROOMS 16; 12 double, twin and triple, 4 with bath, 8 with shower, 4 single with shower
FACILITIES sitting room, dining room, lift, terraces, tiny beach
CREDIT CARDS not accepted
DISABLED access difficult except to restaurant **PETS** not accepted
CLOSED Nov to Easter
PROPRIETORS Marcolini family

LOMBARDIA

GARGNANO

BAIA D'ORO
LAKESIDE HOTEL

Via Gamberera 13, 25084
Gargnano, Brescia

TEL 0365 71171 **FAX** 0365 72568
E-MAIL hotelbaiadoro@gardalake.it
WEBSITE www.gardalake.it/hotel-baiadoro
FOOD breakfast, lunch, dinner
PRICE €€
CLOSED mid-Nov to mid-Mar
PROPRIETORS Terzi family

GIAMBATTISTA TERZI WAS BORN in one of a pair of neighbouring fishermen's cottages built on the edge of the lake in 1780, and his wife was the moving force behind turning them into a hotel in the 1960s. Since then the facilities have slowly been updated. To appreciate the fabulous setting, you should arrive by boat. You can almost dip your hand in the lake from the romantic dining terrace, a splendid vantage point from which to watch night succeed day. The Terzis have gradually redecorated the bedrooms in slightly dubious shades of pink and blue, with painted wooden furniture, shiny fabrics and mirrored glass bedheads. Not to everyone's taste, but they are comfortable.

MILAN

ANTICA LOCANDA DEI MERCANTI
CITY HOTEL

Via San Tomaso 6, 20123 Milano

TEL 02 8054080 **FAX** 02 8054090
E-MAIL locanda@locanda.it
WEBSITE www.locanda.it
FOOD breakfast, snacks
PRICE €€
CLOSED never
MANAGER Alessandro Basta

CENTRALLY LOCATED IN A SMALL SIDE STREET off Via Dante, this is a delightfully decorated hotel in a 17thC building, each room furnished in unique style, some with four-posters, some with wrought iron bedsteads, with beautiful duvet covers and curtains. Some of the rooms are relieved by stencilled borders, others have details (like climbing roses) painted over the base colour. Our inspector thoroughly enjoyed her most recent stay here, but we have received an angry complaint too: tiny, ill-equipped bathrooms, freezing rooms, problems with the booking and the bill, a missing breakfast-in-bed, and, worst of all, 'rude' service. Oh dear. We are investigating, and will report. Let us know your impressions.

LOMBARDIA

MILAN TOWN HOUSE 31
CITY HOTEL

Via Goldoni 31, 20129 Milano

TEL 02 701561 **FAX** 02 713167
E-MAIL townhouse31@townhouse.it
WEBSITE www.designhotels.com
FOOD breakfast **PRICE** €€€
CLOSED 3 weeks around
Christmas and New Year, Aug
PROPRIETOR Ornella Borsato

A DESIGN HOTEL THAT MANAGES to be human as well as cool, the 17-room Town House opened in 2002 and occupies an elegant turn-of-the-century building house in a residential area near Porta Venezia. The style is a relaxed, contemporary take on an 'Out of Africa' idea (reflecting the owner's preferred travel destinations) with neutral colours effectively offsetting some fine antiques, beautiful ethnic pieces, Moroccan throws and artful flower arrangements. The cocktail bar on the back terrace plays host to a sleek crowd at night.

This is a useful (albeit pricey) address for anyone wanting discreet style combined with easy-going personal service.

IL LEONE

RESTAURANT-WITH-ROOMS

*Piazza IV Mortiri, 46030
Pomponesco, Mantova*

TEL 0375 86077/86145
FAX 0375 86770
FOOD breakfast, dinner
PRICE €
CLOSED Jan. restaurant Sun eve
and Mon
PROPRIETOR Signor Pasolini

P OMPONESCO WAS ONCE a flourishing town under the Gonzaga family, and the old part still has faded charm. The Leone lies just off the main *piazza* - a peeling old building once the home of a 16thC nobleman. It is primarily an eating place. There are only seven bedrooms, and by far the most attractive features are the dining areas - the main restaurant has a coffered 16thC ceiling and frieze. Elsewhere, decoration is suitably elegant. The food is among the best in the region, with some unusual combinations of flavour. Beyond the restaurant a courtyard leads to the bedrooms, built around an inviting pool and garden area. They are starkly modern, but comfortable and well maintained.

THE NORTH-EAST

HOTELS IN THE NORTH-EAST

THE REMARKABLE CITY OF VENICE, famed throughout the world for its incomparable beauty, artistic wealth and sheer originality is the focal point of this region. A feast of small hotels are described in the following pages, distilled from our in-depth regional guide, *The Charming Small Hotel Guide to Venice and North-East Italy*. Room prices in Venice are undeniably steep, but if you choose carefully, and secure a canal or lagoon view, you will discover some memorable places in which to stay.

An alternative to staying in Venice itself is to base yourself somewhere on the vast Veneto Plain that fans out from Venice to the foothills of the Dolomites. Here are the great cities of Padua, Treviso, Vicenza and Verona, the villas of Palladio and other attractions, such as the charming little hill towns of Asolo and Follina. You will find some excellent bases from which to explore Venice and the Veneto in these pages. We have reccomended two hotels in Verona; in Treviso you could try the **Alle Beccherie/Campeol** (tel 0422 56601), a traditional restaurant with rooms across the street, and in Padua the **Leon Bianco** (tel 049 8750814). In Vicenza a reader recommends the '50-room, family-run, value-for-money, simple and charming' **Albergo San Raffaele** (tel 0444 545767) with 'almost Tuscan' bedrooms, hidden away on the ascent to the Santuario on Monte Berico. For something smarter you could try **Villa Michelangelo** 7 km away (tel 0444 550300).

The province of Veneto takes in the eastern shores of Lake Garda, where we also have some recommendations. Other hotels on Lake Garda can be found in the Lombardia section of this book. To the east, the Venetian Plain edges into the province of Friuli-Venezia Giulia, where we recommend a couple of places in the south. The north of the province, where it rises to the Carnic Alps with meadows and pine forests, is empty of hotels of our sort, and indeed short on any hotels at all, being little visited by tourists.

Far more popular as a mountainous destination is the province of Trentino-Alto Adige, only a couple of hours' drive but a world away from Venice and its great plain. It feels like Austria, has a special autonomous statute and is largely German-speaking. Owners and staff of the Alpine hotels you will find in its mountains may not even speak Italian... you are more likely to be greeted in German. Place names are extremely confusing, as each town and village, mountain and valley has both an Italian and German name. We have given the Italian translation. Hotels are often Tyrolean chalets, with wooden furniture, ceramic stoves, traditional fabrics; the food too, is mainly Austrian, at least on the simpler menus, while the more sophisticated hotels serve creative variations on the theme. The scenery amongst the Dolomites is beautiful, and there are plenty of activities to pursue both in winter and summer.

THE NORTH-EAST

ASOLO

AL SOLE
~ TOWN HOTEL ~

Via Collegio 33, 31011 Asolo, Treviso
TEL 0423 528111 **FAX** 0423 528399
E-MAIL info@albergoalsole.com **WEBSITE** www.albergoalsole.com

FROM A GLORIOUS POSITION, perched above the Piazza Maggiore on the steep hill up to the massive fortress, the Rocca, this 16thcC villa has a splendid view of the medieval town with its higgledy-piggledy streets. Its deep pink and cream façade is original and appealing, while the trendy, hi-tech interior – hallmark of the dynamic young owner Silvia de Checchi – makes a dramatic contrast.

Almost every room has white rough-cast walls and mellow wood floors, enlivened by daring colour combinations for fabrics and furniture. Although the look is mainly cool and modern, a few antiques and the occasional bowl and pitcher hark back to the past. Recalling former stars in Asolo's firmament, such as 'Eleanor Duse' and 'Gabriele d'Annunzio', the bedrooms are all different; the former has light painted furniture, the latter, ornate church-style pieces. Some rooms have huge claw-foot baths; some have massage showers, just one of the many four-star comforts. Perhaps the ultimate of these are the state-of-the-art loos for the ground floor, which electronically flush, lift and then replace the seat, complete with hygenic paper cover, at the appropriate times. A panoramic restaurant, La Terrazza, has now been opened, and the hotel also has a small fitness centre .

~

NEARBY Palladian villas; Possagno (10 km).
LOCATION at the top of Piazza Maggiore; private car park
FOOD breakfast, dinner
PRICE €€€
ROOMS 23; 14 double and twin, 2 with bath, 12 with shower, 8 single, 2 with bath, 6 with shower, 1 suite with bath; all rooms have phone, TV, air conditioning, minibar, hairdrier, safe
FACILITIES breakfast room, sitting room, dining room, bar, fitness centre, lift, terrace **CREDIT CARDS** AE, MC, V
DISABLED 2 specially adapted rooms **PETS** accepted
CLOSED never
PROPRIETOR Silvia de Checchi

THE NORTH-EAST

ASOLO

VILLA CIPRIANI
~ COUNTRY VILLA ~

Via Canova 298, 31011 Asolo, Treviso
TEL 0423 952166 **FAX** 0423 952095
E-MAIL villacipriani@sheraton.com **WEBSITE** www.sheraton.com/villacipriani

ASOLO IS A BEAUTIFUL MEDIEVAL hilltop village commanding panoramic views, a jewel of the Veneto. The Villa Cipriani, a jewel of the Sheraton Group, now part of the huge Starwood Group, is a mellow ochre-washed house on the fringes of the village, its deceptively plain entrance leading into a warm reception area which immediately imparts the feeling of a hotel with a heart (and a house with a past: it was once the home of Robert Browning). Today it is graced by the prettiest of rose-and-flower-filled gardens, and meals are served on the terrace or in the restaurant overhanging the valley. As for the gracious and comfortable bedrooms, make sure you ask for one with a view, and try for an 'exclusive' rather than a 'superior' double. The latter are not particularly spacious, while the former include a sitting area; two rooms have terraces.

Villa Cipriani is a relaxing country hotel, whose views, comfort, peaceful garden and good food make it particularly alluring. However, some reports complain of prices that were hard to justify, also mentioning intrusive wedding parties and brash clientele. Others have been full of praise.

~

NEARBY Palladian villas; Possagno (10 km).
LOCATION on NW side of village; with garage parking
FOOD breakfast, lunch, dinner; room service
PRICE €€€€
ROOMS 31; 29 double and twin, 2 single, all with bath; all rooms have phone, TV, air conditioning, minibar, hairdrier
FACILITIES sitting room, dining rooms, bar, meeting room, lift, terrace, garden
CREDIT CARDS AE, DC, MC, V
DISABLED access difficult
PETS accepted
CLOSED never
MANAGER Martina Boettcher

THE NORTH-EAST

BANNIA DI FIUME VENETO

L'ULTIMO MULINO
~ CONVERTED MILL ~

Via Mulino 45, 33080 Bannia di Fiume Veneto, Pordenone
TEL 0434 957911 **FAX** 0434 958483
E-MAIL ultimo.molino@adriacom.it **WEBSITE** www.ultimomolino.com

A S THE NAME SUGGESTS, this 17thC building is one of the very last function-ing mills in the area. In use until the 1970s, the three old wooden wheels are still in working condition; indeed, they are set in motion in the evenings for the benefit of guests. The lovely stone house and garden are set in gentle farmland and surrounded by three rivers; the soothing sounds of water are everywhere.

Opened as a hotel in 1994, restoration work has been carried out with great taste and flair, preserving as much as possible of the original charac-ter of the house. The long, open-plan sitting room and bar area have even incorporated the hefty innards of the mill machinery. Throughout, attrac-tive fabrics are teamed with handsome antique furniture, rustic stone and woodwork, and soft, elegant lighting. The comfortable and stylish bed-rooms, while different in layout, are all along similar lines with wooden fit-tings and pale green and cream country fabrics. Those on the second floor have attic ceilings and some have squashy sofas. Bathrooms are in pale grey marble. New owners have recently taken over, and have opened the restaurant for lunch as well as dinner, with fish a speciality.

~

NEARBY Pordenone (10 km); Venice (80 km); Trieste (80 km).
LOCATION 10 km SE of Pordenone, exit from A28 at Azzano Decimo; in own garden with parking
FOOD breakfast, lunch, dinner
PRICE €€€
ROOMS 8 double and twin, 4 with bath, 4 with shower; all rooms have phone, TV, air conditioning, minibar, hairdrier
FACILITIES breakfast room, sitting rooms, dining rooms, bar, music/conference room, garden, terrace
CREDIT CARDS AE, DC, MC, V
DISABLED no special facilities **PETS** accepted
CLOSED 10 days Jan; Aug; restaurant closed Sun eve, Mon
PROPRIETORS Mattarello family

THE NORTH-EAST

BARBIANO

BAD DREIKIRCHEN
~ MOUNTAIN HOTEL ~

San Giacomo 6, 39040 Barbiano, Bolzano
TEL 0471 650055 **FAX** 0471 650044
E-MAIL info@baddreikirchen.it **WEBSITE** www.baddreikirchen.it

THE NAME OF THIS IDYLLICALLY situated hotel, a 14thC chalet owned by the Wodenegg family for 200 years, derives from its vicinity to three small churches which date back to the Middle Ages. The fact that you can only reach the hotel by four-wheel-drive taxi makes for a perfect escape.

The large old building, with its shingled roof and dark wood balconies, has wonderful views and is surrounded by meadows, woods, mountains and quantities of fresh air. There's plenty of space for guests, both inside and out, and the atmosphere is comfortably rustic with an abundance of aromatic pine panelling and carved furniture. A cosy library provides a quiet corner for reading, and simple but satisfying meals are served in the pleasant dining room or on the adjacent veranda, from which the views are superb. Bedrooms in the original part of the house are particularly charming, being entirely wood-panelled.

To sum up, the words of a guest at Bad Dreikirchen in 1908 are still appropriate: 'I stayed for some days ... the weather was continually fine, the position magnificent, and the food good.' Recent guests warmly agree. 'I fell in love with the place. Delightfully relaxed atmosphere, charming young owners.'

~

NEARBY Bressanone (17 km); Val Gardena (10 km).
LOCATION 21 km NE of Bolzano, exit from Brennero Autostrada at Chiusa, head S through Barbiano (6 km); hotel car park on right (call and the hotel will send a jeep to collect you from car park)
FOOD breakfast, lunch, dinner
PRICE €
ROOMS 26; 16 double and twin, 2 family, 8 single, all with bath or shower
FACILITIES sitting rooms, bar, restaurant, games room, library, garden, terraces, swimming pool, table tennis, tennis court (1 km)
CREDIT CARDS MC, V **DISABLED** access difficult **PETS** accepted
CLOSED Nov to mid-May
PROPRIETORS Wodenegg family

THE NORTH-EAST

BRESSANONE

ELEPHANT

~ TOWN HOTEL ~

Via Rio Bianco 4, 39042 Bressanone, Bolzano
TEL 0472 832750 **FAX** 0472 836579
E-MAIL info@hotelelephant.com **WEBSITE** www.hotelelephant.com

BRESSANONE IS A PRETTY TOWN at the foot of the Brenner Pass, more Austrian than Italian in character. The same is true of the charming Elephant, named after a beast which was led over the Alps as a gift from King John of Portugal to Archduke Maximilian of Austria. The only stable big enough for the exhausted animal was next to the inn, so the innkeeper promptly changed its name to celebrate the event.

There is an air of solid, old-fashioned comfort throughout. Corridors decorated in sumptuous colours are lined with heavily carved and beautifully inlaid antiques. The public rooms are all on the first floor: an elegant 18thC-style sitting room, a large light breakfast room, and three dining rooms. The main one is panelled in dark wood with a vast green ceramic stove and stags' heads on the walls. The food is one of the highlights of a stay here. A reporter commented: 'We had a fabulous dinner; the cooking is imaginative but unfussy with lots of fresh herbs and local ingredients, beautifully presented and bountiful.' Bedrooms are large and comfortable, but disappointing compared with the more characterful public areas. Some have antiques, others have none.

~

NEARBY cathedral; Novacella monastery (3 km).
LOCATION at N end of town; in gardens with car parking and garages
FOOD breakfast, lunch, dinner
PRICE €€€
ROOMS 44; 28 double and twin, 27 with bath, one with shower; all rooms have phone, TV, hairdrier
FACILITIES breakfast room, sitting room, bar, dining rooms, lift, garden, swimming pool, tennis courts
CREDIT CARDS AE, DC, MC, V
DISABLED 2 ground floor rooms in annexe
PETS accepted
CLOSED Nov, Jan to Mar
PROPRIETORS Heiss family

THE NORTH-EAST

CALDARO

LEUCHTENBURG
~ COUNTRY GUESTHOUSE ~

Campo di Lago 100, 39052 Caldaro, Bolzano
TEL 0471 960093/960048 **FAX** 0471 960155 **E-MAIL** pensionleuchtenburg@iol.it
WEBSITE www.kalterersee.com/pensionleuchtenburg

THIS SOLID STONE-BUILT 16thC hostel once housed the servants of Leuchtenburg castle, an arduous hour's trek up the steep wooded mountain behind. Today, guests in the *pension* are well cared for by the friendly owners, while the castle lies in ruins. The setting is enviably tranquil, right on Lago di Caldaro, better known (at least to wine buffs) as Kalterer See. Cross a road and you are at the water's edge, where a little private beach is dotted with umbrellas and sunloungers.

Back in the *pension*, the Sparers provide solid breakfasts and three-course dinners of regional cuisine in an unpretentious, homely atmosphere. White-painted low-arched dining rooms occupy the ground floor; above is the reception, with a large table littered with magazines and surrounded by armchairs. There is another sitting area on the first floor, leading to the bedrooms. These have pretty painted furniture and tiled floors (second floor rooms are plainer). Each one tells a story: for example, the 'old smoke room' was where food was smoked. All are large, and some share the views enjoyed from the terrace across vineyards to the lake. Prices could hardly be lower.

~

NEARBY swimming and fishing in lake.
LOCATION 5 km SE of Caldaro, on the edge of the lake; in courtyard with car parking
FOOD breakfast, dinner
PRICE €
ROOMS 19; 15 double and twin, 3 with bath, 12 with shower, 2 single, 2 triple, all with shower; rooms have TV (on request)
FACILITIES sitting area, dining area, bar, terrace, beach
CREDIT CARDS MC, V
DISABLED not suitable
PETS accepted
CLOSED Nov to Easter
PROPRIETORS Sparer family

THE NORTH-EAST

FIÉ ALLO SCILIAR

TURM

~ MOUNTAIN VILLAGE HOTEL ~

Piazza della Chiesa 9, 39050 Fié allo Sciliar, Bolzano
TEL 0471 725014 **FAX** 0471 725474
E-MAIL info@hotelturm.it **WEBSITE** www.hotelturm.it

A SOLID FORMER COURTHOUSE dating from the 12th century, with views across pastures and mountains, Romantik Hotel Turm offers typical Tyrolean hospitality with style and warmth. Now run by dashing Stefan Pramstrahler, who is also the talented chef, the hotel has gained a hip edge in the last couple of years, as well as a wonderful new oriental-style 'wellness' suite and a new wing housing 14 luxurious rooms. Bedrooms are all different and vary considerably in size, but even the smallest has everything you could want for a comfortable stay, including traditional furniture and somewhere cosy to sit. The mini-apartments are excellent value: one, in a little stone tower, is done as a wood-panelled *stübe*, with spiral staircase to a double room and a children's room. The Pramstrahler's fine collection of contemporary art is displayed everywhere, including the new bar/sitting room (with gorgeous sunny terrace) and spills out along the whitewashed corridor walls.

The main dining room is light and spacious, with low wood ceiling and windows overlooking the valley; or you can dine in a romantic little room at the base of the 11thC tower. Either way, the elegant food is superb.

NEARBY Val Gardena; Bolzano (16 km); Castelrotto (10 km).
LOCATION in village, 16 km E of Bolzano; with garden and limited car parking
FOOD breakfast, lunch, dinner; room service
PRICE €€€
ROOMS 35; 29 double and twin, 1 single; all with bath or shower; 5 apartments with kitchen, all rooms have phone, TV, minibar, hairdrier, safe
FACILITIES sitting room, dining rooms, bar, lift, garden, spa and beauty area, outdoor swimming pool, garage
CREDIT CARDS MC, V
DISABLED access possible
PETS accepted
CLOSED Nov to mid-Dec
PROPRIETORS Pramstrahler family

THE NORTH-EAST

FINALE

VILLA SARACENO
~ SELF-CATERING VILLA ~

For all information and booking contact: *The Landmark Trust, Shottesbrooke, Maidenhead, Berkshire SL6 3SW, England* **TEL** 01628 825 925 **FAX** 01628 825417
E-MAIL booking@landmarktrust.co.uk **WEBSITE** www.landmarktrust.co.uk

Highlights of the Veneto are the villas built by the great Renaissance architect Andrea Palladio. If you would like to stay in one, here is your chance. Villa Saraceno, on a plain to the west of the Euganean Hills, is owned by the Landmark Trust, a British organization which acquires and restores buildings of historic interest and then lets them to holidaymakers.

Designed in the mid-16thC as a country retreat as well as a working farm for a well-to-do Vicenzan, Biagio Saraceno, the complex consists of the airy, beautifully proportioned main house as well as other earlier buildings, including the simple Casa Vecchia, in which most of the bedrooms are located. The interior of the Palladian house has been restored to recreate iits original arrangement - a grand sala with two-room apartments opening off it, and huge granaries above. Dim frescoed friezes have been cleaned to reveal scenes of high drama, probably painted for Biagio's son. Saraceno can accommodate up to 16 people. One satisfied tenant wrote to the Landmark Trust: 'a perfect balance between the elegant understatement of the Palladian building and modern-day comforts...'.

~

NEARBY Montagnana (14 km); Vicenza (32 km).
LOCATION in village 32 km S of Vicenza, 12 km N of SS10 between Este and Montagnana
FOOD none
PRICE on application; weekly lets only in high season, shorter stays available at other times
ROOMS accommodates up to 16 in 2 double, 3 twin, 2 single, one family room; 5 bathrooms
FACILITIES kitchen with dishwasher and washing machine, sitting room, dining room, garden, swimming pool
CREDIT CARDS MC, V
DISABLED access difficult
PETS accepted
CLOSED never
PROPRIETORS Landmark Trust

THE NORTH-EAST

FOLLINA

VILLA ABBAZIA
~ TOWN HOTEL ~

Via Martiri della Libertà, 31051 Follina, Treviso
TEL 0438 971277 **FAX** 0438 970001
E-MAIL info@hotelabbazia.it **WEBSITE** www.hotelabbazia.it

THE HOTEL CONSISTS of two buildings: a 17thC *palazzo* and, adjacent, an enchanting little art nouveau villa. Standards of decoration and comfort in both are exceptionally high – rarely have we met hoteliers (brother and sister) more keen to please their guests – and the Abbazia is now a Relais et Châteaux hotel. If you find the lobby and balconied breakfast area a bit much – a sugary pink confection of candy-striped walls strewn with roses, draped tables and floral china – you will not be disappointed by the bedrooms. Each one is individually decorated, and all are delightful: sophisticated and very feminine in English style, full of thoughtful touches. Three rooms have private balconies, at no extra cost. Best of all is the villa with its pillared portico, carved flourishes on its four façades and sweeping staircase. The Abbazia's restaurant, La Corte, is beautifully decorated with stone walls and pillars and an enchanting mural depicting the highlights of the region as seen from a balcony. If you want to eat out, try Da Gigetto in Miane (where you should be sure to visit the wine cellars).

The Zanon's have prepared a helpful list of local information, including routes you can follow on the hotel's bicycles. And they have now opened a second hotel across the street, dei Chiostri (*see p120*).

~

NEARBY 11thC abbey; Palladian villas; Asolo (20 km).
LOCATION in town centre, facing the abbey; car parking
FOOD breakfast, lunch, dinner; room service
PRICE €€€
ROOMS 18; 11 double and twin, 7 suites, all with shower, bath or Jacuzzi; all rooms have phone, TV, safe, hairdrier; 12 have air conditioning
FACILITIES breakfast room, sitting room, dining room, tea room, terrace, garden; garage
CREDIT CARDS AE, DC, MC, V
DISABLED not suitable **PETS** accepted
CLOSED Jan
PROPRIETORS Giovanni and Ivana Zanon

THE NORTH-EAST

GARGAGNAGO

FORESTERIA SEREGO ALIGHIERI
∼ COUNTRY VILLA APARTMENTS ∼

37020 Gargagnago di Valpolicella, Verona
TEL 045 7703622 **FAX** 045 7703523
E-MAIL serego@seregoalighieri.it **WEBSITE** www.seregoalighieri.it

IN 1353, THE SON OF DANTE, who had been exiled in Verona, bought Casal dei Ronchi, and there his direct descendants have lived ever since. Today, overseen by Count Pieralvise Serego Alighieri, the estate is a prosperous producer of Valpolicella wines (much improved in recent years and shaking off their 'cheap and nasty' reputation) as well as olive oil, balsamic vinegar, honey, jams and rice. The family home is a lovely yellow ochre building fronted by formal gardens which overlook the vineyards. Beyond are the former stables, now beautifully converted to make eight apartments, simple yet sophisticated, sleeping two to four people. In each one you find a gleaming chrome kitchen, country furniture, soothing green cotton fabrics, white walls, marble bathrooms. No. 8 spirals up a slim tower: minute sitting room, stairs to a minute kitchen, more stairs to the bedroom. Open a door in the bedhead and there's a tiny window behind. No. 1 is the most spacious, with dining table and elegant chairs. Breakfast is served in a room decorated with old family photographs on the ground floor. Wine tasting can be arranged for eight people or more. There are some good restaurants nearby.

∼

NEARBY Verona (18 km); Lake Garda (14 km).
LOCATION signposted off the road from Pedemonte to San Ambrogio, 18 km NE of Verona; in own extensive grounds with ample car parking
FOOD breakfast
PRICE apartment sleeping 2-4 people €€ per night; weekly rates available
ROOMS 8 apartments for 2, 3 or 4 people, each with kitchen, bathroom with shower, phone, TV, air conditioning
FACILITIES reception, breakfast room, terrace meeting room, estate produce shop
CREDIT CARDS AE, DC, MC, V
DISABLED not suitable
PETS accepted
CLOSED Jan
PROPRIETOR Conte Pieralvise Serego Alighieri

THE NORTH-EAST

DER PUNTHOF
∼ COUNTRY HOTEL ∼

Via Steinach 25, 39022 Lagundo, Bolzano
TEL 0473 448553 **FAX** 0473 449919
E-MAIL www.puenthof.com **WEBSITE** info@puenthof.com

VIA CLAUDIO AUGUSTO, a Roman road to Germany, passed what is now the entrance to Der Pünthof, and the watchtower built to guard the road forms an integral part of the hotel. The main building was a medieval farmhouse and has been in the Wolf family since the 17th century. They opened it as a hotel 40 years ago, housing guests in the barn, but over the decades other buildings have been added. Although Lagundo is a rather dreary suburb of Merano, once inside the hotel's electronic barrier you could be miles from anywhere with only orchards, vineyards and stunning scenery in view.

The public rooms are in the old building: breakfast is served in a pale green *stube* with wooden floor, low ceiling, ceramic stove and traces of the original decoration on the panelled walls. Bedrooms in the barn are modern and comfortable, but uniform, though some have private terraces on to the garden. The most appealing are the rooms in the square tower. One has polished floorboards, a wood ceiling and antique bed. There are five well-equipped self-catering chalets, and six simpler cheaper rooms in another annexe.

∼

NEARBY Bolzano (28 km); Brennero (70 km); the Dolomites.
LOCATION 3 km NW of Merano, outside village; in own grounds with ample car parking
FOOD breakfast
PRICE €
ROOMS 12 double and twin, 2 with bath, 10 with shower; all rooms have phone, TV, minibar, safe
FACILITIES 2 breakfast rooms, sitting room, bar, restaurant, sauna, solarium, garden, tennis courts, swimming pool
CREDIT CARDS AE, DC, MC, V
DISABLED one room on ground floor **PETS** accepted
CLOSED Nov to mid-Mar
PROPRIETORS Wolf family

THE NORTH-EAST

LEVADA

GARGAN
~ COUNTRY GUESTHOUSE ~

Via Marco Polo 2, Levada di Piombino Dese, Padova
TEL 049 9350308 **FAX** 049 9350016
E-MAIL gargan@gargan.it **WEBSITE** www.gargan.it

THE SETTING IS RURAL, on a working farm, and the farmhouse is typical – attractive enough, but not especially prepossessing. A donkey brays in the garden. We walked in quite unprepared for the level of sophistication of this *agriturismo;* it's in a league of its own. The ground floor comprises a hallway with cool white walls and beams painted pale green, plus five interconnecting dining rooms. Furnished only with antiques, these rooms have delicate lace curtains, timbered ceilings, and an array of pictures on their white walls. Our visit coincided with Sunday lunch, and every table was immaculately laid with a white cloth, fine china and gleaming silver; an open fire crackled in the hearth.

The ingredients used in the delicious dinners are mainly produced on the farm. Signora Calzavara is in charge of the cooking and provides a full American breakfast and other meals when required.

The six bedrooms are enchanting. Floors are strewn with rugs; most have wrought-iron bedheads and fine walnut furniture. It's best to book by fax unless you speak Italian.

~

NEARBY Palladian villas; Venice (20 km); Padua (26 km).
LOCATION 20 km N of Venice, in Levada take Via G. Carducci opposite the church and turn left into Via Marco Polo; in own garden with car parking
FOOD breakfast, lunch, dinner
PRICE ©
ROOMS 6; 4 double and twin, 2 family rooms, all with shower; all rooms have TV
FACILITIES dining rooms, sitting area, garden
CREDIT CARDS not accepted
DISABLED access difficult
PETS not accepted
CLOSED Jan, Aug
PROPRIETORS Calzavara family

THE NORTH-EAST

MALCESINE

BELLEVUE SAN LORENZO
~ LAKESIDE HOTEL ~

Loc. Dosde Feri, 37018 Malcesine, Lago di Garda, Brescia
TEL 0457 401598 **FAX** 0457 401055
E-MAIL info@bellevue-sanlorenzo.it **WEBSITE** www.bellevue-sanlorenzo.it

AN ENTHUSIASTIC REGULAR guest of the Bellevue San Lorenzo alerted us to this hotel on the shores of Lake Garda, entreating us to overlook its large number of rooms and its use by (upmarket) tour groups and focus instead on its qualities.

With its own steps down to the Lungolago, the hotel is situated on the main road outside Malcasine (a bit hairy for walkers, as there is no pavement) and consists of the main villa, with public rooms, and attached, the newer restaurant with rooms above. Other bedrooms (less desirable) are in villas in the grounds of mature gardens scattered with contemporary sculpture. Bedrooms are comfortable, if unremarkable. A collection of contemporary art decorates the walls in both the older and the newer buildings.

What stood out for our readers, and subsequently our inspector, was the friendliness of the staff, particularly the hard-working receptionists who both speak several languages and for whom nothing is too much trouble. The grounds are very attractive, and the sun terrace by the pool makes a pleasant place to while away the hours. Food is somewhat variable, but can often be excellent. Most of all, given the standards and facilities, the bill at the Bellevue represents real value for money.

NEARBY Ferry services to villages and towns around Lake Garda.
LOCATION on hill overlooking Lake Garda, 1 km outside Malcesine
FOOD breakfast, lunch, dinner
PRICE €€
ROOMS 50; 46 double and twin, one suite, 3 junior suites, all with bath; all rooms have phone, TV, air conditioning, minibar, safe, hairdrier
FACILITIES sitting room, dining room, bar, lift, terrace, garden, swimming pool, wellness centre, wine room
CREDIT CARDS AE, DC, MC, V
DISABLED no special facilities **PETS** not accepted
CLOSED Nov to Apr
MANAGER Ruggiero Togni

THE NORTH-EAST

CASTEL FRAGSBURG
⌁ CONVERTED CASTLE ⌁

Via Fragsburg 3, 39012 Merano, Bolzano
TEL 0473 244071 **FAX** 0473 244493
E-MAIL info@fragsburg.com **WEBSITE** www.fragsburg.com

A LOVELY DRIVE ALONG A NARROW COUNTRY LANE, through mixed woodland and past Alpine pastures brings you to the east of Merano where Castel Frangsburg – 300 years old and a hotel for more than 100 years – commands splendid views of the Texel massif.

Externally, Fragsburg still looks very much the hunting lodge, with carved wooden shutters and balconies. A terrace along the front of the house, covered with wistaria, is a wonderful place to eat or drink: you seem to be suspended over the mountainside. The adjoining dining room can be opened up in warm weather, and the food – a seven course dinner – is 'very good and carefully served' according to a recent visitor, with a huge breakfast buffet accompanied by Prosecco. In cooler weather you can choose from various Tyrolean-style sitting rooms and a congenial little library. Bathrooms, recently renovated, are modern and spotless and bedrooms all have balconies, carved pine furniture and colourful country fabrics. A wellness centre has now been added to the sauna and gym in the old cellars.

The wooded gardens provide plenty of space for lazing – as well as a wooden shelter reserved for all-over suntanning. Delightful owners.

⌁

NEARBY Promenades along the Passirio river in Merano; Passirio valley, Schloss Rametz; Dolomites.
LOCATION 6 km NE of Merano, in own gardens with ample parking
FOOD breakfast, lunch, dinner
PRICE €€€
ROOMS 20; 6 double and twin, 12 suites, 2 single, all with bath; all rooms have phone, TV, safe, hairdrier
FACILITIES sitting rooms, library, smoking room, dining rooms, terrace, lift, sauna, gym, wellness spa, garden
CREDIT CARDS MC, V
DISABLED one specially adapted room
PETS accepted
CLOSED Nov to Easter
PROPRIETORS Ortner family

THE NORTH-EAST

MERANO

VILLA TIVOLI
~ EDGE-OF-TOWN HOTEL ~

Via Verde 72, 39012 Merano, Bolzano
TEL 0473 446282 **FAX** 0473 446849
E-MAIL info@villativoli.it **WEBSITE** www.villativoli.it

ALMOST IN COUNTRYSIDE, yet close to the town centre, standing in apple orchards, the pale yellow villa is surrounded by an 'exquisite' terraced garden filled with over 2,000 different plants. Inside all is cool and chic, spacious and light, yet not intimidating. The ground floor is open-plan, with a glass-walled dining room; over the bar an extraordinary contemporary fresco of many-breasted Artemis, a recurring theme in the hotel. Another corner holds a sitting area, elegantly furnished with antiques and there is a traditional wood-panelled Tyrolean *stube*. Outside, a terrace with tables shaded by yellow umbrellas – as well as a new rock-lagoon surrounded by cypress and stone – and in the basement, a pool room with gaily painted walls. Bedrooms, named after Mediterranean flowers, are all different, all comfortable, with south-facing balconies. Some are huge, with separate sitting areas; some are furnished with antiques, others are very contemporary. Bathrooms are large, with double basins. Our reporter was hooked: 'Smart but relaxed; staff warm and welcoming, owners genuinely friendly and aiming to please; mountainous breakfast buffet, designed to see you through till evening, and a delicious dinner (half board includes five courses) with excellent local wines.'

~

NEARBY Passirio river promenades; Passirio valley; the Dolomites.
LOCATION on edge of town; in own grounds with ample car parking
FOOD breakfast, lunch, dinner
PRICE €€€
ROOMS 21; 16 double and twin, all with bath or shower, 5 suites with bath; all rooms have phone, TV, hairdrier
FACILITIES sitting room, dining room, bar, library, indoor swimming pool, sauna, lift, terrace, garden
CREDIT CARDS AE, DC, MC, V
DISABLED access difficult **PETS** accepted
CLOSED mid-Dec to mid-Mar
PROPRIETORS Defranceschi family

THE NORTH-EAST

MIRA PORTE

VILLA MARGHERITA
~ COUNTRY VILLA ~

Via Nazionale 416, 30030 Mira Venezia
TEL 041 4265800 **FAX** 041 4265838
E-MAIL hvillam@tin.it **WEBSITE** www.villamargherita.com

THIS COUNTRY VILLA IN THE VENETIAN HINTERLAND stands on the Brenta
Riviera overlooking a flat, industrial landscape but offering peace,
seclusion and acres of real estate for your money, while being well placed
for excursions into Venice, which is just ten kilometres away.

Villa Margherita was built in in the 17th century as a nobleman's country retreat and has been a hotel since 1987, now part of the Romantik
group. Readers are impressed with the standard of furnishings and service; 'not cheap but worth it', comments one. The yellow and blue breakfast room is gloriously light, with French windows on to the garden, while
the sitting room has murals (the principal one portrays a bevy of naked
nymphs cavorting on the banks of the Brenta), an open fireplace and
some beautiful lamps, vases and clocks. You will find fresh fruit and flowers in the thoroughly comfortable bedrooms, the best of which lead to the
breakfast terrace.

The Dal Corso family is the driving force behind the hotel and its highly
regarded restaurant, 200 metres away across a terrifying road. A lively
place, it specializes in mouthwatering seafood dishes. The family have
opened a new deluxe hotel, Villa Francheschi (tel 041 4266531) nearby.

~

NEARBY Venice (10 lm); Padua (20 km).
LOCATION on banks of Brenta at Mira Porte at the E end of Mira, in own grounds
with ample parking
FOOD breakfast, lunch, dinner
PRICE €€
ROOMS 19; 18 double and twin, 3 with bath, 15 with shower; one single with
shower; all rooms have phone, TV, air conditioning, minibar, hairdrier
FACILITIES breakfast room, sitting room, bar, restaurant (200 m away), terrace,
garden, jogging track **CREDIT CARDS** AE, DC, MC, V
DISABLED several rooms on ground floor **PETS** accepted
CLOSED never
PROPRIETORS Dal Corso family

THE NORTH-EAST

MOGLIANO VENETO

VILLA CONDULMER

~ COUNTRY VILLA ~

Via Preganziol 1, 31020 Mogliano Veneto, Treviso
TEL 0471 5972700 **FAX** 0471 5972777
E-MAIL info@hotelvillacondulmer.com **WEBSITE** www.hotelvillacondulmer.com

FOR THE PRICE OF A THREE-STAR HOTEL in Venice you can stay in this impressive 18thC villa 20 minutes away. One very satisfied couple wrote to say that they will do just that whenever they visit the city again.

Flanked by annexes, Villa Condulmer stands four-square in a miniature park designed by Sebatoni. From the moment you walk in you will, like our correspondants, be struck by the sheer scale, not only of the rooms but of the furnishings. The vast central hall is decorated with baroque stucco in subtle colours, inset with murals. Two extravagantly large Murano chandeliers hang from the high ceiling, but comfortable armchairs make it a room to relax in, not just admire. A pair of grand pianos bear witness to Verdi's visits here. The more dilapidated is his; the other, a copy. The dining room ('delicious food') is in restful pale green and white, and there is an intimate stuccoed bar. The most exotic, and expensive, bedrooms are the upstairs suites The double rooms in the main villa are decorated in bright silk damasks, but we prefer the more restrained annexe rooms, where the peace and quiet, the comfortable beds and the heavy linen sheets should guarantee a good night's sleep.

~

NEARBY Palladian villas, Venice (18 km).
LOCATION 12 km S of Treviso, N of road to Mogliano Veneto; in own grounds with ample parking.
FOOD breakfast, dinner
PRICE €€€.
ROOMS 43 double, twin, single, junior suites, 8 apartments, all with bath or shower; all rooms have phone, TV, air conditioning, minibar, hairdrier
FACILITIES breakfast room, bar, sitting rooms, meeting room, TV room, dining rooms, garden, swimming pool, tennis courts, 9- and 18-hole golf
CREDIT CARDS AE, DC, MC, V
DISABLED access difficult **PETS** accepted
CLOSED never
PROPRIETOR Davide Zuin

THE NORTH-EAST

ORTISEI

UHRERHOF DEUR
~ MOUNTAIN CHALET ~

Bulla, 39046 Ortisei, Bolzano
TEL 0471 797335 **FAX** 0471 797457
E-MAIL info@uhrerhof.com **WEBSITE** www.uhrerhof.com

THE NAME MEANS 'HOUSE OF THE CLOCKS', and their ticking and chiming, along with birdsong, are very often the only sounds which break the silence at this traditional chalet set in a tucked-away hamlet 1,600 metres above sea level. Indeed, noise levels hardly rise above a whisper, and Signora Zemmer is at pains to point out that this is a place only for those seeking total peace and quiet. Outside, there is a grassy garden from which to enjoy the wide and wonderful view. Inside, all the rooms, including the balconied bedrooms, are bright, simple and beautifully kept, with plenty of homely details. The core of the chalet is 400 years old, and includes the all-wood *stübe* with working stove. The three adjoining dining rooms have wooden benches round the walls, Tyrolean fabrics for curtains and cushions, bright rugs on terracotta floors and pewter plates displayed in wall racks. Signor Zemmer is the chef, and his simple yet delicious food is elegantly presented on pewter plates.

Underneath the house is a surprisingly smart health complex, with huge picture windows so that you can relax in the open-plan Turkish bath and soak up the view. The hotel is strictly non-smoking.

~

NEARBY Val Gardena; Castelrotto (13 km); Bolzano (26 km).
LOCATION in mountainside hamlet, 13 km E of Castelrotto, off Castelrotto-Ortisei road; garage parking
FOOD breakfast, dinner
PRICE €€
ROOMS 11; 8 double and twin, 4 with bath, 4 with shower, 3 single with shower; 2 apartments for 2-5 with kitchen; all rooms have phone, TV, hairdrier, safe
FACILITIES dining room, bar, sitting room; lift, garden, health centre
CREDIT CARDS MC, V
DISABLED suitable
PETS not accepted
CLOSED Nov to mid-Dec, 2 weeks after Easter
PROPRIETORS Zemmer family

THE NORTH-EAST

PEDEMONTE

VILLA DEL QUAR
～ COUNTRY VILLA ～

Via Quar 12, 37020 Pedemonte, Verona
TEL 045 6800681 **FAX** 045 6800604
E-MAIL info@villadelquar **WEBSITE** www.villadelquar.it

SITUATED IN THE FERTILE VALPOLICELLA valley, this 'typical patrician dwelling' is nowadays a luxury hotel, a member of Relais et Châteaux. The ebullient owner and her family live in the fine main villa, while her hotel occupies the east wing. Public rooms in particular make a great impression. The galleried sitting room, an enclosed arcade with beamed roof, is delightfully light, airy and sophisticated. The Michelin-starred restaurant, Arquade, consists of two dining rooms – resplendent with mirrors, Venetian torches and a vast Murano glass chandelier – is also extremely attractive and makes a delightful place in which to eat. The reception room, doubling as a library and tea room, overlooks the swimming pool. Bedrooms are restrained, masculine, many with lovely old cupboard doors. Bathrooms feel luxurious, swathed in prettily coloured marble. If you take a suite, ask for the one with a terrace, which is no more expensive.

In summer, a white awning covers the terrace and the immaculate pool sparkles invitingly. The villa's setting, though quiet, is in ueventful countryside not quite in keeping with its interior, though it is surrounded by a sea of vines.

～

NEARBY Verona (11 km); Lake Garda (20 km).
LOCATION in Pedemonte follow signs for Verona and hotel at traffic lights; after about 1,500 m turn right for hotel; in own grounds with ample car parking
FOOD breakfast, lunch, dinner; room service
PRICE €€€€€
ROOMS 27; 18 double and twin, 9 suites, all with bath; all rooms have phone, TV, air conditioning, minibar, hairdrier, safe
FACILITIES sitting room, restaurant, breakfast room, bar, terrace, swimming pool, small gym
CREDIT CARDS AE, DC, MC, V
DISABLED rooms on ground floor **PETS** accepted
CLOSED mid-Jan to mid-Mar
PROPRIETORS Evelina Acampora and Leopoldo Montresor

THE NORTH-EAST

PERGINE

CASTEL PERGINE
~ CONVERTED CASTLE ~

38057 Pergine, Valsugana, Trento
TEL 0461 531158 **FAX** 0461 531329
E-MAIL verena@castelpergine.it **WEBSITE** www.castelpergine.it

THIS MEDIEVAL HILLTOP FORTRESS is managed with enthusiasm by an energetic and cultured Swiss couple, Verena and Theo. Past and present coexist happily in a rather alternative atmosphere, and the castle has a truly lived-in feel despite its grand dimensions and impressive history. A recent visit confirmed that this is one of the most affordable and distinctive hotels in the region. Though it must be said that it's an aquired taste: one reader comments on the 'daunting approach, strange modern art, refectory-style dining room and Spartan comfort'.

The route from the car park to the hotel leads you under stone arches, up age-worn steps and through vaulted chambers to the airy, round reception hall where breakfast is also served. The two spacious dining rooms have wonderful views, and the cooking is light and innovative. As you would expect from their price, bedrooms are by no means luxurious, and some are very small, but all are furnished in simple good taste; the best have splendid, heavy, carved wooden furniture and wall panelling.

One of the most enchanting features of the castle is the walled garden. Spend an hour reading a book, or simply watching the mountains through the crumbling ramparts, and you may never want to leave.

~

NEARBY Trento (11 km); Lake Caldonazzo (3 km); Segonzano.
LOCATION off the SS47 Padua road, 2 km SE of Pergine; in own grounds with ample car parking
FOOD breakfast, dinner
PRICE €
ROOMS 21; 13 double and twin, 8 with shower, 4 single, 3 with shower, 4 triple, 3 with shower; all rooms have phone
FACILITIES sitting room, dining rooms, bar, garden
CREDIT CARDS AE, MC, V
DISABLED access difficult **PETS** accepted
CLOSED Nov to Easter
PROPRIETORS Verena Neff and Theo Schneider

THE NORTH-EAST

PIEVE D'ALPAGO

DOLADA
~ RESTAURANT-WITH-ROOMS ~

Via Dolada 21, Plois, 32010 Pieve d'Alpago, Belluno
TEL 0437 479141 **FAX** 0437 478068
E-MAIL dolada@tin.it **WEBSITE** www.dolada.it

A twisting road leads from the Alpago valley to Pieve, and then corkscrews on up to the little hamlet of Plois. Albergo Dolada turns out to be a handsome building with faded apricot walls and green-shuttered windows with a little garden which looks out over snow-capped mountains and the Santa Croce lake and valley far below (there are wonderful walks from the door).

Built in 1923, Dolada has been owned and run as an inn by four generations of the De Prà family. The much vaunted kitchen (one Michelin star, with another in the offing) is overseen by Enzo De Prà, aided by his son Riccardo, while his wife Rossana, a professional *sommelier*, and daughter Benedetta (whose husband is head barman at the Cipriani in Venice) are a cheerful and friendly presence front of house. 'The food' our reporter comments, 'was divine, and the welcome could not have been more friendly. I would recommend the white bedroom, for its spaciousness, if you can get it, but don't worry if not'. The modern bedrooms are named for their colour schemes; the pink one can come as a bit of a shock the morning after an evening of serious over-indulgence in the elegant restaurant, but a long walk in the hills, with wonderful views all around, should sort things out.

~

NEARBY Belluno (20 km); Nevegàl ski area (18 km).
LOCATION in the hamlet of Plois, signposted from Pieve d'Alpago; ample parking
FOOD breakfast, lunch, dinner
PRICE €
ROOMS 7 double and twin, all with shower; all rooms have phone, TV,
FACILITIES restaurant, terrace, garden
CREDIT CARDS AE, DC, MC, V
DISABLED no special facilities
PETS accepted
CLOSED restaurant closed Mon and Tues lunch
PROPRIETORS De Prà family

THE NORTH-EAST

REDAGNO DI SOPRA

ZIRMERHOF
~ MOUNTAIN HOTEL ~

39040 Redagno, Bolzano
TEL 0471 887215 **FAX** 0471 887225
E-MAIL info@zirmerhof.com **WEBSITE** www.zirmerhof.com

SITUATED JUST OUTSIDE the tiny hamlet of Redagno di Sopra, this 12thC *mas* has been in the Perwanger family since 1890. Views are of mountains, green pastures and forests with few signs of civilization to mar the landscape. 'Idyllic', a contented guest tells us. The interior has been carefully restored. The dim, low-ceilinged hall with its intricate wood carving, ticking grandfather clock and old fireplace, immediately plunges you into the atmosphere of an old family home. There is a tiny cosy library, a sitting-cum-breakfast room with an open fire for winter days, and a rustic bar with a grassy terrace, from which to enjoy the superb views. The large wood-panelled dining room houses two elaborate ceramic stoves, and makes a fine setting in which to enjoy the local dishes and sophisticated wines on offer.

The comfortable bedrooms vary enormously in size, but all are attractive with traditional carved furniture (much of it made on the premises) and pretty fabrics; the largest rooms are on the top floor. For the energetic, there's plenty to do, particularly in winter, from skating and curling on the lake to cross-country and downhill skiing.

~

NEARBY Cavalese (15 km).
LOCATION 5 km N of Fontanefredde, off the SS48; in garden with ample car parking
FOOD breakfast, lunch, dinner
PRICE €€
ROOMS 31; 23 double and twin, 2 with bath, 21 with shower, 7 single, 2 with bath, 5 with shower, 1 suite with shower; rooms have TV on request
FACILITIES dining room, sitting room, bar, library, sauna, and steam room, garden, vineyard, riding
CREDIT CARDS MC, V
DISABLED ground floor bedrooms available
PETS accepted
CLOSED early Nov to day after Christmas, after Easter to mid-May
PROPRIETOR Sepp Perwanger

THE NORTH-EAST

SAN FLORIANO DEL COLLIO

GOLF HOTEL CASTELLO FORMENTINI
~ CONVERTED CASTLE ~

Via Oslavia 2, 34070 San Floriano del Collio, Gorizia
TEL 0481 884051 **FAX** 0481 884052
E-MAIL isabellaformentini@tiscalinet.it **WEBSITE** www.golfhotelcastelloformentini.it

WE ASKED FOR FEEDBACK ON THIS HOTEL in our last edition, and we've had plenty. Most speak very positively, praising the 'lovely' rooms ('we lit the little candles in our big modern bathroom'), the 'lavish' breakfast and the 'very reasonable' prices. One, however, criticized the housekeeping: ('the cookie under the nightstand encased in cobwebs was a little scary').

The hotel's name, referring to its nine-hole golf course (closed Mon), gives the impression of something modern, but it is in fact two ancient renovated houses just outside the walls of Castello Formentini, which has belonged to the Formentini family since the 16th century. The present owner, Contessa Isabella Formentini, has filled the rooms of the tiny hotel with family furniture and pictures. Each beautifully decorated and spacious bedroom is named after a prestigious wine, emphasizing the vinous interest of the Formentini family. Three of them are within the castle walls, but all guests are at liberty to use the castle grounds and its swimming pool. The family's restaurant, called Castello Formentini, is open only for groups (minimum 8-10 people) but guests are directed to another excellent, cosy restaurant nearby. This is a charming spot, with gentle, wooded countryside spread out around the hilltop castle.

~

NEARBY Gorizia (4 km); Trieste (47 km).
LOCATION in town, just outside castle walls; private grounds; car parking
FOOD breakfast, all day cold buffet
PRICE €€€
ROOMS 15; 12 double and twin, 2 single, 1 suite in tower, all with bath or shower; all rooms have TV, minibar; 12 rooms have phone; 3 rooms have no phone but air conditioning
FACILITIES sitting room, breakfast room, garden, swimming pool, tennis court, nine-hole golf course
CREDIT CARDS AE, DC, MC, V
DISABLED not suitable **PETS** accepted **CLOSED** Jan
PROPRIETOR Contessa Isabella Formentini

THE NORTH-EAST

SAN OSVALDO

GASTHOF TSCHOTSCHERHOF

~ COUNTRY GUESTHOUSE ~

San Osvaldo 19, 39040 Siusi, Bolzano
TEL 0471 706013 **FAX** 0471 704801
E-MAIL info@tschoetscherhof.com **WEBSITE** www.tschoetscherhof.com

DON'T BE PUT OFF by the unpronounceable name; for lovers of simple, farmhouse accommodation in an unspoiled rural setting, this hostelry could be ideal.

The narrow road from Siusi winds through apple orchards, vineyards and open meadows, eventually arriving at the tiny hamlet of San Osvaldo and this typical 500-year-old farmhouse with its adjacent dark wood barn. The name, painted on the outside of the building, is almost hidden by the clambering vines, and the old wooden balconies are a colourful riot of cascading geraniums. The sun-drenched terrace is a perfect spot for relaxing and eating.

Inside, we were beguiled by smells from the kitchen at the end of the hall, and were drawn to the warmth of the low-ceilinged old *stube* with gently ticking clock, rough wood floor and simple white ceramic stove.

A rustic stone stairway leads up to the modest but tidy bedrooms, some of which have balconies. They have no frills, but after a long day in glorious countryside, we were too tired to notice.

~

NEARBY Castelrotto (5 km); Bolzano (17 km); Sciliar Natural Park (10 km).
LOCATION in hamlet, 5 km W of Castelrotto; with parking
FOOD breakfast, lunch, dinner
PRICE €
ROOMS 8; 7 double and twin, 1 single, all with shower
FACILITIES dining rooms, terrace
CREDIT CARDS not accepted
DISABLED access difficult
PETS accepted
CLOSED Dec to Mar
PROPRIETORS Jaider family

THE NORTH-EAST

San Vigilio

LOCANDA SAN VIGILIO
~ LAKESIDE HOTEL ~

San Vigilio, 37016 Garda, Verona
TEL 045 7256688 **FAX** 045 7256551
E-MAIL info@locanda-sanvigilio.it **WEBSITE** www.locanda-sanvigilio.it

IN GENERAL THE EAST SIDE OF LAKE GARDA is less upmarket than the west but this hotel's idyllic setting, on a lush peninsula, Punta San Vigilio, dotted with olive trees and cypresses, is a conspicuous exception. The property is owned by Conte Agostino Guarienti, who lives in the 16thC villa that dominates the headland. An air of discreet exclusivity pervades the *locanda* (royalty are among regular guests) yet the atmosphere is far from stuffy. Of the public rooms, our favourite is the elegant dining room, right on the lake, with a comfortingly creaky wooden floor. A ceramic stove occupies one corner and sideboards display plates and bottles. You can eat in here, on a little arched veranda or under huge white umbrellas on the terrace where terracotta pots overflow with flowers. Next door is a cosy sitting room.

The seven bedrooms in the main house are all different, though they have beautiful antiques and fabrics in common. Only one has no view. Other bedrooms, or rather suites, are in separate buildings and more rustic in style. In the evening the place comes into its own: with the day trippers gone, guests can wander the peninsula or sit with a drink at one of the Taverna's vine-shaded tables. Whether you arrive by car through an avenue of cypress trees, or, even more magically, by boat, you will find this a gem of a hotel.

~

NEARBY Garda (2 km); Verona (45 km); ferry services (4 km).
LOCATION 2 km W of Garda, on promontory; parking available 150 m away
FOOD breakfast, lunch, dinner
PRICE €€€€€
ROOMS 14; 11 double and twin, 3 suites, all with bath or shower; all rooms have phone, TV, air conditioning, minibar, hairdrier; most rooms have safe
FACILITIES sitting room, dining room, bar, terrace, walled garden
CREDIT CARDS AE, DC, MC, V
DISABLED not suitable
PETS accepted
CLOSED Nov to just before Easter
PROPRIETOR Conte Agostino Guarienti

THE NORTH-EAST

SOLIGHETTO

LOCANDA DA LINO
~ RESTAURANT-WITH-ROOMS ~

Via Brandolini 31, 31050 Solighetto, Treviso
TEL 0438 82150/842377 **FAX** 0438 980577
E-MAIL dalino@trun.it **WEBSITE** www.seven.it/locanda-da-lino

THE CREATION of an inspired chef, Lino Toffolin, this country restaurant became an institution. Championed by the diva Toti Dal Monte, the young Lino was soon cooking for the *glitterati* and being patronized by stars such as Marcello Mastrioni. Although Lino has now died, the place is still run by his family and continues to attract a faithful local following. One long room, with smaller rooms leading off it, can seat 400 for dinner at full stretch. The ceilings are hung idiosyncratically with hundreds of copper pots. A table in the 'inner sanctum' enables you to glimpse food being grilled over a blazing furnace. From a menu of local delicacies, we particularly enjoyed *antipasto misto della Locanda, braciole di vetello ai ferri* and *polpettine in umido con polenta*, and there's an impressive wine list from the beautifully laid-out cellar.

The bedrooms are in annexes and range from comfortable doubles to the extravagantly rococo Elsa Vazzoler suite with its bright blue walls, enormous glilt lamps, and cherubs above the bed. The L-shaped entrance/bar/breakfast area is also furnished with rococo pieces, mixed eclectically but successfully with modern art. A one off.

~

NEARBY Palladian villas; Asolo (20 km).
LOCATION in Solighetto on the Follina road; ample car parking
FOOD breakfast, lunch, dinner
PRICE ⓔ
ROOMS 17; 10 double and twin, 7 suites, all with bath; all rooms have phone, TV, air conditioning, minibar, hairdrier
FACILITIES breakfast area/bar, restaurant, terrace
CREDIT CARDS AE, DC, MC, V
DISABLED several rooms on ground floor
PETS accepted
CLOSED restaurant Mon, Christmas Day, July
PROPRIETOR Marco Toffolin

THE NORTH-EAST

SCORZE

VILLA SORANZO CONESTABILE
~ TOWN VILLA ~

Via Roma 1, 30037 Scorzè, Venezia
TEL 041 445027 **FAX** 041 5840088
E-MAIL vsoranzo@tin.it **WEBISTE** www.villasoranzo.it

STANDING AT THE CENTRE of the hard-working town of Scorzè, this aristocratic villa dates back to the 16th century, but was remodelled in the
18th century in elegant neoclassical style. Visible from its earliest period
(especially if you take room No. 1) are fragments of gorgeous School of
Veronese frescoes. There are also fine ceilings and floors, an impressive
double staircase and a park modelled in the early 19th century in
Romantic English style. The spacious first floor rooms are somewhat staid
but full of character, recalling the last century when they were the bedrooms of the noble Conestabile family, retaining their lofty proportions,
and, in some cases, original *faux* marble walls. Rooms on the second floor,
formerly the household quarters, are plainer but spacious and furnished
in different styles.

On a spring visit our inspector reports that she ate alone in the dining
room, but was comforted by the familial ambience, with copper pans hanging from the ceiling and old dressers laden with wine bottles, and by a
simple but well-prepared set menu. She also notes that her visit was
marred by one of the coolest welcomes in reception that she can remem-
ber. However, other satisfied guests have encountered much friendlier
staff; more reports please.

~

NEARBY Riviera del Brenta; Venice (24 km); Padua (30 km).
LOCATION in Scorzè, 24 km NW of Venice; in own grounds with ample car parking
FOOD breakfast, dinner
PRICE €€€
ROOMS 20; 14 double and twin, 3 single, all with bath or shower, 3 suites; all
rooms have phone, TV
FACILITIES sitting room, dining room, bar, breakfast room, terrace, garden
CREDIT CARDS AE, DC, MC, V
DISABLED not suitable **PETS** accepted
CLOSED restaurant only, Sat, Sun
PROPRIETORS Martinelli family

THE NORTH-EAST

SIUSI ALLO SCILIAR

BAD RATZES
~ MOUNTAIN HOTEL ~

Bagnidi Razzes, 39040 Siusi allo Sciliar, Bolzano
TEL and **FAX** 0471 706131
E-MAIL info@badratzes.it **WEBSITE** www.badratzes.it

LEAVING THE SMALL TOWN OF SIUSI in search of Bad Ratzes, the road winds uphill past green meadows and into a dense forest where Hansel and Gretel would have felt at home. When at last you reach it in a clearing, the hotel, large and modern, looks disconcertingly grim, but the warmth and enthusiasm of the Scherlin sisters will put you immediately at ease. Inside, the decoration is dull 1960s and 1970s, but comfortable. Public areas – including a formal sitting room with open fireplace, a children's playroom and two dining rooms – are extensive. All but four of the spotless bedrooms have balconies.

Food is important at Bad Ratzes: local dishes are carefully prepared and pasta is home made. One of the sisters bakes regularly, and her recipes are recorded in a little booklet. This is one of a group of family hotels in the area and there are many thoughtful child-orientated extras: pots of crayons and paper on the dining tables, a booklet of local bedtime stories, walks for children, a special menu and so on. Adults are not neglected; there is wonderful and varied walking in the neighbourhood and a free ski bus runs to the slopes in winter.

NEARBY Bolzano (22 km); Siusi National Park; skiing (10 km).
LOCATION 22 km NE of Bolzano, 3 km SE of Siusi; in own grounds with ample car parking
FOOD breakfast, lunch, dinner
PRICE €
ROOMS 52; 36 double, 9 single, 7 family rooms, all with bath; all rooms have phone, hairdrier; 18 rooms have TV and safe
FACILITIES dining rooms, sitting rooms, bar, playroom, indoor swimming pool, sauna, garden, garage
CREDIT CARDS not accepted
DISABLED not suitable **PETS** accepted
CLOSED Sunday after Easter to mid-May
PROPRIETORS Scherlin family

THE NORTH-EAST

GARDESANA
~ LAKESIDE HOTEL ~

Piazza Calderini 20, 37010 Torri del Benaco, Verona
TEL 045 7225411 **FAX** 045 7225771
E-MAIL info@hotel-gardesana.com **WEBSITE** www.hotel-gardesana.com

TORRI DEL BENACO IS ONE of the showpiece fishing villages which are dotted along the shore of Lake Garda, and Gardesana, the former harbourmaster's office, is in a plum position. It is a treat to tuck into the chef's speciality fish soup on the delightful first floor dining terrace which overlooks the central *piazza*, 14thC castle and bustling port. The wrought-iron balustrade is decked with cascading geraniums, the tables are elegant, the waiters smartly uniformed, and the food, particularly the fish, fresh and delicious. It makes a perfect vantage point for watching the boats come and go, and the changing colours of the lake. Drinks can also be taken on the ground floor terrace, which extends out on to the *piazza*.

The building has a long history, as its exterior would suggest, with its stone arches and mellow stucco walls; but the entire interior has been smartly modernized in recent years to produce an essentially modern and very comfortable, if simple, hotel. The green and white bedrooms are almost all identical: wooden floors, wooden furnishings, soft fabrics, plenty of little extras. If you can, try to book one of the corner rooms; these have the advantage of facing both the lake and the *piazza*; otherwise choose a third floor room, overlooking the lake with balcony.

NEARBY Bardolino (11 km); Malcesine (21 km); Gardaland.
LOCATION in town centre, on waterfront, in pedestrian zone; unload at hotel, private parking 150 m away
FOOD breakfast, dinner
PRICE €
ROOMS 34; 31 double, 3 single, all with shower; all rooms have phone, TV, air conditioning (Jul and Aug)
FACILITIES dining room, bar, lift, terrace
CREDIT CARDS AE, DC, MC, V
DISABLED no special facilities **PETS** not accepted
CLOSED Nov and Dec
PROPRIETOR Giuseppe Lorenzini

THE NORTH-EAST

TRISSINO

RELAIS CA'MASIERI

∼ RESTAURANT-WITH-ROOMS ∼

Località Masieri, Via Masieri, 36070 Trissino, Vicenza
TEL 0445 490122 **FAX** 0445 490455
E-MAIL info@camasieri.com **WEBSITE** www.camasieri.com

THE COUNTRYSIDE AROUND industrial Arzignano is uninspiring, but things improve as you wind your way to Masieri through willow-fringed meadows. Through wrought-iron gates and at the end of a long drive, the sight of Ca' Masieri itself, a fine old shuttered mansion with swimming pool and shady terrace further lifts the spirits. In our case, they were immediately cast down, because we were late and the chef had just gone home: we had been dreaming of the much-vaunted food all morning. The sight of the charming little restaurant, its walls decorated with delicate 18thC frescoes, only made our disappointment worse. Had we been in time, we might have had the salad of crayfish tails followed by risotto with herbs, and then the casserole of pigeon.

The bedrooms are in an adjacent building which retains its old wooden beamed ceilings, but is otherwise furnished in contemporary style. Two rooms have spiral metal staircases from a sitting area up to the mezzanine beds. No. 201 is huge, with a terrace overlooking the hills and Trissino. There are pretty bedspreads in William Morris leaf-print, curvy modern tables, and stylish bathrooms with walls painted the colour of aluminium.

NEARBY Vicenza (21 km); Verona (49 km).
LOCATION from Trissino, follow signs to Masieri, and in Via Masieri to Ca' Masieri up a private drive; ample car parking
FOOD breakfast, lunch, dinner
PRICE ©€
ROOMS 12; 5 double, 2 single, 5 apartments, all with shower; all rooms have phone, TV, air conditioning, minibar
FACILITIES sitting room, bar, breakfast room, dining room, terrace, swimming pool
CREDIT CARDS AE, MC, V
DISABLED not suitable
PETS accepted
CLOSED never; restaurant closed Sun, Mon lunch
PROPRIETOR Angelo Vassena

THE NORTH-EAST

ACCADEMIA
~ TOWN HOTEL ~

Fondamenta Bollani, Dorsoduro 1058, 30123 Venezia
TEL 041 5210188 **FAX** 041 5239152
E-MAIL info@pensioneaccademia.it **WEBSITE** www.pensioneaccademia.it

STILL ONE OF THE BEST LOVED hotels in Venice, the Accademia continues to
exert its considerable charm on a stream of contented guests. Despite
recent modernisations such as sliding front doors and air conditioning,
both the hotel and its staff have the knack of making guests feel like travellers from another, more genteel, age rather than modern-day tourists.

The Accademia's privileged canalside location is both convenient and
calm, but what really distinguishes the *pensione* is its gardens – the large
canal-side patio, where tables are scattered among plants in classical
urns, and the grassy rear garden where roses and fruit trees flourish. Built
in the 17th century as a private mansion, Villa Maravege retains touches of
grandeur, and most of the furnishings are classically Venetian (the
Murano chandeliers for once tasteful and harmonious). Perfect for sitting
and relaxing is the finely furnished first floor landing, while the bedrooms
have inlaid wooden floors and antiqued mirrors. The airy breakfast room
has crisp white tablecloths and a beamed ceiling; but, weather permitting,
guests will inevitably opt to start their day in the garden.

~

NEARBY Accademia gallery; Scuola Grande dei Carmini.
LOCATION where the Toletta and Trovaso canals meet the Grand Canal; vaporetto
Accademia or water taxi
FOOD breakfast
PRICE €€€
ROOMS 29; 22 double and twin, 9 with bath, 13 with shower, 7 single, 6 with
shower; all rooms have phone, TV; most have air conditioning, hairdrier, safe
FACILITIES breakfast room, bar, sitting room, garden
CREDIT CARDS AE, DC, MC, V
DISABLED no special facilities
PETS accepted
CLOSED never
PROPRIETOR Giovanna Salmaso

THE NORTH-EAST

VENICE

AGLI ALBORETTI

~ TOWN GUESTHOUSE ~

Rio Terrà Foscarini, Dorsoduro 884, 30123 Venezia
TEL 041 5230058 **FAX** 041 5210158
E-MAIL alborett@gpnet.it **WEBSITE** www.aglialboretti.com

THE ALBORETTI IS DISTINGUISHED by its warm welcome, and genuine family atmosphere. Reception is a cosy wood-panelled room with paintings of Venice on the walls and a model of a 17thC galleon in its window; the ground floor sitting room is small, but a second sitting room on the first-floor makes a comfortable retreat (the TV is rarely used); the terrace behind the hotel, entirely covered by a pergola and set simply with tables and chairs, is a delight, especially for a leisurely breakfast in summer. The building's fourth floor is now part of the hotel, and includes another terrace for guests.

The style of the bedrooms is predominantly simple, some with a nautical theme, and most with an antique or two. Like the rest of the hotel, they are well cared for and spotlessly clean, but the bathrooms, though totally renovated, are tiny, as are some of the rooms. None are large, but three are recommended for their garden views, and one also has a balcony on which you can breakfast.

Signora Linguerri runs a sophisticated restaurant next door, where you can eat in the pretty dining room or outside under the pergola; she is an expert on wine and her list offers an interesting selection.

~

NEARBY Accademia gallery; Zattere; Gesuati.
LOCATION alongside the Accademia gallery; vaporetto Accademia
FOOD breakfast, lunch, dinner
PRICE ©©
ROOMS 23; 13 double and twin, 5 single, 5 family rooms, all with bath or shower; all rooms have phone, modem point, TV, air conditioning, minibar, hairdrier
FACILITIES sitting rooms, dining room, bar, lift, terrace
CREDIT CARDS AE, MC, V
DISABLED no special facilities **PETS** accepted
CLOSED Jan occasionally; restaurant Wed, Thurs lunch
PROPRIETOR Anna Linguerri

THE NORTH-EAST

VENICE

AMERICAN

~ TOWN HOTEL ~

Rio di San Vio, Dorsoduro 628, 30123 Venezia
TEL 041 5204733 **FAX** 041 5204048
E-MAIL reception@hotelamerican.com **WEBSITE** www.hotelamerican.com

SET IN A PEACEFUL BACKWATER of Dorsoduro, yet close to the Accademia and the Grand Canal, this is a quiet, dignified hotel with spacious reception rooms and a tiny terrace where you can take breakfast under a pergola in summer. The public areas have a sombre Edwardian air, with wood panelling and silk damask on the walls, tapestry or velvet upholstered chairs, oriental rugs on Venetian mosaic floors, frilly white curtains and potted plants. Corridors are also panelled in wood, with little tables and chairs placed here and there. Bedrooms – all newly renovated – vary in size, as do the bathrooms, and though unexceptional they have pretty Venetian painted furniture (with minibars mercifully disguised as free-standing cupboards), ornate gilt mirrors and pretty Paisley-print bedspreads.

If you choose the American, you should do what you can to secure one of the nine bedrooms that overlook the canal. Nos 101 and 102 are particularly recommended, with three canal-facing French windows on two sides, and narrow balconies from where you can watch the water traffic drift by.

~

NEARBY Accademia gallery; Zattere; Santa Maria della Salute.
LOCATION midway along canal, which runs between Grand Canal and Giudecca Canal; vaporetto Accademia or water taxi
FOOD breakfast
PRICE €€€
ROOMS 28; double and twin and single, all with bath or shower; all rooms have phone, TV, air conditioning, minibar, hairdrier, safe
FACILITIES sitting area, breakfast room, terrace
CREDIT CARDS AE, MC, V
DISABLED no special facilities
CLOSED never
PROPRIETOR Salvatore Sutera Sardo

THE NORTH-EAST

BUCINTORO
~ TOWN GUESTHOUSE ~

Riva San Biagio, Castello 2135, 30122 Venezia
TEL 041 5223240 **FAX** 041 5235224
E-MAIL pensionebucintoro@tin.it

WE MET A COUPLE AT VENICE airport who had splashed out on the Londra Palace (which they liked very much) for the first few days of their stay and then sharply downgraded to the Bucintoro – which they almost preferred. Apart from the wonderful views across St Mark's Basin, which the two hotels share, the contrast could not be greater. Rooms at this basic *pensione*, little changed since the family bought it 30 years ago, are as plain as a pikestaff; breakfast is frugal; and the sitting room, despite its newly upholstered armchairs, remains unappealing.

The secret of its success is its position: every clean and simple room has a lagoon view and is flooded with Venetian light. Corner rooms, beloved by artists, are the best, with windows on to both the lagoon and San Marco (try for Nos 1, 7, 9, 11). Room No. 4 is one of the pleasantest, with large bed, pretty bedspread, airy curtains and the waters of the lagoon gently lapping below. No. 26 can fit up to four people and has a fair-sized bathroom. The modest cement-rendered building with tables outside in summer is conveniently close to the Arsenale vaporetto stop.

~

NEARBY Arsenale; Naval Museum; Piazza San Marco.
LOCATION on the waterfront, at the far end of Riva degli Schiavoni; vaporetto Arsenale or water taxi
FOOD breakfast
PRICE €€
ROOMS 28; 22 double, twin and triple, 17 with bath, 5 with shower, 6 single, 5 with shower, 1 with basin; all rooms have phone, fan on request, hairdrier
FACILITIES breakfast room, sitting room, terrace
CREDIT CARDS MC, V
DISABLED not suitable
PETS not accepted
CLOSED Dec, Jan
PROPRIETORS Bianchi family

THE NORTH-EAST

VENICE

CA' FOSCARI

~ TOWN GUESTHOUSE ~

Calle della Frescada, Dorsoduro 3888-3887/b, 30123 Venezia
TEL 041 710401/710817 **FAX** 041 710817
E-MAIL info@locandacafoscari.com **WEBSITE** www.locandacafoscari.com

YOU WILL NEED HELP FINDING Calle Frescada, a little lane tucked almost out of sight and unmarked on most maps: take Calle Larga Foscari towards the Frari, and at the junction with Crosera, turn right. Calle Frescada runs across the end, and the hotel faces down Crosera. Happily our inspector's maddening search for this little one-star hotel was worth the effort – Ca' Foscari is a cut above. Somehow its charming, modest exterior – smart front door and bell pull, little lantern displaying its name – tells the story, and the interior does not disappoint, nor the welcome from Valter and Giuliana Scarpa.

On the ground floor is a little breakfast room. A couple of flights of stairs, and you are in a fresh, white corridor with white-painted doors leading to the bedrooms. These are modest, as you would expect, but pristine, with lacy curtains and pretty bedspreads and white-tiled minute bathrooms, or, in rooms without bathrooms, decent basins. Note that the communal bathroom only has a shower, not a bath. The metal-framed beds are much more comfortable than they look. An excellent budget hotel in a bustling residential neighbourhood.

~

NEARBY Scuola Grande di San Rocco; Frari; Accademia gallery.
LOCATION between Campo San Tomà and Palazzi Foscari; vaporetto San Tomà
FOOD breakfast
PRICE €
ROOMS 11; 6 double and twin, 3 with shower, 3 with basin only; 1 single with shower, 2 triples without shower, 2 family rooms without shower; communal bathroom with shower
FACILITIES breakfast room
CREDIT CARDS MC, V
DISABLED not suitable
PETS not accepted
CLOSED 15 Nov to 20 Jan, late Jul
PROPRIETOR Valter Scarpa

THE NORTH-EAST

VENICE

LA CALCINA
∼ TOWN HOTEL ∼

Fondamenta Zattere ai Gesuati, Dorsoduro 780, 30123 Venezia
TEL 041 5206466 **FAX** 041 5227045
E-MAIL info@lacalcina.com **WEBSITE** www.lacalcina.com

THE HOUSE WHERE RUSKIN LIVED is hard to resist, both for its historical connection and for its location facing the sunny straits of the Giudecca canal. The simple *pensione*, inherited by a go-ahead young couple, is nowadays a stylish small hotel whose calm, uncluttered rooms provide a welcome antidote to an excess of Venetian rococo. The pretty ground floor reception rooms now including a bar and a cosy, informal bar/restaurant/café, La Piscina.

Unlike many hotels in the city there is a marked difference in price between the rooms at the front, with views across the glittering water, and the darkish back rooms, which have no view, but are equally comfortable. Most expensive are the corner rooms, where the sun streams in from two directions. None of the rooms is large, but all compensate with cool cream walls, warm parquet floors, antiques and gleaming bathrooms with heated towel rails. Meals are served in summer on the terrace in front of the hotel, or the lovely, sunny deck that juts out into the canal (or you can book the romantic roof garden for two), and in winter in the marble-floored restaurant/bar with a picture window, so that even if you opt for a bedroom at the back you can still enjoy the vista.

∼

NEARBY Gesuati church; Accademia gallery.
LOCATION on W side of San Vio canal; vaporetto Zattere or water taxi
FOOD breakfast, light snacks, lunch, dinner
PRICE €€€
ROOMS 29; 3 suites; 19 double and twin, 2 with bath, 20 with shower, 7 single, 1 with bath, 3 with shower, 3 with washbasin; all rooms have phone, air conditioning, hairdrier, safe; apartments also available with space for 2
FACILITIES breakfast room/bar, sitting area, terrace, roof terrace
CREDIT CARDS AE, DC, MC, V
DISABLED not suitable **PETS** not accepted
CLOSED never
PROPRIETORS Alessandro and Debora Szemere

THE NORTH-EAST

VENICE

CA' PISANI
~ TOWN HOTEL ~

Dorsoduro 979/a, 30123 Venezia
TEL 041 2401411 **FAX** 041 2771061
E-MAIL info@capisanihotel.it **WEBSITE** www.capisanihotel.it

BLATANTLY FLYING IN THE FACE of Venetian hotel tradition, the brand new Ca' Pisani, built in the shell of a deep-pink 16thC *palazzo*, is cool, hip and undeniably chic.

Inside, the overall style is designer minimalist, but the odd original feature (brick arches, roof beams, painted coffered ceilings, marble floors), and the collection of fine '30s and '40s beds, mirrors and wardrobes softens this to a certain extent. Decorative themes are consistent throughout both public areas and bedrooms. Silver (above the reception area, in bedroom furniture, in mirror frames, on light fittings, in steel chair frames) is a staple and lightens dark ebony, pale acid-green and pale violet paintwork, and black and orange leather chairs. Warm, hardwood floors and wood doors are all given a contemporary twist. Bathrooms, in either deep mauve or palest grey marble specked with silver, are straight from the pages of a design magazine. The bedrooms have Bang&Olufsen phones and TVs and electrically-operated window blinds. Biscuit-coloured bedcovers and cushions look smart against crisp white linen sheets. Breakfast is served in the basement restaurant where you can also enjoy a light meal. The hotel has opened quite recently; reports would be welcome.

~

NEARBY Accademia gallery; Guggenheim museum.
LOCATION between the Accademia and Zattere; vaporetto Accademia, Zattere
FOOD breakfast, lunch, dinner
PRICE €€€€
ROOMS 29; 23 double and twin, 4 junior suites 2 studios, all with bath; all rooms have phone, TV, air conditioning, minibar, hairdrier
FACILITIES sitting room, internet point, restaurant, bar, Turkish bath, terrace
CREDIT CARDS AE, DC, MC, V
DISABLED 2 specially adapted rooms
PETS accepted
CLOSED never
PROPRIETORS Serandrei family

THE NORTH-EAST

VENICE

FLORA
~ TOWN HOTEL ~

Calle Larga XXII Marzo, San Marco 2283/a, 30124 Venezia
TEL 041 5205844 **FAX** 041 5228217
E-MAIL info@hotelflora.it **WEBSITE** www.hotelflora.it

SUCH IS THE POPULARITY of this small hotel, tucked away down a cul-de-sac close to San Marco, that to get a room here you have to book weeks, even months in advance. You only need to glimpse the garden to know why it is sought after. Creepers, fountains and flowering shrubs cascading from stone urns create an enchanting setting for breakfast, tea or an evening drink in summer.

The lobby is small and inviting, enhanced by the views of the garden through a glass arch; the atmosphere is one of friendly efficiency. There are some charming double bedrooms with painted carved antiques and other typically Venetian furnishings, but beware of other comparatively spartan rooms, some of which are barely big enough for one, let alone two. Coveted rooms include two on the ground floor facing the garden and the three spacious corner rooms, the topmost of which has a marvellous view of Santa Maria della Salute. The venerable Flora has been run by the charming Romanelli family, father, son and grandson, for over 40 years (young Gioele now runs his own place, the excellent Locanda Novecento; see p109). Plaudits continue to flow in to our office, though one mentions that the breakfast room felt crowded in the morning 'though the waiters were quick at juggling seating arrangements'.

~

NEARBY Piazza San Marco.
LOCATION 300 m from Piazza San Marco in cul-de-sac off Calle Larga XXII Marzo; vaporetto San Marco
FOOD breakfast
PRICE €€€
ROOMS 44; 32 double and twin, 6 single, 6 family, all with bath or shower; all rooms have phone, TV, air conditioning, hairdrier, safe
FACILITIES reading room, breakfast room, bar, lift, garden
CREDIT CARDS AE, DC, MC, V
DISABLED 2 rooms on ground floor **PETS** accepted **CLOSED** never
PROPRIETORS Roger and Joel Romanelli

THE NORTH-EAST

LOCANDA AI SANTI APOSTOLI
～ TOWN HOTEL ～

Strada Nova, Cannaregio 4391, 30131 Venezia
TEL 041 5212612 **FAX** 041 5212611
E-MAIL aisantia@tin.it **WEBSITE** www.locandasantiapostoli.com

BE ON THE LOOKOUT FOR A PAIR of handsome dark green doors which herald
the discreet entrance of this converted *palazzo*. Beyond is a scruffy
courtyard and a quirky lift that takes you up to the third floor. What lies in
store for you here is totally unexpected: a lovely apartment that has been
transformed by the Bianchi Michiel family into an elegant, if pricey, B&B,
one of the first, and still one of the best *locandas* to open in recent years
in the city. The sitting room is the epitome of style: oil paintings hang on
glossy apricot walls; heavy lamps rest on antique tables; sofas and chairs
are covered in quiet chintz or swathed in calico. At the far end, a triptych
of wood-framed windows overlooks the Grand Canal. Ornaments and
books left casually around make it feel more like a home than a hotel.

Large and individually decorated, the bedrooms have been done out in
glazed chintzes and stunning strong colours. Like the sitting room, they
are dotted with antiques and pretty china knick-knacks. The two on the
Grand Canal are considerably dearer than the rest. Stefano also owns a
one-bedroom apartment on the second floor, with a vibrant green colour
scheme, no view of the canal, but a sunny roof terrace.

～

NEARBY Ca' d'Oro; Santi Apostoli; Miracoli.
LOCATION just E of Campo Santi Apostoli; vaporetto Ca' d'Oro
FOOD breakfast
PRICE €€€; apartment prices on request
ROOMS 11 double and twin, 6 with bath, 4 with shower; all rooms have phone, TV,
air conditioning, minibar, hairdrier
FACILITIES breakfast room, sitting room, lift
CREDIT CARDS AE, DC, MC, V
DISABLED not suitable
PETS accepted
CLOSED Jan to mid-Feb, 2-3 weeks in Aug, sometimes 2 weeks in Dec
PROPRIETOR Stefano Bianchi Michiel

THE NORTH-EAST

LOCANDA ANTICO DOGE

~ TOWN GUESTHOUSE ~

Campo SS Apostoli, Cannaregio 5043, 30131 Venezia
TEL 041 2411570 **FAX** 041 2443660
E-MAIL info@anticodoge.com **WEBSITE**: www.anticodoge.com

DON'T BE PUT OFF BY FIRST IMPRESSIONS at the Antico Doge. Its entrance may not be to your taste, but the long, wide peach-coloured hallway, decorated with glitzy white Murano glass lights and garish paintings of Venice, gives little hint of the charm and splendour that lies one floor up. Keep going, pausing at the small reception desk (where you will find a friendly and professional welcome) and, mounting the stairs, you will soon arrive on the *piano nobile* of this privately owned *palazzo* with a long history. The central *salone*, which doubles as a breakfast room and bar, is resplendent in gold, with vases of fresh flowers. Bedrooms drip with silk, brocade and damask on walls, windows and beds. Huge chandeliers, gilt mirrors, antique furniture and fine rugs on parquet floors complete the picture. In one suite hangs a picture of a startled looking Doge Marin Falier, whose mansion this once was.

Close to the Rialto, in a delightfully domestic and watery area of Cannaregio, just round the corner from both the Locanda Ai Santi Apostoli (p 104) and the Locanda Leon Bianco (p 108), the Antico Doge is, like them, a cut above many similar bed and breakfast establishments.

~

NEARBY Santi Apostoli; Miracoli; Rialto.
LOCATION across little bridge on W side of Campo Santi Apostoli; vaporetto Ca'd'Oro
FOOD breakfast
PRICE €€€
ROOMS 15, all double or twin, 7 with shower, 8 with bath; all rooms have phone, TV, air conditioning, minibar, safe, hairdrier
FACILITIES bar, breakfast room
CREDIT CARDS AE, MC, V
DISABLED access possible; stairlift **PETS** not accepted
CLOSED never
PROPRIETOR Mariella Bazzetta

THE NORTH-EAST

LOCANDA CIPRIANI

~ RESTAURANT-WITH-ROOMS ~

Torcello, 30012 Burano, Venezia
TEL 041 730150 **FAX** 041 735433
E-MAIL info@locandacipriani.com **WEBSITE** www.locandacipriani.com

THE TINY LAGOON ISLAND OF TORCELLO is the cradle of the Venetian civilization, yet all that remains are two serenely beautiful religious buildings,
the church of Santa Fosca, and the Byzantine cathedral. The latter has a
haunting mosaic of the Madonna, and from its campanile, there is a wonderful view of the lagoon. When the tourists drift home at the end of the
day, Torcello's magic takes hold, and only the half dozen or so residents,
and the handful of guests at the Locanda Cipriani are there to share the
privilege. In the past, these have included Hemingway, Chaplin and Paul
Newman; and the entire British royal family have lunched here. The inn,
opened in 1934 by Giuseppe Cipriani and still in the family, has six bedrooms: simple and homely yet sophisticated, with polished wood floors,
attractive pictures on white walls, writing desks, *objets d'art*, comfortable
sofas and armchairs. Air conditioning has been installed, but mercifully
not televisions, and bathrooms are up to date.

The Locanda's *raison d'être* has always been its restaurant, Though it
is a memorable experience to eat here, either in the rustic dining room or
on the lovely terrace overlooking the cathedral, prices are steep, reflecting not so much the quality of the food, but its long-standing fame.
Romance, however, is guaranteed. In fact, we can think of nowhere more
romantic to stay in all of northern Italy.

~

NEARBY Venice (40 mins); lagoon islands.
LOCATION in centre of island, overlooking the cathedral; vaporetto Torcello (line LN
from Fondamente Nove)
FOOD breakfast, lunch, dinner
PRICE €€€
ROOMS 6; 3 double with sitting rooms, 3 single, all with bath; all rooms have
phone, air conditioning
FACILITIES sitting room, dining room, bar, terrace, garden **CREDIT CARDS** AE, MC, V
DISABLED not suitable **PETS** accepted **CLOSED** Jan to mid-Feb
PROPRIETOR Bonifacio Brass

THE NORTH-EAST

VENICE

LOCANDA DEL GHETTO

~ TOWN GUESTHOUSE ~

Campo del Ghetto Nuovo, Cannaregio 2892, 30131 Venezia
TEL 041 2759292 **FAX** 041 2757987
E-MAIL ghetto@veneziahotels.com **WEBSITE**: www.veneziahotels.com

SURROUNDED ON ALL SIDES BY WATER, the Campo del Ghetto Nuovo is the evocative, rather melancholy heart of what was the world's first Jewish ghetto. Quiet and contemplative, it lies only five minutes walk from heaving Lista di Spagna yet within easy reach of the peaceful Cannaregio backwaters. This stylish, nine-room locanda opened in early 2002, in a building which dates from the 15thC. Several of the rooms have original decorated wooden ceilings.

Seen from the Campo, the reception area glows invitingly from behind big windows under a little portico. On the ground floor is a small breakfast room overlooking the canal while upstairs, the light and airy bedrooms, though varying in shape and size, are all done out in the same elegant, understated style; pale cream walls, honey-coloured parquet floors, pale gold bedcovers and curtains, smart reproduction furniture, brass fittings and soft lighting. Two have small terraces on the Campo while another, (the smallest), has two original Gothic windows and an ancient fireplace serving as a bed head. Bathrooms are super-smart and even equipped with phones.

~

NEARBY Train station; Madonna del Orto; Jewish museum.
LOCATION in Campo del Ghetto Nuovo, ten minutes walk from the train station.
vaporetto Ponte Guglie, San Marcuola
FOOD breakfast
PRICE €€€
ROOMS 9 double and twin, all with bath; all rooms have phone, TV, air conditioning, minibar, safe
FACILITIES breakfast room, sitting area
CREDIT CARDS AE, MC, V
DISABLED one ground floor room **PETS** not accepted
CLOSED never
PROPRIETOR Alessandra Mascharo

THE NORTH-EAST

VENICE

LOCANDA LEON BIANCO

~ TOWN GUESTHOUSE ~

Corte Leon Bianco, Cannaregio 5629, 30131 Venezia
TEL 041 5233572 **FAX** 041 2416392
E-MAIL info@leonbianco.it **WEBSITE** www.leonbianco.it

IF WINDOWS ON TO THE GRAND CANAL are your heart's desire, but you are on a budget, then here is the answer. The Leon Bianco is hidden away in an enclosed courtyard, behind a sturdy door in the wall, and approached by stone steps rising up a cavernous brick-walled stairwell. The spacious, simple rooms have carved mahogany beds, big old cupboards, undulating floors and immense tilted wooden doors. Three look over the Grand Canal, with wonderful views of the Rialto market and the *traghetto* that plies back and forth across the canal, while a fourth, though it lacks a view, is equally romantic, with a dramatic fresco of Moors and camels taken from a painting by Veronese emblazoned across one wall. The locanda, only a few years old, but old-fashioned in feel, occupies one floor of an old *palazzo* and has a reception area and seven large, attractive bedrooms with small, modern bathrooms. Although it doesn't offer the services or address of the ritzy San Marco hotels, the modest prices are irresistible by comparison. A word of warning, however: a reader wrote to us to complain that her booking was cancelled in a preremptory fashion, with little help given to finding alternative accommodation. More reports, please.

~

NEARBY Santi Apostoli; Miracoli; Rialto.
LOCATION in courtyard between Santi Apostoli and Santa Giovanni Crisostomo canals; vaporetto Ca' d'Oro, Rialto
FOOD breakfast
PRICE €€
ROOMS 7; 6 double and twin with shower, one family with bath; all rooms have phone
FACILITIES none
CREDIT CARDS AE, DC, MC, V
DISABLED not suitable
PETS not accepted
CLOSED never
PROPRIETORS Spellanzon family

THE NORTH-EAST

VENICE

METROPOLE

~ TOWN HOTEL ~

Riva degli Schiavoni, Castello 4149, 30122 Venezia
TEL 041 5205044 **FAX** 041 5223679
E-MAIL venice@hotelmetropole.com **WEBSITE** www.hotelmetropole.com

O F THE HALF DOZEN OR MORE HOTELS along the Riva degli Schiavoni, with its matchless views of the lagoon, this is our favourite. Still in private hands, it has endearing touches (the owner, Signor Beggiato, is a collector: everywhere you look are carved angels, lecterns, church pews, corkscrews, crucifixes, cigarette cases, fans) and a core of twinkle-eyed staff who have been there forever. It's a canny choice in winter, when the velvet-hung *salone*, its table heaped with cakes at tea-time, and the intimate wood-panelled and muralled restaurant (a former chapel where Vivaldi taught singing to orphan girls), are most inviting; the latter serves an excellent buffet, making it an intimate and comfortable place in which to lunch or dine.

In the morning, the generous buffet breakfast is served in a pretty room, a vision in candy pink and white, decorated with antique fans. Bedrooms vary from traditional (such as cosy no. 350 with private *altana*) to wildly kitsch (complete with flying cherubs in no. 251). It's a busy tourist hotel in a bustling location, but it has character, atmosphere, and a genuinely warm heart.

~

NEARBY San Marco; Accademia; Rialto.
LOCATION midway along the Riva, next to the church of La Pièta; vaporetto San Zaccaria, Arsenale or water taxi
FOOD breakfast, lunch, dinner; room service
PRICE €€€
ROOMS 72; 56 double and twin, 3 single, 10 junior suites, 3 family; all rooms have phone, TV, air conditioning, minibar, safe, hairdrier
FACILITIES breakfast room, sitting room, dining room, lift, garden
CREDIT CARDS AE, DC, MC, V
DISABLED access possible
PETS accepted
CLOSED never
PROPRIETORS Beggiato family

THE NORTH-EAST

NOVECENTO
~ TOWN HOTEL ~

Campo San Maurizio, San Marco 2683/84, 30124 Venezia
TEL 041 2413765 **FAX** 041 5212145
E-MAIL info@novecento.biz **WEBSITE** www.novecento.biz

OFF CAMPO SAN MAURIZIO, JUST AROUND THE CORNER from the Gritti Palace, the recently opened Locanda Novecento is a wonderful addition to the Venice hotel scene. It's attractive, enveloping, refreshingly different and run with touching commitment by young Gioele Romanelli, and his wife, Heiby. Gioele knows what he is doing: his father owns and runs the excellent Hotel Flora (p103).

It's a bit like walking into a Marrakech *riad*, with furniture, beds and fabrics imported from Morocco, Thailand and Pakistan, and a whiff of incense in the air. There are beamed ceilings, plaster walls, stained bottle glass windows, big cushions on the sitting room floor, amusing beds, superb bathrooms. Music plays in your room at the touch of a button. The old beamed Venetian house, just off the main route between San Marco and the Rialto, lends itself beautifully to its new makeover, which, the Romanellis tell us, is inspired by the great Fortuny, who was himself inspired by the Orient. With just nine bedrooms and a little courtyard garden, the atmosphere is cosy and intimate. We think this new hotel deliciously different compared with the Venice norm.

~

NEARBY San Marco; Accademia; Rialto.
LOCATION off Campo San Maurizio on Calle del Dose; vaporetto Santa Maria del Giglio
FOOD breakfast
PRICE €€€
ROOMS 9 double, 8 with bath, one with shower; all rooms have phone, TV, air conditioning,music, minibar, safe, hairdrier
FACILITIES honesty bar, sitting room, breakfast room, courtyard
CREDIT CARDS AE, DC, MC, V
DISABLED not suitable
PETS accepted
CLOSED never
PROPRIETORS Gioele and Heiby Romanelli

THE NORTH-EAST

VENICE

PALAZZETTO DA SCHIO
~ APARTMENTS IN PRIVATE HOUSE ~

Fondamenta Soranzo, Dorsoduro 316/b, 30123 Venezia
TEL and **FAX** 041 5237937
E-MAIL avenezia@tin.it **WEBSITE** www.palazzettodaschio.it

FONDAMENTA SORANZO IS A TRANQUIL backwater lined with attractive houses, including this red-painted *palazzetto*, home of the da Schio family for the past 300 years. The present incumbent, Contessa da Schio, lives on the ground floor and *piano nobile* while other parts of the house have been converted into four charming and comfortable apartments, available from any period of time from two days to three months. Note, though, that the apartments are considerably less expensive when taken per week or per month, rather than per night. They are largely furnished with family antiques, including pictures and mirrors, with modern bits and pieces to fill the gaps. The topmost apartments (not for those who don't like stairs) has wide views and large sitting rooms, while the apartments on the mezzzanine floor have views on the canal and the garden and cosy, antique-filled living rooms.

The entrance hall of the *palazzetto*, lit by precious Venetian torch lamps and opening on to the garden, is splendid. This, and the fine three-bedroom *piano nobile* apartment, can be hired for parties at any time of the year and is available to stay in for one month in the summer.

~

NEARBY Santa Maria della Salute; Accademia; Zattere.
LOCATION on canal between Grand and Guidecca Canals; vaporetto Salute or water taxi
FOOD none
PRICE €€
ROOMS 4 apartments, 2 with one bedroom, 2 with 2 bedrooms; all with phone, kitchen and bathroom; phone; maid service
CREDIT CARDS not accepted
DISABLED not suitable
PETS not accepted
CLOSED never
PROPRIETOR Contessa Anna da Schio

THE NORTH-EAST

QUATTRO FONTANE
~ SEASIDE HOTEL ~

Via Quattro Fontane 16, 30126 Lido, Venezia
TEL 041 5260227 **FAX** 041 5260726
E-MAIL ILAQuattrofontane@ila-chateau.com **WEBSITE** www.ilachateau.com/quattrof/

THE LONGER WE LINGERED at the Quattro Fontane, the more it grew on us. At first the 150-year-old mock Tyrolean building struck us as rather gloomy and suburban, but we soon warmed to the charmingly decorated reception rooms, particularly the *salone* and the little writing room. Mementos of the owners' travels are dotted around the hotel on walls and shelves – carved wooden figures, painted shells, model ships, porcelain, stamps. In the baronial dining room, with its cavernous hearth and bold red chairs, service was directed with courtesy by the long-serving head waiter. In warm weather you can eat on the wide tree-filled terrace that encircles the hotel.

The bedrooms in the main building have plenty of character and are individually decorated with an assortment of furniture, pictures and fabrics, comfortable if not luxurious. Those in the 1960s annexe are more streamlined, but here too each is different, attractive and cosy, with gaily tiled bathrooms. A dignified hotel, elderly now, but still spruce, and in our opinion the best on the Lido.

~

NEARBY Venice; lagoon islands.
LOCATION set back from seafront on S side of Lido, near Casino; vaporetto Santa Maria Elisabetta
FOOD breakfast, lunch, dinner
PRICE €€€
ROOMS 58; 54 double, 4 single, 35 with bath, 23 with shower; all rooms have phone, TV, air conditioning, hairdrier, safe
FACILITIES sitting room, writing room, dining room, bar; tennis court and beach cabins available
CREDIT CARDS AE, DC, MC, V
DISABLED access difficult
PETS accepted
CLOSED Nov to April
PROPRIETORS Friborg-Bevilacqua family

THE NORTH-EAST

VENICE

LA RESIDENZA
~ TOWN HOTEL ~

Campo Bandiera e Moro, Castello 3608, 30122 Venezia
TEL 041 5285315 **FAX** 041 5238859
E-MAIL info@veniceresidenza.com**WEBSITE** www.veniceresidenza.com

L A RESIDENZA APPEALS to true lovers of Venice who appreciate the chance to stay in the grand Gothic *palazzo* which dominates this dusty and enigmatic square, whose little church, San Giovanni in Bragora is one of the city's most appealing.

Just to enter is an experience: huge doors swing open to reveal an ancient covered courtyard and stone steps leading up to a vast baroque hall with beautifully coloured, lavishly carved plaster walls. Taking breakfast here in the early morning light is a rare treat, though the hushed atmosphere can be a little oppressive.

This, however, is not a grand hotel, but a modest two-star in immodest surroundings. Those devotees – and these were many – who appreciated the combination of grotty, kitsch and antique in the bedrooms under the hotel's former ownership mourn the fact that they have all now been renovated (calm and pretty, but standard); other, more recent guests, appreciate the modernisations and feel that as long as the central hall remains unchanged, La Residenza retains it special appeal.

By the way, the famous smell – of cats? or is it boiled cabbage? – seems to have retreated to the hallway; some say it's gone altogether.

~

NEARBY San Giorgio degli Schiavoni; Arsenale.
LOCATION on small square 100 m behind Riva degli Schiavoni; vaporetto Arsenale, San Zaccaria
FOOD breakfast
PRICE €€
ROOMS 14; 12 double and twin, 2 single, all with bath or shower; all rooms have phone, TV, air conditioning, minibar, safe, hairdrier
FACILITIES sitting room, breakfast area
CREDIT CARDS MC, V
DISABLED not suitable **PETS** accepted
CLOSED never
PROPRIETOR Giovanni Ballestra

THE NORTH-EAST

CA'FAVRETTO SAN CASSIANO

~ TOWN HOTEL ~

Calle della Rosa, Santa Croce 2232, 30135 Venezia
TEL 041 5241768 **FAX** 041 721033
E-MAIL cassiano@sancassiano.it **WEBSITE** www.sancassiano.it

ARRIVING BY BOAT AT SAN CASSIANO's private jetty on the Grand Canal is considerably easier than finding your way by foot through a maze of tortuous, narrow alleyways from the nearest *vaporetto* or *traghetto* point (ask for a brochure to be sent so that you can follow its map). It also means that you can appreciate the 14thC *palazzo's* best feature: its deep red Gothic façade which faces the Grand Canal's greatest glory, the Ca' d'Oro. Inside, the hotel has a rather fusty feel to it, with heavy Venetian furnishings and a fairly lackadaisical staff – characteristics we also found in its sister hotel, the Marconi. What it does have, however, is some endearingly grandiose rooms, and the six facing the canal are splendid, with capacious reproduction antique wardrobes, matching desks and carved bedheads, floating white curtains bordered by velvet or brocade pelmets, and oriental carpets. Sadly, they are no longer the same price as rooms without a view (the management has wised up to their desirability) but you should do all you can to secure one and be tempted to look elsewhere if you can't. The light, elegant breakfast room with huge windows and waterfront views is a delight. In recognition of its historic status as the house of the 18thC Venetian painter, Favretto, the hotel is now officially a 'Residenza d'Epoca', and proud of it.

NEARBY Ca' d'Oro; Rialto markets; Rialto Bridge.
LOCATION on Grand Canal, opposite Ca' d'Oro; vaporetto San Stae or water taxi
FOOD breakfast
PRICE ⒺⒺⒺ
ROOMS 36; 20 double and twin, 12 triple and family, 4 single, all with bath or shower; all rooms have phone, TV, air conditioning, minibar, hairdrier, safe
FACILITIES sitting room, breakfast room, bar
CREDIT CARDS AE, MC, V
DISABLED 2 rooms specially adapted **PETS** accepted
CLOSED never
PROPRIETOR Franco Maschietto

THE NORTH-EAST

VENICE

SAN SAMUELE
~ TOWN GUESTHOUSE ~

Salizzada San Samuele, San Maro 3358, 30124 Venezia
TEL 041 5205165 **FAX** 041 5205165
E-MAIL info@allbergosansamuele.it **WEBSITE** www.albergosansamuele.it

A BUDGET ESTABLISHMENT WITH YOUNG MANAGERS, a fresh lick of paint, 300-year old Venetian marble floors and a pleasant, airy feel to the bedrooms.

The *pensione* is installed on the upper floors of a pretty house in a wide street leading to the San Samuele *vaporetto* and *traghetto* landing stage. Ring the bell for admission, enter a pleasant little courtyard and start climbing the stairs, of which there are quite a few – this hotel is for the young and fit.

On our last visit, all the bedrooms had recently been redecorated, their main decorative feature being a square of pink colour on the wall behind each low, skimpy-looking bed (an inspector informs us that they are adequately comfortable). Bathrooms are modern, each enlivened by a jolly shower curtain. What gives these rooms the edge over others in the same price range, however, is the presence of not one but two large windows with views over the street. The two rooms at the back make up in quiet what they lack in light. Breakfast, if you want it, is served in the rooms.

We have had good reader feedback about this modest, two-star establishment. Run by three friends, it's the sort of places that is much appreciated but hard to find: an affordable hotel that doesn't disappoint.
~

NEARBY Accademia gallery; Frari; Campo Santo Stefano.
LOCATION in quiet area of San Marco, between Campo Santo Stefano and Grand Canal; vaporetto San Samuele.
FOOD breakfast
PRICE €€
ROOMS 10; 8 double, 2 single, 7 with shower; all rooms have phone
FACILITIES sitting room, breakfast room, bar
CREDIT CARDS not accepted
DISABLED not suitable
PETS not accepted
CLOSED never
PROPRIETOR Domenico, Roberto and Bruno

THE NORTH-EAST

VENICE

SEGUSO
~ TOWN GUESTHOUSE ~

Zattere ai Gesuati, Dorsoduro 779, 30123 Venezia
TEL 041 5222340/5286858 **FAX** 041 5222340

SITTING ON THE SUNNY PROMENADE of the Zattere, lapped by the choppy waters of the wide Giudecca canal, gives you the distinct feeling of being by the seaside. This open setting, with a grand panorama across the lagoon, is just one of the charms of the Seguso. A *pensione* in the old tradition, it is family-run, friendly and solidly old-fashioned. And (unlike most hotels in Venice) prices are modest; the Seguso is not noted for its food, but half board here costs no more than bed-and-breakfast alone in hotels of similar comfort closer to San Marco.

The best bedrooms are the large ones at the front of the house, overlooking the canal – though for the privilege of the views and space you may have to forfeit the luxury of a private bathroom (only half the rooms have their own facilities). The main public rooms are the dining room, prettily furnished in traditional style, and the modest sitting room where you can sink into large leather chairs and peruse ancient editions of travel writing and guidebooks. Breakfast is taken on the front terrace – delightful. Fellow guests are often friendly, interesting and great Venice enthusiasts. Group bookings (maximum 30 people) are accepted, though not in September and May.

~

NEARBY Accademia gallery; Gesuati church.
LOCATION 5 mins' walk S of Accademia, overlooking Giudecca canal; vaporetto Zattere or water taxi
FOOD breakfast, lunch, dinner
PRICE €€
ROOMS 36; 31 double and twin, 5 single, 9 with bath, 9 with shower; all rooms have phone
FACILITIES dining room, sitting room, lift, terrace
CREDIT CARDS AE, MC, V
DISABLED access possible **PETS** accepted
CLOSED mid-Dec to mid-Feb
PROPRIETORS Seguso family

THE NORTH-EAST

VERONA

GABBIA D'ORO
~ TOWN HOTEL ~

Corso Portoni Borsari 4a, 37121 Verona
TEL 045 8003060 **FAX** 045 590293
E-MAIL gabbiadoro@easyasp.it **WEBSITE** www.hotelgabbiadoro.it

THIS STYLISH HOTEL in a 17thC *palazzo*, luxurious but never ostentatious, boasts an attention to detail rarely encountered nowadays. A small, beautifully wrapped gift awaits your arrival, and the staff are as charming and polished as the hotel itself. The public rooms, entered through massive wood doors with gilt decoration, are comfortable as well as elegant: there are plenty of places in which to sit and relax, and sofas are large and deep. Wooden floors, beams and brickwork are much in evidence; the sitting room shares one wall with the Gardello Tower. Furnishings, chandeliers, silver-framed photographs, ornaments and antiques are always in keeping. Little lamps lend a glow to the panelled bar, and the new orangery is restful, with its green-and-white colour scheme and view to the terrace.

Frescoes, restored or reproduced from the originals, recur as friezes both downstairs and in the bedrooms. Suites outnumber doubles. In almost all, beds are shrouded in a canopy of antique lace. No. 404, dark red with sloping walls, rafters, and nooks and crannies, is so romantic that it's normally chosen for honeymooners. Prices are high, but we felt justifiably so.

~

NEARBY Piazza delle Erbe; Loggia del Consiglio; Arena.
LOCATION in medieval centre of the city, S of Porta Borsari; garage parking available
FOOD breakfast
PRICE €€€€
ROOMS 27; 8 double and twin, 19 suites, all with bath or shower; all rooms have phone, TV, air conditioning, minibar, hairdrier, safe
FACILITIES breakfast room, sitting room, orangery, bar, meeting room, lift, terrace
CREDIT CARDS AE, DC, MC, V
DISABLED access difficult
PETS accepted
CLOSED never
PROPRIETOR Camilla Balzarro

THE NORTH-EAST

VERONA

TORCOLO
~ TOWN HOTEL ~

Vicolo Listone 3, 37121 Verona
TEL 045 8007512 **FAX** 045 8004058
E-MAIL hoteltorcolo@virgilio.it **WEBSITE** www.hotel.torcolo.it

THE TORCOLO IS AN INEXPENSIVE hotel in an excellent location at the heart of lively Verona. 'Its most outstanding quality,' writes one recent guest, 'was the warmth and friendliness of our welcome and the consistent helpfulness of the staff.' Other positive comments continue to filter through. Every room is individually decorated in varying styles – Italian 18thC, art nouveau, modern – and all are fresher and have more charm than one normally finds at this price. Ours contained a complete set of Liberty-style bedroom furniture which had belonged to owner Silvia Pommari's parents when they first married. It was set off by white linen curtains and a colourful patchwork bedspread. Ceramic tiled bathrooms are somewhat cramped; the best have separate shower cubicles. Rooms are double-glazed against the considerable street sounds (people, not cars) but, despite air conditioning, they can get fuggy, especially in warm weather. Breakfast, including a jug of fresh orange juice, a good assortment of bread and croissants and yoghurt, can be taken in your room, which might be preferable to the rather cramped little breakfast room. In summer, it is served buffet-style in the small off-street courtyard.

~

NEARBY Arena; Via Mazzini, Piazza delle Erbe.
LOCATION just off Piazza Brà; garage parking
FOOD breakfast
PRICE ©©
ROOMS 19; 13 double and twin, 4 single, 2 family, one with bath and 18 with shower; all rooms have phone, TV, air conditioning, minibar, safe, hairdrier; 10 rooms have minibar and safe
FACILITIES sitting area, breakfast room, courtyard, lift
CREDIT CARDS AE, DC, MC, V
DISABLED access difficult
PETS accepted
CLOSED mid-Jan
PROPRIETORS Silvia Pommari and Diana Castellani

THE NORTH-EAST

BARBARANO VICENTINO

IL CASTELLO
COUNTRY VILLA APARTMENTS

Via Castello 6, 36021 Barbarano, Vicenza

TEL and FAX 0444 886055
E-MAIL ilcastello@tin.it
FOOD none
PRICE €
CLOSED never
PROPRIETORS Marinoni family

IL CASTELLO REFERS TO A HANDSOME villa built in the 17thC on the ruins of an ancient castle which looks down over the medieval village of Barbarano Vicentino. Occupied for more than 100 years by the Marinoni family, it retains the original perimeter walls of the castle, and its cellars. There is a formal Renaissance garden. You can choose from three separate apartments, for which reservations must be made on a weekly basis, each with one or two bedrooms, and fully equipped kitchens and bathrooms; or you can take the whole house. Rooms, white-painted and airy, with Venetian marble floors, are somewhat spartan in feel, despite the use of old family furniture throughout.

CORTINA D'AMPEZZO

MENARDI
TOWN HOTEL

Via Majon 110, 32043 Cortina d'Ampezzo, Belluno

TEL 0436 2400 **FAX** 0436 862183
E-MAIL info@hotelmenardi.it
WEBSITE www.hotelmenardi.it
FOOD breakfast, lunch, dinner
PRICE €€ **CLOSED** Oct to mid-Dec, Apr to mid-May
PROPRIETORS Menardi family

THIS FAMILY-RUN HOTEL evolved from a coaching inn when its owners, the Menardi family, began hiring out horses. During the First World War, Luigi Menardi began to transform the rustic inn into a proper hotel. Today the long white building has proliferated carved green wood balconies and tumbling geraniums, plus extra rooms and a separate annexe behind, but the Menardi family can still justifiably proclaim: 'same house, same family, same relaxed atmosphere'. Inside, antique pieces, painted religious statues and old work tools are mixed with local custom-made furnishings which look somewhat dated, but which are nonetheless comfortable. The atmosphere is one of traditional warmth and service is polished.

THE NORTH-EAST

FOLLINA

HOTEL DEI CHIOSTRI
TOWN HOTEL

Piazza IV Novembre 20, 31051 Follina, Treviso

TEL 0438 971805 **FAX** 0438 974217
E-MAIL info@hoteldeichiostri.com
WEBSITE www.hoteldeichiostri.com
FOOD breakfast
PRICE €€
CLOSED mid-Jan to mid-Feb
PROPRIETORS Zanon family

The owners of Follina's Hotel Abbazia (*see p75*), which we have admired ever since it opened a few years ago, have now created a simpler, more modern but no less stylish place to stay right across the street. The Hotel dei Chiostri, built on the ruins of an old monastery, and right beside the lovely cloister of the 11thC abbey, has 15 sophisticated rooms decorated in cool colours with pretty floaty curtains and well-designed contemporary furniture. As at the Abbazia, attention to detail is admirable. Only breakfast is served here; the hotel shares the Abbazia's lovely restaurant, Il Corte.

MADONNA DI CAMPIGLIO

BIO-HOTEL HERMITAGE
MOUNTAIN HOTEL

Via Castelletto Inferiore 63, 38084 Madonna di Campiglio, Trentino

TEL 0465 441558 **FAX** 0465 441618
E-MAIL info@biohotelhermitage.it
WEB www.biohotelhermitage.it
FOOD breakfast, lunch, dinner
PRICE €€ CLOSED Sep to Dec
PROPRIETORS Maffei family

WE WERE ALERTED TO THIS MODERN 'BIO' HOTEL (it was refurbished in 1999 using only natural materials such as solid wood floors and pure wool carpets, ecological water and electricity supply and so on) by an enthusiastic guest who praised everything, but most of all the relaxed 'at home' family atmosphere and the 'superb' food (home-made pumpkin pasta with black truffle, wild rabbit *alla cacciatore*, sweet chestnut mousse). Also: well equipped rooms ('fantasic mattresses'); a parkland setting; shuttle to the town centre and ski slopes; sun terrace; indoor pool; sauna. 'I'm going back', says our correspondent, 'this time for the alpine flowers'.

THE NORTH-EAST

MARLENGO

OBERWIRT
MOUNTAIN RESORT HOTEL

Vicolo San Felice 2, Marlengo,
39020 Merano, Bolzano

TEL 0473 222020 **FAX** 0473 447130
E-MAIL info@oberwirt.com
WEBSITE www.oberwirt.com
Food breakfast, lunch, dinner
PRICE €€
CLOSED mid-Nov to mid-Mar the
PROPRIETORS Waldner family

Originally a simple inn, Oberwirt has been run by the Waldner family since 1749. Today, three generations currently work in the hotel: Signor Waldner's beaming mother, dressed in a *dirndl*, is at reception, while his daughter runs the restaurant. The hotel is often full, and, though it has plenty to recommend it, character and intimacy are not strong features.

The *raison d'être* is the food, which features local produce – highlights include fried duck liver, lamb cutlets in a herb crust and *marscapone* and compote of bitter cherries between layers of strudel pastry. The new kitchen is shown off to guests every Monday before dinner.

MERANO

CASTELLO LABERS
CONVERTED CASTLE

Via Labers 25, 39012 Merano,
Bolzano

TEL 0473 234484
FAX 0473 234146
E-MAIL info@castellolabers.it
WEBSITE www.castellolabers.it
FOOD breakfast, lunch, dinner
PRICE €€ CLOSED Nov to Apr
PROPRIETORS Stapf-Neubert family

ON A HILLSIDE TO THE EAST of Merano, Castello (or Schloss) Labers is immersed in its own lush orchards and vineyards, with direct access to mountain walks through Alpine pastures. The hotel has been in the Neubert family since 1885.

On a bad day, the Castel wouldn't look out of place in an Addams family film, but it has its charm, and the interior is welcoming. Bedrooms vary enormously in size and standard: some elegantly proportioned with antique furniture, others rather too drab and basically furnished.

The ambience? 'Elderly', writes a guest. 'Very pleasant, very quiet, but rather elderly.'

THE NORTH-EAST

MISSIANO

SCHLOSS KORB
CONVERTED CASTLE

Missiano, 39050 San Paolo, Bolzano

TEL 0471 636000
FAX 0471 636033
E-MAIL info@schloss-korb.com
WEBSITE www.schlosskorb.com
FOOD breakfast, lunch, dinner
PRICE €€
CLOSED Nov to Mar
PROPRIETORS Dellago family

RISING UP FROM THE FERTILE VINEYARDS and orchards that surround the outskirts of Bolzano is the 11thC tower which forms the centrepiece of Schloss Korb. The hotel's entrance is a riot of colour – flowering plants set against walls of golden stone and whitewash – and a terrace, awash with plants, hangs out over the valley. The interior is traditional; reception is a cool, dark tiled hall set about with a most eccentric collection of objects, while bedrooms are large, with lovely views over the vineyards. The best are in the tower, as well as the apartment with its carved furniture, though all the rooms in the annexe have balconies. There are two pools, indoor and outdoor. The feel of the place is relaxed, though not intimate.

PINZOLO

CHALET MASO DOSS
MOUNTAIN CHALET

San Antonio di Mavignola 72, 38086 Pinzolo, Trento

TEL 0465 502758 **FAX** 0465 502311
E-MAIL info@masodoss.com
WEBSITE www.masodoss.com
FOOD breakfast, dinner; lunch on request **PRICE** €€; weekly rates available **CLOSED** never
PROPRIETORS Caola family

HERE'S THE REAL THING: A SIMPLE, HEART-WARMING 17thC chalet in the Brenta Valley, set amidst the spectacular landscape of the Adamello-Dolomiti di Brenta National Park. In winter you can explore on cross-country skis, in summer on mountain bikes provided by the chalet, taking a packed lunch if you wish. On your return: wood panelling and simple furniture, check tablecloths and lace curtains, a warm fire, an excellent dinner, a Finnish sauna, and one of six cosy bedrooms with warm duvets and hand-embroidered sheets. Guests gather for a drink before dinner, and the atmosphere is very much that of a welcoming private house.

THE NORTH-EAST

SAN VALBURGA D'ULTIMO

EGGWIRT
MOUNTAIN GUESTHOUSE

*39016 San Valburga d'Ultimo,
Bolzano*

TEL 0473 795319 **FAX** 0473 795471
E-MAIL eggwirt@rolmail.net
WEBSITE www.eggwirt.it
Food breakfast, lunch, dinner
PRICE €
CLOSED mid-Nov to mid-Dec
PROPRIETORS Schwienbacher
family

THE QUIET AND UNSPOILED Val d'Ultima lies 30 kilometres south-west of Merano. In this ideal setting for both summer and winter sports, the Gasthof Eggwirt has existed as a hostelry since the 14th century, and today the Schwienbacher family welcome guests as if to their own home. The hotel is on the edge of the village with a large terrace at the front and superb views all around.

The bright bedrooms have lots of wood and cheerful duvet covers. An inexpensive, relaxed and friendly family hotel offering some excellent ski deals for children.

VENICE

LOCANDA FIORITA
TOWN GUEST-HOUSE

*Campiello Nuovo, Santo Stefano,
San Marco 3457, 30124 Venezia*
TEL 041 523 4754 **FAX** 041 5228043
E-MAIL info@locandafiorita.com
WEBSITE www.locandafiorita.com
Food breakfast **PRICE** €€
CLOSED never
PROPRIETOR Renato Colombera

IF YOU ARE LOOKING FOR BUDGET prices and a quiet yet central location, look no further than this bargain hotel, a red-painted villa tucked away in a quiet, little visited square off Campo Santo Stefano. Rooms are small and functional, with modern white furniture which include desks, bedside tables, even beds. You will find a comfortable bed, but skimpy towels and a lack of shelves, though there is plenty of cupboard space. 'With its beamed ceiling, mint green walls and large windows my room was a perfectly pleasant one in which to wake up,' comments one guest 'especially when one reflects on what it cost'. Breakfast is taken at wooden tables along the wall in the reception area, or, more comfortably, in your room.

THE NORTH-EAST

VENICE

LOCANDA ORSEOLO
TOWN HOTEL

Corte Zorzi, San Marco 1083, 30124 Venezia

TEL 041 5204827 **FAX** 041 5235586
E-MAIL info@locandaorseolo
WEBSITE www.locandaorseolo
FOOD breakfast
PRICE €€€ **CLOSED** never
PROPRIETORS Perruch family

IT'S THE REALLY EXCEPTIONAL WARMTH of the young owners of Locanda Orseolo that really makes it stand out. The hotel, just a few paces from Piazza San Marco, was opened in 2002, one of the new breed of sophisticated places to stay in former private homes, and it was purchased only in 2003 by Matteo, Barbara, Bruno and Francesco, whose genuine warmth and helpfulness towards their guests is a real boon in the hard-nosed world of Venetian hospitality. The hotel itself is smart and spotless; the 15 rooms (which have temperature controls) vary in size, some large, some with bathrooms that are a little cramped. The breakfasts-'eggs any way, excellent coffee'-are praised, but not so much as that wonderful welcome.

VENICE

MARCONI
TOWN HOTEL

Riva del Vin, San Polo 729, 30125 Venezia

TEL 041 5222068
FAX 041 5229700
E-MAIL info@hotelmarconi.it
WEBSITE www.hotelmarconi.it
FOOD breakfast
PRICE €€€ **CLOSED** never
PROPRIETOR Franco Maschietto

THE MARCONI IS A TYPICAL VENICE HOTEL, encapsulating both what is right and what is wrong about many of them. As so often, the location is enviable (right by Rialto Bridge). The building is a 16thC *palazzo* with a 19thC entrance hall, marbled pillars, velvet hangings, and green and gold embossed ceiling. Best of all are the two sought-after rooms with balconies which overlook the Grand Canal, more expensive, but worth it. Bedrooms are fairly simple, but mahogany furniture and damask curtains make them seem old-fashioned. The hotel was renovated only a few years ago, but its dark wood fittings and dated fabrics give it a rather gloomy air.

THE NORTH-EAST

VENICE

PICCOLA FENICE
TOWN HOTEL

Calle della Madonna, San Marco 3614, 30124 Venezia

TEL and **FAX** 041 5204909
E-MAIL
piccolafenice@fenicehotels.it
WEBSITE www.fenicehotels.it
FOOD breakfast **PRICE** €€-
€€€; weekly rates available
CLOSED Jan
PROPRIETOR Michele Facchini

THE TEATRO LA FENICE has at last risen from the ashes after the disastrous fire which rendered it a stark shell. The famous adjacent hotel, Fenice et des Artistes, where performers used to put up, has looked too gloomy and faded for us to include in our guide for some years, but we have always been impressed by its sister hotel, the Piccola Fenice. It consists of seven suites sleeping between two and six people. On the wide first floor landing there is a sitting area with desk and armchairs. The topmost apartment, with little balcony overlooking the rooftops, would be perfect for a family.

VENICE

SERENISSIMA
TOWN HOTEL

Calle Goldoni, San Marco 4486, 30124 Venezia

TEL 041 5200011 **FAX** 041 5223292
FOOD breakfast
E-MAIL info@hotelserenissima.it
WEBSITE www.hotelserenissima.it
PRICE €€
CLOSED after Carnival to mid-Mar
PROPRIETOR Roberto dal Borgo

READERS' REPORTS CONFIRM that this is one of the most endearing and best-kept two-star hotels in town. Our inspector told us that she found it much pleasanter to stay here than in many a more expensive three-star, and, given its central location just a few paces from the Doge's Palace, she deemed it value for money – a rare experience in Venice. Bedrooms are admittedly small (a triple will give two people more room), but neat and pretty, some with purpose-made wooden fittings, others with more attractive Venetian painted headboards, cupboards and bedside tables. There's a charming first floor breakfast room, and corridors are hung with colourful modern paintings.

EMILIA-ROMAGNA

AREA INTRODUCTION

HOTELS IN EMILIA-ROMAGNA

THE VIA EMILIA, THE ROMAN ROAD (now a motorway) stretching along the foothills of the Apeninne mountains from Piacenza to Rimini, gives this region its name. Bounded by the River Po to the north and the wooded slopes of the Apennines to the south, Emilia-Romagna is fertile and prosperous, its countryside a patchwork of fields, hills and plains, with most of its cities strung out along the Via Emilia, with Bologna in the centre.

Bologna, the regional capital, famed for its food, is primarily a business centre with business-style hotels to match; but it is also a city of learning (it has the oldest university in Europe) and of art (including beautiful Renaissance buildings) so there is much to attract the tourist, and we can recommend the four hotels owned by the Orsi family. See pages 127 and 136 for descriptions of the **Corona d'Oro** and the **Commercianti**, and make a note of the **Orologio** (tel 051 231 253) and the new **Novecento** (tel 051 7457311).

In Modena, Bologna's long-time rival with a stunning Romanesque cathedral, we recommend the **Canalgrande** (tel 059 217160). With 78 bedrooms, it is somewhat large for a full entry in this guide, but it is nevertheless a stylish, peaceful and comfortable villa set in beautiful gardens in the middle of the city.

Finding a satisfactory hotel in Parma is also tricky. Our best recommendation is the very central **Torino** (tel 0521 281046). In Ferrara we can thoroughly recommend a homely B&B, **Locanda Borgonuovo** (see page 133) but for something grander, try the **Ripagrande** (tel 0532 675250), a Renaissance *palazzo* converted in 1980, or the luxurious **Duchessa Isabella** (tel 0532 202121). In Reggio Emilia, noted for its Parmigiano Reggiano and its balsamic vinegar, we can recommend the **Hotel Posta** (page 137).

The Adriatic coast of this region is not notable for small hotels, and we have still drawn a blank in Ravenna. You could try the **Bisanzio** (tel 0544 217111) or the simple but central **Centrale Byron** (tel 0544 212225).

Dotted about the region, in small towns or villages and in the countryside, we can recommend a clutch of other hotels, some of which are old favourites, others new discoveries. In addition, a reader writes to thoroughly recommend **Agriturismo Cavaione** (tel 051 589006), a country inn about 15 minutes drive (or bus ride) outside Bologna. 'The room was sunny and comfortable, the views from the balcony gorgeous, and the staff friendly and helpful.' Just what our guide is all about.

EMILIA-ROMAGNA

BOLOGNA

CORONA D'ORO
~ TOWN HOTEL ~

Via Oberdan 12, 40126 Bologna
TEL 051 236456 **FAX** 051 262679
E-MAIL hotcoro@tin.it **WEBSITE** www.bolognahotel.net

THE CORONA D'ORO lies in the historic old city, close to the two famous leaning towers, in a cobbled street which for most of the time is closed to traffic. Enticing food shops (including a wonderful delicatessen) give you some idea of why the city is nicknamed Bologna La Grassa (the Fat).

The Corona d'Oro became a hotel in 1890, though the original building dates back to 1300. It is here that Italy's first printing press was established and there are still a few features surviving from the original *palazzo*. In the early 1980s the hotel was bought by a packaging magnate, who elevated it from a simple hotel to four-star status, successfully combining the old features with the stylish new. The 14thC portico and Renaissance ceilings were preserved, while the plush bedrooms were provided with all modern conveniences. The showpiece was the hallway, with its fine art nouveau frieze supported on columns. Light streaming from above, fresh flowers and lush feathery plants create a cheerful, inviting entrance.

If arriving by car, be sure to get the hotel's route-map; without it, you will never find your way through the Bologna maze.

~

NEARBY Piazza Maggiore; Piazza del Nettuno.
LOCATION in city centre, close to the two leaning towers in Piazza di Porta Ravegnan; with garage parking
FOOD breakfast
PRICE €€€
ROOMS 35; 27 double, 8 single, all with shower; all rooms have phone, TV, air conditioning, minibar, safe
FACILITIES breakfast room, sitting area, bar, TV room
CREDIT CARDS AE, DC, MC, V
DISABLED not suitable
PETS accepted
CLOSED Aug
PROPRIETOR Mauro Orsi

EMILIA-ROMAGNA

BRISIGHELLA

GIGIOLE

~ RESTAURANT-WITH-ROOMS ~

Piazza Carducci 5, 48013 Brisighella, Ravenna
TEL 0546 81209 **FAX** 0546 81275
E-MAIL gigiole.gigiole@tin.it **WEBSITE** www.charmerelax.it/gigiole

BRISIGHELLA IS A PICTURESQUE small town and thermal spa 13 km south-west of Faenza in an area famous for its production of clay and ceramics. The town is also known for its excellent olive oil. The Gigiolè stands across from the main church, a vaguely French-looking shuttered building with a shaded terrace in front.

The French style extends to the food: Tarcisio Raccagni, the chef, has been put on a par with the famous Paul Bocuse. Like Bocuse, he places great stress on using local seasonal ingredients of top quality and the results are superb: succulent meats, delicious soups and imaginative use of vegetables and herbs – all that is best in contemporary Italian cooking, and at affordable prices. The restaurant is a mixture of rustic and elegant; stone arches and walls are hung with copper pots and local ceramics while tables are laid with crisp, white linen and glasses gleam. Our inspectors' only complaint was the loud piped music.

The once sub-standard bedrooms and bathrooms are now thoroughly comfortable and the spacious rooms incorporate a sitting area (one suite has a kitchen). Floors are parquet and the furniture is modern.

~

NEARBY Bologna (50 km); Ravenna (42 km); Faenza (17 km).
LOCATION in centre of town; with public car parking in front
FOOD breakfast, lunch, dinner
PRICE €€
ROOMS 10; 7 double, 2 single, 1 suite, all with shower; all rooms have phone, TV, air conditioning, minibar, hairdrier
FACILITIES restaurant, bar, sitting room, lift, terrace
CREDIT CARDS AE, DC, MC, V
DISABLED no special facilities
PETS accepted
CLOSED hotel closed one month Jan-Feb, restaurant closed Mon
PROPRIETOR Tarcision Raccagni

EMILIA-ROMAGNA

BRISIGHELLA

RELAIS VARNELLO

~ COUNTRY GIESTHOUSE ~

Borgo Rontana 34, 148013 Brisighella, Ravenna
TEL 0546 85493 FAX 0546 83124
E-MAIL info@varnello.it WEBSITE www.varnello.it

A NEWLY CONVERTED FARMHOUSE in the extraordinary, barren-but-beautiful Rontana hills, where you will get (even by the best Italian standards) a great welcome and personal attention. Some Dutch readers discovered it for us and were 'deeply impressed' by the hospitality of the Liverzanis. More accolades have flowed: 'we were flabberghasted, by the hotel's position, the comfort of our rooms and, not least, by the hospitality of the owners' reads one. It really seems that the Liverzanis are natural hosts with a love for their locality, which is full of historical interest.

Everything is in superb new condition and artfully restored. A pleasantly home-like sitting room is furnished with antiques, some from Liverzani family homes. The same private-house feel continues in the four bedrooms, each decorated and equipped differently, with attractive, unobtrusive fabrics, handsome iron bedsteads; one suite has a four-poster with hangings. Two apartments, one with Finnish sauna, are available in an annexe. The grounds are extensive, and it's good walking country. By the way, the Liverzani family have lived in this corner of Italy for 1,000 years and Giovanni was an Olympic rapid-fire pistol shooter. Liana's cooking, despite her insistance that she is not a professional, is also praised.

~

NEARBY Ravenna, Faenza (14 km).
LOCATION about 14 km W of Faenza, in own grounds with private car parking; ask for directions
FOOD breakfast; lunch and dinner by arrangement
PRICE €€
ROOMS 6, 3 double and one single, 2 apartments for 2-5, all with bath and shower; all rooms have phone, TV, air-conditioning, hairdryer, fridge
FACILITIES sitting room, dining room, garden, swimming pool
CREDIT CARDS AE, DC, MC, V
DISABLED no special facilities **PETS** accepted **CLOSED** Jan and Feb
PROPRIETORS Giovanni and Liana Liverzani

EMILIA-ROMAGNA

BRISIGHELLA

TORRE PRATESI

~ COUNTRY HOTEL ~

Via Cavina 11, 48013 Brisighella, Ravenna
TEL 0546 84545 **FAX** 0546 84558
E-MAIL torrep@tin.it **WEBSITE** www.torrepratesi.it

THE SOLID, SQUARE TOWER that forms part of this unusual hotel dates from 1510, while the adjacent farmhouse was added much later. Lovingly restored in 1993, it enjoys a remote and spectacular position on a hill with superb views over vineyards, olive groves and woods. As many of the original features of the building as possible have been preserved, and modernization has been carried out using traditional materials; wood, stone, wrought iron and marble. Modern equipment in the bedrooms is discreetly hidden in drawers and cupboards. Furnishings and colour schemes have been kept simple throughout – terracotta floors, warm, honey-coloured walls, leather armchairs and imaginative contemporary lighting. Bedrooms and bathrooms are surprisingly stylish; those housed in the tower itself enjoy 360° views as each occupies an entire floor.

The Raccagni's encourage a house party atmosphere and are warm and charming hosts. Guests can help themselves from the complimentary bar before a delicious dinner made largely with produce from the estate. There are plenty of spots for relaxing: by a huge stone fireplace, in the library/music room or outside in the lovely grounds.

~

NEARBY Faenza (25 km); Ravenna (50 km).
LOCATION 8 km SW of Brisighella: take the SS302 for Florence, turn off to Valetta just after Fognano and follow signs; car parking including garage
FOOD breakfast, dinner; light lunch on request
PRICE €€
ROOMS 9; 3 doubles and 6 suites, 8 with bath, 1 with shower; 3 rooms in annexe; all rooms have phone, TV, air conditioning, complimentary minibar, hairdrier
FACILITIES sitting rooms, dining room, garden, swimming pool
CREDIT CARDS AE, DC, MC, V
DISABLED 2 adapted suites
PETS accepted
CLOSED never
PROPRIETORS Nerio and Letizia Raccagni

EMILIA-ROMAGNA

CASTELFRANCO EMILIA

VILLA GAIDELLO
~ COUNTRY HOTEL ~

Via Gaidello 18, 41013 Castelfranco Emilia , Roma
TEL 059 926806 **FAX** 059 926620
E-MAIL gaidello@tin.it **WEBSITE** www.gaidello.com

VILLA GAIDELLO CLUB is the creation of three sisters, one an architect, who took on the long neglected land and farm buildings of the old family home, situated in green, peaceful surroundings with a lake full of wildfowl. Today it is still run by one sister, Paola Giovanna Bini (another went to live in the United States, where she runs a similar operation in Middleburg, Virginia). Recent renovation and restoration has resulted in a total of seven apartments, each with kitchen and bathroom, of varying sizes, as well as two double bedrooms. Three of the apartments are in the *casa padronale*, one, for example, occupies the old beamed stable, using the manger for a bedroom. Other apartments are elsewhere on the estate, a couple of minutes' drive away. All display a simple, rustic elegance.

Emphasis at Il Gaidello is on the rural, simple and fresh. The restaurant is in another converted stable, where the food is prepared by *rezdore* (skilled country women) and overseen by Paola. The regional speciality, *tortellini in brodo*, is always on the menu, as well as wonderful *antipasto* and excellent dishes of chicken, rabbit and guineau hen. The food is usually served at long wooden tables. Don't miss Paola's walnut liqueur.

~

NEARBY Modena (10 km); Bologna (25 km).
LOCATION on outskirts of Castelfranco Emilia near the Via Emilia (State Highway 9), between Modena and Bologna; ample car parking
FOOD breakfast, lunch, dinner on request
PRICE €-€€
ROOMS 7 apartments sleeping 2-6 people, 2 double rooms with bath; all rooms have TV, fridge, hairdrier
FACILITIES sitting room, dining room, terrace, garden, lake, solarium
CREDIT CARDS MC, V
PETS not accepted
DISABLED access difficult
CLOSED Aug; restaurant closed Sun eve, Mon
PROPRIETOR Paola Giovanna Bini

EMILIA-ROMAGNA

LOCANDA SOLAROLA

~ COUNTRY RESTAURANT-WITH-ROOMS ~

Via Santa Croce 5, 40023 Castel Guelfo, Bologna
TEL 0542 670102 **FAX** 0542 670222
E-MAIL solarola@imola.queen.it **WEBSITE** www.locandasolarola.com

THE SOLAROLA (situated in the middle of very flat, unvisited part of rural Emilia Romagna) started life in the 1989 as a modest '*agriturismo*' with a few rooms above a rustic eatery. Nowadays its restaurant has a Michelin star for the cooking of owner Antonella Scardovi, who began, after a career as a publicist in Bologna, with no more than her 'natural talent'.

The hotel has now expanded into another building in the farm complex. The decoration might be too 'pretty-pretty' for some tastes; flowers dominate throughout, starting with the reception area. Each bedroom is named after a different flower and has the appropriate floral wallpaper, quantities of lace, painted bedheads, embroidered linens and framed floral prints. Antonella's passion for collecting 'priceless bric-a-brac' results in each room being very individual and full of her personally chosen objects. The comfortable public rooms are crammed with prints and old photos, tiffany lamps, lace cloths, pot plants, books and magazines. Jazz plays softly in the relaxed and cosy restaurant with its sloping, beamed ceilings and low lighting; a fire crackles in the grate in winter. Food is served under a pergola looking on to open fields in summer.

~

NEARBY Bologna (25 km); Ravenna (45 km); Faenza (30 km).
LOCATION 4 km SE of Medicina; A14 motorway exit Castel San Pietro Terme; ample car parking
FOOD breakfast, lunch, dinner
PRICE €€€
ROOMS 15; 14 double and twin, 1 suite, 2 with bath, 13 with shower; all rooms have phone, TV, minibar, hairdrier; 10 have air conditioning
FACILITIES breakfast room, restaurant, bar, sitting rooms, billiard room, library, garden, swimming pool
CREDIT CARDS AE, DC, MC, V
DISABLED ground floor rooms **PETS** accepted
CLOSED restaurant closed Mon, Tues lunch, hotel never
PROPRIETOR Antonella Scardovi

EMILIA-ROMAGNA

FERRARA

LOCANDA BORGONUOVO

~ TOWN BED-AND-BREAKFAST ~

Via Cairoli 29, 44100 Ferrara
TEL 0532 211100 **FAX** 0532 246328
E-MAIL info@borgonuovo.com **WEBSITE** www.borgonuovo.com

A SURPRISING FIND RIGHT IN THE HEART of this old walled city, on which the noble d'Este family (which held sway from the late 13th century until 1598) has left a lasting impression, this is a most welcome place to stay, and makes a pleasant change from normally characterless city-centre accommodation. It's a genuine, family-run private bed-and-breakfast, with four simple rooms available in the house – built inside the walls of a 15thC monastery – of its courteous and friendly owners, the Orlandini's (who speak fluent English and French).

The four bedrooms are soberly furnished with antiques; they are thoughtfully equipped, and one has a kitchenette. In fine weather generous, home-made breakfasts are served on the outdoor patio; in cooler weather you eat at a table in the Orlandini's own living room. Advice is on hand about how to spend your time in Ferarra, and bicycles are provided free of charge to get you about. The Locanda Borgonuovo has a superb location, a few yards from the Castello Estense and the cathedral. Your hosts can also recommend the best places to eat – restaurants, *trattorie* and *osterie*, and they have discount agreements with some restaurants and shops, as well as the local golf course. 'Signora Orlandini is genuinely charming, full of fascinating information about Ferrara...and she serves a brilliant breakfast', runs a recent accolade.

~

NEARBY Castello d'Estense; Palazzo del Comune; cathedral, *teatri*.
LOCATION in pedestrian zone in the centre of Ferrara; with car parking (cars may be brought to the hotel)
FOOD breakfast
PRICE €
ROOMS 4 single, double and twin, 2 apartments for 2-5, all with bath, one with kitchenette; all rooms have phone, TV, air conditioning, minibar, safe, hairdrier
FACILITIES sitting room, breakfast room, patio garden **CREDIT CARDS** AE, MC, V
DISABLED not suitable **PETS** accepted **CLOSED** never
PROPRIETOR Filippo Orlandini

EMILIA-ROMAGNA

MONTEGRIDOLFO

PALAZZO VIVIANI
~ CONVERTED CASTLE ~

Via Roma 38, 47837 Montegridolfo, Rimini
TEL 0541 855350 **FAX** 0541 855340
E-MAIL montegridolfo@montegridolfo.com **WEBSITE** www.montegridolfo.com

Montegridolfo is a beautifully renovated hilltop hamlet dating from the 13th century, only 20 kms from the madness of the Adriatic coast, but light years away in terms of atmosphere. Fashion designer Alberta Ferretti took six years to painstakingly restore the characteristic pale stone buildings and cobbled streets, opening the hotel in 1994.

At the centre is the castle, Palazzo Viviani, housing eight luxurious suites, all furnished with fine antiques; the grandest is frescoed and has a canopied four poster. The decoration fully respects the *palazzo's* origins, while evocative lighting enhances the beauty of the building. The adjacent Casa del Pittore contains seven more modest rooms, while some of the village houses have been converted into self-catering apartments. Breakfast is served in the old *limonaia* of the castle, or in warm weather, on the panoramic ramparts. For other meals, there are four eateries (some closed in winter) within the ancient walls which offer anything from pizza or bread and cheese to the sophisticated dishes based on regional specialities served in the wine cellars of the castle. Concerts and other events are programmed throughout the year.

~

NEARBY Pesaro (18 km); Urbino (25 km); Rimini (28 km); beaches (15 km).
LOCATION 30 km SW of Pesaro; take the Urbino road from Montecchio; in centre of village with parking outside walls
FOOD breakfast, lunch, dinner
PRICE €€€-€€€€€
ROOMS 23; 8 suites in castle, 7 doubles in annexe, 8 apartment for 2-6; all rooms have bath or shower, phone, TV, air conditioning, minibar, hairdrier
FACILITIES breakfast room, restaurants, bar, sitting rooms, garden, swimming pool
CREDIT CARDS AE, DC, MC, V
DISABLED not suitable
PETS accepted
CLOSED never
MANAGER Giuliano Tassinari

EMILIA-ROMAGNA

SORAGNA

AL VECCHIO CONVENTO
~ CONVERTED MONASTERY ~

Via Roma 7, 47010 Portico di Romagna, Forlì
TEL 0543 967053 **FAX** 0543 967157
E-MAIL info@vecchioconvento.it **WEBSITE** www.vecchioconvento.it

PORTICO DI ROMAGNA is a sleepy medieval village centred on a single paved street – the location of the Vecchio Convento. The house was built in 1840 and converted in the mid-1980s into a hotel – with panache that comes as a surprise in this backwater.

The dining room, at the back of the house, is the main focus. With its beamed, pitched ceiling, tiled floor and open fireplace, it has a stylishly rustic air. There is also a stone-flagged family sitting room, with piano, card table, books and games, but in practice your sitting is more likely to be done on the small terrace outside the front door; the bar, just inside the door, offers standing room only.

A severe stone staircase leads up to the bedrooms. Here, the decoration is again plain and classy – but set against that is some glorious antique furniture. The beds are particularly notable – we've rarely seen such a collection of elaborate pieces. (The bases and mattresses, we're pleased to report, modern and firm.) Most rooms are adequately spacious, though some bathrooms at the top of the house have outrageously low ceilings. Signor Cameli cooks traditional dishes with flair – even his chips are a herby delight – while Marisa leads diners through the day's choices with great good humour (and passable English). Sumptuous breakfasts, with home-made preserves. Our readers, this year, heartily endorse the place.

~

NEARBY Faenza (46 km); Ravenna (70 km); Florence (80 km).
LOCATION 30 km SE of Forli, in village; with limited garage parking
FOOD breakfast, lunch, dinner
PRICE €€
ROOMS 15; 12 double and twin, 9 with shower, 3 single, 2 with shower; all rooms have phone
FACILITIES sitting room, dining room, breakfast room, bar, terrace
CREDIT CARDS AE, DC, V **DISABLED** access difficult **PETS** accepted
CLOSED never
PROPRIETORS Marisa Raggi and Giovanni Cameli

EMILIA-ROMAGNA

BOLOGNA

COMMERCIANTI
TOWN HOTEL

Via Pignattari 11, 40124 Bologna

TEL 051 233052 **FAX** 051 224733
E-MAIL commercianti@inbo.it
WEBSITE www.bolognahotel.net
FOOD breakfast
PRICE €€€
CLOSED never
PROPRIETOR Serena Orsi

As its name suggests, the Commercianti caters primarily for the business market, but in a city with few tourist hotels it is a useful place to know about, and several recent visitors have been impressed. It has an excellent position – right in the heart of things, just off Bologna's main square, next to a smart pedestrian shopping street. The hotel exudes an air of efficiency rather than notable character ('rooms aren't particularly memorable but they are very comfortable', says one reporter). The hotel makes a good central base. There is no restaurant – just a café-like breakfast room. Although the Commercianti is situated in a traffic-free zone, guests can gain access by car in order to park in the hotel's garage.

BUSSETO

I DUE FOSCARI
TOWN HOTEL

*Piazza Carlo Rossi 15, 43011
Busseto, Parma*

TEL 0524 930031 **FAX** 0524 91625
FOOD breakfast, lunch, dinner
PRICE € **CLOSED** restaurant
closed Mon, 3rd week Aug
Marco Bergonzi and Roberto
Morsia

It is hard to believe that this Gothic building is in fact only a few decades old, so convincing are its beamed ceilings, heavy antiques and iron candelabras. The hotel is situated on a fine *piazza* in the gentle city of Busseto, home town of Guiseppe Verdi, and also of the illustrious tenor, Carlo Bergonzi, who opened the hotel in 1965. Today it is run by his son, Marco, along with Roberto Morsia, with chef Enrico Piazzi in charge of the kitchen. The *raison d' être* of the place is its traditional restaurant (with terrace). As for wine, the restaurant boasts one of those amazing cellars which you can visit, stocked with more than 750 wines, from humble country bottles to the finest vintages. Bedrooms have been refurbished.

EMILIA-ROMAGNA

POSTA

TOWN HOTEL

Piazza del Monte 2, 42100
Reggio Emilia

TEL 0522 432944
FAX 0522 452602
E-MAIL info@hotelposta.re.it
WEBSITE www.hotelposta.re.it
FOOD breakfast
PRICE €€€
CLOSED never
MANAGER Caroline Salomon

ALTHOUGH ON THE LARGE SIDE for this guide, we draw attention to this city centre hotel for its splendid rococo interior. Built in 1280, the *palazzo* has an austere façade decorated with frescoed coats of arms, but the interior is altogether a diffent story. Best is the bar, whose fittings and furniture were transferred here from a famous 19thC *pasticceria* in nearby Via Emilia more than 30 years ago. Surprisingly for the hotel's size, there is no restaurant; breakfast is taken in a little stucco-decorated hall under a skylight on the first floor. Bedrooms, all different, are prettily decorated, and are well equipped, with comfortable bathrooms.

LOCANDA DEL LUPO

TOWN HOTEL

Via Garibaldi 64, 43019 Soragna,
Parma

TEL 0524 597100 **FAX** 0524 597066
E-MAIL info@locandadellupo.com
WEBSITE www.locandadellupo.com
FOOD breakfast, lunch, dinner
PRICE €€ **CLOSED** Christmas
PROPRIETOR Signor Dioni

BUILT BY THE PRINCELY MELI LUPI FAMILY whose fortress-castle dominates this quiet little Po Valley town, the 18thC Locanda del Lupo has a timeless air, especially in the series of dining rooms which makes up its noted restaurant. Like the rest of the hotel, they are simply decorated, yet remain rather grand, with beamed ceilings, terracotta floors. antiques, old fireplaces and copper pans hanging on whitewashed walls.

The air of quiet refinement is continued through the formal sitting room and the handsome bedrooms. These are mostly spacious, with heavily beamed ceilings and tiled floors, and furnished with antiques. However, we've received a negative comment about the staff: reports please.

TUSCANY

HOTELS IN TUSCANY

No OTHER REGION OF ITALY is as rich in good small hotels as Tuscany. Florence itself is briming with fine places to stay and we have several new entries in the city; **Palazzo Magnani Feroni**, the **Johlea**, **J.K. Place** and the **Relais degli Uffizi**. Also, we have at last found entries in Pisa and Lucca (towns that have hitherto lacked the sort of accomodation that appeals to us). However, it is in the countryside that the greatest number of new places have opened (many of them 'agriturismi' - properties which earn a certain percentage of their income from the land - or 'B & Bs'); it seems that round every bend in the Tuscan countryside there is a notice indicating a place to lay your head. The problem is that many of these are mediocre to say the least, but we have tried to seek out some of the best and have come up with such gems as **Villa Il Poggiale** near San Casciano Val di Pesa and **Relais San Pietro a Polvano** near Castiglion Fiorentino. Of course, there is not room to give all the worthy place full entries, but we also liked the look of the following; **Podere Casato**, Castelnuovo Berardenga (tel 0577 352002), **Palazzo di Luglio**, Sansepolcro (tel 0575 750026) and the **Corte dei papi**, near Cortona (tel 0575 614109).

Along the coast itself, finding welcoming places to stay is more difficult although we have recommendations in Pietrasanta and Pugnano. Another possibility, if you want to sample up-market Italian beach culture in chic Forte dei Marmi is the friendly **Franceschi** (tel 0584 787114) which has a good restaurant. A little further south, in Livorno, you might consider the **Villa Godilonda** (tel 0564 835133), a spotless, modest seaside hotel near two sandy beaches. Right down south, on Monte Argentario, is the smart, spectacularly positioned **Torre di Cala Piccola** (tel 0586 670266) with its own beach while, in pretty Orbetello is the elegant **Relais San Biagio** (tel 0564 860543). Go inland a bit, and there is more choice, especially in the lovely Maremma area. We can recommend the **Podere Le Mezzelune** at Bibbonna (0586 670266) and the **Tenuta La Bandita** at Sassetta (0565 794 224). There is also the **Pereti Country House** (0564 569671), a delightful renovated farmhouse (serving excellent food) immersed in spectacular countryside near Roccatederighi, down towards Grosseto.

The Tuscan island of Elba is big enough to absorb the many summer visitors it attracts without being swamped, although there are few charming small hotels here. There is one hotel which we do not feature in the guide but can recommend: **Capo Sud** (tel 0565 964021) is a complex of small modern villas, scattered among the trees at Lacona, a rather remote part of the island. There is a pool and a private beach. Or get away from it all at **Pardini's Hermitage** (tel 0564 809034) on the island of Giglio where a simple, house party atmosphere prevails (meals all together at a big table) and which can only be reached by boat from the main port.

TUSCANY

ARTIMINO

PAGGERIA MEDICEA

~ COUNTRY HOTEL ~

Viale Papa Giovanni XXIII, 59015 Artimino, Firenze
TEL 055 8718081 **FAX** 055 8751470
E-MAIL artimino@tin.it **WEBSITE** www.artimino.com

ARTIMINO IS A VILLAGE of some distinction, drawing visitors to see its museum and nearby Etruscan tombs. It also has a number of imposing buildings, one being a grand villa built by Ferdinand I of Medici in the 16th century, who was struck by the beauty of the surroundings. Now the outbuildings and servants' quarters of this villa have been converted into an elegant and peaceful hotel.

As befits its aristocratic pedigree, the atmosphere is classy, but unshowy. Furnishings are a stylish, unpretentious mix of new and old, and original features such as sloping rafters, chimneys and ceilings have, where possible, been retained both in bedrooms and in public areas.

A short walk across manicured lawns brings you to the restaurant Biagio Pignatta (named after a celebrated Medici chef). Its specialities are Tuscan dishes 'with a Renaissance flavour' (*pappardelle sul coniglio*, for instance – broad noodles with rabbit sauce), served on a terrace over-looking hillsides of vines and olives. The estate produces its own wine, which is reverently decanted at your table.

~

NEARBY Prato (15 km); Florence (24 km); Etruscan museum.
LOCATION 24 km NW of Florence; car parking
FOOD breakfast, lunch, dinner
PRICE €€
ROOMS 37; 36 double and twin with bath or shower; 1 single with shower; all rooms have phone, TV, air conditioning, minibar; 44 apartments in village with own pool
FACILITIES sitting room, breakfast room, TV room, restaurant, garden, swimming pool, tennis
CREDIT CARDS AE, DC, MC, V
DISABLED ground floor rooms
PETS accepted
CLOSED 10 days Christmas-New Year
MANAGER Alessandro Gualtieri

Tuscany

Il Colombaio
～ COUNTRY HOTEL ～

Via Chiantigiana 29, 53011 Castellina in Chianti, Siena
TEL 0577 740444 **FAX** 0577 740402
E-MAIL info@albergoilcolombaio.it **WEBSITE** www.albergoilcolombaio.it

A NEW ADDITION TO the typically Tuscan farmhouse hotels that cluster around Castellina in Chianti, Il Colombaio is a successful example of a proven formula, and prices are still very reasonable. As you come from Greve in Chianti on the busy Chiantigiana road (SS 222), you will notice Il Colombaio on the right surrounded by lawns, shrubs and trees. Stone-built and capped with the tiled roofs at odd angles to one another so characteristic of Tuscany, the house has a pleasing aspect. It is, however, close to the road.

The restoration has been carried out with attention to detail, using country furniture to complement the rustic style of the building. The sitting room, which used to be the farm kitchen, is spacious and light with beamed ceilings, a traditional open fireplace and, in the corner, the old stone sink now filled with house plants. Breakfast is served in a small stone-vaulted room on the terrace.

The bedrooms have all been furnished with wrought-iron beds and old-fashioned dressing tables; all have modern bathrooms.

The lack of restaurant is not a problem as there are plenty of good eateries nearby.

～

NEARBY Siena (20 km); Florence (40 km); San Gimignano (30 km).
LOCATION just N of Castellina in Chianti; car parking
FOOD breakfast
PRICE €
ROOMS 15 double with bath or shower; all rooms have phone, TV, hairdrier
FACILITIES sitting room, breakfast room, garden, swimming pool
CREDIT CARDS AE, DC, MC, V
DISABLED access possible
PETS not accepted
CLOSED never
MANAGER Roberta Baldini

TUSCANY

CASTELLINA IN CHIANTI

LE PIAZZE
∼ COUNTRY HOTEL ∼

Loc. Le Piazze, 53011 Castellina in Chianti, Siena
TEL 0577 743190 **FAX** 0577 743191
E-MAIL lepiazze@chiantinet.it **WEBSITE** www.locandalepiazze.it

A WELCOME ADDITION TO the booming hotel scene in the area around Castellina in Chianti which, we feel, has the edge on many of its competitors. Although only 6 km from the bustling town, the hotel is in completely secluded countryside reached by a long unsurfaced road which seems to go on forever.

The hotel is, needless to say, a converted 17thC farmhouse, but in this case the owners have deployed more imagination and a greater sense of elegance than usual. The buffet breakfast, for instance, is served on tiled sideboards in a room adjacent to the kitchen and separated from it by a glass partition. Or you can remove yourself to any of the numerous terraces that surround the house for uninterrupted views of classical Chianti countryside.

Rustic antiques have, of course, been used in the furnishing with the usual terracotta, exposed beams and white plaster, but here and there the pattern is broken by pieces from Indonesia. Bedrooms are individually furnished with lavish use of striped fabrics (avoid those in the roof space – they can become unbearably hot); bathrooms are large, with Jacuzzis or walk-in showers big enough for a party.

∼

NEARBY Siena (27 km); Florence (50 km).
LOCATION 6 km W of Castellina in Chianti; car parking
FOOD breakfast; lunch and dinner on request
PRICE ⓔⓔⓔ
ROOMS 20 double and twin with bath or shower; all rooms have phone
FACILITIES sitting room, breakfast room, bar, terraces, garden, swimming pool
CREDIT CARDS AE, DC, MC, V
DISABLED one specially adapted room
PETS quiet dogs accepted by arrangement
CLOSED Nov-April
PROPRIETOR Maureen Skelly Bonini

TUSCANY

CASTELLINA IN CHIANTI

SALIVOLPI

~ COUNTRY GUESTHOUSE ~

Via Fiorentina, 53011 Castellina in Chianti, Siena
TEL 0577 740484 **FAX** 0577 740998
E-MAIL info@hotelsalivolpi.com **WEBSITE** www.hotelsalivolpi.com

FOR NO IMMEDIATELY OBVIOUS REASON, the unremarkable Chianti village of Castellina contains a cluster of Tuscany's most appealing hotels. This welcome addition to the catalogue, open since 1983, offers a much cheaper alternative to its two illustrious neighbours – Tenuta de Ricavo (page 143) and Villa Casalecchi. It occupies two well-restored farm buildings and one new bungalow in a peaceful open position on the edge of the village – supposedly the location of the ancient Etruscan Castellina – affording broad views across the countryside.

There is a Spanish feel to the older of the houses – iron fittings, exposed beams, white walls, ochre tiles – and the spacious rooms are both neat and stylish, with some splendid old beds and other antiques. The whole place is well cared for, and has a calm, relaxed atmosphere.

The garden is impeccably tended, with plenty of space, some furniture and a fair-sized swimming pool. Breakfast ('*molto abbondante*', claims the boss) is served in a crisp little room in the smaller of the houses, and although it is the only meal provided, there is no shortage of restaurants nearby.

~

NEARBY Siena (21 km); San Gimignano (31 km); Florence (45 km).
LOCATION 500 m outside town, on road to San Donato in Poggio; car parking
FOOD breakfast
PRICE €
ROOMS 19 double and twin with bath or shower; all rooms have phone
FACILITIES sitting room, breakfast room, garden, swimming pool
CREDIT CARDS MC, V
DISABLED no special facilities
PETS not accepted
CLOSED never
PROPRIETOR Angela Orlandi

TUSCANY

CASTELLINA IN CHIANTI

TENUTA DI RICAVO
~ COUNTRY HOTEL ~

Loc. Ricavo 4, 53011 Castellina in Chianti, Siena
TEL 0577 740221 **FAX** 0577 741014
E-MAIL ricavo@ricavo.com **WEBSITE** www.ricavo.com

IF AWAY FROM IT ALL IS where you want to get – while retaining the possibility of doing some serious sightseeing – Ricavo is hard to beat. The hotel occupies an entire hamlet, which was deserted in the 1950s when people left the land for the cities in search of work.

The grouping of houses along a wooded ridge in the depth of the countryside might have been conceived as a film-set replica of a medieval hamlet. The main house, facing a little square of other mellow stone cottages, contains some of the bedrooms, and the several sitting rooms, which are comfortably furnished with a pleasant jumble of antique chairs and sofas (one of them with a small library of English, Italian, French and German books). The hotel's restaurant, La Pecora Nera ('The Black Sheep'), is open to non-residents so advance booking is essential.

Breakfast can be taken out-of-doors, on a little piazzetta at the front, weather permitting. At the right time of the year the gardens are bright with flowers, and there are plenty of secluded corners, which make the place seem calm and quiet even when the hotel is full. The small garden pool is ideal for quiet cooling off, the larger one is on a lower terrace.

A visitor pronounces the hotel 'expensive, but professional and worth it', and the food 'very satisfactory'.

~

NEARBY Siena (22 km); Florence (45 km).
LOCATION 4 km N of Castellina in Chianti; car parking
FOOD breakfast, lunch (in summer), dinner
PRICES €€€
ROOMS 23; 13 double and twin, 2 single, 8 suites, all with bath or shower; all rooms have phone, TV, minibar, safe (3-day minimum stay in high season)
FACILITIES sitting rooms, bar, restaurant, terrace, gym, garden, 2 swimming pools, table tennis **CREDIT CARDS** MC, V
DISABLED ground floor rooms available **PETS** not accepted
CLOSED Nov to Easter; restaurant closed Sun
PROPRIETOR Christina Lobrano-Scotoni and Alessandro Lobrano

TUSCANY

CASTELNUOVO BERARDENGA

RELAIS BORGO SAN FELICE
~ HILLTOP HOTEL ~

Loc. Borgo San Felice, 53019 Castelnuovo Berardenga, Siena
TEL 0577 359260/396561 **FAX** 0577 359089
E-MAIL info@borgosanfelice.it **WEBSITE** www.borgosanfelice.com

B ORGO SAN FELICE IS LARGER THAN MOST of the entries in this guide, but we
include it in the guide without hesitation. It is a carefully renovated
hilltop hamlet – like a collection of charming small hotels. Surrounded by
cypresses and the vineyards of the renowned San Felice estate, the peaceful village feels as if it has been suspended in time: no intrusive neon
signs, no lines of cars, just the original Tuscan qualities of perfectly proportioned space setting off simple buildings of brick and stone, and
topped by a jumble of terracotta roofs. Even the swimming pool (which in
these parts all too often resembles a gaping, blue gunshot wound) has
been discreetly tucked away. Gravel paths, carved well heads, pergolas,
lemon trees in gigantic terracotta pots, a church, a bell tower and a
chapel – this is the real Tuscany.

All the original features of the various buildings have been retained:
vaulted brick ceilings, imposing fireplaces, old tiled floors. The furniture is
a stylish mixture of old and modern and the sitting rooms are full of intimate alcoves. An elegant restaurant completes the picture. Top of the
range – with prices to match.

~

NEARBY Siena (17 km).
LOCATION 17 km NE of Siena in former estate village; car parking
FOOD breakfast, lunch, dinner
PRICES €€€€
ROOMS 43; 24 double and twin, 4 single, 15 suites, all with bath or shower; all
rooms have phone, TV, minibar, air conditioning, hairdrier, safe
FACILITIES sitting rooms, conference rooms, billiards room, restaurant, beauty
centre, gym, swimming pool, tennis, bowls, putting and pitching green
CREDIT CARDS AE, DC, MC, V
DISABLED access difficult
PETS not accepted
CLOSED Nov-Apr
MANAGER Birgit Fleig

TUSCANY

CASTIGLION FIORENTINO

RELAIS SAN PIETRO IN POLVANO

~ COUNTRY HOTEL ~

Loc.Polvano 3, 52043 Castiglion Fiorentino, Arezzo
TEL 0575 650100 **FAX** 0575 650255
E-MAIL polvano@technet.it **WEBSITE** www.polvano.com

SITUATED IN THE HILLS above Castiglion Fiorentino, Polvano is a tiny hamlet comprising a clutch of buildings including this solid stone farmhouse, purchased and restored by the Prottis on retirement and opened as a small hotel in 1998 which they run with their family.

The house has been renovated with good taste and a modern, clean touch which does not in any way detract from the inherent rustic characteristics of the building (beamed ceilings, bricked archways, terracotta floors and so on). Solid country furniture goes well with sofas upholstered in pale cream fabric, wicker arm chairs and bright, oriental rugs; two comfortble sitting rooms have open fireplaces. The bedrooms, with their wrought-iron bed heads and white covers, have a similarly uncluttered feel. In cool weather, food is served in the cosy former stables, but in summer you can eat on the wide, partially covered terrace that runs along one side of the building from which views of the open, unspoiled countryside, are stunning. Antonietta and her daughter in law are in charge of the food which, we have heard, is excellent.

This is a delightful place where the emphasis is on peace and tranquility; there are no TV's and children under 12 are discouraged.

~

NEARBY Cortona (20 km); Arezzo (25 km); Lake Trasimeno (20 km).
LOCATION 10 km east of Castiglion Fiorentino in own grounds with parking
FOOD breakfast, dinner
PRICES €€€
ROOMS 10; 4 doubles, 1 single, 5 suites, all with bath or shower; all rooms have phone, air conditioning (suites and 2 doubles), hairdrier
FACILITIES sitting rooms, restaurant, breakfast room, terrace, garden, swimming pool
CREDIT CARDS AE, MC, V
DISABLED no special facilities
PETS not accepted
CLOSED Nov-end Mar
PROPRIETOR Luigi Protti

Tuscany

Cetona

La Frateria
~ Converted convent ~

Convento di San Francesco, 53040 Cetona, Siena
Tel 0578 238015 **Fax** 0578 239220
E-MAIL frateria@fbcc.it **WEBSITE** www.mondox.it

O NE OF THE MORE UNUSUAL entries in this guide and not a hotel in the strict sense but a place of hospitality run by a community that has withdrawn from the world. The buildings, grouped around a hillside church founded in 1212 by St Francis, built of light, golden stone, form a rambling complex. Only seven rooms and suites are available, so, even when it is fully booked, one never has the sensation of being in a busy hotel. There is no swimming pool and none of the rooms has a television.

This may sound monastic, but the setting and furnishings are of the same standard as a top-class hotel: antiques, paintings and colourful wooden carvings (generally religious in theme) and spacious rooms with stone and beige stucco walls. The restaurant is unexpectedly sophisticated (and expensive), serving a mixture of refined and hearty food using fresh produce from the gardens.

A stroll around the monastery with its church and chapel, cloisters and courtyards, and hushed, peaceful atmosphere will help you realize why the young people of this community want to share their peace.

~

Nearby Pienza (40 km); Montepulciano (26 km); Montalcino (64 km).
Location 26 km S of Montepulciano; car parking
Food breakfast, lunch, dinner
Price €€€
Rooms 7; 5 double, 2 suites, all with bath or shower; all rooms have phone, air conditioning, minibar, hairdrier
Facilities sitting rooms, restaurant, terrace, garden
Credit cards AE, MC, V
Disabled no special facilities
Pets not accepted
Closed Jan; restaurant Tue in winter
Manager Maria Grazia Daolio

TUSCANY

LA FOCE

~ COUNTRY APARTMENTS ~

Strada della Vittoria 63, 53042 Chianciano Terme, Siena
TEL and **FAX** 0578 69101
E-MAIL info@lafoce.com **WEBSITE** www.lafoce.com

ANYONE WHO IS FAMILIAR WITH the writing of Iris Origo will be particularly interested in La Foce, the estate whose history during the Second World War is so vividly described in her book, *War in the Val d'Orcia*. Iris died in 1988, but her family still lives on the property in this remote but strangely beautiful corner of Tuscany, running it as a working farm.

Several of the buildings on the large estate have been converted into superior self-catering accommodation, ranging from the delightful two-person Bersagliere to superb and quite grand Montauto which sleeps ten; the latter stands in its own extensive garden with lavender borders and a small pool.

Furnishings throughout the comfortable apartments are in sophisticated and tasteful country style, predominantly antique, but with a few well-chosen modern pieces. There is plenty of colour, provided by bright rugs, cushions and cheerful fabrics. Each has its own piece of private garden and the use of a pool. Music lovers will appreciate the excellent chamber music festival which takes place on the estate each July.

~

NEARBY Pienza (20 km); Montepulciano (10 km).
LOCATION 5 km SW of Chianciano Terme (follow signs for Monte Amiata and Cassia); car parking.
FOOD dinner on request
PRICE appartment sleeping 2 people ⓔ weekly rates from £700; minimum rent 1 week
ROOMS 9 self-catering apartments/houses sleeping 2-14, all with bath and shower; all apartments/houses have phone, TV on request
FACILITIES terraces, garden, swimming pools, tennis, children's playground
CREDIT CARDS MC, V
DISABLED 2 specially adapted rooms
PETS not accepted
CLOSED never
PROPRIETORS Benedetta and Donata Origo

Tuscany

CORTONA

Il Falconiere

~ COUNTRY VILLA ~

Loc. San Martino, 52044 Cortona, Arezzo
Tel 0575 612 679 **Fax** 0575 612 927
E-MAIL info@ilfalconiere.com **WEBSITE** www.ilfalconiere.com

THE PLAIN SURROUNDING Lake Trasimeno, over which Il Falconiere looks, was once the scene of some of Hannibal's fiercest battles against the Romans. Nowadays, the only carnage takes place on the A1 *autostrada* but Il Falconiere is such a haven of civilized living that you will never realize that you are only 20 minutes away from one of Italy's riskiest tourist experiences.

Reached through quiet country lanes, bordered by vineyards, just outside Cortona, the main villa (built in the 17th century around an earlier fortified tower) is set in landscaped grounds of olives, rosemary hedges, fruit trees and roses, which also contain the old lemon house (now a Michelin-starred restaurant) and the still-functioning chapel with an adjoining suite. Meticulous attention has been given to every aspect of decoration and furnishing, from *trompe-l'oeil* number scrolls outside each room to the hand-embroidered window-hangings and finest bed linen. Persian rugs and handsome antiques rest easily on uneven, original terra-cotta floors. In the pigeon-loft of the old tower, reached by a narrow, stone spiral staircase, is a small bedroom with an unsurpassed view of the Valdichiana. A villa nearby has recently been converted to create eight new bedrooms with their own breakfast room and pool. The estate produces its own excellent wine and olive oil and cooking courses are organised too. A recent report praises the hotel unequivocally: 'Everything combines to make this one of the most stylish hotels in Italy.'

~

NEARBY Cortona (3 km); Arezzo (29 km); Lake Trasimeno (10 km).
LOCATION just outside Cortona overlooking Valdichiana; car parking
FOOD breakfast, lunch, dinner
PRICE €€€€ **ROOMS** 19; 13 double, 6 suites, all with bath or shower; all rooms have phone, TV, air conditioning, minibar, hairdrier, safe
FACILITIES restaurant, garden, swimming pools (May-Sep) **CREDIT CARDS** AE, DC, V
DISABLED no special facilities **PETS** accepted **CLOSED** early Jan to mid-Feb
PROPRIETORS Riccardo Baracchi and Silvia Regi

Tuscany

Cortona

San Michele

~ Town hotel ~

Via Guelfa 15, 52044 Cortona, Arezzo
Tel 0575 604348 **Fax** 0575 630147
E-mail info@hotelsanmichele.net **Website** www.hotelsanmichele.net

It might sound like an easy matter to turn a fine 16thC Renaissance palace into a hotel of character, but we have seen too many examples of good buildings that have brutalized by excessive and unwanted luxury, over-modernization and an almost wilful blindness to the original style, not to be delighted when the job has been properly done.

The Hotel San Michele has steered a precise course between the twin dangers of unwarranted adventurousness and lame timidity. White plaster and stark beams are complemented with rich modern fabrics; sofas of the finest leather stand on terracotta floors that seem glazed with a rich wax. Carefully-placed lights emphasize the gracefully interlocking curves of the cortile. The common rooms are full of such stylish features as frescoed friezes and immense carved stone fireplaces.

The bedrooms are more modest in style, with wrought-iron beds and rustic antiques; one report states that they are in need of refurbishment while another says that hers was decidely cramped. Some of the more spacious ones have an extra mezzanine to provide separate sleeping and sitting areas. A recent guest felt that the welcome was somewhat impersonal and that there was 'a faint shadow of the corporate feel' to this hotel.

~

Nearby Diocesan Museum, Arezzo (29 km); Perugia (51 km).
Location in middle of town; garage nearby
Food breakfast
Price €€
Rooms 43; 40 double and twin and 3 suites, all with bath or shower; all rooms have phone, TV, minibar, air conditioning, hairdrier
Facilities sitting room, breakfast room, conference room
Credit cards AE, DC, MC, V
Disabled access possible **Pets** small dogs accepted
Closed mid-Jan to early Mar
Proprietor Paolo Alunno

TUSCANY

FERIOLO

CASA PALMIRA
~ COUNTRY GUESTHOUSE ~

Via Faentina – Loc. Feriolo, 50030 Polcanto, Firenze
TEL and **FAX** 055 8409749
E-MAIL info@casapalmira.it **WEBSITE** www.casapalmira.it

L EAVING FLORENCE, THE OLD Faenza road winds through olive groves and
cypresses before reaching the beautiful and relatively unknown area of
the Mugello, and continuing up and over the Apennines. Casa Palmira is
set just off this road in an oasis of green, a converted barn attached to a
stone farmhouse with medieval origins.

Stefano and Assunta, the warm and charming hosts, have done a beautiful job on converting the barn into a relaxed and comfortable guesthouse. The ground floor sitting room is spacious and welcoming, with a
huge fireplace, squashy sofas and chairs, an open kitchen area where
breakfast is prepared, and a dining area. Upstairs, the bedrooms all lead
off a lovely sunny landing, and while the public areas have terracotta flagstones, the bedrooms all have beautiful chestnut wood floors made by
Stefano (who also made the doors and some of the furniture). Pretty fabrics and patchwork quilts complement warm-coloured walls and dusty
green paintwork. There are mountain bikes and a Smart for guests to hire
and wonderful walking nearby. There is even a hot tub in the garden, and
plans are underway for a Turkish bath. Who needs Florence?

~

NEARBY Florence (16 km); Fiesole (9 km).
LOCATION halfway between Florence and Borgo San Lorenzo just off the SS302, Via
Faentina (from Florence turn right to Feriolo just past Olmo); car parking
FOOD breakfast, dinner on request
PRICE €
ROOMS 6; 4 double and twins, 1 single, 1 triple, 1 with bath, 6 with shower
(although not all are en suite); rooms have hairdrier on request
FACILITIES sitting room, breakfast/dining room, terraces, garden with barbecue,
hot tub
CREDIT CARDS not accepted
DISABLED access difficult **PETS** not accepted
CLOSED Jan-Feb
PROPRIETORS Assunta Fiorini and Stefano Mattioli

TUSCANY

FIESOLE

BENCISTÀ
~ COUNTRY GUESTHOUSE ~

Via B. da Maiano 4, 50014 Fiesole, Firenze
TEL and **FAX** 055 59163
E-MAIL pensionebencista@iol.it

THIS QUINTESSENTIAL FAMILY-RUN *PENSIONE* has provoked both ecstatic and disappointed reports from readers who have either fallen for its slightly faded charms or found it too reminiscent of a boarding house. We love it. Once a monastery, it stands on a hillside overlooking Florence and the surrounding countryside; views from the flower-decked terrace (where breakfast is served in summer) and many of the bedrooms are unforgettable. Added to this are the delights of the building itself, a handsome hall, three salons almost entirely furnished with antiques (including a little reading room with shelves of books and a cosy fire), plus plenty of fascinating nooks and crannies.

No two bedrooms are alike, and each has some captivating feature – a beautiful view, a fine piece of furniture, a huge bathroom or a private terrace. They are nearly all old-fashioned, with plain whitewashed walls and solid antiques; the accent is on character rather than luxury.

The dining room is simple, light and spacious (somewhat reminiscent of a refectory), overlooking the beautiful gardens. The food is totally unpretentious and there is no choice; you will be served with the sort of meal that a Florentine family would eat. One reader complained strongly about dinner while another thought it 'delicious'.

~

NEARBY Roman amphitheatre; cathedral; Florence.
LOCATION 2.5 km S of Fiesole on Florence road; in own grounds with garage and car park
FOOD breakfast, light lunch, dinner
PRICE €€
ROOMS 40; 26 double and twin, 11 single, 3 suite, all with bath or shower; all rooms have phone, hairdrier
FACILITIES sitting rooms, dining room, terrace, garden **CREDIT CARDS** MC, V
DISABLED one adapted room **PETS** accepted
CLOSED sometimes Dec-Jan
PROPRIETOR Simone Simoni

TUSCANY

LE CANNELLE
~ TOWN BED-AND-BREAKFAST ~

Via Gramsci 52-56, 50014 Fiesole, Firenze
TEL 055 5978336 **FAX** 055 5978292
E-MAIL info@lecannelle.com **WEBSITE** www.lecannelle.com

L E CANNELLE'S YOUNG PROPRIETORS Sara and Simona Corsi, have a father with a building business, so who better to restore these two old townhouses on Fiesole's main street, a little way north of the main square. Once finished, he handed over the management of the little bed-and-breakfast to his two daughters who have enthusiastically set about their new activity since opening in November 1999.

The cool hills surrounding Fiesole are studded with spectacular villas, and many of the hotels in the area are correspondingly expensive. We are therefore pleased to include Le Cannelle as a low-cost, but charming, alternative. It has been carefully decorated in simple, yet comfortable style. Bedrooms are quite spacious and one even has a duplex with two single beds at the top. Two offer lovely views of the hills to the north. Those on the somewhat noisy street have double glazing. The blue-and-white bathrooms are spotless. The pretty room where Sara and Simona prepare breakfast is, unfortunately, right on the street.

~

NEARBY Roman Amphitheatre; Florence (8 km).
LOCATION on main street N of the main square; public car parking
FOOD breakfast
PRICE €€
ROOMS 2 double, 1 single, 1 triple, 1 family, all with bath or shower; all rooms have phone, TV, air conditioning
FACILITIES breakfast room
CREDIT CARDS AE, MC, V
DISABLED not suitable
PETS not accepted
CLOSED Jan-Feb
PROPRIETORS Sara and Simona Corsi

TUSCANY

IL TREBBIOLO
~ COUNTRY GUEST HOUSE ~

Via del Trebbiolo 8, 50060 Molino del Piano, Firenze
TEL 055 8300098 **FAX** 055 8300583
E-MAIL iltrebbiolo@libero.it **WEBSITE** www.iltrebbiolo.com

AFTER A LONG PERIOD OF CLOSURE and a change of management, Il Trebbiolo has re-opened in a more relaxed, less up-market guise than before. The simple, ochre-coloured villa dates from the 1400s; it stands on a quiet hillside north of Fiesole, surrounded by acres of woodland, vines and olives. A large gravel terrace in front of the house looks on to open countryside.

The building is flanked by two arched *loggias* under which tables and chairs are grouped; food is served here in the summer. Inside, paintwork in restful colours provides a good backdrop for some handsome antiques and oriental rugs. A bright sitting room is at guests' disposal for cooler weather (in summer, everyone sits outdoors) while a welcoming fire is lit in the lemon-painted restaurant where you can sample local specialities. Half the bedrooms are housed in the main villa. While spacious and comfortable, with big tiled bathrooms, they are quite simply furnished. A smartly-converted annexe houses more bedrooms, a couple of which have kitchennettes.

The new, young owners are enthusiastic and eager to please; thier guest house is comfortable yet unpretentious and enjoys a totally peaceful setting. The visitor's book is full of praise both for the welcome and the food.

~

NEARBY Fiesole (7 km); Firenze (11 km); Mugello.
LOCATION 7 km north of Fiesole on Olmo road; after 7 km turn right for Monteloro. in own grounds with parking
FOOD breakfast, lunch, dinner
PRICE €€
ROOMS 23; 19 doubles and twins, 2 singles, 2 apartments, all with bath or shower; all rooms have phone, TV, hairdrier; rooms in villa have minibar; rooms in annexe have air conditioning
FACILITIES sitting rooms, bar, restaurant, breakfast room, terrace, garden, swimming pool
CREDIT CARDS AE, DC, MC, V
DISABLED adapted rooms **PETS** accepted if small
CLOSED never; restaurant closed Tues lunch and Mon **PROPRIETORS** Roberto Bartolini

TUSCANY

FIESOLE

VILLA SAN MICHELE
∼ COUNTRY VILLA ∼

Via Doccia 4, 50014 Fiesole, Firenze
TEL 055 59451 **FAX** 055 598734
E-MAIL reservations@villasanmichele.net **WEBSITE** www.orient/expresshotels.com

ACCORDING TO ITS BROCHURE, the villa was designed by Michelangelo – which perhaps accounts in part for the high prices. The rooms are among the most expensive in Italy – only a fraction less than those at the hotel's more swanky sister, the Cipriani in Venice – and beyond the reach of most of our readers. But the guide would be incomplete without this little gem on the peaceful hillside of Fiesole – originally a monastery, built in the early part of the 15th century, enlarged towards the end of it, and much expanded recently with the creation of 13 extra suites.

What you get for your money is not extravagant decoration or ostentatious luxury, but restrained good taste and an expertly preserved aura of the past. The rooms are furnished mostly with solid antiques including 17thC masterpieces (religiously maintained every winter, we are told); many of the bedrooms have tiled floors of notable antiquity. Bathrooms, on the other hand, are impressively contemporary. Views from the villa are exceptional. One of the great delights of the place is to dine in the *loggia*, gazing down slopes of olives and cypresses to the city below. The pool terraces share this glorious view. Breakfast is an American buffet feast; half board includes an *à la carte* meal, lunch or dinner.

∼

NEARBY Roman theatre; cathedral; monastery of San Francesco.
LOCATION on Florence-Fiesole road, just below Fiesole; car parking
FOOD breakfast, lunch, dinner
PRICE €€€€€€
ROOMS 40; 25 double and twin, 15 suites, all with bath; all rooms have phone, air conditioning; TV and minibar on request
FACILITIES reading room/bar, piano bar, dining room with *loggia*/terrace, garden, swimming pool (open Jun-Sep)
CREDIT CARDS AE, DC, MC, V
DISABLED access possible **PETS** small dogs accepted
CLOSED late Nov to mid-Mar
MANAGER Maurizio Saccani

TUSCANY

ANNALENA
~ TOWN GUEST HOUSE ~

Via Romana 43, 50125 Firenze
TEL 055 222402 **FAX** 055 222403
E-MAIL annalena@hotelannalena.it **WEBSITE** www.annalena.it

One of Florence's traditional *pensioni* and, in spite of new owners, still very much in the old style, the Annalena is located opposite the back entrance to the beautiful Boboli gardens. Many of the bedrooms look out on to a horticultural centre next door; the best give on to a long veranda Luckily, none have windows on the busy Via Romana.

The 14th century *palazzo* has an intriguing past involving, in its early days, the tragic Annalena (a young noblewoman) and, during the war, foreign refugees fleeing from Mussolini's police. Today, while no luxury hotel, the Annalena offers solid comforts not without a hint of style, and at resonable prices. The huge public room (serving as reception, bar, sitting and breakfast rooms) is a bit dreary, but the bedrooms are lovely: spacious and full of light from tall windows which take full advantage of views of the garden below and the picturesque backs of neighbouring houses. Smart new fabrics and a lick of paint have done wonders for rooms that had been allowed to get a little shabby.

Guests lucky enough to have a room with a terrace should order breakfast there: so much nicer than a rather cramped table in the airless 'salon'.

~

NEARBY Pitti Palace; Boboli Gardens ; Ponte Vecchio; Santo Spiritoi.
LOCATION south of the river, 3 minutes' walk S of the Pitti Palace; public car parking nearby
FOOD breakfast
PRICES €€
ROOMS 20; 16 double and twin, 4 single, all with bath or shower; all rooms have phone, TV, air conditioing, minibar, safe, hairdrier
FACILITIES sitting room/bar/breakfast room
CREDIT CARDS AE, DC, MC, V
DISABLED no special facilities
PETS accepted
CLOSED never
PROPRIETOR Icilio Marazzini

TUSCANY

FLORENCE

APRILE

~ TOWN HOTEL ~

Via della Scala 6, 50123 Firenze
TEL 055 216237 **FAX** 055 280947
E-MAIL relais.uffizi@flashnet.it **WEBSITE** www.venere.it/firenze/aprile

The bust of Cosimo I de' Medici over the door gives a clue to the origins of the 15thC *palazzo* which houses this attractive hotel: it once belonged to the city's most famous family. More stylish use could possibly have been made of its architectural inheritance, but it has a charming, old-fashioned feel to it and the decoration is highly individual.

Public rooms are at the back of the building. The elegant breakfast room has a frescoed ceiling, the bar doubles as sitting room and there is a delightful little garden. Bedrooms vary enormously in shape and size. Although they are all gradually being upgraded, a few are still very traditional. Others have vaulted ceilings, frescoes or fragments of graffiti. The owners have just bought the next-door *palazzo* where sponged paintwork in pale pastels, thick carpets and soft lighting in the bedrooms make for a more modern feel.

Bathrooms in smart grey marble have all been upgraded. Many rooms have a spectacular and unusual view over the rooftops of nearby Santa Maria Novella and its cloister. A free lecture on some aspect of Florence and its history is given on 3 evenings a week for guests.

~

NEARBY Santa Maria Novella; *duomo*; San Lorenzo.
LOCATION just S of Santa Maria Novella station and 10 minutes' walk from the *duomo*; paid car parking nearby
FOOD breakfast
PRICE €€
ROOMS 31; 25 double and twin, 3 single, 6 family, all with bath or shower; all rooms have phone, TV, air conditioning, minibar, hairdrier
FACILITIES sitting room, breakfast room, bar, conservatory, lift, garden
CREDIT CARDS AE, DC, MC, V
DISABLED 2 specially adapted rooms
PETS accepted
CLOSED never
PROPRIETOR Riccardo Zucconi

TUSCANY

FLORENCE

CASCI

~ TOWN HOTEL ~

Via Cavour 13, 50129 Firenze
TEL 055 211686 **FAX** 055 2396461
E-MAIL info@casci.com **WEBSITE** www.hotelcasci.com

MUSIC LOVERS MAY GET A THRILL from the fact that the 15thC *palazzo* which now houses this hotel once belonged to Giacomo Rossini. Located on a busy main road just north of San Lorenzo, the Casci is an unpretentious family-run hotel where you can be assured of the warmest of welcomes from the helpful Lombardis.

The decoration is modern and functional, but painted ceilings in some of the public areas give a clue to the age of the building. The open-plan reception area is bright, cheerful and always busy. The first thing our inspector noticed were two bookcases overflowing with guidebooks and leaflets for guests' use. To the right is the breakfast room, and to the left a bar/sitting area both of which have painted ceilings. The rooms vary in size and shape (some sleep five), and are fairly spartan, but quite attractive with pale yellow walls and modern green wooden furniture.

Many of the bathrooms are new; some have tubs and all have heated towel rails, an unexpected bonus in a two-star hotel. The most peaceful rooms look over a garden at the back of the building; others have double glazing.

~

NEARBY San Lorenzo; Magi chapel; Medici chapels; *duomo.*
LOCATION on busy street N of *duomo*; paid car parking nearby
FOOD breakfast
PRICE €€
ROOMS 26; 14 double and twin, 4 single, 8 family, 7 with bath, 19 with shower; all rooms have phone, TV, air conditioning, hairdrier
FACILITIES breakfast room, bar, lift
CREDIT CARDS AE, DC, MC, V
DISABLED one specially adapted room
PETS small ones accepted
CLOSED Jan
PROPRIETORS Lombardi family

TUSCANY

CLASSIC
~ TOWN HOTEL ~

Viale Machiavelli 25, 50125 Firenze
TEL 055 229351 **FAX** 055 229353

STANDING IN ITS OWN LUSH GARDEN and rubbing shoulders with some of the most impressive residences in Florence, this pink-washed villa is on a leafy avenue just five minutes from Porta Romana, the old gate into the south of the city. A private residence until 1991, the house was rescued from decay and turned into a comfortable and friendly hotel which maintains admirably reasonable prices.

Bedrooms vary in size, but all are fairly spacious, with parquet floors, original plasterwork, antique furniture and pretty bedspreads. Two have frescoes, and another hosts an impressive fireplace. The high ceilings on the first floor allow for a duplex arrangement with extra space for beds or sitting areas on a higher level, while top floor rooms have sloping, beamed attic ceilings and air conditioning. A romantic annexe suite tucked away in the garden, complete with tiny kitchen area, offers extra privacy for the same price as a standard double.

In warmer weather, breakfast is served outside under a pergola, but even in winter the conservatory allows for a sunny – possibly even a warm – start to the day.

~

NEARBY Pitti Palace; Piazzale Michelangelo; Museo La Specola.
LOCATION in residential area 5 minutes' walk from Porta Romana; car parking
FOOD breakfast
PRICE €€
ROOMS 20; 17 double and twin, 2 single, 1 suite, all with bath or shower; all rooms have phone, TV, air conditiong, safe, hairdrier
FACILITIES breakfast room, conservatory, garden
CREDIT CARDS AE, DC, MC, V
DISABLED no special facilities
PETS accepted
CLOSED 2 weeks Aug
PROPRIETOR Corinne Kraft

TUSCANY

FLORENCE

HELVETIA AND BRISTOL
~ TOWN HOTEL ~

Via dei Pescioni 2, 50123 Firenze
TEL 055 26651 **FAX** 055 288353
E-MAIL information.hbf@royaldemeure.com **WEBSITE** www.hotelhelvetiabristolfirenze.it

THE HELVETIA WAS ORIGINALLY a Swiss-owned hotel right in the centre of Florence which added the name Bristol to attract 19thC British travellers. Illustrious past guests include Stravinsky, Bertrand Russel and Gabriel d'Annunzio. After 1945, it gradually fell into decay until new management took it over and began restoration in 1987, sparing no expense in their imaginative recreation of a 19thC luxury hotel.

Those with classical tastes, used to the stark simplicity of the Tuscan style, may find the results cloying and indigestible, but others will enjoy the rich colour schemes and heavy, dark antiques. The least overwhelming room is a 1920s winter garden where food is served; it is full of handsome cane furniture and potted palms, with a green-tinted glass ceiling. The bedrooms are, if anything, even more ornate than the public rooms. Antiques, Venetian mirrors and chandeliers plus swathes of rich fabric add to the opulence. One of the finest features of the hotel is its extensive collection of prints and pictures. Staff and service are smooth and professional. In 2000 the hotel extended into the next-door building, adding 18 new doubles and three suites.

~

NEARBY Ponte Vecchio; Uffizi; Palazzo Vecchio.
LOCATION in the centre of town, opposite Palazzo Strozzi, W of Piazza Repubblica; public car parking nearby
FOOD breakfast, lunch, dinner
PRICES €€€€€
ROOMS 67 double and twin, single and suites, all with bath or shower; all rooms have phone, TV, CD player, hairdrier, minibar, air conditioning
FACILITIES sitting rooms, restaurant, bar, winter garden
CREDIT CARDS AE, DC, MC, V
DISABLED some facilities
PETS not accepted
CLOSED never
MANAGER Pietro Panelli

TUSCANY

FLORENCE

HERMITAGE
~ TOWN HOTEL ~

Vicolo Marzio 1, Piazza del Pesce, 50122 Firenze
TEL 055 287216 **FAX** 055 212208
E-MAIL florence@hermitagehotel.com **WEBSITE** www.hermitagehotel.com

THE LOCATION, JUST NORTH OF the Ponte Vecchio, is highly central, and highly favoured: few hotels this close to Florence's main drag could be described as peaceful, but this Lilliputian-scale retreat is not inappropriately named. There is an air of tranquillity about it – helped by a judicious, although not always sufficient, amount of double glazing on the busier riverside aspect.

Everything about the Hermitage is small, like a doll's house – only upside down, with neat, graceful bedrooms on the lower floors, while the reception desk and public rooms are on the fifth floor, overlooking the Arno. It's worth the climb: both bar-sitting room and breakfast room are delightfully domestic, in cool lemony yellows made intimate and welcoming with flowers and pictures.

The Hermitage was once no more than one of the typical, older-style *pension* that are becoming rare in Florence. But it has had a marked facelift and, as a recent inspection revealed, is now more tasteful, well-kept - and expensive - than average. It also has touches of luxury; all rooms have Jacuzzi baths or showers. A flower-filled roof terrace offers views across Florence's red rooftops – an appealing place for breakfast.
~

NEARBY Uffizi; Ponte Vecchio.
LOCATION in heart of city, facing river; garage
FOOD breakfast, snacks
PRICES €€€
ROOMS 28 double and twin, 24 with bath, 4 with shower; all rooms have phone, TV, air conditioning, hairdriers, safe
FACILITIES breakfast room, bar/sitting room, roof terrace
CREDIT CARDS MC, V
DISABLED access difficult
PETS small dogs accepted
CLOSED never
PROPRIETOR Vincenzo Scarcelli

TUSCANY

FLORENCE

J AND J
~ TOWN HOTEL ~

Via di Mezzo 20, 50121 Firenze
TEL 055 2345005 **FAX** 055 240282
E-MAIL jandj@dada.it **WEBSITE** www.hoteljandj.com

A CONVERTED MONASTERY provides the setting for this cool, chic hotel some distance east of the Duomo, on the way to the Sant' Ambroggio market. The street is comparatively quiet, and inside, the hotel feels a haven from heat and dust, so effective is its air conditioning and so peaceful is its ambience.

Many original features of the building are still intact – columns, vaulted ceilings, frescoes and wooden beams – and furnishings, though stylishly modern in places, are sympathetic to the spirit of the antique setting, and certainly not lacking personality. A small, pretty patio garden at the rear of the hotel, with elegant white parasols and plants in tubs, tempts breakfast-eaters to venture out through the plate-glass doors, though the interior option, with its decorated, vaulted ceiling, is almost as inviting.

Bedrooms vary. All are of high standard; some exceptionally spacious, with split-level floors and seating areas, and high ceilings with exposed beams. A recent visitor felt that their eclectic style made them more like private rooms than hotel ones.

A word of warning; the stairs are very steep and there is no lift.

~

NEARBY *Duomo*; church of Santa Croce.
LOCATION E of *duomo*, N of Santa Croce; garage parking nearby
FOOD breakfast
PRICES €€€€
ROOMS 19; 12 double and twin, 7 suites, all with bath; all rooms have phone, TV, air conditioning, minibar, hairdrier
FACILITIES sitting room, bar
CREDIT CARDS AE, DC, MC, V
DISABLED no special facilities
PETS not accepted
CLOSED never
PROPRIETORS Cavagnari family

TUSCANY

FLORENCE

J.K.PLACE
~ TOWN HOTEL ~

Piazza Santa Maria Novella 7, 50123 Firenze
TEL 055 2645181 **FAX** 055 2658387
E-MAIL jkplace@jkplace.com **WEBSITE** www.jkplace.com

OCCUPYING A TALL, elegant town house on Piazza Santa Maria Novella, and opened in May 2003, J.K. Place is Florence's newest and most captivating boutique hotel. To the right is Alberti's glorious symmetrical church façade; you can almost ignore the shabbiness of the square itself. Once inside the discreet entrance, the cares of the world and the dust of the city really do seem to fade into the restful cream and grey colour scheme, the soft music, the heady scent of flowers, the flickering candle light and the bend-over-backwards-to-help attention of the charming staff. While not for those on a lean budget, and much beloved by the fashion crowd, this hotel is not at all stuffy or intimidating.

The decoration is a seductive contemporary take on neo-classical style. Rooms are filled with comfortable furniture, interesting art and covetable *objets*. A fire burns in the cosy sitting room where arm chairs and sofas are draped with cashmere throws. Breakfast is served at a big polished antique table in the glassed-in courtyard or in your room. Bedrooms continue along the same stylish lines (although some are very small) while bathrooms are naturally magnificent. Views from the rooftop terrace take in the whole city.

~

NEARBY Santa Maria Novella; Ponte Vecchio; Uffizi; Palazzo Vecchio.
LOCATION in the centre of town with lift; private garage nearby
FOOD breakfast, snacks
PRICES €€€€€
ROOMS 20; 13 double and twin, 7 suites, all with bath or shower; all rooms have phone, TV, DVD, CD, air conditioning, minibar, safe, hairdrier
FACILITIES sitting rooms, breakfast room, bar, roof terrace
CREDIT CARDS AE, DC, MC, V
DISABLED adapted rooms
PETS accepted if small
CLOSED never
GENERAL MANAGER Omri Kafri

TUSCANY

FLORENCE

LOGGIATO DEI SERVITI
∼ TOWN HOTEL ∼

Piazza SS Annunziata 3, 50122 Firenze
TEL 055 289592 **FAX** 055 289595
E-MAIL info@loggiatodeiservitihotel.it **WEBSITE** www.loggiatodeiservitihotel.it

ONE OF FLORENCE'S NEWEST charming hotels is in one of its loveliest Renaissance buildings, designed (around 1527) by Sangallo the Elder to match Brunelleschi's famous Hospital of the Innocenti, opposite. Until a few years ago the building housed a modest *pensione* and the beautiful square was a giant car park. But the Loggiato is now elegantly restored and, thanks to the city council's change of heart, much more peaceful.

The decoration is a skilful blend of old and new, all designed to complement the original vaulting and other features with a minimum of frill and fuss. Floors are terracotta-tiled, walls rag-painted in pastel colours. Bedrooms are individually decorated with sympathy and flair. There is a small, bright breakfast room in which to start the day (with fruit juice, cheese and ham, *brioches*, fruit and coffee) and a little bar where you can recover from it, browsing glossy magazines and sipping a Campari.

A recent reporter praised the 'admirable' comfort and standards, 'individual' welcome and service, and 'calm, comfortable and quiet' atmosphere. They provided 'the best breakfast we have had in Italy' and 'excellent' value for money. His sole quibble was 'slightly gloomy lighting'.

∼

NEARBY Church of Santissima Annunziata; Foundlings' Hospital.
LOCATION a few minutes' walk N of *duomo*, on W side of Piazza SS Annunziata; garage service on request
FOOD breakfast
PRICES €€€
ROOMS 29; 19 double and twin, 6 single, 4 suites, all with bath or shower; all rooms have phone, TV, air conditioning, minibar, hairdrier, safe
FACILITIES breakfast room, bar
CREDIT CARDS AE, DC, MC, V
DISABLED not suitable
PETS accepted
CLOSED never
PROPRIETOR Rodolfo Budini-Gattai

TUSCANY

MORANDI ALLA CROCETTA
~ TOWN GUEST HOTEL ~

Via Laura 50, 50121 Firenze
TEL 055 2344747 **FAX** 055 2480954
E-MAIL welcome@hotelmorandi.it **WEBSITE** www.hotelmorandi.it

KATHLEEN DOYLE ANTUONO first moved into this lovely former convent in the 1920s; in the early '80s, she opened the house to guests. She, sadly, is no more (although her portrait as an 18-year-old beauty hangs in the breakfast room), but the hotel continues to be successfully run by her son Paolo.

Situated near Piazza Santissima Annunziata along with Brunelleschi's famous Spedale degli Innocenti, the house is decorated throughout with taste and care. Antique Tuscan furnishings, patterned rugs, interesting pictures and fresh flowers abound. You may spot corbels carved with coats of arms in the reception hall, ancient painted tiles or fragments of fresco in the bedrooms. A recent inspector was impressed not only by her lovely frescoed room, but by the attention to detail, such as the thoughtful lighting, heated towel rail and even a phone in the bathroom. Another recent visitor, however, complained about the 'businesslike' atmosphere and the 'disgraceful' breakfast. The latter is included in the room price, but is not obligatory; try instead the excellent Pasticceria Robiglio in nearby Via dei Servi. We like the unpretentious Morandi, and it is convenient for exploring Florence's *centro storico*. Be warned: the stairs up to the reception are steep, especially if you are carrying luggage.

~

NEARBY *Duomo*; archaeological museum; San Marco, Accademia.
LOCATION in quiet street NW of Piazza del Duomo with private garage
FOOD breakfast
PRICE €€
ROOMS 10; 6 double and twin, 2 single, 2 family, all with shower; all rooms have phone, TV, air conditioning, minibar, hairdrier, safe
FACILITIES sitting room, breakfast room
CREDIT CARDS AE, DC, MC, V
DISABLED access difficult **PETS** small well-behaved dogs accepted
CLOSED never
PROPRIETORS Paolo Antuono

TUSCANY

FLORENCE

PALAZZO CASTIGLIONI
~ TOWN BED-AND-BREAKFAST ~

Via del Giglio 8, 50123 Firenze
TEL 055 214886 **FAX** 055 2740521
E-MAIL pal.cast@flashnet.it **WEBSITE** www.florenceby.com

THE ONLY SIGN BETRAYING the existence of this smart little B&B is a tiny, discreet brass plaque next to the bell. The solid 16thC *palazzo* is situated on one of the side streets which runs into the San Lorenzo market area.

The hotel is on the second floor where a warmly-lit reception area doubles as sitting and breakfast room. The colour scheme is elegant pale green and cream. Sofas and chairs are upholstered in a smart brocade with co-ordinating curtains and paintwork. Several of the six bedrooms are frescoed. One particularly pretty room is entirely covered in pastoral scenes, while another is a *trompe l'oeil* of a castle courtyard complete with coats of arms, suits of armour in niches and birds circling in the sky above. All the rooms are furnished with a mixture of antiques and reproduction pieces and have armchairs, padded bedheads and curtains in handsome fabrics; two are big enough to be called 'junior suites'.

Bathrooms are a refreshing step away from the white-tiled hotel norm, with yellow and pale blue sponged paintwork, deep blue ceramic-tiled floors, and prints and painted mirrors on the walls.

~

NEARBY San Lorenzo; Medici chapels; Santa Maria Novella.
LOCATION between *duomo* and station; paid car parking next door
FOOD breakfast
PRICE €€
ROOMS 6 double, 1 with bath, 5 with shower; all rooms have phone, TV, air conditioning, minibar, hairdrier
FACILITIES sitting room, breakfast room, lift
CREDIT CARDS AE, MC, V
DISABLED no special facilities
PETS small ones accepted
CLOSED Christmas
PROPRIETOR Giancarlo Avuri

TUSCANY

FLORENCE

PALAZZO MAGNANI FERONI

~ TOWN HOTEL ~

Borgo San Frediano 5, 50124 Firenze
TEL 055 2399544 **FAX** 055 2608908
E-MAIL info@florencepalace.it **WEBSITE** www.florencepalace.com

IF YOU WANT THE ROMANCE and atmosphere of a grand Renaissance *palazzo* combined with the facilities of an upmarket hotel (and you have a fat wallet), this could be for you. Situated in the lively Oltrarno district south of the river, the *palazzo* was home to the owner's family until he decided to convert it into a hotel. He has maintained all the characteristics of its noble origins, however, and you will find grand salons filled with fine family antiques and pictures, elaborate frescoes, original boxed ceilings, old terracotta floors and glittering chandeliers.

There is no lack of communal space for guests who can choose between a plant-filled courtyard, a billiard room, various sitting rooms (including one on the top floor with rather incongruous fake zebra print-covered chairs) and a fabulous rooftop terrace with views all over the city and way beyond. The ten luxourious suites are enormous; each has a seperate sitting room furnished with squashy arm chairs and sofas and a fair spattering of antiques too. Our inspector particularly liked the cheapest room in the place: a beautiful and romantic little room with floor-to-ceiling frescoes and a small private garden. Bathrooms (complete with robes and slippers) are suitably opulent. You will even be asked to choose the scent of your soap on arrival.

~

NEARBY Pitti Palace; Santo Spirito; Ponte Vecchio.
LOCATION south of the river in centre of own, west of Ponte Vecchio with lift and private garage
FOOD breakfast, snacks
PRICE €€€€€€
ROOMS 11; 1 double and 10 suites all with bath; all rooms have phone, TV, air conditioning, minibar, safe, hairdrier
FACILITIES sitting rooms, bar, breakfast room, billiard room, gym, terrace
CREDIT CARDS AE, DC, MC, V
DISABLED access difficult **PETS** not accepted **CLOSED** never
PROPRIETOR Alberto Giannotti

TUSCANY

FLORENCE

RELAIS DEGLI UFFIZI
~ TOWN GUEST HOUSE ~

Chiasso de' Baroncelli/Chiasso del Buco 16, 50122 Firenze
TEL 055 2676239 **FAX** 055 2657909
E-MAIL info@relaisuffizi.it **WEBSITE** www.relaisuffizi.it

IT IS EASY TO GET LOST among the warren of narrow passageways that lead off the south side of Piazza della Signoria, and there is no helpful sign to guide you to the Relais degli Uffizi. Look out for a pale stone arch that will lead you to its doorway, through which you will see a pretty lunette fresco of a rooftop scene. Make straight for the comfortable sitting room which has a fabulous view over the piazza. A few minutes of watching the comings and goings in this historic square, sizing up the vast outline of the Palazzo Vecchio, and then pondering the extraordinary silhouette of the cathedral dome to the north will immediately give you a flavour of the city.

The ten bedrooms, each different from the next, are arranged on two floors. All, however, are tastefully decorated and furnished: pastel colours on the walls, a mix of antique and traditional Florentine painted pieces, and original features such as boxed ceilings, creaky parquet floors and even an enormous fireplace that acts as a bed head (this was the kitchen in the original 16th century house). Several rooms have modern four-poster beds hung with filmy white curtains. Bathrooms have recently been re-vamped.

~

NEARBY Ponte Vecchio; Palazzo Vecchio; the Uffizi.
LOCATION in a narrow lane off the south side of Piazza Signoria with lift and paid parking nearby
FOOD breakfast
PRICE €€€
ROOMS 10 doubles and twins, 1 single all with bath or shower; all rooms have phone, TV, air conditioning, minibar, safe (in some), hairdrier
FACILITIES sitting room/breakfast room
CREDIT CARDS AE, DC, MC, V
DISABLED adapted rooms
PETS accepted if small
CLOSED never
PROPRIETOR Elisabetta Matucci

TUSCANY

FLORENCE

RESIDENCE JOHANNA CINQUE GIORNATE
~ TOWN GUESTHOUSE ~

Via delle Cinque Giornate 12, 50129 Firenze
TEL and **FAX** 055 473377
E-MAIL cinquegiornate@johanna.it **WEBSITE** www.johanna.it

THE JOHANNA IS UNDER THE SAME OWNERSHIP as the Johlea (see page 169)
and offers the same excellent value for money - of which we thoroughly approve.

Some way north-west of the centre of the city, but on several bus routes, the Johanna's existence is announced by a discreet brass plaque next to a solid iron gate; the pleasant building stands in its own small gravelled garden.

Inside, you find yourself in an elegant private house, with cool, cream-coloured walls, and high ceilings throughout give a sense of space. At the back of the house, a comfortable sitting room doubles as the reception.

The bedrooms are all fairly large (one particularly so), and are furnished with large beds and a mixture of antiques and modern pieces. Tasteful fabrics, of predominantly pale green-and-cream stripes, add style. The bathrooms vary in size, but even the smallest is adequate. Each room has the wherewithal for a simple DIY breakfast: electric kettle, coffee, tea, biscuits and *brioche*.

~

NEARBY Santa Maria Novella; Fortezza da Basso.
LOCATION in residential area 15 minutes' walk NW of the station; limited car parking
FOOD breakfast
PRICE €
ROOMS 6; 5 double and twin, 1 family, 1 with bath, 5 with shower; all rooms have TV; 3 have air conditioning
FACILITIES sitting room, small garden
CREDIT CARDS not accepted
DISABLED no special facilities, but 3 ground floor rooms
PETS accepted
CLOSED never
PROPRIETOR Lea Gulmanelli

TUSCANY

RESIDENZA JOHLEA UNO
∼ TOWN GUESTHOUSE ∼

Via San Gallo 76, 50129 Firenze
TEL 055 4633292 **FAX** 055 4634552
E-MAIL cinquegiornate@johanna.it **WEBSITE** www.johanna.it

IN A CITY WHERE HOTEL PRICES HAVE sky-rocketed over the past few years, it is difficult to believe that a guest house can offer three-star comforts at one-star prices, but that's just what the Johlea does. The *residenza* occupies an elegant apartment in a solid *palazzo* just north of the Duomo. The atmosphere is of a gracious private house: indeed, there is no hotel sign on the street and you will be given your own key to come and go. There's no breakfast room either, but rooms are supplied with the wherewithal for a simple breakfast laid out on laquer trays. The bedrooms are stylishly decorated in soft pastel colours and comfortably furnished, partly with antiques. The bathrooms are excellent too.

Upstairs is a cosy little sitting room with an honesty fridge from which guests can help themselves to (and sign for) cold drinks, yoghurts and so on. Up another staircase is the Johlea's crowning glory, a small roof terrace from which there are 360° views of the city. If there is no room at the inn, there is always the Johlea II, a couple of doors down the road which is equally pleasant, offers the same value for money, but has no terrace.

∼

NEARBY *Duomo*; San Marco; Accademia Gallery.
LOCATION in centre of city, directly north of the duomo with garage parking nearby (extra charge); lift
FOOD breakfast (in room)
PRICE €
ROOMS 6; 5 double and twin, 1 family, 1 with bath, 5 with shower; all rooms have TV; 3 have air conditioning
FACILITIES sitting room, roof terrace
CREDIT CARDS not accepted
DISABLED no special facilities
PETS accepted
CLOSED never
PROPRIETOR Lea Gulmanelli

TUSCANY

FLORENCE

TORNABUONI BEACCI
~ TOWN GUESTHOUSE ~

Via Tornabuoni 3, 50123 Firenze
TEL 055 212645/268377 **FAX** 055 283594
E-MAIL info@torabuonihotels.com **WEBSITE** www.tornabuonihotels.com

ONE COULD NOT ASK FOR more in terms of location. Via Tornabuoni is one of Florence's most elegant and central shopping streets, where leading designers such as Gucci, Ferragamo, Pucci and Prada have their stores, and within easy walking distance are all the main sights of the city. Yet its position on the fourth and fifth floors of the 15thC Palazzo Minerbetti Strozzi, at one corner of Piazza Santa Trinita, makes it a haven from Florence's crowded, noisy streets.

The *pensione* has a turn-of-the-century atmosphere. Fans of E.M. Forster's *A Room with a View* will find this a close approximation of the Edwardian guesthouse described in the novel. Many of the rooms have views, but none so fine as the rooftop terrace, with its plants and pergola, which looks over the city to the towers and villas of the Bellosguardo hill. Even in the hot, still days of July and August, you may catch a refreshing breeze here.

The decoration and furnishings are old-fashioned but well maintained, like the house of a maiden aunt. Parquet floors and plain-covered sofas are much in evidence. Rooms vary – some are quite poky – but new management has been making improvements.

~

NEARBY Santa Trinita; Ponte Vecchio; Palazzo della Signoria.
LOCATION in centre of town; garage nearby
FOOD breakfast, dinner, snacks (in summer)
PRICES €€€
ROOMS 28; 20 double and twin, 8 single, all with bath or shower; all rooms have phone, TV, air conditioning, minibar, hairdrier
FACILITIES sitting room, restaurant, roof terrace
CREDIT CARDS AE, DC, MC, V
DISABLED access difficult
PETS small dogs accepted
CLOSED never
PROPRIETOR Francesco Bechi

TUSCANY

FLORENCE

TORRE GUELFA
~ TOWN BED-AND-BREAKFAST ~

Borgo SS Apostoli 8, 50123 Firenze
TEL 055 2396338 **FAX** 055 2398577
E-MAIL torre.guelfa@flashnet.it **WEBSITE** www.hoteltorreguelfa.com

THERE CAN BE FEW BETTER SPOTS in Florence in which to enjoy a quiet *aperitivo* after a hard day's sightseeing: this is the tallest privately-owned tower in the city, dating from the 13th century and enjoying a 360° view over a jumble of rooftops, taking in all the most important landmarks and the countryside beyond.

The hotel is very popular, particularly with the fashion crowd during trade fair season. The Italian-German owners have created a comfortable and unstuffy atmosphere rejecting a heavy, Florentine look for a lighter touch. Bedroom walls are sponge-painted in pastel shades and curtains are mostly fresh, embroidered white cotton. Furniture is a mixture of wrought iron and prettily-painted pieces with some antiques. Bathrooms are in smart grey Carrara marble.

One room has its own spacious terrace complete with olive tree; be prepared to fight for it. A glassed-in *loggia* provides space for a sunny breakfast room and the double 'salon', with its boxed-wood ceiling and little bar, is a comfortable and quiet place in which to relax.

~

NEARBY Ponte Vecchio; Vecchio and Pitti palaces.
LOCATION in centre of town in traffic-limited area; garage nearby
FOOD breakfast
PRICE ⓔⓔ
ROOMS 16; 13 double and twin, 1 single, 2 family, all with bath or shower; all rooms have phone, TV, air conditioning, minibar, hairdrier (some)
FACILITIES sitting room, breakfast room, bar, terraces
CREDIT CARDS AE, EC, MC, V
DISABLED one specially adapted room
PETS small ones accepted
CLOSED never
PROPRIETOR Giancarlo Avuri

TUSCANY

FLORENCE

VILLA AZALEE
~ TOWN HOTEL ~

Viale Fratelli Rosselli 44, 50123 Firenze
TEL 055 214242 **FAX** 055 268264
E-MAIL villaazalee@fi.flashnet.it **WEBSITE** www.villa-azalee.it

CONVENIENT FOR THE STATION, but slightly remote from the monumental district (about 15 minutes by foot) Villa Azalee will appeal to visitors who prefer family-run hotels with some style to larger, more luxurious operations; and by the standards of most hotels in Florence, prices are very reasonable. The hotel consists of two buildings: the original 19thC villa and, across the garden, a new annexe, full of the potted azaleas that give the place its name.

A highly individual style has been used in the decoration and furniture: some will find the results delightful, others excessively whimsical. Pastel colours, frilly canopies and matching curtains and bedcovers characterize the bedrooms. They are all air conditioned, with spotless, new bathrooms. The public rooms are more restrained with an interesting collection of the family's paintings. Breakfast is served either in your room, in the garden (somewhat noisy) or in a separate breakfast room.

One of the drawbacks of the hotel is its location on the *viali* (the busy traffic artery circling Florence). Sound-proofing has been used, but rooms in the annexe, or overlooking the garden, are preferable.

~

NEARBY Santa Maria Novella; Ognissanti; San Lorenzo; *duomo.*
LOCATION a few minutes' walk W of the main station, towards Porta al Prato; garage nearby
FOOD breakfast
PRICES ©©
ROOMS 25; 23 double and twin, 2 single, all with bath or shower; all rooms have phone, TV, air conditioning, minibar, hairdrier
FACILITIES sitting room, bar, garden
CREDIT CARDS AE, DC, MC, V
DISABLED 2 adapted rooms
PETS accepted by arrangement
CLOSED never
PROPRIETOR Ornella Brizzi

TUSCANY

FLORENCE

VILLA BELVEDERE
~ COUNTRY VILLA ~

Via Benedetto Castelli 3, 50124 Firenze
TEL 055 222501 **FAX** 055 223163
E-MAIL reception@villa-belvedere.com **WEBSITE** www.villa-belvedere.com

THIS FAMILY-RUN HOTEL lies in a pleasant hilly residential district on the southern outskirts of the city, commanding excellent views through classically Tuscan cypress trees when Florentine smog permits. The building itself is no great beauty, being practical and modern, but its well-kept gardens and small swimming pool are a great boon in hot weather, and its peaceful surroundings, away from any passing traffic, a relief from the city centre at any time of the year.

The Ceschi-Perotto family manage their business with welcoming enthusiasm and efficiency and have recently completed an ambitious programme of refurbishment. Bedrooms and bathrooms are traditionally decorated in a smart matching scheme of *fleur de lys* motifs, racing greens and high-quality solid wood furnishings. Bathrooms gleam, with white tiles offset by restrained geometric friezes. Public areas are light, spacious and comfortable – and the breakfast room makes the best of the garden.

A limited evening snack menu is available until 8.30 pm – particularly useful after a tiring day's sightseeing, since there are few restaurants within easy walking distance.

~

NEARBY Pitti Palace; Boboli gardens.
LOCATION 3 km S of city; car parking
FOOD breakfast, snacks
PRICES €€
ROOMS 26; 21 double and twin, 2 single, 3 suites, all with bath or shower; all rooms have phone, TV, air conditioning, safe, hairdrier
FACILITIES 2 sitting rooms, breakfast room, bar, TV room, veranda, garden, swimming pool, tennis
CREDIT CARDS AE, DC, MC, V
DISABLED no special facilities **PETS** not accepted
CLOSED Dec-Feb
PROPRIETORS Ceschi-Perotto family

TUSCANY

FLORENCE

VILLA POGGIO SAN FELICE
~ HILLTOP VILLA ~

Via San Matteo in Arcetri 24, 50125 Firenze
TEL 055 220016 **FAX** 055 2335388
E-MAIL info@villapoggiosanfelice.com **WEBSITE** www.villapoggiosanfelice.com

THE HILLS IMMEDIATELY to the south of Florence are full of grand and beautiful villas, many of them erstwhile summer residences of wealthy Florentine families. The 15thC Villa Poggio San Felice is such a house; perched on a little *poggio* or hill, it could be in the heart of Chianti but is, in fact, only ten minutes from the city centre. The villa was bought by Gerardo Bernardo Kraft – a Swiss hotelier – in the early 19th century and was recently inherited and restored by his descendants.

The mellow old villa is set in a lovely garden designed by Porcinai in the late 1800s. Inside, the feeling is very much of an elegant private house, but it is not at all stuffy. Cheerful fabrics and interesting colours give a young feel to the place while blending nicely with family antiques and pictures. The day starts in the long, high-ceilinged breakfast room where French windows open on to the garden. For relaxation, there is a pretty, partially arched *loggia*, plenty of seats dotted around the grounds or a sitting room for cooler weather. The comfortable and spacious bedrooms – each different from the next – lead off a landing on the first floor; two have working fireplaces. The suite has a little reading room and a terrace overlooking the city.

~

NEARBY San Miniato, Piazzale Michelangelo.
LOCATION S of Porta Romana, follow the signs for Arcetri; car parking
FOOD breakfast
PRICE ©©©
ROOMS 5; 4 double, 1 twin, 4 with bath, 1 with shower; all rooms have phone; hairdrier on request
FACILITIES sitting room, breakfast room, terraces, garden, free shuttle service to and from Ponte Vecchio
CREDIT CARDS AE, DC, MC, V
DISABLED access difficult **PETS** small pets accepted
CLOSED Jan-Mar
PROPRIETORS Livia Puccinelli and Lorenzo Magnelli

TUSCANY

LECCHI IN CHIANTI

SAN SANO

∾ COUNTRY HOTEL ∾

Loc.San Sano Gaiole in Chianti, 53010 Siena
TEL 0577 746130 **FAX** 0577 746156

THE MEDIEVAL HAMLET OF SAN SANO, a clutter of stone houses with uneven terracotta roofs, has at its heart an ancient defence tower, destroyed and rebuilt many times. Now, in its latest incarnation, this imposing structure forms the core of a delightful, family-run hotel in a relatively little visited, authentic part of Chianti.

The various buildings surrounding the tower (which houses some of the bedrooms; others have direct access to the grounds) give the hotel a rambling character, connected by narrow passageways, steep stairways and unexpected courtyards. The restoration has been meticulous and restrained. The decoration is in classic, rustic Tuscan style but with individual touches: carefully chosen antiques, colourful pottery and plenty of flowers The dining-room, in the former stables, spanned by a massive stone arch and still with the feeding trough, is a cool haven from the summer sun. Each bedroom has its individual character (one with nesting birds in its perforated walls, now glassed off) and gleaming, almost surgical bathrooms. Outside is a stone-paved garden at the foot of the tower and, at a slight remove, a hill-side swimming pool.

∾

NEARBY Radda in Chianti (9 km); Siena (25 km); Florence (60 km).
LOCATION hilltop hamlet in open countryside with own car parking
FOOD breakfast, dinner
PRICE ©©
ROOMS 14; 12 double and twins, 2 single, all with shower, 2 with bath; all rooms have phone, TV, air conditioning, minibar, hairdrier
FACILITIES sitting areas, breakfast and dining room, garden, swimming pool
CREDIT CARDS AE, DC, MC, V
DISABLED 2 adapted rooms
PETS accepted
CLOSED mid-Nov to mid-Mar
PROPRIETORS Marco Amabili

TUSCANY

GREVE IN CHIANTI

VILLA DI VIGNAMAGGIO
~ COUNTRY VILLA ~

Greve in Chianti, 50022 Firenze
TEL 055 8544840 **FAX** 055 8544468
E-MAIL agriturismo@vignamaggio.com **WEBSITE** www.vignamaggio.com

CHIANTI HAS MORE THAN ITS SHARE OF hilltop villas and castles, now posing as hotels, or, as in this case, self-catering (*agriturismo*) apartments. Vignamaggio stands out from them all: one of those rare places that made us think twice about advertising it. The villa's first owners were the Gherardini family, of which Mona Lisa, born here in 1479, was a member. This could even have been where she and Leonardo met. More recently, it was the setting for Kenneth Branagh's film of Shakespeare's *Much Ado About Nothing*.

Villa di Vignamaggio is a warm Tuscan pink. A small formal garden in front gives way to acres of vines. The pool, a short distance from the house, is among fields and trees. The interior is a perfect combination of simplicity and good taste, with the emphasis on natural materials. Beds, chairs and sofas are comfortable and attractive. Old wardrobes cleverly hide small kitchen units. The two public rooms are equally pleasing, and breakfast there or on the terrace is thoughtfully planned, with bread from the local bakery and home-made jam. The staff were charming and helpful when we visited. 'Service' is kept to a minimum ("This is not a hotel.").

~

NEARBY Greve (5 km); Florence (19 km); Siena (38 km).
LOCATION 5 km SE of Greve on the road to Lamole from the SS222; car parking
FOOD breakfast; dinner 2 evenings a week
PRICE €€
ROOMS 21 rooms, suites, self-catering apartments for 2-4 people, all with bath; all rooms/apartments have phone; air conditioning
FACILITIES sitting room, bar, gym, terrace, garden, 2 swimming pools, tennis court, children's playground
CREDIT CARDS AE, MC, V
DISABLED one specially adapted apartment
PETS accepted
CLOSED mid Nov-mid Mar
PROPRIETOR Gianni Nunziante

TUSCANY

LOCANDA L'ELISA
~ COUNTRY VILLA ~

Via Nuova per Pisa (SS 12 bis), Massa Pisana, 55050 Lucca
TEL 0583 379737 **FAX** 0583 379019
E-MAIL info@locandalelisa.com **WEBSITE** www.locandalelisa.com

A FRENCH OFFICIAL OF THE NAPOLEONIC times who accompanied the Emperor's sister, Elisa Baciocchi, to Lucca acquired this 18thC villa for his own residence. Perhaps that accounts for the discernibly French style of the house that makes it unique among Tuscan hotels. A square building, three storeys high, painted in an arresting blue, with windows and cornices picked out in gleaming white, the villa stands just off the busy old Pisa-Lucca road.

The restorers have fortunately avoided the oppressive Empire style (which, in any case, the small rooms would not have borne) and aimed throughout at lightness and delicacy. The entrance is a symphony in wood, with geometrically patterned parquet flooring and panelled walls, and the illusion of space created with large mirrors. To the right is a small sitting room, furnished with fine antiques and Knole sofas. A round 19thC conservatory is now the romantic restaurant; the food is unpretentious and excellent, with an emphasis on fish. Each suite has been individually decorated using striped, floral and small-check patterns, canopied beds and yet more antiques – no expense has been spared. A glorious mature garden insulates it from the main road.

~

NEARBY Lucca (3 km); Pisa (15 km).
LOCATION 3 km S of Lucca on the old road to Pisa; car parking
FOOD breakfast, lunch, dinner
PRICE €€€€€
ROOMS 10; 1 double, 1 single, 8 suites, all with bath or shower; all rooms have phone, TV, air conditioning, minibar, safe, hairdrier
FACILITIES sitting rooms, restaurant, garden, swimming pool
CREDIT CARDS AE, DC, MC, V
DISABLED ground floor rooms available
PETS small dogs accepted
CLOSED early Jan to early Feb
MANAGER Leonardo Iurlo

TUSCANY

MERCATALE VAL DI PESA

SALVADONICA
～ COUNTRY ESTATE ～

Via Grevigiana 80, 50024 Mercatale Val di Pesa, Firenze
TEL 055 8218039 **FAX** 055 8218043
E-MAIL info@salvadonica.com **WEBSITE** www.salvadonica.com

THIS DELIGHTFUL ASSEMBLY OF RUSTIC buildings amid olive groves and vine-yards will gladden the heart of any lover of Tuscan scenery. Two entre-preneurial young sisters have energetically converted a family home, on what was until recently a feudal estate, into a thriving bed-and-breakfast and *agriturismo* business. Past visitors have found the place enchanting.

Now the two main buildings of the farm – one rich red stucco, the other mellow stone and brick – offer five well-equipped, comfortable guest rooms and ten apartments to let. They have clay-tiled floors and wood-beamed ceilings, and range from the merely harmonious and comfortable to the positively splendid (in the case of a brick-vaulted former cowshed).

From the paved terraces surrounding the buildings, you look over an olive grove to the neat swimming pool area with Jacuzzi. A tennis court and riding stables offer alternative pastimes. Breakfast, with a changing variety of cakes and breads, is served in a pleasant stone-walled dining room or on a sunny terrace overlooking unspoiled sweeps of countryside, where the local Gallo Nero Chianti and excellent olive oil are still produced.

～

NEARBY Florence (20 km).
LOCATION 20 km S of Florence, E of road to Siena; car parking
FOOD breakfast
PRICE €€
ROOMS 5 double, 10 apartments, all with shower; all rooms have phone; apartments have fridge
FACILITIES billiards room, TV room, garden, swimming pool, tennis
CREDIT CARDS AE, DC, MC, V
DISABLED one specially-adapted room and one apartment
PETS if small (extra charge)
CLOSED Nov-Feb
PROPRIETORS Baccetti family

TUSCANY

MONTE SAN SAVINO

CASTELLO DI GARGONZA
∼ CONVERTED CASTLE ∼

Gargonza, 52048 Monte San Savino, Arezzo
TEL 0575 847021 **FAX** 0575 847054
E-MAIL gargonza@gargonza.it **WEBSITE** www.gargonza.it

Nᴏᴛ sᴏ ᴍᴜᴄʜ ᴀ ᴄᴀsᴛʟᴇ as an entire 13th century fortified hamlet, Gargonza was once a working farm where Dante Alighieri was a guest. Perched high above typical, unspoilt Tuscan landscape, it has been beautifully (but not overly) restored; the ancient walls encircle a cluster of buildings including a tower, a church and an octagonal well. Its paved alleyways are traffic free, although you can drive in with your luggage.

The *foresteria*, or guest house, has seven fairly Spartan rooms rentable for a minimum of three days in high season. Twenty five self-catering apartments (named after past occupants) have recently been refurbished; these are let on a weekly basis and offer good value for groups of families. They are comfortable and mostly spacious, with new bathrooms, pretty co-ordinating fabrics, working fireplaces and cleverly concealed kitchen units. Note that housekeepng is only available on request.

Breakfast is served in the *frantoio* (the old olive press) which also houses a sitting room graced with the only TV on the premises. Just below the walls, a rustic restaurant serves excellent local specialities including homemade *pici* with duck sauce and superb Chainina beef. The recent addition of a large pool, on a terrace bordered by rosemary hedges, is very welcome.

∼

NEARBY Arezzo (25 km); Chianti; Val di Chiana.
LOCATION 35 km E of Siena on SS73, 7 km W of Monte San Savino; car parking outside walls
FOOD breakfast, lunch, dinner
PRICE €€
ROOMS 10 double in main guesthouse all with bath or shower; 25 self-catering houses; all rooms have phone, hairdrier; main guesthouse rooms have minibar
FACILITIES sitting rooms, TV room, breakfast room, restaurant, meeting rooms, garden, swimming pool (open mid May-mid Sept)
CREDIT CARDS AE, DC, MC, V
DISABLED access difficult **PETS** not accepted
CLOSED 3 weeks Nov **PROPRIETOR** Conte Roberto Guicciardini

Tuscany

Montefiridolfi

Il Borghetto

~ Country villa ~

Via Collina S Angelo 23, Montefiridolfi, S. Casciano Val di Pesa, 50020 Firenze
Tel 055 8244442 **Fax** 055 8244247
e-mail ilborghetto@studio-cavallini.it

Discretion, taste and refinement are the key characteristics of this family guesthouse, much appreciated by a discerning (and returning)
clientele that enjoys civilized living in a peaceful, bucolic setting.

A manicured gravel drive leads past the lawn, with its rose beds and
cypress trees, to the main buildings, which include the remains of two
15thC military towers. From a covered terrace, where breakfast is
improved by views of miles of open countryside, a broad-arched entrance
leads to the open-plan ground floor of the main villa. Within, the usual
starkness of the Tuscan style, has been softened by the use of muted tones
in the wall colours and fabrics. Comfortable furniture abounds without
cluttering the spacious, airy quality of the public areas. Upstairs, in the
bedrooms (some of which are not particularly large), floral wallpaper and
subdued lighting create a balmy, relaxed atmosphere. No intrusive phone
calls or blaring televisions.

Even the refined like a swim; but for those who consider swimming
pools raucous, there is a soothing water garden.

Cookery courses are organized here at certain times of the year.

~

Nearby Florence (18 km); Siena (45 km); San Gimignano (40 km).
Location 18 km S of Florence, E of Siena road; on right before village; car parking
Food breakfast; lunch and dinner if requested by enough people
Price €€€ (2-day minimum stay)
Rooms 8; 6 doubles, 2 suites all with shower
Facilities sitting room, dining room, terrace, garden, swimming pool
Credit cards not accepted
Disabled one suitable room
Pets not accepted
Closed Nov-Mar
Manager Antonio Cavallini

TUSCANY

MONTERIGGIONI

MONTERIGGIONI

~ VILLAGE HOTEL ~

Via 1 Maggio 4, 53035 Monteriggioni, Siena
TEL 0577 305009/305010 **FAX** 0577 305011
E-MAIL info@hotelmonteriggioni.net **WEBSITE** www.hotelmonteriggioni.net

VISITORS TO TUSCANY HAVE BEEN increasingly keen to drop by well-preserved, medieval Monteriggioni and spend a couple of hours relaxing in the *piazza* (where a bar serves snacks), browsing the antique shops or sampling the menu of Il Pozzo, one of the finest restaurants in the Siena area. Finally, somebody had the bright idea that a small hotel would not go amiss, especially since the town is peaceful and well placed for exploring the locality.

A couple of old stone houses were knocked together and converted with sure-handed lightness of touch to make this attractive hotel. The former stables now make a large, light and airy public area used as reception, sitting room and breakfast room.

At the back, a door leads out to a well-tended garden running down to the town walls and containing what is possibly the smallest swimming pool in Tuscany. The bedrooms are perfectly acceptable, furnished to a high rustic-antique standard with stylish hypermodern bathrooms.

~

NEARBY Siena (10 km); San Gimignano (18 km); Florence (55 km); Volterra (40 km).
LOCATION within the walls of Monteriggioni, 10 km N of Siena; car parking available nearby
FOOD breakfast
PRICES €€€
ROOMS 12; 10 double, 2 single, all with shower; all rooms have phone, TV, minibar, air conditioning, safe
FACILITIES sitting area, breakfast room, bar, garden, swimming pool
CREDIT CARDS AE, DC, MC, V
DISABLED no special facilities
PETS not accepted
CLOSED Jan-Feb
MANAGER Michela Gozzi

TUSCANY

MONTEVETTOLINI

VILLA LUCIA

~ FARMHOUSE BED-AND-BREAKFAST ~

Via dei Bronzoli 144, 51010 Montevettolini, Pistoia
TEL 0572 617790 **FAX** 0572 628817
E-MAIL lvallera@tin.it **WEBSITE** www.bboftuscany.com

LUCIA VALLERA ALSO CALLS her delightful hillside farmhouse the 'B&B of Tuscany' and runs her establishment along English bed-and-breakfast lines – guests and family mingle informally, eating together in the traditional Tuscan kitchen or at the huge wooden table in the dining room if numbers require.

A strong Californian influence can be detected in the cooking and in the laid-back, elegant style of the place. (Lucia is an American of Italian extraction who has returned to Italy after living in the States.) There are plenty of up-to-date touches: CD player, satellite TV, computer. The clientele, too, is mainly American – lawyers, doctors and so on – often on return visits.

The dining room has various dressers crammed with colourful china and glass; there is a double sitting room with comfortable sofas and armchairs in traditional fabrics, plus shelves of books. Bedrooms are attractive, with working fireplaces, patchwork bedspreads, terracotta floors and antique furniture. Bathrooms, either adjoining or across the hall from the bedrooms, are decked in blue and white tiles, and spotlessly clean. The house has a lovely garden, and looks up to the old town of Montevettolini.

~

NEARBY Montecatini Terme (5 km); Lucca (30 km); Pisa (50 km).
LOCATION on hillside outside Montevettolini; car parking
FOOD breakfast; dinner on request
PRICE €€
ROOMS 5 double, 2 apartments for 2, all with bath; all rooms have phone, TV, air conditioning
FACILITIES sitting room, conference room, terraces, garden, swimming pool
CREDIT CARDS not accepted
DISABLED no special facilities
PETS accepted
CLOSED Nov-Apr
PROPRIETOR Lucia Vallera

TUSCANY

MONTICHIELLO DI PIENZA

L'OLMO

~ COUNTRY GUESTHOUSE ~

53020 Montichiello di Pienza, Siena
TEL 0578 755133 **FAX** 0578 755124
E-MAIL info@lolmopienza.it **WEBSITE** www.olmopienza.it

THE INITIAL IMPRESSION GIVEN by this solid stone building set on a hillside overlooking the rolling hills of the Val d'Orcia towards Pienza is a little stark. A few trees would soften the lines. Once inside, however, the elegant, comfortable sitting room with its oriental rugs, low beamed ceiling, antiques and glass-topped coffee table laden with books dispels any such feeling. When we visited, there was a fire roaring in the grate and Mozart playing softly in the background.

The spacious bedrooms and suites (two of which have fireplaces) are individually and stylishly decorated in smart country style with floral fabrics, fresh white cotton bedcovers, botanical prints, soft lighting and plenty of plants and dried flowers. One room has the floor-to-ceiling brick-grilled wall (now glassed in) that is so typical of Tuscan barns. The wrought-iron fixtures throughout are by a local craftsman. Two suites have private terraces leading on to the large garden.

The pool has a wonderful view and the arched courtyard makes a pleasant spot for an aperitif.

~

NEARBY Siena (50 km); Pienza (7 km); Montepulciano (12 km).
LOCATION 7 km S of Pienza; car parking
FOOD breakfast, dinner on request
PRICE €€
ROOMS 6; 1 double, 5 suites, all with bath; all rooms have phone, TV, minibar, hairdrier, safe; 1 apartment
FACILITIES sitting room, breakfast/dining room, terraces, garden, swimming pool
CREDIT CARDS AE, MC, V
DISABLED one ground floor room available
PETS not accepted
CLOSED mid Nov to end Mar
PROPRIETOR Francesca Lindo

TUSCANY

VILLA LE BARONE
~ COUNTRY VILLA ~

Via San Leolino 19, 50020 Panzano in Chianti, Firenze
TEL 055 852621 **FAX** 055 852277
E-MAIL info@villalebarone.it **WEBSITE** www.villalebarone.it

LE BARONE, THE ATTRACTIVE 16thC country house of the della Robbia family (of ceramics fame), became a hotel in 1976, but still feels very much like a private home.

The small scale of the rooms helps, but there are several other factors. The antique furniture is obviously a personal collection; reception amounts to little more than a visitors' book in the hall; there are plenty of books around – including English ones – and there are always fresh flower arrangements in the elegant little sitting rooms; and you help yourself to drinks, recording your consumption as you do so. In the past a minimum stay of three nights has further contributed to the low-key house-party atmosphere; but the rule has now been dropped.

Guests who are not out on sightseeing excursions have plenty of space to themselves in the peaceful woody garden or by the lovely pool, which gives a glorious panorama of the surrounding hills of Tuscany.

The restaurant and some of the rooms are in converted outbuildings. Recent reports have praised the setting, the service and the food and concluded that the price is justified.

~

NEARBY Siena (31 km); Florence (31 km).
LOCATION 31 km S of Florence off SS222; covered car parking
FOOD breakfast, lunch, dinner
PRICE €€€
ROOMS 28; 27 double and twin, 22 with bath, 6 with shower, 1 single with shower; all rooms have phone, hairdrier; 15 rooms have air conditioning
FACILITIES 3 sitting rooms, TV room, self-service bar, dining room, breakfast room, garden, table tennis, swimming pool, tennis
CREDIT CARDS AE, MC, V
DISABLED ground floor rooms
PETS not accepted
CLOSED Nov-Mar
MANAGER Caterina Buonamici

TUSCANY

VILLA ROSA
~ COUNTRY GUESTHOUSE ~

Via S. Leolino 59, Panzano in Chianti, Firenze
TEL 055 852577 **FAX** 055 8560835
E-MAIL villa.rosa@flashnet.it **WEBSITE** www.resortvillarosa.com

A RECENT ADDITION TO the countless hotels and guesthouses in this part of
Chianti, Villa Rosa is a solid structure dating from the early 1900s.
Looming over the road from Panzano to Radda, its appearance makes a
refreshing change from the usual rustic stone Tuscan farmhouse formula:
it is painted bright pink.

Inside, a light touch is evident in the decoration. The terracotta floors
and white walls downstairs are typical, but bedrooms have pastel-
coloured, sponged paintwork, wrought-iron four poster beds and a mixture
of wicker furniture, together with antique pieces here and there. The
attractive, rather quirky, light fittings are by a local craftsman. Bathrooms
also have touches of colour and heated towel rails add a hint of luxury.

The building is too near the road to be ideally situated, but at the back
there is a peaceful, partially shaded terrace for open-air eating, while the
garden slopes up the hillside to a pleasant pool and open, vine-striped
countryside. Reasonable prices and a relaxed style of management make
this hotel very popular; the food is good, too. A recent report remarks on
the 'interesting local fare' and 'good value'.

~

NEARBY Florence (34 km); Siena (28 km).
LOCATION 3 km SE of Panzano on Radda road; car parking
FOOD breakfast, dinner
PRICE €
ROOMS 16 double and twin with bath or shower; all rooms have phone, TV,
minibar
FACILITIES sitting room, restaurant, terraces, garden, swimming pool
CREDIT CARDS AE, DC, MC, V
DISABLED one specially adapted room, but access difficult
PETS accepted
CLOSED mid-Nov to just before Easter
PROPRIETOR Sabine Buntenbach

TUSCANY

PANZANO IN CHIANTI

VILLA SANGIOVESE

~ COUNTRY VILLA ~

Piazza Bucciarelli 5, 50020 Panzano in Chianti, Firenze
TEL 055 852461 **FAX** 055 852463
E-MAIL villa.sangiovese@libero.it **WEBSITE** www.wel.it/villasangiovese

THE BLEULERS USED TO MANAGE the long-established Tenuta di Ricavo at Castellina (see page 143). They opened their doors in Panzano, a few miles to the north, in 1988 after completely renovating the building, and winning high praise from our readers.

The main villa is a neat stone-and-stucco house fronting directly on to a quiet back street; potted plants and a brass plate beside the doorway are the only signs of a hotel. Attached to this house is an old, rambling, stone building beside a flowery, gravelled courtyard-terrace offering splendid views. The landscaped garden below includes a fair-sized pool.

Inside, all is mellow, welcoming and stylish, with carefully chosen antique furnishings against plain, pale walls. Bedrooms, some with wood-beamed ceilings, are spacious, comfortable, and tastefully restrained in decoration. The dining room is equally simple and stylish, with subdued wall lighting and bentwood chairs on a tiled floor.

A limited but interesting *à la carte* menu is offered, which changes each night – service on the terrace in summer. A reporter praises the food and the wine.

~

NEARBY Greve (5 km); Siena (31 km); Florence (31 km).
LOCATION on edge of town, 5 km S of Greve; car parking
FOOD breakfast, lunch, dinner
PRICE €€€
ROOMS 19; 16 double, 1 single, 2 suites, all with bath or shower; all rooms have phone; rooms facing the *piazza* have air conditioning, TV on request
FACILITIES 2 sitting rooms, library, dining room, bar, terrace, garden, swimming pool
CREDIT CARDS MC, V
DISABLED no special facilities
PETS not accepted
CLOSED 15 Dec-end Feb; restaurant Wed
PROPRIETORS Ulderico and Anna Maria Bleuler

TUSCANY

PELAGO

LA DOCCIA
~ COUNTRY GUESTHOUSE ~

19-20 Ristonchi, 50060 Pelago, Firenze
TEL 055 8361387 **FAX** 055 8361388
E-MAIL ladoccia@tin.it **WEBSITE** www.ladocciawelcomes.com

EDWARD AND SONIA MAYHEW opened their beautifully converted stone farmhouse to guests in May 1999. Stunningly situated high up in the hills in a refreshingly undiscovered corner of Tuscany, the style is comfortable rustic with handmade terracotta flagstones, beamed ceilings, stone staircases and brick arches. Warm colours on the walls make a welcome change from the usual stark white. The furniture is a successful mix of locally made pieces and the Mayhews' own English antiques while books, pictures on the walls and knick-knacks give it the feel of a private house. This style is continued in the comfortable bedrooms and self-contained apartments, which are carefully furnished and have particularly smart bathrooms; two of the appartments have open fires for added cosiness in winter.

There are two sitting rooms, both with fireplaces (one is enormous), and an honesty bar. Breakfast and dinner (the latter prepared by Edward) are served at a long communal table. The house stands at 630 metres above sea level, so the long stone terrace, shaded by large, white umbrellas and bordered by lavender and roses, has fabulous views over the hills and down to Florence far below.

~

NEARBY Florence (27 km); Vallombrosa (8 km).
LOCATION 27 km E of Florence, 5 km S of Pelago; car parking
FOOD breakfast; lunch and dinner by arrangement
PRICE €€
ROOMS 5 double, 4 apartments for 2-4 people, all with bath or shower
FACILITIES sitting rooms, dining room, bar, terraces, garden, swimming pool
CREDIT CARDS AE, MC, V
DISABLED no special facilities
PETS accepted
CLOSED B & B rooms Dec-Feb; apartments never
PROPRIETORS Edward and Sonia Mayhew

TUSCANY

IL CHIOSTRO DI PIENZA
~ CONVERTED MONASTERY ~

Corso Rossellino 26, 53026 Pienza, Siena
TEL 0578 748400 **FAX** 0578 748440
E-MAIL ilchiostrocdipienza@virgilio.it **WEBSITE** www.relaisilchiostrodipienza.com

IN THE MODEST WAY OF Renaissance popes, Pius II renamed his home town of Corsignano after himself and made it a model of 15thC urban planning. So it is appropriate that the modern tourist-pilgrim should find lodgings in this stylishly converted monastery. The entrance is located at the back of the austere white cloister that gives the hotel its name and on to which half the rooms look; the other half face away, over the serenely magnificent hills of Val d'Orcia.

Many of the original features of the monks' cells have been retained: frescoed, vaulted ceilings and tiled floors. The furniture, however, breaks with monkish antiquity and concentrates on modern comfort without sinning against the character of the building. Bathrooms, though hardly spacious, are fully equipped.

The sitting rooms, with their old beamed ceilings, and the restaurant give on to a delightful terrace garden, where a pool has recently been built – a great bonus in a town. There could be no more agreeable place for an evening aperitif than its shady peace. A recent guest found the atmosphere, welcome and service fautless; 'I wouldn't mind moving in for life' she says.

~

NEARBY Palazzo Piccolomini; *duomo*; Siena (52 km), Montepulciano.
LOCATION centre of town next to Palazzo Piccolomini; public car parking outside walls
FOOD breakfast, lunch, dinner
PRICE €€€
ROOMS 37; 19 doubles and twins, 9 singles, 9 suites, all with bath; all rooms have phone, TV, air conditioning, minibar, safe, hairdrier
FACILITIES sitting rooms, bar, restaurant, garden, swimming pool
CREDIT CARDS AE, DC, MC, V
DISABLED 2 adapted rooms
PETS accepted
CLOSED Jan-Mar; restaurant Mon
MANAGER Massimo Cicala

TUSCANY

LA SARACINA
~ COUNTRY GUESTHOUSE ~

Strada Statale 146, 53026 Pienza, Siena
TEL 0578 748022 **FAX** 0578 748018
E-MAIL info@lasaracina.it **WEBSITE** www.lasaracina.it

BY THE TIME THE McCOBBS retired from La Saracina to return to the U.S.A. in 1996, they had created an extremely comfortable guesthouse. With the attention to detail that seems to be a characteristic of foreigners who go into the business, they turned an old stone farmhouse and its outbuildings, set in glorious countryside, into something special.

Refinement and good taste predominates: the bedrooms, all with their own entrance from out of doors, are spacious and elegant; suites have sitting areas. Antique furnishings mingle well with bright Ralph Lauren fabrics and there is a distinct leaning towards American country style. The luxurious bathrooms are fitted with marble sinks and Jacuzzis – several are enormous. Breakfast is served on the terrace in warm weather or in a neat breakfast room. There is an attractive swimming pool surrounded by smooth lawns.

We have no reason to believe that the new young owner has not maintained the high standards of this upmarket place and that her enthusiasm and fresh approach have not been winning through. Reports please.

~

NEARBY Pienza (7 km); Montepulciano (6 km).
LOCATION on quiet hillside, 7 km from Pienza on Montepulciano road; car parking
FOOD breakfast
PRICES €€€
ROOMS 5; 2 double, 3 suites, all with bath or shower; all rooms have phone, TV, minibar; one self-catering apartment
FACILITIES breakfast room, garden, swimming pool, tennis
CREDIT CARDS AE, MC, V
DISABLED no special facilities, but all rooms are on ground floor
PETS not accepted
CLOSED never
PROPRIETOR Simonetta Vessichelli

TUSCANY

PIETRASANTA

ALBERGO PIETRASANTA
~ TOWN HOTEL ~

Via Garibaldi 35, 55045 Pietrasanta, Lucca
TEL 0584 793726 **FAX** 0584 793728
E-MAIL a.pietrasanta@versilia.toscana.it **WEBSITE** www.albergopietrasanta.com

PIETRASANTA (THE 'SAINTED STONE') has long been associated with the marble industry. The world-famous quarries at Carrara are nearby, and the attractive little town thrives on marble studios, bronze foundries, and a subculture of artists from all over the world. Recently, tourism here has moved upmarket, and the Albergo Pietrasanta is a response to this development. Opened in 1997, the hotel occupies elegant 17thC Palazzo Barsanti-Bonetti in the centre of town. The interior maintains many of the embellishments of a nobleman's house: intricate plasterwork, delicate frescoes, a couple of superbly-carved marble fireplaces, spacious rooms and antiques. However, the addition of the owners' contemporary art collection adds a totally new dimension.

The comfortable, unfussy bedrooms have warm, parquet floors, armchairs, smart fabrics and varying colour schemes. Thoughtful extras (cool linen sheets, plenty of mirrors, well-designed lighting and the tray of *vin santo* and biscuits) impressed our inspector. Downstairs, the winter garden doubles as breakfast room and bar while the pretty gravelled garden, dominated by three old palm trees, is a cool spot in summer.

~

NEARBY Pisa (25 km); Lucca (25 km); beaches (4 km).
LOCATION on pedestrian street in town centre; private garage
FOOD breakfast
PRICES €€€€
ROOMS 19; 8 double and twin, 1 single, 10 suites, all with bath or shower; all rooms have phone, TV, minibar, air conditioning, safe
FACILITIES sitting rooms, bar, breakfast room/winter garden, gym, Turkish bath, garden
CREDIT CARDS AE, DC, MC, V
DISABLED 2 specially adapted rooms
PETS accepted by arrangement
CLOSED early Jan to Mar
MANAGER Marisa Giuliano

TUSCANY

PISA

ROYAL VICTORIA

~ TOWN HOTEL ~

Lungarno Pacinotti 12, 56126 Pisa
TEL 050 940111 **FAX** 050 940180
E-MAIL eds@royalvictoria.it **WEBSITE** www.royalvictoria.it

FAMOUS WORLDWIDE FOR ITS NOW not-so-leaning tower, Pisa has a long history as a tourist destination, having been an important stop on the Grand tour. These days, its hotels are disappointingly short on charm with the exception of the Royal Victoria, a relic of that golden age of travel which occupies a *palazzo* on the north bank of the Arno. It attraction lies in the rather funky retro atmosphere as opposed to its creatue comforts, but it has many fans and we are pleased to include it.

The hotel dates back some 160 years although the *palazzo* itself is very much older. The old fashioned lobby is adorned with potted palms and the walls are hung with framed letters from past guests who include Dickens, the Duke of Wellington and Ruskin. Upstairs, the bedrooms are fairly spartan with lumbering old furniture and 60s bathrooms (due to be renovated), but mattresses and fabrics are new. Room 202 is extraordinary, with creaky old parquet, floor-to-ceiling medieval-style *trompe l'oeil* frescoes and painted furniture. The breakfast room belongs to the same rather dreamy, bygone age. There are several sitting areas, but far the best place to relax with a book and an aperitivo is the plant-filled roof terrace.

~

NEARBY Palazzo Reale; Piazza dei Cavalieri; Leaning Tower.
LOCATION on north bank of Arno with private garage and lift
FOOD breakfast
PRICES €€€
ROOMS 48 doubles and twin, all but 8 with bath or shower; all rooms have phone, TV, hairdrier on request
FACILITIES sitting room, breakfast room, roof terrace
CREDIT CARDS AE, DC, MC, V
DISABLED no special facilities
PETS accepted
CLOSED never
PROPRIETORS Nicola and Maurizio Piegaja

TUSCANY

PISTOIA

PIEVE A CELLE
~ COUNTRY GUESTHOUSE ~

TEL 0573 913087 **FAX** 0573 910280
E-MAIL info@tenutadipieveacelle.it **WEBSITE** www.tenutadipieveacelle.it

LITTLE VISITED PISTOIA IS A JEWEL of a town which offers easy access to Florence, Lucca and Pisa. This new agriturismo is situated near the zoo; at night the silence may be broken by the incongruous sounds of wild animal noises. Set in 1,700 acres of land planted with olives, vines and woods broken by walking paths and mountain bike tracks, the house is a typically solid Tuscan rural building. Inside, the usual rustic formula of terracotta floors, beamed ceilings and so on has been brightened up by warm colours on the walls and some imaginative furnishings. An open fire burns in the sitting room to welcome guests in cold weather while upstairs, the bedrooms are charmingly decorated with pretty fabrics (designed by the owner, who is in the textile business) and mainly furnished with antiques. Wrought-iron four poster beds are hung with white linen while bright kilims and African textiles sit well with warm sand coloured walls.

Bordered by wooden decking, the substantial pool is surrounded by vineyards and utterly peaceful views. The Paccentis' style is very relaxed and they are warm hosts. Although there are good places to eat in Pistoia, you should stay in at least once to sample Fiorenza's excellent cooking.

~

NEARBY Pistoia (3 km); Montecatini Terme (10 km); Florence (30 km).
LOCATION 3 km NW of Pistoia in own grounds with parking; take the Abetone road from the autostrada, come off at Pistoia Ovest, follow signs to Montagnana; the entrance is after 2 km on the right
FOOD breakfast, diner on request
PRICE €€
ROOMS 5 double, all with shower; all rooms have TV, air conditioning, hairdrier
FACILITIES sitting room, breakfast room, terraces, garden, swimming pool, mountain bikes
CREDIT CARDS MC, V
DISABLED ground floor room **PETS** not accepted
CLOSED never **PROPRIETOR** Fiorenza and Cesare Saccenti

TUSCANY

PISTOIA

VILLA VANNINI
~ COUNTRY VILLA ~

Villa di Piteccio, 51030 Pistoia
TEL 0573 42031 **FAX** 0573 42551
E-MAIL info@volpe-uva.it **WEBSITE** www.volpe-uva.it

WE HAVE RECEIVED MORE READER'S letters about Villa Vannini than any other hotel in the guide, and they have all been exuberant in their praise. Situated in a remote and delightfully peaceful setting high on the hill not far from the lively little town of Pistoia, access is via a narrow road which winds up through unspoilt countryside. The venerable Signora Vannini handed over the hotel several years ago to the charming Bordonaro family who offer a warm welcome and fabulous food. They have left the villa largely as it was and maintained the relaxed and totally unpretentious atmosphere.

There are various little sitting areas with large vases of flowers, chintz-covered or chunky modern seats, prints and watercolours and the sort of antiques that complete a family home. The dining room, with its white-washed walls, polished parquet and soft background jazz makes an elegant setting for Luigi Bordonaro and his daughter Francesca's 'inspirational and exquisitely fresh' cooking based on Tuscan specialities: there is nothing to be gained from eating out.

Bedrooms are beautifully and individually furnished with flowery fabrics and fine antiques; bathrooms are mainly spacious and old-fashioned. In front of the house, a simple terrace provides a haven after a day's sightseeing. Although children are allowed, this is not a very suitable place for youngsters.

~

NEARBY Pistoia (6 km); Florence (35 km); Lucca (45 km).
LOCATION 6 km N of Pistoia, take Abetone road from Pistoia and branch right; the hotel is 2 km above Piteccio
FOOD breakfast, lunch, dinner
PRICE €
ROOMS 8 double and twin with bath (not all baths en suite)
FACILITIES 2 sitting rooms, games room, dining room, terrace, garden
CREDIT CARDS AE, DC, MC, V
DISABLED no special facilities **PETS** not accepted **CLOSED** never
MANAGERS the Bordonaro family

TUSCANY

PRATO

VILLA RUCELLAI
~ COUNTRY VILLA ~

Via di Canneto 16, 59100 Prato, Firenze
TEL and **FAX** 0574 460392

THIS IS A QUINTESSENTIAL charming small hotel. Industrial Prato creeps almost to the doors of the mellow old villa, and the railway line skirts the property, but this should not stop you from visiting a very special place. Its origins date back to a medieval watchtower, and it has been in the venerable Rucellai family since 1740. The unsightly views from the lovely terrace – filled with lemon trees – and the *loggia*, are more than compensated for by the atmosphere of the house, the warm welcome and the modest prices. Behind the property rise the beautiful Pratese Hills, which can be explored on foot from the house.

Guests have the run of the main part of the house, with its baronial hall and comfortable sitting room, filled with pictures and books. Breakfast is self-service and is taken around a communal table in the homely dining room. The bedrooms are simply furnished and full of character; they reflect the rare attribute of the place – that of a well-run hotel which gives no hint of being anything but a cultivated family home. Recent algae problems in the swimming pool seem to have been solved.

~

NEARBY Prato; Florence (20 km).
LOCATION down a narrow street, in Bisenzio river valley, 4 km NE of Prato (keep parallel with river and railway line on your left); car parking
FOOD breakfast
PRICE €
ROOMS 11; 10 double and twin, 1 family, all with bath or shower
FACILITIES sitting room, TV room, dining room, gym, terrace, garden, swimming pool
CREDIT CARDS not accepted
DISABLED not suitable
PETS not accepted
CLOSED never
PROPRIETORS Rucellai Piqué family

TUSCANY

PUGNANO

CASETTA DELLE SELVE
~ COUNTRY BED-AND-BREAKFAST ~

56010 Pugnano, Pisa
TEL and **FAX** 050 850359

YET ANOTHER ELEVATED Tuscan farmhouse, but this one has a personality all of its own thanks to the owner, Nicla Menchi, a most unusual hostess. The approach to the white building is through a thick chestnut wood. Once at the top of the rough 2-km drive, the peaceful surroundings, the flower-filled garden and the wonderful views from the red-tiled terrace start to work their magic.

The interiors are very different from the norm. For a start, Nicla's own vivid paintings occupy much of the wall space. The house is exceptionally well maintained and the bedrooms have bold, bright colour schemes involving bedheads, rugs, bedspreads (all handmade by Nicla) and, of course, her pictures. It might be a little fussy for some tastes; even the coat hangers are colour co-ordinated. However, public areas are a little more restrained, but still full of pictures, books and ornaments. Breakfast (including fresh eggs, home-made cakes and jams) is, when possible, served on the terrace.

Nicla Menchi's enthusiasm for her home and her guests is infectious and many leave as her friend. Not suitable for children under 12.

~

NEARBY Lucca (10 km); Pisa (12 km); beaches (15 km).
LOCATION in countryside 2 km off SS12, E of Pugnano, 10 km SW of Lucca; car parking
FOOD breakfast
PRICE € (minimum 3-day stay)
ROOMS 6 double with bath or shower (2 are adjacent)
FACILITIES sitting room, terrace, garden
CREDIT CARDS not accepted
DISABLED not suitable
PETS accepted
CLOSED never
PROPRIETOR Nicla Menchi

TUSCANY ·

RADDA IN CHIANTI

RELAIS FATTORIA VIGNALE
∼ COUNTRY HOTEL ∼

Via Pianigiani 15, 53017 Radda in Chianti, Siena
TEL 0577 738300 **FAX** 0577 738592
E-MAIL vignale@vignale.it **WEBSITE** www.vignale.it

THIS HAS ALWAYS BEEN a favourite with our inspectors, and recent visits have left their enthusiasm undimmed. The house is built on a slope down from the middle of the village. On the main 'ground' floor are four interconnecting sitting rooms, each on a domestic scale, and beautifully furnished with comfy sofas, antiques, muted rugs on polished terracotta floors, walls (either white and dotted with paintings or covered by murals) and one or two grand stone fireplaces. The bedrooms above are similarly classy, with waxed wooden doors, white walls and antique beds. The sitting rooms, the back bedrooms and the pool all share a grand view across the Radda Valley. Ten rooms are housed in a heated annexe across the road.

A recent addition to the Relais Fattoria Vignale is the lovely breakfast terrace; in cool weather there is a neat breakfast room in a brick vault beneath the hotel, where an excellent buffet is set out, and coffee and extras are served by friendly waitresses. There is also a *taverna* for light dinners.

Three hundred metres from the hotel (and under the same ownership) is the Vignale Restaurant which serves excellent (but pricey) creative Italian dishes.

Although they are tolerated, children will not be popular here unless they are as quiet as mice.

∼

NEARBY Siena (31 km); Florence (52 km).
LOCATION in middle of village, 31 km N of Siena; car parking
FOOD breakfast, snacks
PRICE €€€
ROOMS 40; 31 double and twin, 4 single, 2 family rooms, 3 suites, all with bath or shower; all rooms have phone, air conditioning, minibar
FACILITIES 3 sitting rooms, breakfast room, bars, conference room, terrace, garden, swimming pool **CREDIT CARDS** AE, MC, V
DISABLED access difficult **PETS** not accepted
CLOSED 3 weeks Dec, early Jan to mid-Mar **MANAGER** Silvia Kummer

TUSCANY

REGGELLO

VILLA RIGACCI

~ HILLTOP VILLA ~

Vággio 76, 50066 Reggello, Firenze
TEL 055 8656718/562 **FAX** 055 8656537
E-MAIL hotel@villarigacci.it **WEBSITE** www.villarigacci.it

THIS CREEPER-COVERED 15thC farmhouse, in the second decade since its transformation from private home to charming small hotel, is in a beautiful secluded spot – on a hilltop surrounded by olive groves, pines, chestnut trees and meadows – yet only a few kilometres from the Florence-Rome *autostrada*, and a short drive from Florence and Arezzo.

Many of the original features of the house have been preserved – arched doorways, beamed bedrooms, tiled or stone-flagged floors – and it is furnished as a cherished private house might be. The sitting room has an open fire in chilly weather. The bedrooms – the best (though not all) of them gloriously spacious – are full of gleaming antiques, and overlook the gardens or swimming pool, which is of fair size, with a pleasant tile-and-grass surround and woodland views. For relaxation, there are plenty of quiet, shady spots in the park, which contains some magnificent trees.

These days, the food is predominantly Tuscan with some French influences - it used to be rather upmarket French, which wasn't to everybody's taste. Families are offered special rates and are well catered for in that there is a small playground area and part of the new pool is given over to kids.

~

NEARBY Florence (30 km); Arezzo (45 km).
LOCATION 300 m N of Vággio, 30 km SE of Florence (exit Incisa from A1); car parking
FOOD breakfast, lunch, dinner
PRICE €€€
ROOMS 28; 20 double and twin, 3 single, 5 suites, all with bath or shower; all rooms have phone, TV, minibar, air conditioning
FACILITIES sitting rooms, library, dining room, garden, swimming pool
CREDIT CARDS AE, DC, MC, V
DISABLED not suitable **PETS** small ones accepted
CLOSED never
PROPRIETORS Frederic Pierazzi

TUSCANY

SAN CASCIANO DEI BAGNI

SETTE QUERCE
∼ VILLAGE GUESTHOUSE ∼

53040 San Casciano dei Bagni, Siena
TEL 0578 58174 **FAX** 0578 58172
E-MAIL settequerce@ftbcc.it **WEBSITE** www.settequerce.it

SEVERAL GENERATIONS OF Daniela Boni's family have run the local bar in this tiny spa town, located high in the hills in a remote corner of southern Tuscany. The family business expanded in 1997 to include this delightful and original hotel, and, most recently, the bar has extended into an excellent restaurant (located 100 m from the main building).

The name derives from the fact that the rambling townhouse backs on to an oak wood. The contemporary interior design is a refreshing change from the Tuscan norm. At ground level, earth tones, vivid reds and pinks prevail. Bedrooms on the second floor are in sunny yellows and greens, and, at the top, shades of blue predominate. The cheerful fabrics on chairs, curtains, cushions and duvets are by Designers Guild. The rooms are all dotted with ornaments (old irons, rustic ceramics, basket ware) while framed black-and-white photos depicting the history of the town hang on the walls. Each bedroom has a comfortable sitting area (compensating for the lack of public sitting room) and a cleverly-designed kitchenette. Bathrooms are immaculate and several have Jacuzzis.

∼

NEARBY Thermal baths; Orvieto (40 km); Montepulciano (40 km).
LOCATION on street just outside town; public car parking next door
FOOD breakfast
PRICE €€
ROOMS 9 suites with bath; all rooms have phone, TV, air conditioning, minibar, hairdrier
FACILITIES bar, restaurant, terraces
CREDIT CARDS AE, DC, MC, V
DISABLED 2 specially adapted suites
PETS small ones accepted
CLOSED 2 weeks Jan
PROPRIETORS Daniela, Maurizio and Silvestro Boni

TUSCANY

SAN CASCIANO VP

FATTORIA LA LOGGIA
~ COUNTRY ESTATE ~

Via Collina 40, Loc. Montefiridolfo, 50026 San Casciano, Firenze
TEL 055 8244288 **FAX** 055 8244283
E-MAIL info@fattorialaloggia.com **WEBSITE** www.fattorialaloggia.com

MONTEFIRIDOLFI IS SET in classic Chianti countryside scattered with ancient estates producing wine and olive oil. Many of the mellow, stone farm buildings hereabouts are being turned into tourist accommodation of one sort or another, and Fattoria la Loggia is one of the most successful of its type: a range of spacious and attractive apartments agreeably housed in a hamlet-like collection of rural dwellings, in a hilltop setting with views over gloriously peaceful surroundings. The apartments are let daily or weekly. But this is not simply a self-catering complex – cooking lessons and dinners with wine tastings are sometimes organized in the cellar.

Each unit is carefully furnished with country-style pieces and many personal touches; kitchens and bathrooms, however, are efficiently modern, and are finished to a very high standard. Visitors can swim, ride, or walk on the estate, which produces its own wine and olive oil. La Loggia has recently established an artists' studio, with a permanent museum of contemporary art, as well as providing a venue for concerts and theatre.

~

NEARBY Florence (18 km), San Gimignano (40 km), Siena (45 km).
LOCATION 18 km S of Florence, E of road to Siena; car parking
FOOD breakfast
PRICES ©©
ROOMS 4 double, 11 apartments for 2-6 people, all with bath or shower; all rooms/apartments have phone, fridge, safe, TV
FACILITIES garden, solarium, swimming pool, table tennis, barbeque
CREDIT CARDS not accepted
DISABLED one adapted apartment
PETS accepted by arrangement
CLOSED never
PROPRIETOR Giulio Baruffaldi

TUSCANY

SAN CASCIANO VAL DI PESA

VILLA IL POGGIALE
~ COUNTRY VILLA ~

Via Empolese 69, 50026 San Casciano Val di Pesa, Firenze
TEL 055 828311 **FAX** 055 8294296
E-MAIL villailpoggiale@villailpoggiale.it **WEBSITE** www.villailpoggiale.it

FAMILY HOME OF ONE OF THE OWNERS until quite recently, Il Poggiale is a pale salmon-coloured villa dating from the 16th century. At the front of the house, a gracious Renaissance loggia overlooks an expanse of green lawn protected by ancient cypress trees. It opened as a hotel in April 2003 after careful restoration, but still maintains the feeling of a private house.

On arrival, guests are shown into a spacious, elegant salon dominated by a vast chandelier; family portraits hang on the walls while soothing classical music plays in the background. Drinks are laid out on a table to which guests can help themselves and sign a chit. Generous breakfasts (with home-made breads, cakes and jams) are served in a pretty dining room with pink and white striped tablecloths.

The bedrooms, each different from the next, are beautifully furnished and romantically decorated (several have four posters) in dusty blues and pinks with filmy white curtains and colourful bedspreads and rugs. Bathrooms are gorgeous too; one (entirely frescoed) has a claw-foot bath. Outside, a long terrace runs along the west wall of the villa. Breakfast is served here in summer, but it is also a glorious spot from which to enjoy spectacular sunsets.

~

NEARBY Florence (17 km); Siena (55 km); Chianti.
LOCATION 2 km SW of San Casciano off Empoli road in own grounds with parking
FOOD breakfast, light lunch on request when pool is open
PRICES ©©
ROOMS 21; 19 double and twin, 2 suites and 3 self-catering apartments all with bath or shower; all rooms have phone, TV, air conditioning, fridge, kettle, safe, hairdrier
FACILITIES sitting rooms library, breakfast room, terraces, garden, swimming pool
CREDIT CARDS DC, MC, V
DISABLED access difficult **PETS** not accepted **CLOSED** Feb
GENERAL MANAGER Caterina Piccolominii

TUSCANY

SAN GIMIGNANO

L'ANTICO POZZO
~ TOWN GUESTHOUSE ~

Via San Matteo 87, 53037 San Gimignano, Siena
TEL 0577 942014 **FAX** 0577 942117
E-MAIL info@anticopozzo.com **WEBSITE** www.anticopozzo.com

THE ANCIENT BRICK WELL in question (*pozzo* means well) is in the entrance hall of this fine, 15thC townhouse situated on one of the pedestrian streets leading up to San Gimignano's central Piazza del Duomo. The building was beautifully restored in 1990, and is now, in our view, possibly the best hotel in town.

A stone staircase leads up to the large first floor bedrooms and the breakfast room, the latter known as the *sala rosa*, thanks to its deep pink walls. The waxed and worn terracotta tiles on this floor are original, as are the high, beamed ceilings. Several rooms have delicate frescoes; in one, the walls and ceiling are entirely painted with garlands of flowers and elegant, dancing figures.

Rooms on the upper floors are smaller, but still most attractive. Those at the top have attic ceilings and views of the famous towers or countryside to compensate for their small size.

The furnishings throughout are in simple good taste; carefully-chosen antiques mix well with the wrought-iron beds; colours are muted. A pretty, walled terrace is an added bonus.

Recent reports on Il Pozzo have been generally very positive although several mention steep stairs (there is also a lift) and a lack of public sitting areas.

~

NEARBY *duomo*; Museo Civico; Torre Grossa.
LOCATION on pedestrian street in centre of town; public car parking (300 m)
FOOD breakfast
PRICE €€
ROOMS 18; 17 double and twin, 1 single, all with bath or shower; all rooms have phone, TV, air conditioning, minibar
FACILITIES bar, breakfast room, terrace, lift **CREDIT CARDS** AE, DC, MC, V
DISABLED 2 specially adapted rooms **PETS** not accepted
CLOSED 6 weeks in winter
PROPRIETOR Emanuele Marro

TUSCANY

SAN GUSME

VILLA ARCENO
~ COUNTRY VILLA ~

Loc. Arceno, San Gusme, 53010 Castelnuovo Berardenga, Siena
TEL 0577 359292 **FAX** 0577 359276
E-MAIL mail@relaisvillarceno.com **WEBSITE** www.realisvillarceno.com

VILLA ARCENO ORIGINALLY SERVED as a hunting lodge for a Tuscan noble family, but 'lodge' is too humble a word to describe this aristocratic building. A long, private road winds through the thousand-hectare estate (which has many farmhouses converted into apartments) to the square, rigidly symmetrical villa with its overhanging eaves, surrounded by lawns, gravel paths and flower-filled terracotta urns. In front of the villa is a separate, walled park in the Romantic style, with shady paths leading down to a small lake.

Inside, a cool, elegant style prevails: off-white walls and vaulted ceilings contrast with the warmth of terracotta floors (strewn with Persian carpets), reproduction antique furniture and light yellow drapes. The atmosphere is formal, but not stiffly so: the highly professional staff make guests feel more than welcome.

Upstairs, the guest rooms, which are all light and spacious, have been individually decorated. Particularly attractive is the suite, which has a bay of three arched windows. Some rooms have their own terraces. You should also ask to see the spiral stairway of the central tower that finishes in a rooftop gazebo.

The hotel does not accept children under 12.

~

NEARBY Siena (25 km); Florence (85 km).
LOCATION 30 km NE of Siena; car parking
FOOD breakfast, light lunch, dinner
PRICE €€€€
ROOMS 16; 12 double, 4 suites, all with bath; all rooms have phone, TV, air conditioning, minibar
FACILITIES sitting rooms, restaurant, garden, tennis, swimming pool, mountain bikes
CREDIT CARDS AE, DC, MC, V
DISABLED not suitable **PETS** small dogs accepted by arrangement
CLOSED mid-Nov to Mar
PROPRIETOR Gualtiero Mancini

TUSCANY

SANTA MARIA DEL GIUDICE

VILLA RINASCIMENTO
~ COUNTRY VILLA ~

Loc. Santa Maria del Giudice, 55058 Lucca
TEL 0583 378292 **FAX** 0583 370238
E-MAIL info@villarinascimento.it **WEBSITE** www.villarinascimento.it

ALMOST EXACTLY HALFWAY between Pisa and Lucca, this hillside villa presents, at first sight, something of an architectural conundrum. On the right-hand side is a rosy coloured, rustic Renaissance villa, three storeys high, constructed with a mixture of brick and stone. Its main feature is a lovely corner *loggia*, enclosed by four brick arches supported by Doric columns in stone. On the left, it is joined by a much simpler farmhouse structure. The two are united by a long, paved terrace with lemon trees in large terracotta pots. One can breakfast here, or take an *aperitivo* in the evening.

Inside, a more uniform rustic style prevails. The public rooms all face the terrace, and are distinguished by exposed-beam or brick-vaulted ceilings, and include interesting features such as the remnants of an old stone olive press. Bedrooms are carefully furnished; the four attic rooms are simpler in style; some of the bathrooms are small, but adequate.

Up the hill from the villa is the annexe, with some more modern rooms and studios, and a pool designed to exploit to the full its hillside position.

A recent guest was very disappointed with the food and felt that the hotel did not offer good value: more reports please.

~

NEARBY Lucca (9 km); Pisa (11 km).
LOCATION 9 km SW of Lucca; car parking
FOOD breakfast, dinner
PRICE €€
ROOMS 17 double and twin all with bath or shower (one room has bathroom across landing); all rooms have phone, TV, air conditioning, 6 studios (one-week minimum) in annexe
FACILITIES sitting rooms, bar, restaurant, garden, swimming pool, tennis
CREDIT CARDS MC, V
DISABLED one suitable room in annexe **PETS** accepted by arrangement
CLOSED Nov-Mar
PROPRIETOR Carla Zaffora

TUSCANY

ANTICO CASALE DI SCANSANO
~ COUNTRY HOTEL ~

Scansano, 58054 Grosseto
TEL 0564 507219 **FAX** 0564 507805
E-MAIL info@anticocasalediscansano.com **WEBSITE** www.anticocasaldiscansano.com

TWO WIDELY-TRAVELLED readers wrote in enthusiastic terms to draw our attention to this captivating hotel in the coastal region of Tuscany known as the Maremma, south-east of Grosseto. We can scarcely improve on their verdicts: 'Rooms sweetly decorated with country antiques and a lovely restaurant with terrace overlooking a spectacular green valley with vineyards and olive groves; a truly relaxing experience.' And: 'In four months touring the country, we thought this hotel number one; we were impressed by the welcome and hospitality, the surroundings – even the beds were the best we encountered in Italy.' A recent report praised the food, which is 'local and delicious'.

The Antico Casale is a beautifully restored, 200-year-old farmhouse which retains more of its origins than most such places. The Macereto estate of which it is part produces a range of *grappa*, olive oil and wines (including the Morellino di Scansano DOC); many surrounding farms produce olive oil, and the Casale's stables are in very active use: riding holidays are offered (with instruction if you need it), and the hotel even offers special 'DB&B and horse' rates. Wine-tasting and cookery courses too.

~

NEARBY Thermal spa of Saturnia; Argentarian coast.
LOCATION in countryside 30 km SE of Grosseto; car parking
FOOD breakfast, lunch, dinner, snacks
PRICE €€
ROOMS 32; 21 double, 6 single, 1 family room all with shower, 4 suites with Jacuzzi bath; all rooms have phone, TV, air conditioning, minibar, hairdrier
FACILITIES sitting room, dining room, bar, terrace, swimming pool, horse riding
CREDIT CARDS AE, DC, MC, V
DISABLED 2 adapted rooms
PETS accepted if well behaved
CLOSED never; restaurant closed mid Jan-mid Feb
PROPRIETOR Massimo Pellegrini

TUSCANY

SIENA

2006

PALAZZO RAVIZZA
~ TOWN HOTEL ~

Pian dei Mantellini 34, 53100 Siena
TEL 0577 280462 **FAX** 0577 221597
E-MAIL bureau@palazzoravizza.it **WEBSITE** www.palazzoravizza.it

SIENA IS NOTORIOUS FOR its dearth of decent hotels in the centre of town, so we were delighted to see that Palazzo Ravizza has undergone a facelift and is now a very pleasant place in which to stay. Fortunately, the old-fashioned, slightly faded charm has not been sacrificed to modernization. The bedrooms still have their heavy – at times quirky – period furniture and polished parquet or terracotta floors, but the fabrics have been smartened up and bathrooms are all shining new with heated towel rails. Some even have double Jacuzzis.

Downstairs, the public rooms (in part with smart black and white floor tiles) have pretty painted ceilings and comfortable armchairs and sofas. There is a cosy library, as well as a smart new bar and an elegantly-appointed (now independent) restaurant; the 'obligatory half board in high season' rule no longer applies.

The garden at the back is a great asset and has recently been re-designed in formal Italian style: it provides a cool and shady respite from the city heat, and tables are laid outside for breakfast and dinner in the summer.

~

NEARBY *Duomo*; Ospedale Santa Maria della Scala.
LOCATION just SW of town centre in residential street; car parking
FOOD breakfast, dinner
PRICE €€
ROOMS 40; 30 double and twin, 3 single, 7 suites, all with bath or shower; all rooms have phone, TV, minibar, hairdrier
FACILITIES sitting rooms, bar, restaurant, garden
CREDIT CARDS AE, DC, MC, V
DISABLED adapted room
PETS accepted
CLOSED never
PROPRIETOR Francesco Grotanelli de Santi

TUSCANY

SINALUNGA

LOCANDA DELL'AMOROSA
∼ COUNTRY INN ∼

53048 Sinalunga, Siena
TEL 0577 679497 **FAX** 0577 632001
E-MAIL locanda@amorosa.it **WEBSITE** www.amorosa.it

THE LOCANDA DELL'AMOROSA is as romantic as it sounds. An elegant Renaissance villa-cum-village, within the remains of 14thC walls, has been converted into a charming country inn.

The old stables, beamed and brick-walled, have been transformed into a delightful rustic (but pricey) restaurant serving refined *nouvelle*-style versions of traditional Tuscan recipes, using ingredients from the estate, which also produces wine.

Only a fortunate few can actually stay here – either in apartments in the houses where peasants and farmworkers once lived, or in ordinary bedrooms in the old family residence. The bedrooms are cool, airy and pretty, with whitewashed walls, terracotta floors, antique furniture and Florentine curtains and bedspreads – and immaculate modern bathrooms.

To complete the village there is a little parish church with lovely 15thC frescoes of the Sienese school. While certainly not an authentic feature, the recently installed pool, surrounded by vineyards and enjoying marvellous views of the rolling countryside, is a great asset. With discreet, attentive service, the Locanda is a paradise for connoisseurs of Tuscany, for gourmets and for all romantics. It is, however, popular with up-market tour groups.

∼

NEARBY Siena (45 km); Arezzo (45 km); Chianti.
LOCATION 2 km S of Sinalunga; car parking
FOOD breakfast, lunch, dinner
PRICE €€€€
ROOMS 25; 17 double, 8 suites, all with bath or shower; all rooms have phone, TV, air conditioning, minibar
FACILITIES sitting room, dining room, bar
CREDIT CARDS AE, DC, MC, V
DISABLED access difficult
PETS not accepted
CLOSED mid-Jan to mid Mar; restaurant Mon, Tue
MANAGER Carlo Citterio

TUSCANY

SORANO

HOTEL DELLA FORTEZZA

~ CASTLE GUESTHOUSE ~

Piazza Cairoli, 58010 Sorano, Grosseto
TEL 0564 632010 **FAX** 0564 632012
E-MAIL fortezza@fortezzahotel.it **WEBSITE** www.fortezzahotel.it

FOR ENTHUSIASTS OF ARCHAEOLOGY, this remote corner of the Maremma – with its abundance of Etruscan remains – is a dream. The ancient, picturesque town of Sorano is built on a tufa outcrop and is surrounded by the hills of the Alta Maremma. The imposing 11thC Orsini fortress is dramatically situated on the edge of the town and now partially occupied by a stylish hotel. After dark, the place is floodlit, and the approach to the hotel across an old suspension bridge and through several courtyards is like taking a step back into the Middle Ages.

Once inside, however, the comforts are very much of this century although the tasteful and careful restoration has been carried out with full respect for the building's origins. The solid walls are pale throughout, warmed by soft lighting while beamed ceilings and terracotta floors are in tone with the surroundings. A collection of 19thC antiques blend well with fine reproduction pieces and fabrics in deep blue and gold. There are some wonderful old beds in the comfortable bedrooms which vary enormously in shape and size. All have fabulous views over the rooftops of unspoiled countryside.

~

NEARBY Pitgliano (9 km); Lake Bolsena (20 km).
LOCATION 9 km NE of Pitigliano, on edge of town; car parking
FOOD breakfast
PRICE €€
ROOMS 16; 14 double and twin, 2 suites, all with bath; all rooms have phone, TV, minibar, hairdrier
FACILITIES breakfast room, sitting room, terraces
CREDIT CARDS AE, MC, V
DISABLED one specially adapted room
PETS small ones accepted
CLOSED early Jan to Mar
PROPRIETOR Luciano Caruso

TUSCANY

BORGO PRETALE
~ HILLSIDE HAMLET ~

Loc. Pretale, 53018 Sovicille, Siena
TEL 0577 345401 **FAX** 0577 345625
E-MAIL info@borgopretale.it **WEBSITE** www.borgopretale.it

A LONG, WINDING, UNSURFACED road through wooded hills brings you to this group of grey stone houses clustered around a massive 12thC watch-tower. Local historians claim that it was part of a system of such towers, spread across the Sienese hills, all within line of sight, to communicate quickly any news of approaching invaders and to provide protection against their rampages. Nowadays, this civilized retreat offers a haven from the stresses of modern life.

Every detail has been considered in the restoration and decoration. The harshness of the medieval structure has been lessened by the use of well-chosen antiques, mellow lighting and rich, striped fabrics. A serenely beautiful 15thC carved wooden Madonna, bearing the Infant Christ, stands in a brick-framed niche.

Every bedroom contains a different blend of the same artful ingredients, each splendid in its own way, though we particularly liked those in the tower. The stylish restaurant serves a limited choice of dishes (but all well prepared) and has an extensive wine list on which a *sommelier* can offer advice. And tucked away, close to the edge of the woods, is an inviting pool.

~

NEARBY Siena (20 km); San Gimignano (28 km).
LOCATION 20 km SW of Siena on quiet hillside; car parking
FOOD breakfast, lunch (buffet by pool Jun-Sep), dinner
PRICE €€€
ROOMS 35; 32 double, 3 suites, all with bath or shower; all rooms have phone, TV, air conditioning, minibar, safe
FACILITIES sitting room, restaurant, bar, sauna, garden, swimming pool, tennis, archery, gym, mountain bikes
CREDIT CARDS AE, DC, MC, V
DISABLED not suitable **PETS** not accepted
CLOSED Nov to early Apr
MANAGER Daniele Rizzardini

TUSCANY

VICCHIO

VILLA CAMPESTRI

~ COUNTRY VILLA ~

Via di Campestri 19, 50039 Vicchio di Mugello, Firenze
TEL 055 8490107 **FAX** 055 8490108
E-MAIL villa.campestri@villacampestri.it **WEBSITE** www.villacampestri.it

GET CLEAR DIRECTIONS before you set off for this hilltop villa: it is in an isolated location, some way south of the village of Vicchio di Mugello.

The house looks classically Renaissance, but actually dates back to the 13th century. It overlooks sloping hillsides of mown grass, and miles of unspoiled countryside – much of it part of the villa's own estate. Inside, many original features remain: an old chapel, 14thC frescoes, massive interior doors, and timbered ceilings. Furnishings blend with this venerable setting, including some valuable antiques, notably a vast and regal four-poster bed and an 18thC sofa. Plain white walls offset the dark wood of beams and furniture. Most of the bedrooms are handsomely furnished and spacious – some might find them too grand for comfort. Although one satisfied guest found them 'very comfortable indeed' and 'well worth' the high prices. Bathrooms are beautifully tiled in blue and white. The open-plan sitting room and dining room are traditionally furnished and fairly formal; the restaurant is renowned, and local dignitaries make the long trek to enjoy its food. Breakfast was a disappointment for one visitor, though. The staff are kind and welcoming, and if you're lucky the owner may entertain you with a little piano music after dinner.

~

NEARBY Florence (35 km).
LOCATION in countryside 3 km S of Vicchio, 35 km NE of Florence; car parking
FOOD breakfast, dinner; snacks
PRICE €€€
ROOMS 21; 14 double and twin, 1 single, 6 suites, all with bath or shower; all rooms have phone, TV, minibar
FACILITIES sitting room, dining room, garden, swimming pool
CREDIT CARDS MC, V
DISABLED 4 specially adapted bedrooms
PETS accepted by arrangement
CLOSED mid Nov-mid Mar
PROPRIETOR Paolo Pasquali

TUSCANY

VOLPAIA

LA LOCANDA
~ COUNTRY GUESTHOUSE ~

Loc. Montanino, Volpaia, 53017 Radda in Chianti, Siena
Tel 0577 738832 **Fax** 0577 739263
E-MAIL info@lalocanda.it **WEBSITE** www.lalocanda.it

THE BEVILAQUAS (HE NEAPOLITAN, SHE MILANESE) began their search for the ideal spot in which to set up their guesthouse four years ago. In April 1999, what was once a collection of ruined farm buildings high up in the Chianti hills finally opened for business, and you would be hard pressed to find a more beautiful setting. At 600 m above sea level, views from the terraces, garden, pool and some of the rooms are of layers of hills, striped with vines and shaded with woods; in the foreground is the mellow old fortified hamlet of Volpaia.

The restoration of the pale stone buildings has been done with unerring good taste. Interiors, while maintaining many of the rustic features, have a refreshingly contemporary look with an imaginative use of colour throughout to offset plenty of terracotta and wood.

The comfortable bedrooms have an uncluttered feel, and the bathrooms are spacious and gleaming. One end of the long, sunny living room is dominated by a massive stone fireplace, and filled with colourfully-upholstered sofas and armchairs.

~

NEARBY Florence (48 km); Siena (38 km).
LOCATION 4 km W of Volpaia (signed from *piazza* in the village) follow signs to the hotel; car parking.
FOOD breakfast, dinner on request
PRICE €€€
ROOMS 7; 6 double and twin, 1 suite, all with bath; all rooms have phone, TV, hairdrier, safe
FACILITIES sitting rooms, bar, dining room, terraces, garden, swimming pool
CREDIT CARDS AE, DC, MC, V
DISABLED ground floor rooms available
PETS not accepted
CLOSED mid-Nov to mid-Mar
PROPRIETORS Guido and Martina Bevilaqua

TUSCANY

BARBERINO VAL D'ELSA

IL PARETAIO
COUNTRY GUESTHOUSE

Loc. San Filippo, 50021
Barberino Val d'Elsa, Firenze

TEL 055 8059218 **FAX** 055 8059231
E-MAIL ilparetaio@tin.it
WEBSITE www.ilparetaio.it
FOOD breakfast, dinner
PRICE €€
CLOSED never
PROPRIETORS Giovanni and
Cristina de March

A GREAT ADDRESS FOR THOSE interested in horse riding but not to be dis-
missed by any traveller in search of the country life. Strategically
located between Florence and Siena, in hilly surroundings, Il Paretaio is a
17thC stone-built farmhouse on its own large estate. The accommodation
is simple but attractive. The ground floor entrance and sitting area was
originally a work room, and still retains the old stone paving. A huge brick
arch spans the central space and brick-vaulting contrasts with the plain
white walls. Upstairs, the rustic style is continued in the exposed-beam
ceilings and worn terracotta floors.

CASTELLINA IN CHIANTI

PALAZZO SQUARCIALUPI
TOWN HOTEL

Via Ferruccio 26, 53011
Castellina in Chianti, Siena

TEL 0577 741186 **FAX** 0577 740386
E-MAIL info@chiantiandrelax.com
WEBSITE www.chiantiandrelax.com
FOOD buffet breakfast; snacks in
the bar
PRICE €€
CLOSED Nov to mid-Mar
PROPRIETORS Targioni family

P ALAZZO SQUARCIALUPI IS SET in the medieval village of Castellina in
Chianti, and when our reporter first came here, she was struck by the
friendly, peaceful atmosphere and the lovely rooms. It is a 14thC stone
building with arched doors and windows, which was formerly an imposing
farmhouse. It has been renovated in a simple, stylish way, while retaining
its traditional farm character. There are 17 large bedrooms and suites
with plain white walls, beamed ceilings and dark wooden furniture.
Downstairs there is a rustic sitting room in muted tones of white, cream
and terracotta, and another elegant room with frescoes.

TUSCANY

CASTELNUOVO BERARDENGA

VILLA CURINA
COUNTRY VILLA

Loc. Curina, 53019 Castelnuovo Berardenga, Siena

TEL 0577 355630
FAX 0577 355610
E-MAIL info@villacurina.it
WEBSITE www.villacurina.it
FOOD breakfast, dinner
PRICE €€€
CLOSED Nov-Mar/Apr
MANAGER Andrea de Agostini

A VIVACIOUS, CONVIVIAL ATMOSPHERE pervades this hotel-and-apartment complex set in low, rolling countryside north of Siena. When we visited, it was full of activity, with people enjoying themselves in the pool, playing tennis or setting off for bike rides. The main villa, surrounded by ornamental gardens and trees, is a large, cream-coloured, 18thC building and contains the guest bedrooms as well as the principal public rooms. Most of the apartments are in three old stone farmhouses with small, brown-shuttered windows and connected by pathways of Siena brick. An attractive restaurant, spanned by strong brick arches, serves fresh produce from the estate.

GAIOLE IN CHIANTI

CASTELLO DI SPALTENNA
CASTLE HOTEL

Gaiole in Chianti, 53013 Siena

TEL 0577 749483 **FAX** 0577 749269
E-MAIL info@spaltenna.it
WEBSITE spaltenna.it
FOOD breakfast, lunch, dinner
PRICES €€€
CLOSED early Jan to late Mar
MANAGER Guido Conti

A DRAMATICALLY SITUATED, fortified monastery on a hilltop next to the medieval church of Santa Maria di Spaltenna, built round a central courtyard. The present management has been in place for some years now and has carried out extensive redecoration and renovation. Cosy standard rooms are in what were the monk's cells, while suites and de luxe rooms (done out in up-market country style) are housed in various outbuildings. There is a plethora of facilities (pools, sauna, gym, Jacuzzis and so on) but a dearth of atmosphere. The food, served in a rather formal room, is good but expensive.

TUSCANY

GAIOLE IN CHIANTI

CASTELLO DI TORNANO

CASTLE HOTEL

Gaiole in Chianti, 53013 Siena

TEL 0577 746067 **FAX** 0577 746094
E-MAIL info@castelloditornano.it
WEBSITE www.castelloditornano.it
FOOD breakfast, lunch, dinner
PRICES €€€
CLOSED never
PROPRIETORS Francesco Giuffrede

ONE OF THE COUNTLESS DEFENCE and watchtowers that dot Tuscany and solidly built in grey stone with commanding views of the surrounding countryside, the Castello di Tornano has undergone something of a transformation recently. There are still self-catering apartments for rent in an adjoining farmhouse, but these are rather drab compared to the luxurious rooms that are now available in the castle and tower itself. The style is rather theatrical with a medieval feel; deep red brocaded fabrics, mezza corona beds, elaborated wrought iron light fittings, luxourious (unmedieval) bathrooms. The restaurant serves Tuscan specialities and there is a hot tub on the top of the tower.

LUCCA

ALLA CORTE DEGLI ANGELI

CASTLE HOTEL

Via degli Angeli 23, 55100 Lucca

TEL 0583 469204
FAX 0583 991989
E-MAIL
info@allacortedegliangeli.com
WEBSITE
www.allacortedegliangeli.com
FOOD breakfast
PRICE €€
CLOSED never
MANAGER Pietro Bonino

THE LOVELY WALLED TOWN of Lucca makes an excellent base for a few days: you can explore the town itself, visit nearby villas, drive up to the verdant Garfagnana or spend a day on the beach. This small, upmarket guest house is one of the few 'charming' places to stay within the walls. Downstairs, a reception area includes a small dining room (it must be said that we have had one negative comment about the breakfast) while on the upper floor, the six bedrooms (named after flowers) are elegantly and comfortably furnished and painted in pastel shades. Bathrooms all have Jacuzzi tubs.

TUSCANY

MASSA E COZZILE

VILLA PASQUINI
COUNTRY VILLA

Via Vacchereccia 56, Margine Coperta, 51010 Massa e Cozzile, Pistoia

TEL 0572 72205 **FAX** 0572 910888
Food breakfast, dinner
Price €€
Closed late Nov to mid-Mar
PROPRIETORS Innocenti family

Stay at Villa Pasquini and you step back into the 19th century. Little has changed here, either in furnishings, or decoration, since then. Until seven years ago, it was the autumn retreat of an aristocratic Roman family, the Pasquinis; then it was bought, fully furnished, by the present incumbents, who have lovingly preserved it, combining a family home with a most unusual hotel. The bedrooms are, of course, all different, some quite grand with canopied beds. Bathrooms are old-fashioned, but well equipped. In the attractive dining room – originally the entrance hall – the emphasis is on traditional recipes. Our reporter chose the fixed-price menu (five delicious courses) and thought the price very reasonable.

MONTEFOLLONICO

LA CHIUSA
COUNTRY GUESTHOUSE

Via della Madonnina 88, 53040 Montefollonico, Siena

TEL 0577 669668 **FAX** 0577 669593
E-MAIL info@ristorantelachiusa.it
WEBSITE www.ristorantelachiusa.it
Food breakfast, lunch, dinner
PRICE €€€€
CLOSED Jan-Mar; restaurant Tue
PROPRIETORS Dania Masotti and Umberto Lucherini

Several of the better small hotels in this guide started off as restaurants which, over the years have converted a few rooms for overnight visitors, with such success that they have extended this side of their business. But on the whole the restaurant remains the centre of the enterprise. Not that at La Chiusa, a stone farmhouse and *frantoio* (olive press), the comfort of guests is secondary. The greatest care and attention has been given to the bedrooms and suites each has been individually furnished with antiques. Bathrooms are superb. Dania Masotti is justifiably proud of her achievements as a cook, and meals in the elegant (and pricey) restaurant are gastronomic experiences although the word locally is that standards have slipped recently.

TUSCANY

MONTIGNOSO

IL BOTTACCIO
RESTAURANT WITH ROOMS

Via Bottaccio 1, 54038
Montignoso, Massa

TEL 0585 340031 **FAX** 0585 340103
E-MAIL bottaccio@bottaccio.it
WEBSITE www.bottaccio.it
Food breakfast, lunch, dinner
Price €€€€
Closed never
PROPRIETORS Stefano and
Elizabeth D'Anna

IL BOTTACCIO LIES IN ITS OWN GROUNDS a few kilometres inland from the chic beaches of Forte dei Marmi, but amid the rather ugly suburban sprawl of Massa, a town dominated by the marble industry. It is primarily a restaurant serving 'creative dishes inspired by Mediterranean tradition' and cooked by Nino, who also manages the place. Originally an oil mill some of the undeniably luxurious rooms actually incorporate bits of the old olive press, but there is a vague feeling of having seen better times about it. However, the hotel is unique in its way and the food is good (though expensive).

PIEVE SANTO STEFANO

LOCANDA LA PERGOLA
COUNTRY INN

Via Tiberina 177, Pieve Santo
Stefano, 52036 Arezzo

TEL 0575 797053
Food breakfast,lunch, dinner
Price €
Closed never; restaurant closed
Wed
PROPRIETORS Marida Gorini and
Loreana Marini

A USEFUL ADDRESS FOR ANYONE taking the road from central Tuscany to Ravenna, this local inn is run by three capable women; Marida, Oriana and Valeria. Previous owners restored the house with real panache in classy country style: rustic antiques and painted reproduction pieces sit on polished tiled floors in the bedrooms. Shower rooms are compact but smart. The dinng room shows the same simple good taste, but the real attraction here is Marida's exquisite country cooking which includes a daily batch of superb ravioli made with local ricotta. The busy new superstrada across the narrow valley doesn't seem to be a major problem.

TUSCANY

RADICOFANI

LA PALAZZINA
COUNTRY GUESTHOUSE

*Loc. Le Vigne, Celle sul Rigo,
53040 Radicofani (Siena)*

TEL & FAX 0578 55771
E-MAIL fattorialapalazzina@virgilio.it
WEBSITE
www.fattorialapalazzina.com
Food breakfast
Price € (minimum 3 nights in
high season)
Closed 1 Nov-mid Mar
PROPRIETOR Nicoletta Innocenti

A 17TH CENTURY HILLTOP HUNTING lodge, La Palazzina is situated on a big farm in the remote and captivating south-eastern corner of Tuscany amidst rolling hills. Approached by an alley of cypress trees, the house is set in manicured gardens with a pristine swimming pool to one side overlooking wide vistas. Inside, pale pastel colours and smart black and white tiled floors downstairs give a clean cool look, while antiques and carefully chosen fabrics add style. The bedrooms have beamed ceilings and wrought-iron beds; a few have their own terraces. A generous breakfast includes produce from the farm.

SAN GIMIGNANO

LE RENAIE
COUNTRY HOTEL

*Loc. Pancole, 53037 San
Gimignano, Siena*

TEL 0577 955044 **FAX** 0577 955126
E-MAIL lerenaie@iol.it
WEBSITE www.hotellerenaie.com
FOOD breakfast, lunch, dinner
PRICE €€
CLOSED Nov
PROPRIETOR Leonetto Sabatini

A SIMPLE, WELL-RUN COUNTRY HOTEL – built up over the years by the present owners from a bar and restaurant – which makes a respectable base within a short drive of San Gimignano. The building is no architectural masterpiece, but a typical example of a modern rustic construction. Inside, modern terracotta flooring and cane furniture make for a light, fresh atmosphere. The restaurant, Da Leonetto, is popular with locals (especially for large functions) but gets mixed notices from reporters. Upstairs are the bedrooms, which have a mixture of modern, built-in furniture and reproduction rustic. Guests seem to appreciate the peaceful location, services (including a swimming pool and access to a tennis court).

TUSCANY

SESTO FIORENTINO

VILLA VILLORESI
TOWN VILLA

*Via Ciampi 2, 50019 Colonnata
di Sesto Fiorentino, Firenze*

TEL 055 443212 **FAX** 055 442063
E-MAIL cvillor@tin.it
WEBSITE www.villavilloresi.it
FOOD breakfast, lunch, dinner
PRICE €€
CLOSED never
PROPRIETOR Contessa Cristina Villoresi

THE ARISTOCRATIC VILLA VILLORESI looks rather out of place in what is now an industrial suburb of Florence, but once in the house and gardens you suddenly feel a million miles away from the modern, bustling city. Contessa Cristina Villoresi is a warm hostess who has captured the hearts of many transatlantic and other guests. It is thanks to her that the villa still has the feel of a private home – all rather grand, if a little faded. Bedrooms are remarkably varied – from the small and quite plain to grand apartments with frescoes and Venetian chandeliers. Some look over the courtyard, others on to the pool and garden. We are assured that the food is now better than it was.

SOVICILLE

BORGO DI TOIANO
COUNTRY HOTEL

Loc. Toiano, 53018 Sovicille, Siena

TEL 0577 314639
FAX 0577 314641
E-MAIL toiano@sienanet.it
WEBSITE www.sienanet.it/toiano
FOOD breakfast, snacks
PRICE €€
CLOSED Nov-Mar
MANAGER Pierluigi Pagni

MOST OF THE ABANDONED rural hamlets (*borgi*) that once housed small farming communities and have since been converted into distinctive hotels were located on steep hills or jumbled together behind secure walls. Borgo di Toiano, by contrast, has a pleasant open aspect: a few old stone houses, superbly restored, are spread out across acres of stone and terracotta terraces. The main public rooms also have a spacious, unclut-tered feel. Bedrooms have the same mixture of rustic and modern. Swimming pool.

UMBRIA AND MARCHE

AREA INTRODUCTION

HOTELS IN UMBRIA AND MARCHE

VISITORS ARE DISCOVERING that there is more to Umbria than Assisi; but it nonetheless remains the main tourist highlight of the region. Choices of hotel here are strictly limited: there are many that are mediocre, and some of the more comfortable are too big for a full entry here; of these, the **Subasio** (tel 075 812206) is a 70-room, polished, rather formal place, but notable for the views from its better bedrooms and beautiful flowery terraces. We continue to recommend the **Umbra** (page 239) in town, and **Le Silve** (page 221) in the countryside, and we have added **L' Orto degli Angeli** in Bevagna, 24 km away (page 222).

Perugia is not nearly so well known as Assisi, but well worth a visit if you can penetrate the infuriating defences of its traffic system. Since its massive expansion to over 90 bedrooms, we have dropped our entry for the **Brufani** (tel 075 5732541), though it's worth knowing about, if expensive. Just along from the Brufani is **La Rosetta** (tel 075 5720841); though also large, it is not worryingly impersonal, and better value. Another possibility as a base for exploring the area is the **Da Sauro** (tel 075 826168), a family hotel on the peaceful island of Maggiore in Lake Trasemino. We have a new recommendation for the centre of Orvieto, and there's plenty of choice for relaxing hotels in the Umbrian countryside.

Marche's coast, like the rest of the Adriatic, offers large resorts with plenty of hotels, but not many suitable for this guide. Pesaro, though a big town, is a more interesting mixture of old town and beach resort than many along this coastline; along with the **Villa Serena** (page 236) we have added **Villa La Torraccia** (page 241), and we might also mention the **Vittoria**, a stylish, well-equipped hotel on the seafront (tel 0721 34344). Ancona, regional capital of the Marche and a big seaport, is definitely not the place to stay but 12 km down the coast, at the popular resort of Portonovo, we have the **Emilia** and, as a back-up address can also suggest the **Hotel Monteconero** (tel 071 9330592). this hotel is built around a 11thC Benedictine monastery and perched on a cliff, 550 m above the sea in the middle of the Monteconero national park. Further south at Numana, the **Eden Gigli** (tel 071 933 0652) is a smart, modern hotel in a beautiful setting overlooking the sea.

Inland from Pesaro, the Renaissance art city of Urbino is an essential place to visit, and we have a new entry just outside; the **Locandadi Valle Nuova**. If you want to stay in the centre of things, however, our best suggestion is the **Raffaello** (tel 0722 4896), a straightforward 19-room place; it has no restaurant but this is not a problem since it is right in the middle of the town.

Gubbio is an equally compelling place to visit: try the **Bosone** (tel 075 9220688), or alternatively the **Torre dei Calzolari Palace** (tel 075 925 6327), which is some 7 km away. Also slightly out of town are the **Villa Montegranelli** (tel 075 9220185), a severe stone-built villa in hillside grounds, or the extravagant **Park Hotel ai Cappuccini** (tel 075 9234).

UMBRIA AND MARCHE

AMELIA

PICCOLO CARLENI
~ RESTAURANT WITH ROOMS ~

Via Pellegrino Carleni 21, 05022 Amelia, Terni
TEL 0744 983925 **FAX** 0744 978143
E-MAIL carleni@tin.it **WEBSITE** www.giubileoitalia.com/carleni

IT IS THOUGHT THAT THE LITTLE hill town of Amelia was founded as early as the 12thC B.C., making it amongst the oldest settlements in Italy. It has a beautiful setting on the ridge that divides the Nera and Tiber valleys.

The Carleni has just changed hands, and the new English owner is still a little uncertain of its future. What she does know, however, is that the restaurant (two inviting rooms with warm yellow walls and an open fire), which serves creative renditions of Umbrian *cuisine*, will continue to be the heart of the place. For now, the charming accommodation has been divided into two two-bedroom apartments which share a big kitchen and living room on the ground floor plus a delightful walled garden. The top floor apartment has a private terrace with spectacular views. Each has a small kitchenette (useful for making breakfast which is not provided); the style is comfortable rustic with beamed ceilings and tasteful mix of country antiques and pine or wicker pieces. The walls, here too, are a warm yellow and duvets add a touch of luxury. The Carleni is a delightful little place and we really hope that it will continue to offer some kind of lodging in the future.

~

NEARBY Orvieto (32 km); Spoleto (40 km); Viterbo (30 km).
LOCATION 20 km SW of Terni, in centre of town; public car parking 100 m from hotel
FOOD lunch, dinner
PRICE €€€€€ per week; one week minimum let April-Sept
ROOMS 2 2-bedroomed self-catering apartments each with 2 bathrooms; all rooms have phone, TV, air conditioning, safe, hairdrier
FACILITIES restaurant, living room, kitchen, garden
CREDIT CARDS AE, DC, MC, V
DISABLED no special facilities
PETS not accepted
CLOSED 3-4 weeks around Jan, Feb
PROPRIETOR Cate Thomas

UMBRIA AND MARCHE

POGGIO D'ASPROLI
~ COUNTRY GUEST-HOUSE ~

Loc. Asproli 7, 06059 Todi, Perugia
TEL and **FAX** 075 8853385
E-MAIL poggiodasproli@email.it

IF YOU ARE TIRED OF NAPLES, you may not be tired of life – just in need of peace and quiet. Such was the case with Bruno Pagliari, so he sold his large hotel in southern Italy to continue his career as an artist in the tranquility of Umbria's leafy valleys. But the tradition of hospitality remained, and he has opened up his hillside farmhouse so that his guests can also enjoy this oasis.

The rambling building of local stone is packed full of an arresting mixture of antiques and Bruno's own modern art. The main sitting room, with its great fireplace and white couches, is flanked by a long terrace where one can eat or just relax, listening to birdsong from the wooded hills.

In the rest of the house, stone and brick arches frame decoratively painted doors and parchment-shaded lights illuminate old coloured wooden carvings. The bedrooms will inspire many a pleasant dream.

The atmosphere is hushed, but in a relaxed rather than reverent manner and, birdsong aside, the only sound is of operatic arias gently playing in the background.

~

NEARBY Todi (7km); Oriveto (29 km).
LOCATION country house in its own grounds
FOOD breakfast, dinner on request
PRICE ⓔⓔ
ROOMS 7 double, 2 suite all with shower or bath, phon, heating
FACILITIES pool, garden, terrace, sitting room
CREDIT CARDS AE, MC, V
CHILDREN not suitable
DISABLED difficult
PETS not accepted
CLOSED mid-Jan to mid-Mar
LANGUAGES English, French, German
PROPRIETOR Bruno Pagliari

UMBRIA AND MARCHE

ASSISI

LE SILVE

~ COUNTRY HOTEL ~

Loc. Armenzano, 06081 Assisi, Perugia
TEL 075 8019000 **FAX** 075 8019005
E-MAIL hotellesilve@tin.it **WEBSITE** www.lesilve.it

EVEN IF YOU ARE NOT PLANNING to stay at this sophisticated gem, the road up to Le Silve is worth exploring for its own rewards – or perhaps avoiding if you are the nervous sort. It winds up over a series of hills and passes until you reach the house, set on its own private hill-ridge, 700 m above sea level. The views are wonderful.

Le Silve is an old farmhouse (parts of it very old indeed – 10th century) converted to its new purpose with great sympathy and charm. There is a delightfully rambling feel to the place, with rooms on a variety of levels. The rustic nature of the building is preserved perfectly – all polished tile floors, stone or white walls, beamed ceilings, the occasional rug – and it is furnished with country antiques. Public rooms are large and airy, bedrooms stylishly simple. The self-contained suites are in villas about 1.5 km from the main house.

We have had conflicting reports of the food, which uses produce from the associated farm. Recently, a reader praised the 'very modern Italian cooking' (also pointing out that portions were small) while a previous guest complained about the 'pretentious *cuisine minceur* at astronomical prices'. What do you think? Le Silve is close enough to Assisi for sightseeing expeditions but remote enough for complete seclusion – and with good sports facilities immediately on hand (fair-sized pool). But it's not for vertigo sufferers.

~

NEARBY sights of Assisi.
LOCATION in countryside 12 km E of Assisi, between S444 and S3; ask hotel for directions; ample car parking
FOOD breakfast, lunch, dinner; room service
PRICE €€€
ROOMS 18; 11 double, 3 single, 4 self-contained suites, all with bath; all rooms have phone, TV, minibar, safe **FACILITIES** 2 sitting rooms, dining room, bar, terrace, swimming pool, tennis, sauna, riding, archery, mini-golf, motorbike
CREDIT CARDS AE, DC, V **DISABLED** no special facilities **PETS** not accepted
CLOSED mid-Nov to mid-Jan **MANAGER** Daniela Taddia

UMBRIA AND MARCHE

BEVAGNA

L'ORTO DEGLI ANGELI

~ TOWN HOTEL ~

Via Dante Alighieri, 06031 Bevagna, Perugia
TEL 0742 360130 **FAX** 0742 361756
E-MAIL ortoangeli@ortoangeli.it **WEBSITE** www.ortoangeli.it

BEVAGNA IS ANOTHER OF THOSE SLEEPY little Umbrian places full of artistic gems, this time on the old Via Flaminia. Situated in the centre of town, l'Orto degli Angeli is a 17thC property which is remarkable for two features. The delightful hanging garden occupies the site of a Roman amphitheatre, and one rough stone wall of the pretty, lemon-painted restaurant is a remnant of a first century temple to Minerva.

The grandly-named Antonini Angeli Nieri Mongalli family have restored their fascinating home with much care. Its dimensions are grand, too, complete with frescoes, aged terracotta floors and vast stone fireplaces are still there, but it manages to be homely and comfortable too – anything but overwhelming. The bedrooms are imaginatively decorated with great style; smart fabrics blend with the original terracotta floor tiles, gorgeous family antiques and painted woodwork. Modern equipment is carefully hidden from view. The menu in the restaurant changes every week, and Tiziana Antonini oversees the cooking. She bakes fresh bread daily, and even grinds her own flour. The jams and cakes served at breakfast are home made.

~

NEARBY Assisi (24 km); Perugia (45 km); Spello (13 km).
LOCATION 8 km SW of Foligno, in centre of town; public car parking 100 m
FOOD breafast, lunch, dinner
PRICE ⓔⓔⓔ
ROOMS 14; 5 double and 9 suites, 7 with bath, 7 with shower; all rooms have phone, TV, air conditioning, minibar, safe, hairdrier
FACILITIES breakfast room, restaurant, sitting room, reading room, garden
CREDIT CARDS AE, DC, MC, V
DISABLED not suitable
PETS accepted on request
CLOSED mid-Jan to mid-Feb
PROPRIETORS Tiziana and Francesco Antonini Angeli.Nieri Mongalli

UMBRIA AND MARCHE

CAMPELLO SUL CLITUNNO

IL VECCHIO MOLINO

~ CONVERTED MILL ~

Loc.Pissignano, Via del Tempio 34, 06042 Campello sul Clitunno, Perugia
TEL 0743 521122 **FAX** 0743 275097
E-MAIL vecchiomolino@perugiaonline.com **WEBSITE** www.perugiaonline.com

IT IS A MYSTERY HOW THIS INN, so close to the busy Perugia-Spoleto road, remains so peaceful. Almost the only sound is of gurgling brooks winding through the leafy gardens. As befits an old mill, all the buildings live in close harmony with the river: the drive sweeps around the mill pond to a creeper-covered building against which old grinding-stones rest. The gardens are a spit of land, with weeping willows dipping into streams on both sides. Water even runs through some of the old working parts, where the mill machinery has been built into the decorative scheme.

There seems to be no end to the number of public rooms, all furnished in a highly individual manner: elegant white sofas in front of a big brick fireplace, surmounted by carved wooden lamps; tables with lecterns bearing early editions of Dante's *Purgatorio*; mill wheels used as doors. The bedrooms were, we were relieved to note, pleasingly dry and decorated in a restrained manner with fine antiques, the white walls lit up by parchment-shaded lamps; TV's are absent as a matter of principle.

It's worth remembering that the hotel is popular in the wedding season and during the Spoleto festival.

~

NEARBY Spoleto (11 km); Perugia (50 km).
LOCATION 50 km SE of Perugia between Trevi and Spoleto; in own grounds by the Clitunno river; ample car parking
FOOD breakfast
PRICE €€
ROOMS 13; 6 double, 2 single, 5 suites, all with bath or shower; all rooms have phone, minibar, air conditioning
FACILITIES sitting rooms, bar, TV room, gardens
CREDIT CARDS AE, DC, MC, V
DISABLED access difficult
PETS accepted
CLOSED Nov-Mar
PROPRIETOR Paolo Rapanelli

CANALICCHIO

RELAIS IL CANALICCHIO
~ HILLTOP HOTEL ~

Via della Piazza 13, 06050 Canalicchio, Perugia
TEL 075 8707325 **FAX** 075 8707296
E-MAIL relais@relaisilcanalicchio.it **WEBSITE** www.relaiscanalicchio.it

One of the paradoxes of modern Italy is that what were once the modest homes of farmers and artisans have become, with careful restoration, exemplars of modern taste and comfort. What makes this possible is the Italian genius for combining everyday materials of quality – brick, wood, plaster, terracotta – with style and flair.

The owners of Relais Il Canalicchio have taken over most of the semi-fortified, hilltop town of the same name and created a hotel that not only respects the native Umbrian qualities but imaginatively enhances them with contemporary Italian panache. Public rooms are in the old working areas of the mill: brick arches and the massive grinding stones set off thecomfortable, elegant furniture. The plain plaster walls are decorated with English prints, oil portraits and brilliant local ceramics. An old wine-press remains.

Each bedroom has been individually furnished; some have terrace gardens and many have superb views. Sixteen new 'country suites', situated about 100 metres from the main house and arranged around their own pool, have recently been added. The restaurant serves exquisitely prepared produce from its own farm. There is a new chef, so we would welcome reports. If you feel guilty about such hedonism, there is a gym, a pool and a sauna.

~

Nearby Perugia, Assisi, Gubbio, Todi (all within 40 km).
Location quiet hilltop village 30 km SE of Perugia; car parking
Food breakfast, lunch, dinner
Price €€€
Rooms 49; 32 double; 17 suites, all with bath or shower; all rooms have phone, TV, air-conditioning, minibar, safe
Facilities sitting rooms, restaurant, billiard room, gym, sauna, terraces, gardens, swimming pool, tennis court, mountain bikes
Credit cards AE, DC, MC, V
Disabled some rooms suitable **Pets** accepted
Closed never

UMBRIA AND MARCHE

CASTEL RIGONE

RELAIS LA FATTORIA
～ TOWN HOTEL ～

Via Rigone 1, 06060 Castel Rigone, Lago Trasimeno, Perugia
TEL 075 845322 **FAX** 075 845197
E-MAIL info@relaislafattoria.com **WEBSITE** www.relaislafattoria.com

O N THE HILLS BEHIND LAKE TRASIMENO lies the small medieval town of
Castel Rigone, a mere handful of houses grouped about a handsome
piazza. Right at its centre is this pleasant, family-run hotel occupying
what was once a manor house.

You feel a sense of welcome the moment you step inside the reception
area, which has a wooden ceiling, stone walls and comfortable Knole
sofas. Keen young staff are on hand to make you feel at home. The public
rooms are tastefully decorated, with Persian rugs on the polished cork
floors and bright modern paintings on the white walls. The only addition
to the building that has been allowed by the Italian Fine Arts Ministry is a
restaurant perfectly in keeping with the original style. Dishes include
fresh fish from the lake.

Bedrooms have been designed with an eye more to modern comfort
than to individual style and some have lake views. The bathrooms are
bright and new.

Along the front of the house is a terrace with sitting areas and a small
swimming pool. An excellent, extensive buffet breakfast (home-made
bread and jams, cheeses and cured meats) is served here in fine weather.

～

NEARBY Perugia (27 km); Assisi (35 km); Gubbio (50 km).
LOCATION 27 km NW of Perugia, in centre of town; car parking nearby
FOOD breakfast, lunch, dinner
PRICE €€
ROOMS 29; 23 double, 3 single, 3 junior suites, all with bath or shower (suites with
Jacuzzis); all rooms have phone, TV, minibar
FACILITIES sitting room, restaurant, terrace/garden, swimming pool
CREDIT CARDS AE, DC, MC, V
DISABLED no special facilities
PETS accepted
CLOSED hotel never; restaurant only, Jan
PROPRIETORS Pammelati family

UMBRIA AND MARCHE

LA GIOIA
~ COUNTRY HOUSE HOTEL ~

Cole del Marchese 60, 06044 Castel Ritaldi, Perugia
TEL 0743 254068 **FAX** 0743 254046
E-MAIL benvenuti@lagioia.biz **WEBSITE** www.lagioia.biz

HAVING RUN HER OWN interior decorating business in Zurich, Marianne Aerni-Kühne was in an ideal position to restore this 300-year-old oil and grain mill and indeed, she and her husband Daniel have done a beautiful job. La Gioia is situated in gentle countryside near several of Umbria's bigger towns, but also within easy reach of such undiscovered gems as Bevagna and Montefalco. The pale stone building stands in its own extensive grounds, which include an attractive pool, lawns, terraces and plenty of sitting areas where big white umbrellas provide shade. Inside, typical rustic features (*cotto* floors, beamed ceilings, exposed brickwork and so on) have been tastefully enhanced by the use of earthy, Mediterranean colours, a mix of old and new furniture, bright fabrics and soft lighting. The bedrooms have been individually decorated with much attention to detail: underfloor heating and duvets on the beds make them very cosy in cooler weather. Some are split level with either a bed or sitting area on the top level, while others have a private terrace overlooking the garden. At La Gioia, food and wine are considered to be an important part of your stay (the chef uses home-grown or local produce), and half board is encouraged, especially during high season.

~

NEARBY Assissi (35km); Spoleto (13km); Todi (35km); Terni (45km).
LOCATION 13 km NW of Spoleto; in ample grounds with car parking
FOOD breakfast, dinner; light lunch on request
PRICE €€; €€€ half board
ROOMS 12; 11 double, 1 single, all with bath or shower; all rooms have phone, TV, safe, hairdrier
FACILITIES bar, sitting room, library, restaurant, terraces, garden, swimming pool
CREDIT CARDS MC, V
DISABLED adapted rooms
PETS accepted
CLOSED Nov, Jan-Feb
PROPRIETORS Marianne and Daniel Aerni-Kühne

UMBRIA AND MARCHE

CENERENTE

CASTELLO DELL'OSCANO

~ CASTLE VILLA ~

06134 Loc. Cenerente, Perugia
TEL 075 690125 **FAX** 075 690666
E-MAIL info@oscano.com **WEBSITE** www.oscano.com

AT FIRST SIGHT CASTELLO DELL'OSCANO appears like a fairytale medieval castle: ivy-clad turrets, battlements and crenellated towers rise above a steep, hillside pine forest. The two main towers date from the 15thC; they were incorporated into the 18thC re-building by an American tycoon.

The interiors are finely proportioned, spacious and light. The hall rises the entire height of the castle, with an imposing carved stairway, polished wood floors and neo-Gothic windows. One public room leads into another, all filled with the castle's original furniture: a library which will entrance any bibliophile with its carved classical bookcases and 18thC volumes; sitting rooms with wooden panelling, tapestries and sculpted fireplaces; a dining room with old display cases full of Deruta pottery.

Upstairs, the floors are of geometrically patterned, black-and-white marble. There are only ten bedrooms in the castle, each with its own antique furnishing. The remainder, in the Villa Ada next door, are less exciting and cheaper. The most spectacular (but strictly for the agile) is in the turret, with a four-poster bed and a door to the ramparts which look over the romantic gardens below.

~

NEARBY Perugia (5 km); Assisi (28 km); Gubbio (40 km).
LOCATION on a hillside in its own grounds; ample car parking
FOOD breakfast, dinner
PRICE €€€-€€€€
ROOMS 11 double (Castello), 8 double, 2 single (Villa Ada), all with bath or shower; all rooms have phone, TV, air conditioning, minibar, hairdrier, safe
FACILITIES sitting rooms, dining room, library, bar, gardens, swimming pool
CREDIT CARDS AE, DC, MC, V
DISABLED 1 suitable bedroom
PETS on request
CLOSED never; restaurant only, mid-Jan to mid-Feb
MANAGER Michele Ravano

UMBRIA AND MARCHE

FATTORIA DI VIBIO

~ FARM GUESTHOUSE ~

Loc. Buchella 1a, 9-Doglio, 05010 Montecastello Vibio, Perugia
TEL 075 8749607 **FAX** 075 8780014
E-MAIL info@fattoriadivibio.com **WEBSITE** www.fattoriadivibio.com

OCCASIONALLY, THE WHOLE ATMOSPHERE of a place is captured by a small detail: here it is the hand-painted pottery used to serve Signora Saladini's delicious food which sums up the relaxed elegance of this reno-vated 18thC farmhouse. The style is modern rustic Italian, with pleasing open spaces, defined by white walls that contrast with the colourful fab-rics and ceramics. Light, airy and well proportioned, there is an feeling of effortless simplicity which, you quickly realize, required a great deal of taste and effort. Most of the bedrooms, of similar style, are in the house next door.

The Saladini family are serious about their visitors' comforts and well-being, starting in the kitchen. Much of what goes into the guests comes out of the farm or the market garden and the preparation is a spectacle in itself, open to all. The mandatory half board should not prove a penance. If you need to lose calories, you can swim (even in winter thanks to the new indoor pool) , play table tennis, ride or walk in the magnificent countryside around. Or just relax in the quiet of the garden. Otherwise, there is not much to do – but then that is the whole point of this soothing guesthouse.

~

NEARBY Todi (15 km); Orvieto (30 km); Perugia (40 km).
LOCATION on quiet hillside off S448 road between Todi and Orvieto; ample car parking
FOOD breakfast, lunch, dinner
PRICE €€; half board obligatory; 1-week minimum stay in Aug and over Easter
ROOMS 14 double and twin, all with bath or shower; TV, phone; 2 self-catering cottages
FACILITIES sitting room, dining room, terrace, garden, swimming pools, bicycles, riding, fishing, archery, tennis
CREDIT CARDS AE, DC, MC, V
DISABLED one suitable room
PETS accepted
CLOSED Jan and Feb
PROPRIETORS Gabriella, Giuseppe & Filippo Saladini

UMBRIA AND MARCHE

VILLA PAMBUFFETTI
~ VILLA HOTEL ~

Viale della Vittoria 20, 06036 Montefalco, Perugia
TEL 0742 379417 **FAX** 0742 379245
E-MAIL info@villapambuffetti.com **WEBSITE** www.villapambuffetti.com

LIKE HEMINGWAY IN SPAIN, the poet D'Annunzio seems to have stayed everywhere in Italy; however, in the case of Villa Pambuffetti the claim is better justified than most. Not only did he dedicate a poem to the delightful medieval walled town of Montefalco (a 5-min walk), from where the views are breathtaking, but the villa itself has a turn-of-the-century elegance that fits the poet's legend.

Ten thousand square metres of shady garden surround the main building. Inside, furniture and decoration have been kept almost as they were at the start of the 1900s when the Pambuffetti family began taking 'paying guests': floors and panelling of seasoned oak, bamboo armchairs, Tiffany lampshades and old family photographs in art nouveau frames pay tribute to a century that started optimistically. Many of the bedrooms are furnished with the family's older and finer antiques and all have bathrooms which, though recent, are stylistically nearly perfect. If you like a room with a view, try the tower, which has one of the six-windowed, all-round variety. The food, based proudly on local seasonal ingredients, is excellent. All in all, a gem.

~

NEARBY Montefalco; Assisi (30 km); Todi (30 km).
LOCATION just outside Montefalco, in its own grounds; with ample car parking
FOOD breakfast, dinner
ROOMS 15; 11 double and twin, 1 single; 3 suites, 2 with bath, 13 with shower; all rooms have phone, TV, air conditioning, minibar, hairdrier
PRICE €€€
FACILITIES sitting room, bar, restaurant, *loggia*, garden, swimming pool
CREDIT CARDS AE, DC, MC, V
DISABLED 2 rooms on ground floor
PETS not accepted
CLOSED never
MANAGERS Argentina, Alessandra and Mauro Pambuffetti

UMBRIA AND MARCHE

PODERE COSTA ROMANA
~ COUNTRY APARTMENTS ~

SS Flaminia, Strada per Itieli
TEL 0744 722495/335 5738210 **FAX** 0823 797118
E-MAIL costaromana@virgilio.it **WEBSITE** www.podercostaromana.com

A NNA MARIA GIORDANO decided in the late Nineties to swap the chaos of
her native Naples for the peace of this south-western corner of
Umbria. She brought and lovingly restored an 18thC stone farmhouse,
keeping a piece for herself and conveting the rest into apartments, which
she opened to guests in 2002. The property is immersed in a wooded hillside just outside the fine old town of Narni, once an important station on
the Roman Via Flaminia. Inside the house, the large communal sitting
room, with its open fireplace, allows guests to mingle. There is a garden,
too, for general use and a pool overlooking the hills. The apartments,
sleeping up to five, are carefully decorated in comfortable rustic style:
warm pastels on the walls, dark wood floors and beamed ceilings,
wrought-iron fittings, old country furniture and thoughtful lighting. Each
has a kitchenette and some kind of private outside space.

~

NEARBY Narni (3km); Terni (15km); Todi (40km).
LOCATION in open countryside off the SS3 (to Rome) south of Narni
FOOD breakfast
ROOMS 6 self-catering apartments sleeping from 2-5, all with bath or shower; all
rooms have TV
PRICE €€, minimum two nights
FACILITIES sitting room, garden, terraces, swimming pool
CREDIT CARDS not accepted
DISABLED access difficult
PETS not accepted
CLOSED never
PROPRIETOR Anna Maria Giordano

UMBRIA AND MARCHE

LA BADIA
~ CONVERTED ABBEY ~

Loc. La Badia, 05019 Orvieto, Terni
TEL 0763 301959 **FAX** 0763 305396
E-MAIL labadia.hotel@tin.it **WEBSITE** www.labadiahotel.it

ARRIVING AT TWILIGHT AT LA BADIA is like landing in a scene from a Gothic novel: ruined arches, rooks cawing from a crenellated bell tower, dark cypresses silhouetted against the sky and, across the valley, the evening profile of Orvieto's cathedral, secure on its fortress crag. But the golden stone monastery on the hill, surrounded by Umbria's intense green countryside, soon reveals itself as an outstanding hotel that would have delighted any Renaissance cardinal.

Restraint is the hallmark of this fine building's conversion into a distinctive hotel. The robust architecture of the old abbey is always allowed to speak for itself, and modern embellishments have been kept to a minimum. The heavy wooden period furniture goes well with the massive stone walls; wrought-iron lights illuminate vaulted ceilings; floors are either of plain or geometrically-patterned terracotta. Here and there, an unexpectedly-placed church pew reminds the guest of what once was.

On the hill behind is a pool fit for a pope. In front of the abbey, beside the famous 12-sided tower, is a peaceful garden where the meditative visitor can contemplate the view of Orvieto.

~

NEARBY Orvieto (5 km); Todi (40 km); Viterbo (45 km).
LOCATION on quiet hillside, 5 km S of Orvieto; own car parking
FOOD breakfast, lunch, dinner
PRICE €€€
ROOMS 28; 21 double, 7 suites, all with bath or shower; all rooms have phone, air-conditioning, minibar, hairdrier, TV
FACILITIES sitting room, breakfast room, bar, restaurant, tennis, swimming pool
CREDIT CARDS AE, V, MC
DISABLED ground floor rooms
PETS not allowed
CLOSED Jan, Feb
PROPRIETOR Luisa Fiume

UMBRIA AND MARCHE

ORVIETO

PALAZZO PICCOLOMINI
~ TOWN HOTEL ~

Piazza Ranieri 36, 05018 Orvieto, Terni
TEL 0763 341743 **FAX** 0763 391046
E-MAIL piccolomini.hotel@orvienet.it **WEBSITE** www.hotelpiccolomini.it

AT LAST A DECENT HOTEL has been created in the centre of this remarkable town which sits on a pedestal of tufa some 300 m above sea level. Orvieto is a charming place with a fabulous, candy-striped cathedral, an atmospheric *centro storico*, a choice of restaurants serving fine, regional food and last, but not least, an excellent local white wine.

Pale pink Palazzo Piccolomini (so-named after the family who built it at the end of the 16th century) is situated at the heart of the old city and was beautifully restored as a hotel in 1998. Inside, there is a wonderful sense of calm throughout the cool, vaulted rooms, which have been furnished with what some might call Spartan good taste. In the spacious salon, wrought-iron candelabras and white covers on sofas and chairs are stylish against white walls and polished terracotta floors; filmy white curtains ripple in the breeze and filter the sunlight. The bedrooms, although varying in shape and size, are similar, with modern, dark wooden furniture and the odd splash of deep blue. Some have rooftop views. You eat breakfast in a vaulted basement room which has Etruscan origins.

~

NEARBY cathedral; underground caves.
LOCATION on the S side of town near Porta Romana; public car parking 200 m away
FOOD breakfast
PRICE €€
ROOMS 31; 22 double and twin, 6 single, 3 suites, all with shower; all rooms have phone, TV, air conditioning, minibar, hairdrier
FACILITIES breakfast room, sitting room, bar, lift
CREDIT CARDS AE, DC, MC, V
DISABLED some adapted rooms
PETS accepted
CLOSED 1 week Jan
MANAGER Liliana Achilli

UMBRIA AND MARCHE

ORVIETO

VILLA CICONIA

~ COUNTRY VILLA ~

Loc. Ciconia, Via dei Tigli 69, Oriveto, 05018 Terni
TEL *0763 305582/3* **FAX** *0763 302077*
E-MAIL *villaciconia@libero.it* **WEBSITE** *www.bellumbria.net-hotel*

PROTECTED FROM THE NEARBY busy road and the encroachments of Oriveto's new suburbs by its tree-filled gardens, La Ciconia is a small, attractive 16thC grey stone villa with two bays of windows flanking an arched entrance. Inside, you'll find a variety of styles, from the spacious ground floor public rooms with geometric, polychrome tiled floors, massive stone fireplaces and frescoed friezes to the simpler but more restful sitting rooms on the upper floor, where leather couches add a zestful note of modernity.

The bedrooms are in a more rustic style, with wrought-iron or four-poster beds and antique chests that combine well with the exposed roof-beams and warm, terracotta floors. Bathrooms are spanking new and most have a shower rather than a bath.

The gardens are a delight, bounded by two streams and there is now a pool, but suffer unfortunately, from some noise from the road outside. The restaurant serves Umbrian specialities with oil and wine from the owner's farms - popular for weddings, so it may get busy at weekends.

A pleasant alternative to La Badia (page 231) if the latter is full or you find it too expensive.

~

NEARBY Oriveto (3km); Todi (33 km); Perugia (78 km).
LOCATION just outside Oriveto in its own grounds, ample car parking
FOOD breakfast, lunch, dinner
PRICE €€€
ROOMS 9 double, 1 single, all with bath (one with Jacuzzi), phone, satellite TV, minibar, air-conditioning
FACILITIES sitting rooms, dining room, breakfast room, garden, swimming pool
CREDIT CARDS AE, DC, MC, V
CHILDREN welcome
DISABLED not suitable **PETS** please check first
CLOSED mid-Jan to mid-Feb; restaurant only, Mon **LANGUAGES** English
PROPRIETOR Valentino Petrangeli

UMBRIA AND MARCHE

PANICALE

LE GROTTE BOLDRINO DI
~ TOWN HOTEL ~

Via Virgilio Cappari 30, 06064 Panicale, Perugia
TEL 075 837161 **FAX** 075 837166
E-MAIL grottediboldrino@libero.it **WEBSITE** www.grottediboldrino.com

THE FORMER PALAZZO BELLESCHI-GRIFONI, hewn into the walls of the medieval brick-built hill town of Panicale, was converted only in 1990 to its present use. In contrast to its stern front, the interior is small and intimate, designed in the finest contemporary manner, with particularly imaginative use of iron and wood.

The hotel can be entered through a doorway from one of the narrow passageways of the old *borgo* or, more conveniently, via the lower restaurant entrance on the road which encircles the town. A warren-like corridor takes you to the parquet-floored bedrooms. In surprising contrast to their modern finish, they are furnished with imperious late-19thC furniture – towering walnut bedheads, and so on. Noteworthy also is the gentle use of lighting.

New owners took over in spring 2003 and have spruced the place up a bit, adding minibars, hairdriers and so on in the bedrooms. We would welcome reports from readers, particularly about the rustic restaurant which serves Umbrian specialities: are its high standards being maintained?

~

NEARBY Castiglione del Lago (15 km); Città della Pieve (25 km).
LOCATION built into the town walls; car parking nearby
FOOD breakfast, lunch, dinner
PRICE ⓔ
ROOMS 11; 9 double and twin, 2 single, all with bath or shower; all rooms have phone, TV, hairdrier, minibar, safe
FACILITIES sitting room, breakfast room, restaurant
CREDIT CARDS AE, DC, MC, V
DISABLED access difficult
PETS small pets accepted
CLOSED never, restaurant closed wed
PROPRIETOR Laura Nicchiarelli

UMBRIA AND MARCHE

PANICALE

VILLA DI MONTESOLARE

~ COUNTRY VILLA ~

Loc. Colle San Paolo, 06070 Panicale, Perugia
TEL 075 832376 **FAX** 075 8355462
E-MAIL info@villamontesolare.it **WEBSITE** www.villamontesolare.it

HIGH WALLS KEEP OUT the arid scenery around, enclosing the stuccoed villa in a green oasis. The present building dates back to 1780, although the 16thC chapel in the garden suggests a much earlier house was on the site. When the present owners bought it, they set about restoring the 19thC garden (and the secret garden behind it), building the swimming pool a discreet distance away, and converting the villa without interfering with its patrician character.

The result is one of the most comfortable country retreats of the Trasimeno area. The bedrooms of the villa retain their original character – beamed ceilings, quarry tile floors and whitewashed walls, furnished in squirely fashion with turn-of-the-century high-backed beds, cabinets and wardrobes. The cool blue sitting room on the *piano nobile* certainly is noble, while the dining rooms and the bar are situated more humbly, downstairs. Since 1994 Rosemarie Strunck and her husband Filippo have converted several '*case coloniche*' and other outbuildings which stand outside the walls by the hotel's second swimming pool. These contain suites and superior doubles which are furnished in country style.

~

NEARBY Panicale (12 km); Città della Pieve (24 km); Perugia (25km).
LOCATION 3 km N of the SS220, direction Colle S. Paolo; ample car parking
FOOD breakfast, lunch, dinner
PRICE €€€
ROOMS 28 rooms; 21 doubles and 7 suites, all with bath or shower; all rooms have air conditioning, hairdrier, phone, minibar (not in main villa), TV, safe
FACILITIES 2 dining rooms, sitting room, bar, 2 swimming pools, tennis court
CREDIT CARDS AE, DC, MC, V
DISABLED one suitable apartment
PETS accepted
CLOSED never
PROPRIETOR Rosemarie Strunk and Filippo Iannarone

UMBRIA AND MARCHE

PESARO

VILLA SERENA
~ COUNTRY VILLA ~

Via San Nicola 6/3, 61100 Pesaro
TEL 0721 55211 **FAX** 0721 55927
E-MAIL info@villa-serena.it **WEBSITE** www.villa-serena.it

THE ADRIATIC COAST south of Rimini is not short of hotels, but it is very short of our kind of hotel, which makes this one a real find – a handsome 17thC mansion with some token castellations, standing in a wooded park high above the hubbub of the coast.

The villa has always belonged to one family – the counts Pinto de Franca y Vergaes, who used it as a summer residence until, in 1950, they turned it into a small hotel to be run like a family home. A natural host, Renato Pinto does the cooking, producing delicious, well-presented dishes (order in advance out of high season). Stefano and Filippo see to guests and reception, while their mother, Signora Silvana, busies herself in the house and garden, with its terracotta pots and orange trees; all the family are reassuringly down-to-earth. The emphasis is on character, simplicity and peace, not luxury. There are salons of baronial splendour, and corridors delightfully cluttered with bric-à-brac and potted plants. A few faded corners reinforce the villa's appealing air of impoverished aristocracy. No two bedrooms are alike, but antiques and fireplaces feature in most. A couple could do with painting and some trees could well be lopped to let in light.

~

NEARBY Pesaro (4 km); Urbino (40 km).
LOCATION 4 km SE of Pesaro and beach, in a large wooded park on hillside, with private car parking
FOOD breakfast, lunch, dinner
PRICE €€
ROOMS 9 double and twin, 1 suite, all with bath or shower; all rooms have phone and hairdrier
FACILITIES sitting rooms, dining room, bar, terrace, swimming pool
CREDIT CARDS AE, DC, V
DISABLED access difficult
PETS accepted
CLOSED 2 weeks early Jan
PROPRIETOR Renato Pinto

UMBRIA AND MARCHE

GATTAPONE
~ TOWN VILLA ~

Via del Ponte 6, 06049 Spoleto, Perugia
TEL 0743 223447 **FAX** 0743 223448
E-MAIL info@hotelgattapone.it **WEBSITE** www.hotelgattapone.it

THERE ARE TWO THINGS you can do in this hotel just outside Spoleto's centre. The most obvious is to gape at the unparalleled views of the 13thC Bridge of Towers spanning the Tessino Valley. The other is to enjoy the quaintness of its Sixties jet-set decoration, all wood, glass, chrome and leather. If you tire, as some do, of the oh-so-prevalent rustic antique look, then you will enjoy the now dated, but meticulously maintained 'modern' style of the much-loved Gattapone.

The hotel is a favourite of the Spoleto Festival crowd, and the walls of the American Bar are festooned with pictures of the famous and would-be famous who throng its salons late into the evening. Even if you do not stay at the Gattapone, you will notice it. From the outside it looks like a solid, two-storey villa with classic ochre walls and green shutters. Inside, one becomes aware how the original building and its more modern extension have been constructed downwards to exploit the hillside position. Many of the bedrooms have large picture windows to capture the panorama.

We have visited the hotel in low season and enjoyed the peace and quiet. During the Festival (Jun-Jul), rooms are hard to get.

~

NEARBY Assisi (48 km); Todi (42 km); Perugia (63 km).
LOCATION on hillside, just outside historic centre of Spoleto; no private car parking facilities
FOOD breakfast
PRICE €€
ROOMS 14; 7 double and twin, 7 junior suites, all with bath or shower; all rooms have phone, TV, air conditioning, minibar
FACILITIES sitting room, breakfast room, bar, terrace
CREDIT CARDS AE, DC, MC, V
DISABLED no special facilities
PETS accepted
CLOSED never
PROPRIETOR Pier Giulio Hanke

UMBRIA AND MARCHE

LE TRE VASELLE
~ VILLAGE HOTEL ~

Via Garibaldi 48, 06089 Torgiano, Perugia
TEL 075 9880447 **FAX** 075 9880214
E-MAIL 3vaselle@3vaselle.it **WEBSITE** www.3vaselle.it

THREE MONASTIC WINE JUGS discovered during the restoration of the original 17thC *palazzo* are what give this exceptional hotel its name and its theme: wine. Owned by the Lungarotti family, makers of Umbria's finest vintages, the *palazzo* is packed with still lifes of grapes, prints of the gods carousing and statues of Bacchus. However, nothing but sober professionalism characterizes the day-to-day management.

Bedrooms, some in a more modern building behind the main one and others in a luxury annexe a short walk away, are all furnished to the highest standards: comfortable striped sofas, antique chests, individually chosen prints and lamps give an air of unrushed elegance. Public rooms are open and spacious, spanned by sweeping white arches and softly lit. Breakfast, an extensive buffet, is served on a secluded back terrace. The restaurant is outstanding, with a wine list the size of a telephone directory.

A recent visitor to Le Tre Vaselle could report only improvements. It could not be more professional; you could not feel more at home.

~

NEARBY Deruta (5 km); Perugia (8 km); Assisi (16 km).
LOCATION in quiet street in village of Torgiano, 13 km SE of Perugia; car parking in nearby *piazza*
FOOD breakfast, lunch, dinner; room service
PRICE ©©©
ROOMS 61; 52 double and twin, 2 singles, 7 suites, most with bath, some with shower; all rooms have phone, TV, air conditioning, hairdrier
FACILITIES sitting rooms, dining rooms, breakfast room, bar, lift, terrace, swimming pool, sauna
CREDIT CARDS AE, DC, MC, V
DISABLED access possible
PETS not accepted
CLOSED never
MANAGER Giovanni Margheritini

UMBRIA AND MARCHE

UMBRA
TOWN HOTEL

Via degli Archi 6, 06081 Assisi, Perugia

TEL 075 812240 **FAX** 075 813653
E-MAIL info@hotelumbra.it
WEBSITE www.hotelumbra.it
FOOD breakfast, lunch, dinner
PRICE €
CLOSED Dec, mid Jan-mid Feb
PROPRIETOR Alberto Laudenzi

TUCKED AWAY DOWN AN ALLEY off Assisi's main square, this family-run hotel consists of several small houses with a small courtyard shaded by a pergola. The interior is comfortable and in parts more like a private home than a hotel; there is a bright little sitting room and an elegant dining room although meals are served outside in warm weather. However, we have had several negative reports about the housekeeping and general upkeep, particularly in the simple bedrooms. Readers have appreiciated the modest prices, the central location and the views but have been disappointed with the food and their rooms. Parking is a major problem.

BASCHI

POMURLO VECCHIO/LE CASETTE
COUNTRY GUESTHOUSE

Loc. Pomurlo Vecchio, 05023 Baschi, Terni

TEL 0744 950190/950475 **FAX** 0744 950500 **FOOD** lunch, dinner **PRICE** €; minimum stay 1 week in Aug **CLOSED** never **PROPRIETOR** Lazzaro and Daniela Minghelli

LAZZARO MINGHELLI'S 350-ACRE FARM estate stretches from the shores of Lago di Corbara almost to Baschi. His romantic family home, Pomurlo Vecchio, is an eccentric 12thC tower, jutting out of a wooded hillock. It also has four small apartments: they are homely, though when we last visited we felt they were rather frayed at the edges. The principal guest accommodation, Le Casette, stands on the other side of the estate. Three stone cottages have been rebuilt around a swimming pool. Though lacking the patina of age, they provide a summer oasis particularly suitable for families. Rooms are simply decorated. The restaurant, overseen by daughter Daniela, is noteworthy.

UMBRIA AND MARCHE

NARNI

DEI PRIORI
TOWN HOTEL

*Vicolo del Comune 4,Narni, 05035
Narni, Terni*

TEL 0744 726843 **FAX** 0744 726844
E-MAIL loggiadeipriori.it
WEBSITE info@loggiadeipriori.it
FOOD breakfast, lunch, dinner
PRICE €
CLOSED never
PROPRIETOR Maurizio Bravi

Tucked away in a quiet alley in the medieval heart of one of southern Umbria's unsung towns, this friendly small hotel provides an ideal staging post for travellers who prefer the 'backroads' route along the via Flaminia to Rome. As well as the magnificent Piazza dei Priori, the town's Romanesque *duomo* and the 14thC Palazzo del Podestà provide ample reason for an overnight detour. A lift, or a grandiose black oval staircase, takes you up to the comfortable modern bedrooms which look out into the central courtyard or over the pantiled roofs of the medieval *borgo*. A few have small balconies. Downstairs, the "La Loggia" restaurant spills out into the courtyard in the summer months. Its menu is mainly Umbrian and includes truffles in season.

NARNI

LOCANDA DI VALLE NUOVA
FARM GUESTHOUSE

*La Cappella 14, Sagrata di
Fermignana, 60133 Pesaro-
Urbino*

TEL & FAX 0722 330303
E-MAIL info@valenuova.it
WEBSITE www.vallenuova.it
FOOD breakfast, dinner
PRICE €
CLOSED mid Nov-mid June
PROPRIETOR Savini family

The Savini family moved to Umbria from Milan 20yrs ago because they loved the area; now, their 185 acre organic farm is thriving as is their delightful little guesthouse. Set in rolling hills just outside Urbino, the farm prodces its own wine, wheat, fruit and veg plus beef, pork and poultry, much of which features in the delicious meals prepared by mother and daughter. The six simple but stylish bedrooms are named after their colour schemes; all have a little sitting area. This is a relaxing place with a nice pool; there is horse riding on the property, and sightseeing nearby. Neither smokers nor credit cards are accepted.

UMBRIA AND MARCHE

OSPEDALICCHIO DE BASTIA

LO SPEDALICCHIO
MEDIEVAL MANOR

Piazza Bruno Buozzi 3, 06080
Ospedalicchio de Bastia, Perugia

TEL and **FAX** 075 801 0323
E-MAIL info@lospedalicchio.it
WEBSITE lospedalicchio.it
FOOD breakfast, lunch, dinner
PRICE €
CLOSED never
MANAGER Signor Costarelli

DESPITE THE ATTRACTIONS OF ASSISI, for the touring motorist there is much to be said for staying out of town. This one is the best around: a four-square manor house on the road to Perugia. The ground-floor rooms have high, vaulted brick ceilings and tiled floors with the occasional rug. The restaurant (which enjoys a high local reputation) is on one side – stylishly set out; in contrast, the sitting room-bar area is traditionally sparse with exposed stone walls. Bedrooms vary widely – some high-ceilinged, some two-level affairs with sitting space. The staff are courteous and helpful; their French is better than their English. We are pleased to hear that the noisy church bells are now stopped during the night.

PESARO

VILLA LA TORRACCIA
COUNTRY VILLA

Strada Torraccia 3, 61100 Pesaro

TEL and **FAX** 0721 21852
E-MAIL info@villatorraccia.it
WEBSITE www.villatorraccia.it
FOOD breakfast
PRICE € €
CLOSED never
PROPRIETOR Antonio Galeazzi

VILLA LA TORRACCIA is an unusual structure: a solid, rectangular house with a tower which seems to grow out of its middle. The 13thC building was constructed as a watchtower and later used as an of inland lighthouse which lit the way to Pesaro. This spot could make an ideal base for anyone who wants a bit of culture (Urbino and other art sights are within easy reach) combined with a bit of beach (coast, 4 km). Extensive restoration work was done in 1994 using traditional building materials. The rather intimidating dimensions of the house are softened by comfortable furnishings and some clever duplex arrangements in the spacious bedroom suites. These are all different, furnished with antiques and rustic pieces.

UMBRIA AND MARCHE

PORTUNUOVO

EMILIA
SEASIDE HOTEL

Collina di Portonuovo 149/A,
Portonuovo, 60020 Ancona

TEL 071 801145 **FAX** 071 801 330
E-MAIL info@hotelemilia.com
WEBSITE www.hotelemilia.com
FOOD breakfast, lunch, dinner
PRICE €€€
CLOSED Nov-Mar
PROPRIETOR Rafaella Fiorini

WE HAVE HAD MIXED reports about the Emilia recently, but have decided to keep it because of its wonderful position above the Adriatic, its relaxed atmosphere and the 'excellent seafood' served in the restaurant. The building itself is modern and undistinguished, but has a distinctive appeal inside thanks to the scores of paintings adorning the walls, left by artists in lieu of payment. The décor is bright, sunny and modern with big windows taking full advantage of views across verdant lawns to the sea. many of the bedrooms share this view and each has a balcony. Jazz and classical concerts are held on the lawn in summer.

SPOLETO

SAN LUCA
TOWN HOTEL

Via Interna delle Mura 21, 06049
Spoleto, Perugia

TEL 0743 223399
FAX 0743 223800
E-MAIL sanluca@hotelsanluca.com
WEBSITE www.hotelsanluca.com
FOOD breakfast
PRICE €€
CLOSED never
PROPRIETOR Daniela Zuccari

WHEN POPE INNOCENT II came to this spot in 1198, his presence is reputed to have caused a fountain to begin spouting, giving renewed strength to himself and his retinue. Today the site is occupied by an impressive 19thC building, with soft yellow painted exterior walls, which was transformed into an elegant hotel in 1995. The yellow colour scheme continues inside in the light, sunny hallway and sitting areas. Several of the pastel-toned bedrooms have a balcony or terrace; all of them are soundproofed and have a large bathroom. Right in the centre of Spoleto, but peacefully set in lush gardens, the San Luca also has a roof garden and a spacious courtyard, filled with flowers and olive trees.

LAZIO AND ABRUZZO

HOTELS IN LAZIO AND ABRUZZO

ALTHOUGH ROME IS A CITY of grand hotels rather than small and charming ones, we have made a couple of interesting discoveries for this new edition. These are the stylish **Locanda Cairoli**, in a converted *palazzo* (page 248), and the pretty **Sant' Anna**, conveniently near the Vatican and with the bonus of an attractive courtyard garden (page 267). A recent inspection confirmed that many of our favourites are going from strength to strength: among them, the delightful **Due Torri** (page 251) and its smart sister, **Fontanella Borghese** (page 252), friendly **La Residenza** (page 259), and the newly refurbished **Scalinata di Spagna**. We have not included the luxurious 37-room **Lord Byron** (tel 06 3220404), at the top end of the market (and of the Spanish Steps) or **Caesar House** (tel 06 6792674), a new and very sophisticated boutique hotel in Via Cavour, both are certainly less impersonal than most smart Rome hotels, but still impressively ritzy – and not really right for this guide. If you want to rub shoulders with the glitterati, the **de Russie** (tel. 06 328881), off Piazza del Popolo, is the place to stay. One-time haunt of well-to-do Russians, it opened after a total revamp in 2000; pricey but with fabulous terraced gardens and a spa.

Only 38 km north-west of Rome in Anguillara Sabazia and new to the guide, we have discovered **I Due Laghi**, a friendly country four-star (page 266). Also within easy driving distance of Rome to the north just outside Poggio Mirteto Scalo is the country-club-style **Borgo Paraelios** (page 246), and, on the coast outside Palo Laziale, **Posta Vecchia** is the 17thC mansion that once belonged to Jean Paul Getty (page 266). A stay here surrounded by the fabulous artworks and faded grandeur is an expensive but unique experience. Within day-trip range of the capital to the east are **Palestrina** (birthplace of the 16thC composer) and **Tivoli** (villas of Emperor Hadrian and the 16thC Cardinal d'Este). If you want to stay overnight in Palestrina, go for the **Stella** – an excellent, modern restaurant with clean spacious bedrooms (tel 06 9538172).

North of Rome is the pretty wooded countryside around the ancient city of Viterbo and Lago di Vico, the homeland of the Etruscans. Here we have another new find, a charming 17thC farmhouse, **La Meridiana** (page 267). East of Rome, **Antico Borgo** is a simple bed-and-breakfast in the medieval village of Fumone (page 245), and further north-west near Farnese, **Il Voltone** retains its appeal, set in gloriously unspoiled country (page 244). To the south, on Lazio's coast at San Felice Circeo, there's **Punta Rossa** (page 265), a pleasant holiday hotel, and on the nearby island of Ponza, **Gennarino a Mare** (page 247) is a delight.

Abruzzo is a wild and wooded mountainous region, forming part of the Apennine mountains. Charming small hotels are thin on the ground here and you might do best to explore the area from a base nearer Rome. Nevertheless you could try the tiny **Villa Vignola** on the coast at Vasto (tel 0873 310050), the medieval **Castello di Balsorano** at Balsorano (tel 0863 951236), and in Scanno, the friendly chalet, **Mille Pini** (tel 0864 74387), or **Del Lago** (tel 0864 74343), in a lakeside setting 3 km outside the town.

L'Aquila, the capital of the region, is a big town further north but still in the heart of the mountains. Though mainly a business centre today, the surrounding mountains and the imposing historical buildings within the town itself still make it an interesting place to stay. Try the **Grand Hotel del Parco** (tel 0862 413248), which with 36 rooms is smaller and less business-oriented than most of the hotels in the town.

LAZIO AND ABRUZZO

FARNESE

IL VOLTONE
~ COUNTRY HOTEL ~

Il Voltone, 01010 Farnese, Viterbo
TEL and **FAX** 0761 422540
E-MAIL info@voltone.it **WEBSITE** www.voltone.it

HARDLY ANYONE ARRIVES at Il Voltone without getting lost (make sure you have precise directions and don't give up on a road that seems never-ending); or without falling in love at first sight with this charming, individual hotel. A clutch of beautifully restored 17thC buildings – including a small church – colour-washed in pinks, yellows and creams, it stands high in the middle of a 465-hectare estate. Rolling hills, vineyards, woods and fields stretch out on three sides – scenery you can admire from reception rooms, bedrooms and even the swimming pool.

The unfussy decoration is more Tuscan than Roman with warm, fresh colours that echo the exterior. Floors are terracotta-tiled, scattered with the occasional Persian carpet. Almost everywhere table lamps cast a warm, flattering light. Bedrooms are graced with a few handsome pieces of furniture, and some have lovely old beams.

In the dining room, choose from a range of local dishes, made from the freshest ingredients, and drink wine from the estate's own vineyards. For relaxing outside, there is a terrace with tables and chairs, shaded by horse chestnuts and parasols. There is so much to see locally that the thoughtful Parenti sisters have planned itineraries for guests who want to explore.

~

NEARBY Farnese (12 km); Lake Bolsena.
LOCATION N of Farnese off the Ischia di Castro-Latera road; car parking
FOOD breakfast, lunch, dinner
PRICE €€
ROOMS 30 double and twin, triple and family, all with bath or shower; all rooms have phone, TV, hairdrier
FACILITIES sitting room, breakfast room, terrace, garden, swimming pool
CREDIT CARDS MC, V
DISABLED ground floor room with special facilities
PETS accepted by arrangement
CLOSED early Nov to early Apr
PROPRIETORS Daniela and Donatella Parenti

LAZIO AND ABRUZZO

FUMONE

ANTICO BORGO

~ VILLAGE BED-AND-BREAKFAST ~

Via del Fico 5, 3010 Fumone , Frosinone
TEL and **FAX** 0775 49791
E-MAIL lisaeagles@infinito.it **WEBSITE** www.italiaabc.it/az/anticoborgo

LITTLE SEEMS TO HAVE CHANGED over the centuries in the charming medieval fortress village of Fumone (the name means 'big smoke', after the smoke signals sent up from here to warn Rome of imminent invasion from Naples). No cars are permitted inside the old walls, still intact and with only two entrances: one facing Rome, the other, Naples. So if you arrive by car, you must park outside and walk through the labyrinthine streets until you reach this simple, friendly B&B in one of the ancient village houses. Once inside, all is airy and bright. Upstairs and down, the plain white-walled rooms are lifted by warm terracotta floors and attractive timberwork. There are wooden panels on the bar, wooden stairs, doors and even ceilings.

Don't worry about the lack of a dining room. There is a choice of restaurants and pizzerias in the village, two of them only a couple of minutes' walk away. Guests will be helped and advised by their delightful English host, Lisa Eagles, who, with her Italian husband Giampaolo, provides a very personal service. They will even pick up and drop off at Rome airport or local stations. In an area where this guide has no other hotels, we feel that Antico Borgo is a real find.

~

NEARBY Frosinone (21 km); Lake Canterno.
LOCATION in centre of Fumone, 12 km N of Ferentino; public car park outside fortress walls.
FOOD breakfast 50E
PRICE €
ROOMS 8; 7 double and twin, 1 with bath, 6 with shower, 1 single with shower; all rooms have TV
FACILITIES sitting/breakfast room
CREDIT CARDS not accepted
DISABLED access difficult **PETS** not accepted
CLOSED Nov to Mar
PROPRIETOR Lisa Eagles

LAZIO AND ABRUZZO

POGGIO MIRTETO SCALO

BORGO PARAELIOS

~ COUNTRY VILLA ~

Valle Collicchia, 02040 Poggio Mirteto Scalo, Rieti
TEL 0765 26267 **FAX** 0765 26268
E-MAIL borgo@fabaris.it

A 19THC VILLA IS AT THE HEART of this attractive country club-style development in the hills halfway between Rome and Rieti, with most of the
immaculately furnished rooms and suites spread around the beautiful gardens and courtyards, ensuring peace and seclusion for their occupants.
Each room also has its own terrace. Decoration varies from room to room,
but the predominant style is Italian 'rustic chic' – a blend of warm
colours, chintzes and period furniture. Some also have exposed rafters and
brass beds. The numerous public rooms are grander: don't be surprised to
spot a Canaletto or an Attardi among the fine paintings on their walls.
This show of wealth is not off-putting, however, and the place exudes
warmth and hospitality, thanks in great measure to the friendly staff.

One of the most relaxing places to sit is the huge covered terrace with
splendid views of the hills and masses of padded wicker chairs. Whenever
possible, food is served outside, and consists largely of simple but tasty
local specialities.

An excellent range of facilities includes indoor and outdoor pools,
sauna, Turkish bath and a minibus service to Rome.

~

NEARBY Rome (40 km); Marmore Falls; Lake Piediluco.
LOCATION 4 km N of Poggio Mirteto off SS313; car parking
FOOD breakfast, lunch, dinner
PRICE €€€€
ROOMS 18; 16 double and twin, 2 suites, all with bath or shower; all rooms have
phone, TV, air conditioning, hairdrier
FACILITIES sitting rooms, restaurant, games rooms, meeting room, spa, garden,
indoor and outdoor swimming pool, tennis, golf
CREDIT CARDS AE, DC, MC, V
DISABLED access difficult
PETS small dogs accepted
CLOSED never; restaurant Tues
PROPRIETORS Salabe family

LAZIO AND ABRUZZO

GENNARINO A MARE

~ WATERFRONT RESTAURANT-WITH-ROOMS ~

Via Dante 64, 04027 Ponza , Latina
TEL 0771 80071/80593 **FAX** 0771 80140
E-MAIL gennarinoamare@yahoo.it

THE *RAISON D'ETRE* OF THE Gennarino a Mare is its popular, buzzing restaurant, spread out over a covered timber deck, perched on piles, jutting into the sea. There are no prizes for guessing what the cuisine is based on – seafood, including fish and shellfish of all descriptions. The Gennarino provides moorings so, in the holiday season, hotel guests rub shoulders with yachties who come ashore to sample the daily catch.

A small blue-painted box-shaped building, with a backdrop of Ponza's colourful houses climbing the cliffside, the hotel is modest but full of sunlight. White-walled rooms are simply furnished with ceiling fans, brightly co-ordinating curtains and bedspreads, and balconies overlooking the sea; the best have large terraces with table and deckchairs.

The hotel had its genesis in the tiny *pensione* run by the parents of the present owner Francesco Silvestri, who has lived here all his life. A charming man, for whom nothing is too much trouble, he will direct you to the island's many natural treasures: beaches, cliffs, caves and grottoes. There are other hotels on Ponza but this one has the edge, combining a terrific restaurant, character and unbeatable prices.

~

NEARBY Chiaia di Luna beach; Pilatus caves.
LOCATION on waterfront opposite harbour; garage for 30 cars
FOOD breakfast, lunch, dinner
PRICE €€€
ROOMS 12 double and twin with bath; all rooms have phone, TV, minibar
FACILITIES sitting room, restaurant, bar
CREDIT CARDS AE, DC, MC, V
DISABLED access difficult
PETS not accepted
CLOSED never
PROPRIETOR Francesco Silvestri

LAZIO AND ABRUZZO

ROME

LOCANDA CAIROLI

~ TOWN HOTEL ~

Piazza Benedetto Cairoli 2, 00186 Roma
TEL 06 68809278 **FAX** 06 68892937
E-MAIL cairolo@tin.it

THE COLD STAIRCASE INSIDE the entrance to this *palazzo* doesn't prepare you for such a charming hotel on the first floor. 'Welcome Home' heads the brochure, which says it all: this *locanda* is deeply comfortable and fitted out in serious style. Opened in 2000, it was designed and is clearly loved by its architect owner Signor Chasini, who lives in part of the building. The atmosphere is bright and warm and the staff are welcoming and professional.

Opposite reception is a funky, small kitchen – all granite surfaces and 'Smeg' appliances. In the stunning room next-door, a simple breakfast is served at a long glass dining table, in front of a huge and beautiful hand-painted dresser. There are pale sofas, fresh flowers, and an impressive contemporary collection of art and sculpture, including works by the owner's family. All the woodwork is natural, and complemented by terra-cotta floors and tapestry rugs. Bedrooms are smart, with crisp mono-grammed linen, navy and white furnishings, Aubusson carpets, and high-spec bath and shower rooms.

It may not be ideal for families, but this little hotel is a comfortable and sophisticated address in central Rome.

~

NEARBY Campo di Fiori; Pantheon; Trastevere.
LOCATION SE of Campo di Fiori, on the SW side of Lago Argentina; public car parking nearby
FOOD breakfast
PRICE €€€
ROOMS 13; 11 double, 4 with bath, 7 with shower, 2 single with shower; all rooms have phone, TV, video, air-conditioning, hairdrier
FACILITIES sitting/breakfast room, communal minibar, lift
CREDIT CARDS AE, DC, MC, V
DISABLED no special facilities
PETS not accepted
CLOSED never
PROPRIETOR Luciano Chasini

LAZIO AND ABRUZZO

ROME

CELIO
~ TOWN HOTEL ~

Via SS Quattro 35/C, 00184 Roma
TEL 06 70495333 **FAX** 06 7096377
E-MAIL info@hotelcelio.com **WEBSITE** www.hotelcelio.com

THE MASSIVE BULK of the Colisseum stands guard at the end of the
quiet, largely residential street where stands the Hotel Celio. Those
two reasons – the quiet, and the proximity of the amazing ancient
arena (plus important nearby remains of the ancient city), make the
Celio a prime base in central Rome. Ease of parking (own small drive,
and a garage nearby), is a bonus, too, and driving in from Ciampino airport is no big deal – as quick as half an hour on the Via Appia. The
rooms aren't large, but they are rather fun if you don't mind deep red
brocade on the walls, and paintings and mirrors created by an artist
from Brescia to look at least 200 years older than they actually are. The
floors are wonderful: high-quality imitation ancient mosaic, designed
by the owner, Roberto Quattrino. There is no lift to the bedrooms, and
it is a moderate climb to the roof where guests can sunbathe and where
there is a penthouse suite, complete with own roof terrace and views
across Rome to St Peter's. Breakfast is served in fine weather in a
courtyard imaginatively roofed in with a tent.

~

NEARBY Colisseum, Roman forums.
LOCATION central Rome, near Colisseum
FOOD breakfast
PRICE €€€€
ROOMS 19 doubles and suites, all with en suite bath, shower; all rooms have
phone, TV, hairdryer, air-conditioning
FACILITIES roof terrace, breakfast area, sitting area
CREDIT CARDS AE, DC, MC, V
DISABLED no lift
PETS small ones by arrangement
CLOSED never
PROPRIETOR Roberto Quattrini

LAZIO AND ABRUZZO

ROME

CONDOTTI
~ TOWN HOTEL ~

Via Mario De' Fiori 37, 00187 Roma
TEL 06 6794661 **FAX** 06 6790457
E-MAIL hotelcondotti@italyhotel.com **WEBSITE** www.hotelcondotti.com

THE OWNERS CONTINUE to make improvements to this appealing little hotel located in an attractive street in the heart of Rome's chicest shopping zone. The warmly-lit reception hall looks inviting from the street side of the double glass doors; guests are greeted at an antique table, often by a professional and helpful Canadian. The reception incorporates a smart sitting area, where deep, squashy sofas in yellow and blue stacked with cushions are made for lounging, and there's a table laden with magazines and newspapers. Down a marble staircase is the attractive breakfast room where cream-coloured walls, touches of blue and soft lighting make the very best of a windowless basement. Here, unfortunately our inspector ate a disappointingly minimalist breakfast.

Most of the bedrooms (divided into two categories – standard and superior) have been refurbished, and now look tasteful and smart, though some of the standard ones are smallish and bland. The superior rooms are more appealing, with much larger bathrooms and terraces. Blue and gold predominate (a favourite colour scheme in Roman hotels) on fabrics and carpets while furniture and bedheads are in rich cherry wood. Five rooms in an annexe round the corner help satisfy demand for this rightfully popular hotel.

~

NEARBY Spanish Steps; Via del Corso; Villa Borghese.
LOCATION between Via del Corso and Piazza di Spagna; public car park nearby
FOOD breakfast
PRICE €€€
ROOMS 17 double and twin, 12 with bath, 5 with shower; all rooms have phone, TV, air conditioning, minibar, hairdrier
FACILITIES reception, breakfast room, lift
CREDIT CARDS AE, DC, MC, V
DISABLED access difficult **PETS** not accepted
CLOSED never
PROPRIETOR Massimo Funaro

LAZIO AND ABRUZZO

ROME

DUE TORRI
~ TOWN GUESTHOUSE ~

Vicolo del Leonetto 23, 00186 Roma
TEL 06 68806956 **FAX** 06 68805531
E-MAIL hotelduetorri@interfree.it **WEBSITE** www.hotelduetorriroma.com

THIS STYLISH LITTLE HOTEL in a quiet, cobbled lane just north of Piazza
Navona is a real discovery. The fresh, painted façade offers a foretaste
of the neat interior where the spacious reception area leads into a series
of comfortable public rooms. Marble floors gleam and provide a suitable
setting for some lovely antiques while chairs and sofas are upholstered in
red velvet or smart red and beige, a colour scheme which is continued
throughout the house. There are some fine antique mirrors (including a
huge one on each landing), old lamps and attractive prints, all of which
are offset by cool, cream walls.

The bedrooms (each with its own brass doorknocker) are arranged on
five floors and reached by an elegant marble staircase with *fin-de-siècle*
iron banister (or there's a lift). None of them is very large (one or two are,
in fact, quite small), but all are pretty and comfortable. Bedheads,
valances, curtains and bedcovers are all in co-ordinated red and beige;
attractive but never fussy. Some rooms have great views over rooftops and
terraces, excellent for an inside glimpse of Roman domestic life. Four –
including a single – have terraces equipped with tables and chairs.

A recent report describes the Due Torri as 'spotless and professionally
run ... a hotel, where guests receive very personal service'.

~

NEARBY Piazza Navona; Piazza di Spagna; Via del Corso.
LOCATION in quiet side street just N of Piazza Navona; public car park nearby
FOOD breakfast
PRICE €€€
ROOMS 26; 15 double and twin, 7 single, 4 family, all with shower; all rooms have
phone, TV, air conditioning, minibar, hairdrier
FACILITIES sitting rooms, breakfast room, lift
CREDIT CARDS AE, DC, MC, V
DISABLED no special facilities **PETS** accepted
CLOSED never
PROPRIETOR Cinzia Giordani Pighini

LAZIO AND ABRUZZO

ROME

FONTANELLA BORGHESE
~ TOWN GUESTHOUSE ~

Largo Fontanella Borghese 84, 00186 Roma
TEL 06 68809504 **FAX** 06 6861295
E-MAIL fontanellaborghese@interfree.it **WEBSITE** www.fontanellaborghese.com

O CCUPYING THE TOP TWO FLOORS of a graceful 16thC building, which once belonged to the Borghese princes, this elegant, modern hotel is under the same ownership as the more modest Due Torri (see page 251). A neo-classical courtyard separates it from the bustle of the busy road and a discreet lift whisks you up to the hotel.

The open-plan reception area gives a taste of the style of the establishment: smart marble floors, cool cream walls, leafy pot plants, some fine antiques and plenty of light. The space is dominated by a sweeping, open staircase in wrought iron, brass and marble, and behind this are several comfortable sofas which make a sunny spot for relaxing with a magazine. The owner has kept the decoration of the stylish bedrooms simple; co-ordinating fabrics (in green and cream on the lower floor, blue and cream upstairs), dark parquet floors, neutral cream walls, brass light fittings, some antique furniture and prints on the walls. Our latest inspector noticed some rather tired-looking decoration, but was assured that there is an ongoing programme of refurbishment. Bathrooms (off-white with the appropriate-coloured trim) are smart and well equipped.

This is a classy, inviting hotel, with an enthusiastic owner and loyal clientele, which offers reasonable prices for the standard of accommodation it provides.

~

NEARBY Augustus Mausoleum; Piazza di Spagna; Pantheon.
LOCATION N of the Pantheon between Via del Corso and Via di Ripeta; public car park nearby
FOOD breakfast
PRICE €€€
ROOMS 29; 21 double and twin, 5 single, 3 suites, all with bath or shower; all rooms have phone, TV, air conditioning, minibar, hairdrier
FACILITIES sitting room, breakfast room, lift **CREDIT CARDS** AE, DC, MC, V
DISABLED access possible **PETS** accepted **CLOSED** never
PROPRIETOR Cinzia Giordani Pighini

LAZIO AND ABRUZZO

ROME

GREGORIANA

~ TOWN GUESTHOUSE ~

Via Gregoriana 18, 00187 Roma
TEL 06 6797988 **FAX** 06 6784258

I N A PLEASANT SHUTTERED HOUSE, a mere 30 seconds from the top of the celebrated Spanish steps, Gregoriana makes a homely, and not prohibitively expensive, base in this very pricey part of Rome. Our recent inspector was also struck by the warmth of the welcome.

Her visit coincided with the start of six months of major improvement works, principally to create a breakfast room in the cellar. There was virtually no public space before, and breakfast had to be served in the bedrooms. As we went to press we learned that the hotel was due to reopen in August 2004.

Our inspector was told that much of the decoration – an extraordinary mix of rather dated Chinoiserie and art deco – will remain the same. A woven bamboo effect covers walls and ceiling in the tiny reception area while carpets are deep, Siamese pink. Upstairs, one landing is covered in leopard print, and another in William Morris. Inside the simple rooms, walls are light pink and Chinese-red lacquer furniture is mixed with rather dated seventies-style pieces. The best are at the back of the building where three have small private terraces and others enjoy peaceful rooftop views. Bathrooms are refreshingly normal with pretty floral wallpapers and white tiles. We look forward to seeing this attractively quirky little hotel after its renovation.

NEARBY Spanish Steps; Via del Corso; Trevi Fountain.
LOCATION just SE of the top of the Spanish Steps; public car park nearby
FOOD breakfast; room service
PRICE €€€
ROOMS 20 double and twin with bath or shower; all rooms have phone, TV, air conditioning, hairdrier
FACILITIES breakfast room, lift
CREDIT CARDS not accepted
DISABLED no special facilities **PETS** accepted
CLOSED never
PROPRIETOR Maria Novella Panier Bagat

LAZIO AND ABRUZZO

ROME

LOCARNO

~ TOWN HOTEL ~

Via della Penna 22, 00186 Roma
TEL 06 3610841 **FAX** 06 3215249
E-MAIL info@hotellocarno.com **WEBSITE** www.hotellocarno.com

To STEP INSIDE THE FINE *fin-de-siècle* doors of this stylish, wisteria-clad hotel just north of the Piazza del Popolo is to enter a time warp, somewhat faded, but with a dark, mysterious appeal that makes it a perennial favourite with musicians, artists and film-makers. The ground floor public rooms house the owner's impressive collection of original art nouveau and art deco pieces; fabulous lamps, Thonet bentwood furniture, old posters and, in reception, a grandfather clock with a resonant chime. The bar leads into a spacious sitting room where a fire burns in winter.

A birdcage lift creaks up to the bedrooms, each one different from the next, but all furnished with antiques, original lamps and rich fabrics. The spotless bathrooms are mostly in marble. New rooms and suites in the 1905 villa next door are more luxurious with opulent fabrics and more marble, though some guests might miss such modern practicalities as reading lights and power showers.

There is plenty of outside space, too; in warm weather, breakfast is served until 11.30 am either on the stunning roof terrace or in the pretty garden. And a fleet of bicycles is available for guests' use. The laid-back feel to this hotel and its understated glamour ensure that it is almost always full, even in winter.

~

NEARBY Piazza del Popolo; Villa Borghese; Via del Corso.
LOCATION in side street just N of Piazza del Popolo; public car parking nearby
FOOD breakfast, lunch, dinner
PRICE €€€
ROOMS 65; 51 double and twin, 13 single, one suite, all with bath or shower; all rooms have phone, TV, air conditioning, minibar, hairdrier; de luxe rooms have video and stereo
FACILITIES sitting room, breakfast room, dining room, bar, meeting room, lift, roof garden, terrace, free bicycles **CREDIT CARDS** AE, DC, MC, V
DISABLED some adapted rooms **PETS** not accepted **CLOSED** never
PROPRIETOR Maria-Teresa Celli

LAZIO AND ABRUZZO

ROME

MOZART

~ TOWN HOTEL ~

Via dei Greci 23b, 00187 Roma
TEL 06 36001915 **FAX** 06 36001735
E-MAIL info@hotelmozart.com **WEBSITE** www.hotelmozart.com

IDEALLY PLACED FOR SHOPAHOLICS on one of the narrow, cobbled streets that run between Via del Corso and Via del Babuino, the Mozart is one of the pleasantest of the numerous hotels in the area. It expanded a few years ago into the adjacent building, so there is an 'old' part and a 'new' part, two sets of stairs and lifts, and rather confusing warren-like corridors.

The lobby is a calm expanse of cool, creamy archways, marble floors and stylish parlour palms. On the first floor, a long, comfortable sitting room has pale yellow walls, dark hardwood floor broken by oriental rugs, invitingly squashy sofas, and handsome antique furniture. An open fire cheers up chilly evenings. Although small, the bedrooms, off light corridors, are smart and well-equipped, with pale terracotta floors and dark cherry wood furniture as well as the odd antique piece; the pokey singles are best avoided. In the bathrooms, chrome fittings gleam; one even opens on to a little terrace. The suites also have their own spacious terraces, and there is a delightful roof garden on two levels, equipped with stylish garden furniture and white umbrellas, from where you can see most of Rome. There is a little bar up there, too – a superb spot for an *aperitivo*.

Signs requesting that guests refrain from lingering over breakfast made our recent inspector worry that the hotel might have outgrown itself.

~

NEARBY Piazza di Spagna; Piazza del Popolo; Villa Borghese.
LOCATION in side street between Via del Corso and Via del Babuino; public car parking nearby
FOOD breakfast
PRICE €€€
ROOMS 56; 45 double and twin, 9 single, 2 suites, all with bath or shower; all rooms have phone, TV, air conditioning, minibar, hairdrier
FACILITIES sitting room, breakfast room, bar, roof garden
CREDIT CARDS AE, DC, MC, V
DISABLED some adapted rooms **PETS** not accepted **CLOSED** never
PROPRIETOR Mario Pinna

LAZIO AND ABRUZZO

PENSIONE PARLAMENTO
~ TOWN GUESTHOUSE ~

Via delle Convertite, Roma 00187
TEL 06 6792082 **FAX** 06 69921000
E-MAIL hotelparlamento@libero.it **WEBSITE** www.hotelparlamento.it

ONE OF A HANDFUL OF TWO-STAR establishments that we feature in Rome, this friendly family-owned *pensione* on the third and fourth floors of a 17thC *palazzo*, has an excellent central location for those on a budget. Anyone interested in the contortions of Italian politics can stroll over to the Quirinale in nearby Piazza del Parlamento to watch the comings and goings of politicians and officials.

On our latest visit, we were particularly impressed by the infectious enthusiasm of the Chini family and their staff. Their front door opens on to the tiled reception, where collages of postcards from grateful clients cover the walls. Murals brighten the next-door breakfast room, where the odd elegant touch (such as a glittering chandelier) softens the modern decoration. Bedrooms – where pale, dusty pink predominates – vary in size from quite large to tiny. Bedcovers are monogrammed, furniture is simple reproduction. Singles are amongst the best we have seen in Rome (try for Nos 92 or 109), and double windows keep the street noise at bay.

Some changes were being planned as we went to press, including the transformation of the rather scruffy roof terrace, and the creation of some new bedrooms opening on to it. Breakfast is always served here in the summer months. (The *pensione* will remain open throughout the building works.) Not ritzy or glitzy, but comfortable and clean, and perfect for families (particularly rooms 76, 82 and 108).

NEARBY Via del Corso; Spanish Steps; Pantheon.
LOCATION between Via del Corso and Piazza San Silvestro; public car park nearby
FOOD breakfast
PRICE €€
ROOMS 25; 15 double and twin, 4 single, 6 family, all with bath or shower; all rooms have phone, TV, hairdrier; some have air-conditioning
FACILITIES breakfast room, communal minibar, roof garden **CREDIT CARDS** AE, DC, MC
DISABLED not suitable **PETS** accepted **CLOSED** never
PROPRIETOR Plinio Chini

LAZIO AND ABRUZZO

ROME

PORTOGHESI
~ TOWN HOTEL ~

Via dei Portoghesi 1, 00186 Roma
TEL 06 6864231 **FAX** 06 6876976
E-MAIL info@hotelportoghesiroma.com **WEBSITE** www.hotelportoghesiroma.com

JUST NORTH OF LOVELY PIAZZA Navona and situated in the heart of what was the Portuguese quarter of 17thC Rome, the Portoghesi has an attractively old-fashioned look to it from the outside. Until a few years ago, it was pretty old-fashioned on the inside too, but major refurbishment has brought increased comfort although possibly at the expense of character.

Bedrooms (a few are large enough to be called suites) have been thoroughly modernized with quality reproduction furniture mixed with some antiques, padded bedheads, pleasant wallpapers and co-ordinated fabrics in rich colours. The new bathrooms sparkle. Depending on which floor you are on, views may include the neighbour's washing hanging out to dry or little terraces tucked away among the rooftops. The pretty glassed-in breakfast room, decked out in sunny, modern fabrics, and adjoining flower-filled terrace are at the top of the building, and look on to the ancient 'Torre della Scimmia' or 'Tower of the Monkey', so named from a legend which claims that a baby was rescued and carried to the top by a monkey in the 17th century.

A reader recently wrote to praise this small hotel's 'central yet quiet location' and 'delightful, sunny breakfast room', where she enjoyed 'a wide choice of fresh fruit and yogurt, croissants, cereal, juice and coffee'.

~

NEARBY Piazza Navona; Pantheon; Castel Sant' Angelo.
LOCATION in a side street just N of Piazza Navona; public car parking nearby
FOOD breakfast
PRICE €€€
ROOMS 28 double and twin, single and suites, 5 with bath, 23 with shower; all rooms have phone, TV, air conditioning, hairdrier
FACILITIES breakfast room, roof garden, lift
CREDIT CARDS MC, V
DISABLED access difficult **PETS** not accepted
CLOSED never
PROPRIETORS Claudio and Marco Trivellone

LAZIO AND ABRUZZO

ROME

RAPHAËL

~ TOWN HOTEL ~

Largo Febo 2, 00186 Roma
TEL 06 682831 **FAX** 06 6878993
E-MAIL info@raphaelhotel.com **WEBSITE** www.raphaelhotel.com

CLOAKED IN STALACTITES OF IVY, the Raphaël stands back from the bustle of Piazza Navona and belongs, instead, to the quiet refinement of the antiques and antiquarian bookshops and local *trattorias* of Via dei Coronari which runs beside it. The discreet façade conceals one of the most evocative and theatrical lobbies in the city. The dazzling white marble floor provides a dramatic contrast with the Byzantine icons, Old Master paintings, prints by the Italian Futurists and ceramics by Picasso displayed in baroque furniture; modern sofas add comfort. The dining room is equally immaculate, and the German manager has introduced an impressive new breakfast buffet. In fact, nothing disappoints here.

Bedrooms are slowly but constantly being updated, and, since our last inspection, some of the smaller ones have been combined to make fewer, more spacious, rooms. Older bedrooms drip in paisley fabrics, with co-ordinated padded headboards and bedspreads, and parquet floors. Newer ones are more modern and minimal, but not so beautiful, with bedcovers and sofas in Fendi's deep purple and black stripes and well-lit pale walls. Bathrooms, new and old, in white marble, are all stunning. Its final incomparable asset is the roof terrace, which offers magnificent views over almost the entire city. Book early to dine up here in the summer months.

~

NEARBY Piazza Navona; Palazzo Altemps; Santa Maria della Pace.
LOCATION at the N end of Via dell' Anima behind Piazza Navona; public car park nearby
FOOD breakfast, lunch, dinner
PRICE €€€€€
ROOMS 56; 49 double and twin, 7 suites, all with bath; all rooms have phone, TV, air conditioning, minibar, hairdrier; some rooms have stereo, safe
FACILITIES breakfast room, dining room, bar, conference room, fitness centre, roof dining terrace **CREDIT CARDS** AE, DC, MC, V
DISABLED no special facilities **PETS** accepted **CLOSED** never
PROPRIETOR Roberto Vannoni

LAZIO AND ABRUZZO

ROME

LA RESIDENZA
~ TOWN HOTEL ~

Via Emilia 22, 00187 Roma
TEL 06 4880789 **FAX** 06 485721 **E-MAIL** la.residenza@thegiannettihotelsgroup.com
WEBSITE w.thegiannettihotelsgroup.com

FASHIONABLE VIA VENETO is home to some of Rome's grandest hotels. La Residenza is not one of these, but its position, just a block away from the sweeping, tree-lined avenue, is only one of its advantages. It is a traditional, well-managed, good value hotel with an impressive entrance and exceptionally welcoming and professional staff. A bar and sitting rooms lead off the front hall on the elevated ground floor. Smartly kitted out in a deep-pink striped fabric, with cream on the walls, these have a mixture of modern and antique furniture, sofas, attractive paintings and a calm atmosphere. But in the stylish downstairs breakfast room our inspector found the service rather slow and the food a little tired-looking.

Bedrooms are very comfortable with huge beds, though bathrooms could be updated. Some have a glassed-in bath which might challenge the physically less agile. There are some homely personal touches, such as a fruit bowl and tea and coffee making facilities. The singles are very small and tend to be dingy. The larger doubles or suites are ideal for families; some have fair-sized terraces.

Unfortunately, due to new laws, the air-conditioning system has been relocated to the roof terrace, and almost entirely blocks what used to be a stunning view over Rome.

~

NEARBY Spanish Steps; Villa Borghese; Via del Corso.
LOCATION in side street off Via Veneto; limited car parking
FOOD breakfast
PRICE €€€
ROOMS 29; 17 double and twin, 7 suites, all with bath, 5 single with shower ; all rooms have phone, TV, air conditioning, minibar, hairdrier, safe
FACILITIES sitting rooms, breakfast room, bar, lift, patio, terrace
CREDIT CARDS MC, V
DISABLED access difficult **PETS** small ones accepted
CLOSED never
MANAGER Paolo D'Angelo

LAZIO AND ABRUZZO

ROME

SCALINATA DI SPAGNA

~ TOWN GUESTHOUSE ~

Piazza Trinità dei Monti 17, 00187 Roma
TEL 06 6793006 **FAX** 06 69940598
E-MAIL info@hotelscalinata.com **WEBSITE** www.hotelscalinata.com

FOR MANY VISITORS TO ROME, the Spanish Steps represent the heart of the city, a popular, lively rendezvous. At their summit stand two hotels which represent the epitomes of their respective markets: the Hassler, one of the city's grandest establishments, and this individual little *pensione* which, now more than ever, wins our accolade for genuine charm.

A major and recently completed programme of redecoration, by the proprietor's daughter, Claudia, has brought about some very pleasing changes. Rooms are now coated in pretty blue and gold floral fabrics and illuminated by Murano chandeliers. Neoclassical scroll sofas and small tables enhance a mood of comfort and intimacy. Although every room is done out in the same fabrics and colour scheme, individual pieces of furniture, large oil paintings and gilded mirrors make each seem distinctive. The new bathrooms are modern and well-equipped. The tiny entrance hall and corridors have been redesigned, too, with a new reception desk and polished stucco walls. Inevitably, prices have risen and are now among the highest of hotels in this category.

The breakfast area has also been refurbished, and here, on a recent visit, our reporter enjoyed a variety of fresh pastries, juices, fruit and coffee, although she was slightly disappointed that there was nobody on hand to make her a *cappuccino*. There are just 16 rooms, so book well ahead.

~

NEARBY Piazza di Spagna; Villa Medici; Villa Borghese.
LOCATION at top of Spanish Steps; public car parking nearby
FOOD breakfast
PRICE ⓔⓔⓔⓔ
ROOMS 15 double and twin, one triple, all with bath; all rooms have phone, TV, air conditioning, minibar, hairdrier, safe
FACILITIES sitting room, breakfast room, roof terrace **CREDIT CARDS** AE, DC, MC, V
DISABLED no special facilities **PETS** accepted
CLOSED never
PROPRIETOR Renato Bellia

LAZIO AND ABRUZZO

ROME

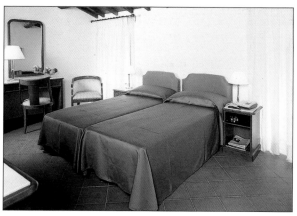

TEATRO DI POMPEO
~ TOWN GUESTHOUSE ~

Largo del Pellaro 8, 00186 Roma
TEL 06 6872812 **FAX** 06 68805531
E-MAIL hotel.teatrodipompeo@tiscali.it **WEBSITE** www.hotelteatrodipompeo.it

TUCKED AWAY IN A LITTLE FREQUENTED corner off the rather shabby but nonetheless picturesque Campo di Fiori, this is a relaxed, but very efficient, modest family-run hotel, where Paolo Cavarocchi, nephew of the owner, Lorenzo Mignoni, has taken over as manager. It has one unique and extraordinary feature: it is built on the site of the Teatro di Pompeo which dates from 55 B.C., and the breakfast room is hewn from the ancient tufa walls. The adjoining sitting room shares the same setting but is rather spoiled by ugly lighting; however, a table is thoughtfully laden with guidebooks, novels and magazines.

Upstairs, the bedrooms are simple, homely and appealing; padded bed-heads and bedspreads in attractive fabrics, the odd antique combined with good reproduction furniture and filmy white curtains add a touch of style to white walls and standard terracotta flagstones. However a recent visit revealed some bedrooms and bathrooms in need of a lick of fresh paint in places. Rooms on the top floor are cosier, with beamed, attic ceilings and those at the front of the building have a bird's-eye view, through efficiently double-glazed windows, of the sometimes noisy comings-and-goings in the *piazza* below.

~

NEARBY Campo dei Fiori; Piazza Navona; the Vatican.
LOCATION just E of Campo dei Fiori; car parking nearby
FOOD breakfast
PRICE €€€
ROOMS 12 double and twin, 6 with bath, 6 with shower; all rooms have phone, TV, air conditioning, minibar, hairdrier
FACILITIES sitting rooms, breakfast room, bar, lift
CREDIT CARDS AE, DC, MC, V
DISABLED no special facilities
PETS not accepted
CLOSED never
PROPRIETOR Lorenzo Mignoni

LAZIO AND ABRUZZO

VILLA FLORENCE
~ TOWN VILLA ~

Via Nomentana 28, 00161 Roma
TEL 06 4403036 **FAX** 06 4402709
E-MAIL villa.florence@flashnet.it **WEBSITE** www.venere.it/roma/villa_florence

THIS POPULAR HOTEL, LOCATED in a 19thC house on the busy Via Nomentana just beyond Porta Pia to the north-east of the centre of Rome, has emerged sparkling from a major refurbishment. Not only are the rooms now freshly and stylishly decorated but air conditioned and sound-proofed, with a number of new features such as modem plugs, trouser presses and Jacuzzis.

The newly-pointed façade is now an elegant pale yellow. The public areas have been refitted in a traditional style, suited to the period of the villa, with brocade wallpaper and heavy curtains. The bedrooms, once merely functional, are now considerably more elegant and comfortable, decked in richly-coloured, elegant fabrics (on walls, beds and curtains) with the colour schemes changing depending on the floor. The furniture is mostly good quality neoclassical-style reproduction which blends well with original features such as fine walnut bedroom doors. The smart bathrooms are also new.

There is a small, secluded terrace behind the house, on to which some of the bedrooms (in outbuildings) have direct access, and where breakfast is served on warm days. The private car parking – albeit limited – is a big plus in this city.

~

NEARBY Villa Borghese; Via Veneto; Piazza di Spagna.
LOCATION about 1 km NE of Via Veneto, NE of Porta Pia; private car parking in garden
FOOD breakfast
PRICE €€€
ROOMS 32; 27 doubles, 2 singles, 3 family, all with bath or shower; all rooms have phone, TV, air conditioning, minibar, hairdrier
FACILITIES sitting room, breakfast room, bar, lift, roof terrace, garden
CREDIT CARDS AE, DC, MC, V
DISABLED ground floor rooms available **CLOSED** never
PROPRIETORS Tullio and Fabio Capelli

LAZIO AND ABRUZZO

ROME

VILLA DEL PARCO
~ TOWN VILLA ~

Via Nomentana 110, 00161 Roma
TEL 06 44237773 **FAX** 06 44237572
E-MAIL info@hotelvilladelparco.it **WEBSITE** www.hotelvilladelparco.it

OUR INSPECTOR WAS FULL of enthusiasm after her visit to this mellow, 1910 villa situated in a little oasis of calm off the busy Via Nomentana and a 20-minute bus ride from the centre of Rome. It was worth the journey: she had found a delightful hotel with a truly warm welcome and very reasonable prices.

The pretty walled gardens to either side (where breakfast is served in summer) only partially protect against traffic noise, but once inside, all is peaceful and elegant. The reception lobby emanates a cosy glow with deep yellow sofas and armchairs grouped around a coffee table laden with magazines. An old grandfather clock, some fine oil portraits and a collection of covetable antiques add to the feeling of well-being. From here, steps lead down to a series of sunny rooms: a bar, two breakfast rooms and a sitting area. The ambience, here too, is both restful and tasteful; more antiques, green fabrics, plants and a mass of nicely-framed pictures. Bedrooms vary in size: some are quite small, others larger but all have touches of elegance. Six attic rooms were added a few years ago, and they are charmingly decorated in fresh greens and cream. Excellent value.

~

NEARBY Villa Torlonia; Villa Borghese; Catacombe of S. Agnese.
LOCATION in residential area, NE of city centre (Porta Pia); public car parking nearby
FOOD breakfast
PRICE €€
ROOMS 29; 15 double and twin, 14 single, all with bath or shower; all rooms have phone, TV, air conditioning, minibar, hairdrier
FACILITIES 2 sitting rooms, breakfast rooms, bar, lift, garden
CREDIT CARDS AE, DC, MC, V
DISABLED ground floor room available
PETS accepted
CLOSED never
PROPRIETOR Elisabetta Bernardini

LAZIO AND ABRUZZO

ROME

VILLA DELLE ROSE
~ TOWN VILLA ~

Via Vicenza 5,00185 Roma
TEL 06 4451788 **FAX** 06 4451639
E-MAIL villadellerose@flashnet.it **WEBSITE** www.villadellerose.it

THE AREA ROUND TERMINI TRAIN STATION is scruffy, but Via Vicenza is a once-elegant street lined with mellow old villas set in attractive gardens. Despite the presence of a few shady-looking characters, the location of Villa delle Rose is convenient for those who arrive in Rome by train. The warmth and enthusiasm of the Filippo family give it a friendly atmosphere and, ambitious for their hotel, they are continually improving its comfort and style. The bar-sitting room is surprisingly grand, with marbled columns, elaborate plasterwork and a frescoed ceiling. The basement breakfast room is somewhat stark, but is due to be updated this year, and serves a better-than-average buffet.

Recent improvements have brought two of the 37 rooms up to a much higher standard (Nos 110 and 111). More luxurious than the rest, they have green carpet, padded headboards and matching covers, large sofas and modern desks. The new bathrooms are tiled in co-ordinating colours. The other bedrooms vary (some have balconies), but they, their bathrooms and the corridors all have a lingering Sixties decoration that cries out for updating: apparently this is planned to take place over the next year or two. The pretty garden is a welcome and unusual feature so close to the station.

~

NEARBY Termini station; Villa Borghese; Roman Forum.
LOCATION in a residential street just N of Termini station; limited free car parking
FOOD breakfast
PRICE €€
ROOMS 37; 28 double and twin, 3 single, 6 family, all with bath or shower; all rooms have phone, TV, air-conditioning, hairdrier, safe
FACILITIES sitting room, breakfast room, bar, lift, garden
CREDIT CARDS AE, DC, MC, V
DISABLED ground floor rooms available **PETS** accepted
CLOSED never
PROPRIETORS Claude and Frank Filippo

LAZIO AND ABRUZZO

SAN FELICE CIRCEO

PUNTA ROSSA
~ SEASIDE HOTEL ~

Latina, 04017 San Felice Circeo
TEL 0773 548085 **FAX** 0773 548075
E-MAIL punta_rossa@iol.it **WEBSITE** www.puntarossa.it

SAN FELICE IS AN AMIABLE VILLAGE at the foot of the 550-metre Monte Circeo, which is an isolated lump of rock at the seaward point of a flat area, once marshland but now drained, except for zones which have been declared a national park. The Punta Rossa curves around the mountain in a secluded setting above an exposed and rocky shore, laid out like a miniature village. Reception is in a lodge just inside an arched gateway, and beyond that is a little *piazza* enclosed by white-walled buildings in rough Mediterranean style. Public rooms are light and beautifully decorated. Bedrooms are spread around in low buildings at or near the top of a flowery garden which drops steeply to the sea. All of them are pleasant, with balconies and sea views; but sizes vary, and, at our last inspection, some of the colour schemes looked dated. The main attraction of the suites is their generous size. The restaurant (food is 'exceptional' according to our latest report) is some-way down the garden towards the sea and glorious sea-water pool. In another rave report, a guest says his only regret was 'not to stay longer'.

~

NEARBY Terracina (20 km); Circeo national park.
LOCATION 4 km W of San Felice, isolated on rocky shore; private car parking
FOOD breakfast, lunch, dinner 350E
PRICE €€€
ROOMS 34; 27 double, 7 suites, all with bath or shower; all rooms have phone, TV, air-conditioning, minibar
FACILITIES bar, dining room, spa, terrace, garden, swimming pool
CREDIT CARDS AE, DC, MC, V
DISABLED access difficult
PETS not accepted
CLOSED never
MANAGER Maria Fiorella Battaglia

LAZIO AND ABRUZZO

ANGUILLARA SABAZIA

I DUE LAGHI
COUNTRY HOTEL

Loc. Le Cerque, 00061 Anguillara Sabazia

TEL 06 99607059 **FAX** 06 99607068
E-MAIL info@iduelaghi.it
WEBSITE www.iduelaghi.it
FOOD breakfast, lunch, dinner
PRICE €€€
CLOSED never
PROPRIETOR Matteo Marzano

IF YOU WANT TO BE WITHIN striking distance of Rome but based in the countryside, with a swimming pool in the garden and riding, tennis, golf and sailing on your doorstep, consider this friendly rural hotel. Originally a simple *agriturismo*, it has grown into a fully-fledged hotel, which still feels relaxed despite its four stars. It has a delightful hands-on owner, willing staff, and a reputation for excellent food, served in a large homely dining room or on a leafy terrace. The bedrooms tend to be uniform, with unexciting decoration but lovely views over the surrounding woods and fields. In addition to the 25 bedrooms, there are seven suites which open on to the garden.

PALO LAZIALE

POSTA VECCHIA
COUNTRY VILLA

Palo Laziale, 00055 Ladispoli, Roma

TEL 06 9949501 **FAX** 06 9949507
E-MAIL info@lapostavecchia.com
WEBSITE www.lapostavecchia.com
FOOD breakfast, lunch, dinner
PRICE €€€€€
CLOSED Nov to Mar
MANAGER Barbara Panzero

THE TYRRHENIAN SEAFRONT mansion that belonged to John Paul Getty and which he filled with fabulous artworks and antiques makes one of Italy's most remarkable hotels. Staying here, surrounded by priceless *objets* but with none of the formality that you might expect from a grand hotel, is a unique experience. While excavating the indoor pool, the remains of a Roman villa were discovered, which are now on display in a mini museum, visible through glass panels in the floor. The setting is spectacular, with six hectares of parkland and a formal garden on one side and the water lapping the dining terrace on the other – a wonderfully romantic place to dine on a warm summer's evening.

LAZIO AND ABRUZZO

ROME

SANT' ANNA
TOWN HOTEL

Borgo Pio 133, 00193 Roma

TEL 06 68801602
FAX 06 68308717
E-MAIL santanna@travel.it
WEBSITE
www.travel.it/roma/santanna
FOOD breakfast
PRICE €€€
CLOSED never
PROPRIETOR Viscardo Scialanga

O N A COBBLED STREET JUST OUTSIDE the Vatican walls, this pretty hotel is ideal for those who want to beat the daily crowds. Its lobby is carpeted and plush, with faux marbling, 16thC-style portraits and antique mirrors. A marble-floored sitting area, with leather sofas, leads out to a charming courtyard, where white iron tables, orange trees in pots and a lion head fountain make an attractive backdrop for breakfast. Bedrooms, though comfortable and well equipped, lack character, with built-in furniture and dull colour schemes. Those with murals have more panache. The marble bathrooms are immaculate, and rooms facing the road have balconies. Murals of Roman scenes brighten the subterranean breakfast room.

VITERBO

LA MERIDIANA
COUNTRY APARTMENTS

Strada Cimina 17, 01100 Viterbo

TEL 0761 344917 **FAX** 0761 306230
E-MAIL agriturismo@
lameridianastrana.com
WEBSITE
www.lameridianastrana.com
FOOD none
PRICE €
CLOSED never
PROPRIETOR Giandomenico
Ranucci

T HE SETTING IS IDYLLIC: a 17thC farmhouse at the foot of Mount Pallanzana, surrounded by 30 acres of olive groves, woods, lakes and rivers, 3.5 km outside Viterbo, an Etruscan city and storehouse of seven centuries of architecture. The five self-catering apartments are simply but tastefully decorated in rustic style. Rooms have terracotta floors, white walls enlivened by prints, timber ceilings and country furniture. In winter, there are open fires to keep you snug; in summer, you can throw open the doors to the garden, and there's a shared pool. Bedrooms are pretty, with calico curtains and wrought-iron beds. It's the perfect place for keen equestrians: the excellent Club Roncone riding school is next door.

CAMPANIA

AREA INTRODUCTION

HOTELS IN CAMPANIA

CAMPANIA HAS FOUR DISTINCT parts: the frantic, magnificent, decaying city of Naples; the fabulous coastline between Sorrento and Ravello; the islands of Capri and Ischia; and the coast and countryside north of Naples.

Don't fight shy of Naples. Plunge down its central artery, Spaccanapoli, if you do nothing else. An authentic pizza for lunch, and a more refined dinner at **La Cantinella**, next door to the **Miramare** (page 278) and owned by the same family, makes a good combination. The owner of our other recommendation in Naples, the **Soggiorno Sansevero** (page 279), has recently opened a new hotel, the **Palazzo Doria d'Angri** (tel 081 7901000/fax 081 211698) with its own dining room. Or, if you don't mind being some way from the centre, the **San Francesco Monte** opened in 2001 with 50 rooms in an impressive looking former convent on a hillside above the city (tel 081 2512461/fax 081 2512485).

Unless you are there for its thermal baths, crowded Ischia is less appealing than Capri, whose natural beauty is liberally doused in glitz. Ischia is harder work for the seeker of small hotels than Capri, but we recommend two. If these are full, you could try the 85-room **Hotel Terme San Michele** above the little car-free village of Sant' Angelo (tel 081 999276/fax 081 999149). Capri has a good selection, and we can also recommend the **Luna** (tel 081 8370433/fax 081 8377459) or, if money is no object, the exclusive **Scalinatella** (tel 081 8370633/fax 081 8378291) and, at the other end of the spectrum, **Villa Helios** (tel/fax 081 8370240), as a budget option. All our recommendations are in or just outside car-free Capri town (you walk to your hotel and your luggage is transported from the ferry by porter); we don't have any recommendations for Anacapri.

Hotels on the Sorrento and Amalfi coasts are well represented in the pages that follow. Sadly, the famous **Cappuccini Convento** in Amalfi has closed; and the **Caruso Belvedere** in Ravello (tel 089 857111) has new owners and has been closed for restoration for several years. We have been told that it will reopen in 2005. Positano, the famously pretty fomer fishing village has dozens of hotels; we believe that our selection is the best of the bunch. We haven't included the famous **San Pietro**, too plush for our purposes, but nonetheless a memorable place.

If you want to avoid staying in the tourist centres, you could opt for **Capo la Gala**, a neat modern hotel in Vico Equense below the Sorrento coast road (tel 081 8015758/fax 081 8798747), or the **Belvedere** at Conca dei Marini, once a stopover on the Grand Tour and with breathtaking views (tel 089 831282/fax 089 831439). We have made three new discoveries for this edition of the guide on or near the still unspoilt Cilento coast south of Naples; they are **Domus Laeta** (page 276), **Palazzo Belmonte** (page 293) and **Albergo Il Castello** (page 295).

Along the coast and in the countryside north of Naples we have just two recommendations, one on the coast at Baia Domizia, and one in the medieval village of Dragoni.

CAMPANIA

AMALFI

LIDOMARE

~ SEASIDE BED-AND-BREAKFAST ~

84011 Amalfi, Salerno
TEL 089 871332 **FAX** 089 871394
E-MAIL lidomare@amalficoast.it **WEBSITE** www.lidomare.it

L OCKED IN A TIME WARP, you might suspect this modest two star of being fusty; in fact, it has its share of charm. Floor tiles are burnished to such a gleam you can see your reflection; huge bookcases are bursting with battered leather-bound volumes; miniature figures are displayed in a glass-fronted cabinet; and the large high-ceilinged rooms are full of family antiques and traditional hand-painted furniture. From the entrance you can glimpse, through the family's own parlour, the charming old tiled kitchen where breakfast is prepared. It is served in the only reception room, where guests sit at little wooden tables between a grand piano and potted plants. With the exception of the minibar and satellite TV in every bedroom, and new Jacuzzi baths in every bathroom – grating additions to our mind – little seems to have changed at the Lidomare for the last 100 or so years.

Though the entrance to the 15thC house is off a little square, the front faces the sea and the best rooms, with small balconies, are on this side. The others have no view to speak of save the peace of the *piazzetta*. All are simple and spotless. From the moment you step inside, you know that this is not only a family hotel but a home, and the warmth of the owners resonates through the quirky old-fashioned rooms and corridors.

~

NEARBY cathedral and Paradise cloisters; Ravello (6 km).
LOCATION in *piazzetta* off Piazza del Duomo; public car parking nearby
FOOD breakfast
PRICE €
ROOMS 15 double and twin with bath; all rooms have phone, TV, air conditioning, minibar
FACILITIES sitting/breakfast room
CREDIT CARDS AE, DC, MC, V
DISABLED not suitable **PETS** accepted
CLOSED never
PROPRIETORS Camera family

CAMPANIA

AMALFI

LUNA CONVENTO

~ CONVERTED MONASTERY ~

Via P. Comite 33, 84011 Amalfi, Salerno
TEL 089 871002 **FAX** 089 871333

SINCE THE CLOSURE OF the famous Cappuccini Convento, the Luna Convento has become the most appealing Amalfi hotel. A five-minute walk uphill from the bustling town centre, it occupies two separate buildings, divided by the winding coast road – one of them an old Saracen tower perched right on the sea.

The hotel opened in 1822 (it is the oldest in Amalfi), and has been in the same family for five generations. But you only have to step inside to see that the building's history goes back much further than the 19th century. The unique feature is the Byzantine cloister enclosing a garden and ancient well. The arcade serves as a quiet and civilized sitting area and breakfasts are served within the actual cloister – a delightful spot to start the day. You have the choice of modern or traditional bedrooms, and for a premium you can have your own private sitting room. Lunch and dinner are taken either in the vaulted restaurant in the main building, where large arched windows give beautiful views of the bay, or better still across the road where the terrace and parasols of the tower restaurant extend to the water's edge. The swimming pool forms part of the same complex. The hotel is well known for its week-long cooking courses.

~

NEARBY cathedral and Paradise cloisters; Ravello (6 km).
LOCATION 5 minutes walk uphill from town centre, overlooking sea; car parking
FOOD breakfast, lunch, dinner; room service
PRICE €€€€
ROOMS 45; 40 double and twin, 2 single, 3 suites, all with bath; all rooms have phone, TV, hairdrier
FACILITIES sitting room, 2 dining rooms, 2 bars, cloister, swimming pool, disco
CREDIT CARDS AE, DC, MC, V
DISABLED not suitable
PETS not accepted
CLOSED never
MANAGER Signor Ciccone

CAMPANIA

BAIA DOMIZIA

HOTEL DELLA BAIA

~ SEASIDE HOTEL ~

81030 Baia Domizia, Caserta
TEL 0823 721344 **FAX** 0823 721566
E-MAIL info@hoteldellabaia.it **WEBSITE** www.hoteldellabaia.it

BAIA DOMIZIA IS A MODERN and quite sophisticated seaside resort, stretching along a splendid, broad, sandy beach north of Naples. But at the Hotel della Baia you are unaware of being in a resort at all. It is a low-lying white building, standing well away from the main development, and its lush gardens lead straight past the tennis court to the beach.

The hotel was opened about 35 years ago by the three Sello sisters from Venice, who have successfully reproduced the peaceful atmosphere of a stylish, if rather large, private villa. Spotless white stucco walls, cool tiled floors and white sofas are offset by bowls of fresh flowers and potted plants, and the antique and modern furnishings blend well together. The house feels lived-in, with books and magazines around, and an interesting range of pictures on the walls.

Bedrooms are no less attractive; many have balconies. A smartly furnished veranda links the house to the garden, and deckchairs and extravagant white parasols are set out on the lawn.

The hotel has traditionally aimed high with its food, and new reports, praising both the chef and the friendly restaurant and bar staff, confirm it as a most congenial place in which to eat.

~

NEARBY Gaeta (29 km); Naples within reach.
LOCATION in S part of resort, with gardens leading down to long sandy beach; ample car parking
FOOD breakfast, lunch, dinner; room service
PRICE €€
ROOMS 56; 54 double, 18 with bath, 36 with shower, 2 single, 1 with bath, 1 with shower; all rooms have phone, TV, air conditioning
FACILITIES 2 sitting rooms, TV room, dining room, bar, terrace, garden, tennis, beach
CREDIT CARDS AE, DC, MC, V
DISABLED no special facilities **PETS** accepted
CLOSED Oct to mid-May
PROPRIETORS Elsa, Velia and Imelde Sello

CAMPANIA

CAPRI

LA PAZZIELLA
~ TOWN VILLA ~

Via P. R. Giuliani 4, 80073 Capri, Napoli
TEL 081 8370044 **FAX** 081 8370085
E-MAIL info@hotellapazziella.com **WEBSITE** www.hotellapazziella.com

THE SCENT OF EXOTIC flowers greets you on the path leading up to this low white bougainvillea-draped villa set in a romantic garden of lawns, lemon trees and classical statues. Despite being so close to Capri town, birdsong is the only sound likely to disturb you here. Our inspectors liked La Pazziella: a smart yet well-priced hotel (at the lower end of its price bracket) that has successfully side-stepped Capri's glitter and gloss and strikes all the right chords.

The decoration is fresh and bright. Plain white walls and blue-and-white-tiled floors set off attractive polished wood furniture. Moorish arches, a recurring theme both inside and out, link one area to another, form niches and alcoves and announce flights of steps. Plants and flowers add colour to the ground floor sitting area and arched picture windows frame the garden. Breakfast is served on a glorious covered terrace.

Decorated in the same vein, the bedrooms are stylish and comfortable. Even the standard doubles have dainty writing tables and large antique chests. The superior rooms have their own balcony or terrace. The icing on the cake is the large pool with plenty of sunbathing space – quite a rarity on this island.

~

NEARBY Capri town; monastery of San Giacomo.
LOCATION off Le Botteghe Fuoriovado, 5 minutes' walk E of Capri town
FOOD breakfast
PRICE €€€
ROOMS 19; 17 double and twin and suites, 2 single, all with bath; all rooms have phone, TV, air conditioning, minibar, hairdrier, safe
FACILITIES sitting area, terrace, garden, shared swimming pool
CREDIT CARDS AE, DC, MC, V
DISABLED not suitable
PETS not accepted
CLOSED Oct to Mar
MANAGER Silvio del Pizzo

CAMPANIA

CAPRI

VILLA BRUNELLA
~ TOWN HOTEL ~

Via Tragara 24a, 80073 Capri, Napoli
TEL 081 8370122 **FAX** 081 8370430
E-MAIL villabrunella@capri.it **WEBSITE** www.villabrunella.it

THE VILLA BRUNELLA IS a great find on Capri because it perfectly combines the warmth and friendliness of a small, family-run hotel with Capri-style glamour and all the services of a much larger establishment. The drawback is the very long flight of steps to and from the bedrooms; if you can face those, you are on to a winner.

The hotel consists of a series of tumbling terraces, ending in a garden, with fabulous views of sea and coast across to Marina Piccolo. It begins with its restaurant, whose entrance is on narrow Via Tragara. With picture windows and a romantic atmosphere, it is staffed by friendly waiters and a characterful *maitre d'*, and the food is good. The hotel then continues down the hillside, accessed by the steps. Next comes the cosy, cluttered reception area, presided over by the charming and welcoming Ruggiero family, with the kitchen open to view next door. Then the glamour begins: first at the pool, with its spacious sun terrace where poolside lunches are served, and then, further down, in the bedrooms. These are a great surprise: very Capri, with silk materials, marble bathrooms, terraces, Jacuzzis, fancy bedheads and gladioli by the vaseful.

Here is a small, personal hotel, with all the advantages of the nearby Grand Hotel Quisisana, but much less formal; we loved it, steps and all.

~

NEARBY monastery of San Giacomo; Punta Tragara.
LOCATION on lane leading to Punta Tragara, 10 minutes walk from Capri town
FOOD breakfast, lunch, dinner
PRICE €€€€
ROOMS 20; 8 double, 12 suites, all with bath; all rooms have phone, TV, air conditioning, minibar, hairdrier, safe
FACILITIES sitting area, bar, restaurant, terrace, garden, swimming pool
CREDIT CARDS AE, DC, MC, V
DISABLED not suitable **PETS** not accepted
CLOSED Nov to Easter
PROPRIETORS Vincenzo and Brunella Ruggiero

CAMPANIA

CAPRI

VILLA SARAH

~ TOWN VILLA ~

Via Tiberio 3a, 80073 Capri, Napoli
TEL 081 8370122 **FAX** 081 8370430
E-MAIL info@villasarah.it **WEBSITE** www.villasarah.it

IT'S A STIFF UPHILL WALK out of town (on the road to Emperor Tiberius's palace, (Villa Jovis) to Villa Sarah, surrounded by a large, abundant kitchen garden. (As with all Capri town hotels, you can arrange to have your luggage carried by porter from the ferry.) The reward is peace and simplicity in a calm family-run hotel far removed from the bustle and vulgarity of the town.

Villa Sarah, set back from the road, is a spacious whitewashed villa whose bedrooms have old pictures and prints on white walls, plain curtains on wooden poles, dark wood furniture, tiled floors and simple bathrooms. The best have balconies and sea views. Breakfast is served in a no-frills dining room or on the terrace, with a good selection of rolls and croissants, home-made jam, yoghurts, cold meats and cereals. Afterwards, you can lounge on the terrace, and then take a turn around the garden. This is the pride and joy of Signor de Martino: vine-covered paths skirt trees laden with fruit, including oranges and lemons, as well as beds stuffed with aubergines, peppers, tomatoes and much more. The de Martino's love to treat their guests, allowing them to pick what they want themselves.

~

NEARBY Villa Jovis, Capri town.
LOCATION on lane leading to Villa Jovis, 15 minutes' walk from Capri town
FOOD breakfast
PRICE €€€
ROOMS 19; 14 double with bath, 5 single with shower; all rooms have phone, TV, air conditioning, minibar, hairdrier
FACILITIES sitting area, bar, breakfast room, terrace, garden
CREDIT CARDS AE, DC, MC, V
DISABLED not suitable
PETS not accepted
CLOSED Nov to Easter
PROPRIETORS de Martino family

CAMPANIA

DRAGONI

VILLA DE PERTIS
~ COUNTRY VILLA ~

Via Ponti 30, 81010 Dragoni , Caserta
TEL and **FAX** 0823 866619
E-MAIL info@villadepertis.it **WEBSITE** www.villadepertis.it

ORIGINALLY A NOBLEMAN'S country residence dating back to the 17th century, Villa de Pertis has been restored to provide plain but comfortable and very reasonably priced accommodation in the form of five bedrooms and two suites. Its owner, Nicola de Pertis, is a charming host and very knowledgeable about the area. This is a place in which to wind down: there is little to do other than to walk or bicycle (bikes provided) in the Matese mountains, or to wander around the medieval village of Dragoni with its fine church, and the nearby village of Baia e Latina. On your return you might be diverted by a game of billiards or table tennis. Dinner, featuring regional dishes in a firelit room, was 'special' according to one reader's report; others wrote that 'an excellent dinner was arranged, at short notice, almost exactly in line with our requests', and 'dinner was left to the chef and was simple but delicious'.

One of the same correspondents reports that her room was clean, cool and large, with a comfortable bed, a good bathroom and a wonderful view on to a small square in the centre of Dragoni where 'it seems time has stood still'. There is also a charming terrace overlooking the Matese hills.

~

NEARBY Matese lake (30 km); Naples (55 km).
LOCATION in small town of Dragoni, overlooking countryside; car parking
FOOD breakfast, dinner
PRICE €
ROOMS 7; 5 double and 2 suites, all with bath; all rooms have phone; suites have TV and hairdrier
FACILITIES sitting room, dining room, billiard room, table tennis, terrace, garden, free bicycles
CREDIT CARDS AE, V
DISABLED access difficult
PETS accepted
CLOSED mid-Jan to mid-Mar, 2 weeks end Nov
PROPRIETOR Nicola de Pertis

CAMPANIA

GIUNGANO

DOMUS LAETA
~ TOWN BED-AND-BREAKFAST ~

Via Gioia 1, 84050 Giungano, Salerno
TEL 082 8880177 **FAX** 081 7645862
E-MAIL domuslaeta@libero.it **WEBSITE** www.domuslaeta.com

BESIDE THE MAIN SQUARE AND the church in the small inland town of Giungano, but with a distant view of the sea, Domus Laeta has been the home of the aristocratic Aulisio family since it was built in the 17th century. The house is well preserved, with watchtowers, walls punctuated by loopholes, stables and mangers, a stone-built oil mill, cellars and bread ovens. In the lovely gardens a glorious swimming pool (with hydromassage) has been created from an old reservoir, fed by a spring-water well.

Inside, the house is tasteful and cultured; the tiled floors and timbered ceilings of the public rooms, unchanged over the centuries. The Aulisio family's heritage is evident everywhere: in the antiques and *objets d'art*, the portraits and other paintings, and the 3,000 rare books that fill the library bookcases. Occupying the original rooms, and some with historic names ('The Bishop's Antechamber' and 'The Bishop's Chamber'), the bedrooms are simple yet attractive.

Good value prices include a generous continental breakfast, and the Aulisios, always charming and accommodating hosts, will organize dinner specially if you request it in advance. There are also a number of *trattorie* nearby, serving simple local food.

~

NEARBY Cilento national park; Punta Licosa; Agropoli (10 km); Paestum (10 km).
LOCATION in centre of town; with public car park nearby
FOOD breakfast; dinner on request
PRICE €
ROOMS 5; 3 double, one twin, one suite, all with bath; one room has air conditioning
FACILITIES dining room, sitting areas, library, TV room, gym, terrace, garden, swimming pool **CREDIT CARDS** MC, V
DISABLED not suitable
PETS accepted
CLOSED mid-Jan to mid-Mar
PROPRIETOR Camilla Aulisio

CAMPANIA

ISCHIA

LA VILLAROSA
~ TOWN VILLA ~

Via Giacinto Gigante 5. Porto d'Ischia, 80077 Ischia , Napoli
TEL 081 991316 **FAX** 081 992425
E-MAIL hotel@lavillarosa.it **WEBSITE** www.lavillarosa.it

THIS IS A SHARP CONTRAST to our other hotel on the island, Il Monastero (page 295), in every way: it is immersed in a jungle of a garden right in the heart of the little town of Ischia, and its great attraction – apart from the garden and pleasant thermal pool – is its series of delectable sitting rooms, which are beautifully furnished with comfortable armchairs and ornate antiques. The bedrooms are furnished with 19thC pieces of Neopolitan, Sicilian and French origin.

The light, welcoming restaurant upstairs leads out on to a terrace over-looking the garden and the rooftops of Ischia, and meals are served there in summer. At one time only full board terms were offered, but we are pleased to report that Signor Amalfitano now offers 'room only' and half-pension terms as we have no evidence about the standard of cooking: whenever we have tried to send someone to stay, the hotel has been fully booked. Readers' reports would therefore be especially welcome.

Like many hotels on the island, the Villarosa offers thermal treatments of various sorts – with a private 'thermalist physician' on hand to super-vise – but the atmosphere is far removed from that of the traditional spa hotel, and those not seeking a *kur* will feel quite at home.

~

NEARBY Port of Ischia (500 m); Castello d'Ischia (2 km).
LOCATION 200 m from lido; with limited car parking
FOOD breakfast, lunch, dinner
PRICE €€€
ROOMS 40; 34 double and twin, 20 with bath, 14 with shower; 6 single, all with shower; all rooms have phone
FACILITIES sitting room, dining room, TV room, bar, lift, terrace, swimming pool, sauna
CREDIT CARDS AE, DC, MC, V
DISABLED access difficult
PETS not accepted
CLOSED Nov to Mar
PROPRIETOR Paolo Amalfitano

CAMPANIA

NAPLES

MIRAMARE
~ WATERFRONT HOTEL ~

Via Nazario Sauro 24, 80132 Napoli
TEL 081 7647589 **FAX** 081 7640755
E-MAIL info@hotelmiramare.com **WEBSITE** www.hotelmiramare.com

THERE ARE TWO COMPELLING REASONS for choosing the Miramare as your
Naples base. The first is its owners, Enzo and Bibi Rosolino (attended
by their comic-serious Skye terrier, Gavroche), whose warmth and charm
filters through to their loyal, attentive staff. The second is the rooftop terrace, with sunloungers, capacious hammock and terrific views across the
Bay of Naples to the Sorrento coast, Vesuvius and Capri. You will have to
ignore the roar of traffic on the *lungomare* below; this is Naples after all.
In summer 'an abundant and delicious' breakfast, according to a reporter,
is served here; you could also have a romantic *dinner à deux*, with dishes
brought in from Cantinella, the excellent Michelin-starred restaurant
belonging to Enzo's brother next door (discount for hotel guests).

The building, dating from 1914, is a gracious Liberty-style villa which
served as the American Consulate before becoming a hotel, well known for
its piano bar, The Shaker Club, in 1944. Nowadays the lobby and breakfast
room, in high romantic Neopolitan style, are resplendent in green, gold
and red Venetian and Florentine silks. Bedrooms, which have been carefully redecorated in the same mood, are compact, but they have high ceilings and tall windows, as well as effective air conditioning and thoughtful
extras such as kettles for tea and coffee and a supply of videos. The
best have sea views. The façade of the building and the ground floor bedrooms
were being renovated as we went to press.

~

NEARBY Piazza dei Plebiscito; Castel dell' Ovo; ferry ports.
LOCATION on waterfront road, 10 minutes' walk from city centre, close to ferry
ports; adjacent garage parking
FOOD breakfast; lunch and dinner available on request; room service
PRICE ⓔⓔⓔ **ROOMS** 30; 27 double and twin, 3 single, all with bath or shower; all
rooms have phone, TV, video, air conditioning, minibar, hairdrier
FACILITIES sitting room, breakfast room, bar, lift, roof terrace
CREDIT CARDS AE, DC, MC, V **DISABLED** access difficult **PETS** not accepted **CLOSED** never
PROPRIETORS Enzo and Bibi Rosolino

CAMPANIA

NAPLES

SOGGIORNO SANSEVERO

～ TOWN GUESTHOUSE ～

Piazza San Domenico Maggiore 9, 80134 Napoli
TEL 081 7901000 **FAX** 081 211698
E-MAIL albergo.sansevero@libero.it **WEBSITE** www.albergosansevero.it

PEACE REIGNS IN THIS no-frills guesthouse circling the internal courtyard of an old *palazzo*, but it hasn't always been so. In 1590, here in the home of the Princes of Sansevero, the troubled madrigal composer Carlo Gesualdo murdered his wife and her lover in a frenzied attack. But we didn't feel the presence of any ghosts in the newly painted cream bedrooms or their modern grey bathrooms. The decoration is modest – mosaic floors, functional furniture – but the rooms are spacious and prices rock-bottom. Our favourite is No. 6, 'Marechiaro', vast with a vaulted ceiling and more character than the others, and it only costs more. The owner, Armida Auriemma, a kindly Italian woman who speaks no English, is an unlikely property magnate, but she owns three other guesthouses in Naples: Albergo Sansevero, similar in style, and Albergo Sansevero (Degas), aimed at students, and her latest acquisition, Doria D'Angri, in Piazza VII Settembre, which occupies the *piano nobile* of an 18thC *palazzo* and serves dinner in a stunning frescoed dining room.

Breakfast is not provided at the Soggiorno Sansevero, but you'll find Scaturchio, one of the best known cafés in the city, in the colourful *piazza* below. Don't miss the Sansevero chapel next door to (and once part of) the *palazzo*, which contains an extraordinary, spooky sculpture, *Shrouded Christ* by Sanmartino.

～

NEARBY Capella Sansevero; Santa Chiara.
LOCATION in heart of city at Spaccanapoli; car parking at Albergo Sansevero
FOOD none
PRICE €
ROOMS 6; 4 double and twin and triple, all with shower, 2 single with shared shower; all rooms have phone, TV, air conditioning, hairdrier
FACILITIES none **CREDIT CARDS** AE, DC, MC, V
DISABLED not suitable **PETS** small dogs accepted
CLOSED never
PROPRIETOR Armida Auriemma

CAMPANIA

POSITANO

CALIFORNIA
~ TOWN BED-AND-BREAKFAST ~

Via C. Columbo 141, 84017 Positano, Salerno
TEL 089 875382 **FAX** 089 812154
E-MAIL info@hotelcaliforniapositano.it **WEBSITE** www.hotelcaliforniapositano.it

DIRECTLY OPPOSITE THE SIRENUSE (see page 285), this is another Neapolitan nobleman's *palazzo*, built in 1677, but in all other respects completely different. Come here if you want atmosphere, a warm welcome and (for Positano) budget prices. The *châtelaine* is Mary Cinque (English first name, but 100 per cent Italian *mamma*) who now runs the hotel opened by her father-in-law in 1968 and named after his much-missed sister who had emigrated to California. "I want my guests to be happy," she says, and she means it. Mary tries hard to keep up with modern requirements and a programme of renovation has recently been completed. Luckily most of the rooms, though plain, still retain an old-fashioned charm, and all have a balcony or terrace. No. 54 is large, with green tiled floor and high painted ceiling. No. 55 is even bigger. No. 61 is one of the rooms in which Mary has proudly installed a Jacuzzi, and benefits from windows on two sides.

The hotel's star feature, notwithstanding Mary herself, is the upper-floor terrace which stretches along the front of the building. It has a pure turn-of-the-century feel, leafy, elegant, dotted with wrought-iron and wicker furniture. There are no other public spaces; breakfast is served here or in your room. As the Eagles sang of another *Hotel California*, we thought it was 'a lovely place' - but we'd be reassured by some positive readers' letters, especially as we haven't yet been able to stay the night.

~

NEARBY Amalfi (17 km); Ravello (23 km).
LOCATION on road leading into/out of town, overlooking town and sea, 10 minutes' walk from waterfront; car parking
FOOD breakfast
PRICE €€
ROOMS 15 double and twin with bath; all rooms have phone, TV, air conditioning, minibar, hairdrier
FACILITIES terrace **CREDIT CARDS** AE, DC, MC, V
DISABLED not suitable **PETS** not accepted **CLOSED** mid-Nov to Mar
PROPRIETOR Mary Cinque

CAMPANIA

POSITANO

LA FENICE
~ SEASIDE BED-AND-BREAKFAST ~

Via G. Marconi 8, 84017 Positano , Salerno
TEL 089 875513 **FAX** 089 811309

GUESTS SHOULD BE ISSUED with a health warning before arriving at this unusual B&B. Some 400 steps (and a main road) separate the beach from the breakfast terrace, reception-sitting area and main bedrooms. Only the fit should attempt the climb (though a section can be done by stair lift). The rest of the bedrooms are in cottages that cascade down the steep cliff, reached by little staircases and narrow paths, ending with a glorious salt water swimming pool and waterfall, hewn out of the rock face. The pool was built by Costantino Mandara, the enterprising owner, who gave up being a vet in 1982 to turn his family home into a hotel. But Solomon the myna bird, Asuaro the dog, Tiberius the cat and a flock of geese – mementoes of his earlier life – are still in residence.

Handsome antique beds, huge *armoires* and family heirlooms fill the modest bedrooms, whose white walls and vaulted ceilings keep them beautifully cool with no need for air conditioning. Some of the cottages have private patios (we liked the one belonging to No 2). The trek from here up to the flowery terrace for breakfast is well rewarded by Signora Mandara's delicious home-made jams and Solomon's cheery *'buon giorno'*.

~

NEARBY Amalfi (17 km); Ravello (23 km).
LOCATION on Amalfi road, 15 minutes' walk E of centre of town; car parking
FOOD breakfast
PRICE €
ROOMS 12 double and twin, 6 with bath, 6 with shower; 1 apartment for 4; all rooms have phone
FACILITIES sitting area, terraces, swimming pool, private beach, fishing
CREDIT CARDS not accepted
DISABLED not suitable
PETS not accepted
CLOSED Christmas
PROPRIETOR Costantino Mandara

CAMPANIA

POSITANO

MARINCANTO

~ TOWN HOTEL ~

Via Cristoforo Colombo 56, 84017 Positano, Salerno
TEL 089 875130 **FAX** 089 875595
E-MAIL info@marincanto.it **WEBSITE** www.marincanto.it

WHEN WE VISITED THIS UNPRETENTIOUS B&B a few years ago, we were utterly charmed by it. Now it has undergone a dramatic transformation, emerging as a much sleeker, glossier and pricier three-star establishment. The entrance through the car park is unprepossessing, but once the lift has whisked you down to the main floor and a huge tiled room overlooking the sea across a flowery terrace, its charms become clear. From its stunning position, perched on a cliff on the outskirts of Positano, there is a panoramic view stretching out to sea and of the whole little town as it clings to the cliff face. The delightful Vespoli family have owned and run the hotel for several generations, and they and their friendly staff take great trouble to look after their guests, with small services such as turning down beds at night – a rare luxury even in much grander establishments.

Newly renovated in pale colours, with creamy curtains and attractive wooden furniture, bedrooms are divided between the main building, the best of which have balconies with sea views, and an annexe. The annexe rooms are larger and several have lovely secluded terraces. Steps lead down to the beach past a succession of terraces, some with sunloungers for everyone's use. Breakfast – outside in fine weather, inside if it's cold or wet – is an impressive buffet of cereals, juices, rolls, cake and cold meat.

~

NEARBY Amalfi (17 km); Ravello (23 km).
LOCATION on road leading into/out of town, overlooking town and sea, 10 minutes' walk from waterfront; car parking
FOOD breakfast
PRICE €€€
ROOMS 25 double and twin, triple and family, one suite, all with bath or shower; all rooms have phone, TV, air conditioning, minibar, hairdrier
FACILITIES sitting area, lift, terraces **CREDIT CARDS** AE, DC, MC, V
DISABLED access possible **PETS** accepted
CLOSED Nov to week before Easter
PROPRIETOR Celeste Vespoli

CAMPANIA

POSITANO

MIRAMARE

~ TOWN BED-AND-BREAKFAST ~

Via Trara Genoino 25-27, 84017 Positano Salerno
TEL 089 875002 **FAX** 089 875219
E-MAIL miramare@starnet.it **WEBSITE** www.starnet.it/miramare

WHATEVER BEDROOM YOU ARE GIVEN at the Miramare, an appealingly understated, discreet hotel and baby sister of the Palazzo Murat (see opposite), it will have a private sea-facing terrace, shaded by vine or
bougainvillea and furnished with table and deckchairs. The rooms were
revamped a few years ago and look stunning with white walls, terracotta
floors, elegant fabrics and antiques; minibar and safe kept well out of
sight. Bathrooms (Nos 209 and 210 with sea views themselves) are spacious, and decorated with hand-painted tiles.

The sitting room is an attractive area with a vaulted ceiling, more terracotta tiles, antique and pale upholstered furniture and plenty of plants
and flowers. The breakfast room is a delight: a glassed-in terrace with
bougainvillea hanging from the ceiling in great swathes, and views to the
beach far below.

Set on the steep hill to the west of the beach, down seven or eight
flights of steps (more steps lead to the seafront), the Miramare is a series
of old fishermen's houses joined to make what recent visitors call a 'positively gorgeous' hotel but they also warn that, 'It's not for people who can't
negotiate lots of stairs two or three times a day.' This was less of a problem
a few years ago when it had its own restaurant.

~

NEARBY Amalfi (17 km); Ravello (23 km).
LOCATION 3 minutes' walk W of main beach; car parking
FOOD breakfast
PRICE €€€
ROOMS 15 double and twin with bath; all rooms have phone, TV, air conditioning,
minibar, hairdrier, safe
FACILITIES sitting room, dining room, bar
CREDIT CARDS AE, DC, MC, V
DISABLED not suitable **PETS** accepted
CLOSED Nov to week before Easter
PROPRIETORS Attanasio family

CAMPANIA

POSITANO

PALAZZO MURAT
~ TOWN HOTEL ~

Via dei Mulini 23, 84017 Positano, Salerno
TEL 089 875177 **FAX** 089 811419
E-MAIL info@palazzomurat.it **WEBSITE** www.palazzomurat.it

MOST HOTELS IN POSITANO are ranged up the steep hills on either side of the ravine leading down to the sea. The Palazzo Murat, in contrast, is right in the heart of things – just inland of the *duomo*, and on a pedestrian alley lined with trendy boutiques.

The main building is a grand L-shaped 18thC *palazzo*. Within the L is a charming courtyard – a well in the middle, bougainvillea trained up the surrounding walls, palms and other exotic vegetation dotted around – occupied by the gorgeous, but pricey Al Palazzo restaurant, recently taken over by the hotel and specializing in Mediterranean cuisine. Breakfast is served here (though in spring early risers will find it sunless) and it makes a romantic spot for dinner. Along one side of this courtyard run the inter-connecting sitting rooms, beautifully furnished with antiques.

Bedrooms in the *palazzo* itself are attractively traditional in style – some painted furniture, some polished hardwood – and have doors opening on to token balconies (standing room only). Rooms in the more modern extension on the seaward side of the main building have the attraction of bigger balconies.

Positano's many restaurants are mainly congregated behind the beach, a short stroll away. 'Excellent value, stunning location', was one visitor's verdict.

~

NEARBY Amalfi (17 km); Ravello (23 km).
LOCATION in heart of resort; public car park nearby
FOOD breakfast
PRICE ©©©
ROOMS 30 double and twin with bath; all rooms have phone, TV, air conditioning, minibar, hairdrier, safe
FACILITIES sitting rooms, bar, terrace
CREDIT CARDS AE, DC, MC, V
DISABLED access difficult **PETS** small ones accepted **CLOSED** early Jan to first week Mar
PROPRIETORS Attanasio family

CAMPANIA

POSITANO

SIRENUSE
~ TOWN HOTEL ~

Via C. Colombo 30, 84017 Positano Salerno
TEL 089 875066 **FAX** 089 811798
E-MAIL info@sirenuse.it **WEBSITE** www.sirenuse.it

WE DIDN'T INCLUDE THE FAMOUS Sirenuse in the first editions of this guide, believing it too grand, and with too many bedrooms for our purposes; but our latest visit made us think again. It is, simply, too beautiful to ignore, filled with so many lovely things that it feels like a mix between a living museum of decorative arts and the private home of an aristocratic family – which is exactly what it was. Though until recent times Positano was a simple fishing village, it was always a popular summer destination for Neapolitan nobility, and this 18thC *palazzo* was the residence of Marchese Sersale. At the end of the Second World War, it was used as a rest house for a British guards regiment, some of whose members later wanted to return with their families. It became a hotel, still to this day owned and run by the Sersale family. Over the years, the *palazzo* has expanded to include more rooms (not all with views), a web of public and private terraces, a delightfully pretty swimming pool (which can become crowded in summer), and a glamorous restaurant with top-flight food.

The cool, white-walled bedrooms are heavenly, especially those in the old house. They are liberally endowed with family heirlooms – including fine paintings and delightful Venetian and Neapolitan furniture – which complement the original ceramics.

~

NEARBY Amalfi (17 km); Ravello (23 km).
LOCATION on road leading into/out of town, overlooking town and sea, 10 minutes' walk from waterfront; car parking
FOOD breakfast, lunch, dinner; room service
PRICE €€€€€
ROOMS 63 standard and de luxe double and twin bedrooms and suites, with or without view; all rooms have phone, TV, air conditioning, minibar, hairdrier, safe
FACILITIES sitting room, dining room, bar, lift, terraces, swimming pool
CREDIT CARDS AE, DC, MC, V **DISABLED** not suitable **PETS** not accepted
CLOSED sometimes in Jan
PROPRIETORS Sersale family

CAMPANIA

POSITANO

VILLA FRANCA

~ TOWN HOTEL ~

Via Pasitea 318, 84017 Positano, Salerno
TEL 089 875655 **FAX** 089 875735
E-MAIL info@villafrancahotel.it **WEBSITE** www.villafrancahotel.it

PROVIDED YOU ARE NOT WORRIED by heights, or by remoteness from the centre of things, this smartly traditional hotel has much to commend it. The position, high on the western side of the Positano ravine, gives an excellent view of the resort and the coast beyond from the windows and terraces – but does mean that the walk down to the resort centre and beach takes a few minutes and that the walk back up is exhausting. Happily, there is a private bus to and from the beach at certain times.

If the hotel's panoramic position is its first attraction, the second is its smart, cool sitting area – a series of interconnecting spaces with white-tiled floors and white-painted walls, linked by arched doorways. Comfortable armchairs with vivid blue covers are grouped around low tables, punctuated by enormous potted plants. The dining room has the same decorative style, and the food – mostly local specialities – is 'fresh, unpretentious and really delicious', according to our reporter.

Bedrooms are fresh, pretty and comfortable, though the standard rooms are small; the best have their own sea-view balconies. The glorious rooftop pool and terrace share the view.

We've had a number of very enthusiastic reports about this friendly hotel, which started life as a bar and has been in Mario Russo's family for several generations. He is now helped by his niece and a team of willing, welcoming staff, many of whom have been here for years.

~

NEARBY Amalfi (17 km); Sorrento (17 km); Ravello (23 km).
LOCATION on main road above town; car parking (paid valet service)
FOOD breakfast, snacks, dinner; room service
PRICE €€€
ROOMS 26 double and twin with bath or shower, 10 rooms in annexe; all rooms have phone, TV, air conditioning, minibar, hairdrier, safe
FACILITIES sitting room/bar, dining room, fitness centre, lift, swimming pool
CREDIT CARDS AE, DC, MC, V **DISABLED** access difficult **PETS** small ones accepted
CLOSED Nov to Mar **PROPRIETOR** Mario Russo

CAMPANIA

POSITANO

VILLA ROSA

~ TOWN BED-AND-BREAKFAST ~

Via C. Colombo 127, 84017 Positano, Salerno
TEL 089 811955 **FAX** 089 812112
E-MAIL info@villarosapositano.it **WEBSITE** www.villarosapositano.it

VILLA ROSA IS THE PARENT of the chirpy young Villa La Tartana (see opposite), by dint of the fact that its owners, the Caldieros, are the parents of Beniamino, the chirpy young owner of La Tartana. Although it lacks the freshness and zest of La Tartana, Villa Rosa has plenty to impress, and makes an excellent choice for a very reasonably priced stay in Positano. Its greatest assets are undoubtedly its spacious private terraces, all with fabulous views over the town and the Mediterranean. Its drawbacks are the many thousands of steps (well it seems that way) that lead from the road up to the reception lobby. However, as long as you are averagely fit you will cope, and luggage is taken for you.

Apart from the reception lobby with comfortable sitting area, there are no other public rooms, but the terraces more than compensate. The bedrooms are arranged on three tiers looking out to sea. Four have particularly huge terraces, which feel like a second room. Our favourite, however, has a charming lime tree plum in the middle, shading the patio table and chairs. There is also one family room, with two extra beds and a large outside table, and an apartment with two double rooms and a roof terrace.

Villa Rosa has the feel of a comfortable old house. Bedrooms are simply but pleasantly decorated, some with original tiled floors and large French windows. Breakfast is served in your room or on the terrace. The Caldieros have recently opened a restaurant, Caffè Positano, with a breathtaking view, a 10-minute walk from the hotel.

~

NEARBY Amalfi (17 km); Ravello (23 km).
LOCATION on road leading into/out of town, overlooking town and sea, 10 minutes' walk from waterfront; public car parking nearby
FOOD breakfast **PRICE** ⓔⓔ **ROOMS** 12 double all with terrace, 11 with shower, one with bath; one apartment; all rooms have phone, TV, air conditioning, fridge, hairdrier **FACILITIES** sitting area, garden **CREDIT CARDS** AE, DC, MC, V
DISABLED not suitable **PETS** not accepted **CLOSED** Nov to Easter
PROPRIETORS Franco and Virginia Caldiero

CAMPANIA

POSITANO

VILLA LA TARTANA
~ TOWN BED-AND-BREAKFAST ~

Via Vicolo Vito Savino 6/8, 84017 Positano , Salerno
TEL 089 812193 **FAX** 089 8122012
E-MAIL info@villalatartana.it **WEBSITE** www.villalatartana.it

DELICIOUSLY FRESH AND CLEAN, with simple bedrooms that feel good to wake up in and are a joy to come home to, this modern *pensione* has made a terrific addition to the hotel scene in Positano since it opened in 2000. The owner, Beniamino Caldiero, may be young, but he has the touch.

Villa La Tartana is pristine as well as admirably simple, and its good vibrations emanate from the fact that all the decorative elements have been chosen with attention to detail and an eye for quality, and all locally made, from the charming ceramic wall lights to the carved and painted bedheads and hand-painted bathroom tiles. Gaily tiled floors, white walls, floaty white curtains, a vase of flowers, a little terrace with pretty table and chairs overlooking the sea where breakfast is served ... delightful.

Villa La Tartana (*tartana* means fishing boat) can be found right at the base of Positano, near the main square and the beach. The sherbet lemon tiled reception lobby, reached via a flight of stairs next to the Caldieros' clothing and ceramics shop, sets the tone. The same zingy yellow tiles are continued throughout the corridors, which, teamed with plain white walls, account for much of the place's feel-good factor. Along with charming staff, and a good breakfast, well presented, we could hardly find a fault.

~

NEARBY Amalfi (17 km); Ravello (23 km).
LOCATION beside the church of Santa Maria Assunta, overlooking the beach and sea; public car parking nearby
FOOD breakfast
PRICE €€
ROOMS 12 double all with shower, 9 with sea view; all rooms have phone, TV, air conditioning, fridge, hairdrier, safe
FACILITIES sitting area
CREDIT CARDS AE, DC, MC, V
DISABLED not suitable **PETS** not accepted
CLOSED Nov to Easter
PROPRIETOR Beniamino Caldiero

CAMPANIA

RAVELLO

PALUMBO

~ CONVERTED *PALAZZO* ~

Via S. Giovanni del Toro 16,84010 Ravello , Salerno
TEL 089 857244 **FAX** 089 858133
E-MAIL reception@hotelpalumbo.it **WEBSITE** www.hotelpalumbo.it

ALTHOUGH IT HAS LONG been in our guide, we have not perhaps done jus-
tice to this lovely hotel, very much our kind of place in the luxury
bracket. It stands next to the much-vaunted Palazzo Sasso, but is in every
way different: while the international-style Sasso could be anywhere, the
Palumbo oozes individuality, panache and understated elegance. It feels
like a private house – or rather a private Moorish-style 12thC *palazzo* –
which is what it was until converted by its Swiss-Italian owners, the
Vuilleumier family.

Public rooms focus on the core of the *palazzo*, an inner courtyard
where Corinthian-topped columns, a dazzling deep blue-and-white tiled
floor, imaginative modern wall ceramics in the bar area, and comfortable
sofas and chairs create a strong first impression. The first floor-restaurant
is equally elegant, graced by lovely antiques and paintings including a
(school of) Caravaggio. Or you can eat on the terrace, with views over
vineyards to the dazzling blue sea below. Half board is compulsory in high
season, but this is no hardship. Bedrooms, accentuated by antiques and
rugs, are elegant and unpretentious, as are the bathrooms, some with
quite elderly fittings. We don't mind: if you want state-of-the-art, go to
Palazzo Sasso. Bedrooms in the annexe are much less appealing, and
much cheaper. More reports please.

~

NEARBY Villa Rufolo; Villa Cimbrone; Amalfi (7 km).
LOCATION perched on cliffs, close to town centre, 200 m from the main square;
garage parking
FOOD breakfast, lunch, dinner; room service
PRICE ©©©©© **ROOMS** 11 in main house; 8 double and twin, 3 suites, all with
bath; 7 double and twin in annexe, all with bath; all rooms have phone, TV, air
conditioning, minibar, hairdrier, safe **FACILITIES** sitting room, dining room, bar,
terrace, garden, swimming pool (by arrangement at nearby hotel) **CREDIT CARDS**
AE, DC, MC, V **DISABLED** access difficult **PETS** accepted **CLOSED** never
PROPRIETOR Marco Vuilleumier

CAMPANIA

RAVELLO

PARSIFAL

~ CONVERTED MONASTERY ~

Viale G. d'Anna 5, 84010 Ravello , Salerno
TEL 089 857144 **FAX** 089 857972
E-MAIL info@hotelparsifal.com **WEBSITE** www.hotelparsifal.com

THE PARSIFAL (WHICH WAGNER composed in Ravello) retains a certain monastic simplicity along with its 13thC cloister. The former convent is still owned by nuns, but for many years now has been a family-run hotel. On a recent visit we discovered that the place has changed hands, and is now run by Antonio Mansi and his young family. Signor Mansi comes from Ravello, and worked at the Parsifal as a teenager. He went on to become manager of the famous Danieli in Venice, before returning home to pursue his dream of owning his own small-scale hotel. It couldn't be more different than the Danieli: though professional, the family are particularly friendly and willing to please.

While gradually upgrading the Parsifal (the hotel had become very tired), Signor Mansi wants to retain its simple feel. Certainly the panoramic but dowdy dining room could do with his attention, but it has heart-stopping views. Here, and on the creeper-clad terrace, honest food with creative touches is served (half-board is compulsory for three nights or less). Bedrooms are plainly furnished, and some are smallish: ask for the one with the terrace and sea view. Recent reports have been positive.

~

NEARBY Villa Rufolo; Villa Cimbrone; Amalfi (7 km).
LOCATION overlooking the town and sea, 5 minutes' walk from main square; parking in street or public garage nearby
FOOD breakfast, lunch, dinner
PRICE €€
ROOMS 19; 18 double and twin, 1 single, 10 with bath, 9 with shower, 8 with sea view; all rooms have phone, TV
FACILITIES sitting room, dining room, bar, terrace, garden
CREDIT CARDS AE, DC, MC, V
DISABLED not suitable
PETS accepted
CLOSED never
PROPRIETOR Antonio Mansi

CAMPANIA

RAVELLO

VILLA CIMBRONE
~ TOWN VILLA ~

Via Santa Chiara 26, 84010 Ravello Salerno
TEL 089 857459/858072 **FAX** 089 857777
E-MAIL info@villacimbrone.it **WEBSITE** www.villacimbrone.it

IT'S HARD TO IMAGINE a more romantic setting than the Villa Cimbrone's, in the fabulous gardens laid out by English aristocrat Lord Grimthorpe in the early 19th century. A formal network of paths and beds with wilder landscaped areas, they boast a belvedere, from where you can admire 'the most beautiful view in the world', according to Ravello *habitué* Gore Vidal. The villa is equally enchanting. A 12thC building, revived by Grimthorpe and recently restored again, it has kept all its period features including splendid stone fireplaces and tiled floors, and is crammed with knick-knacks, books, oil paintings and antiques. Through white Gothic doors, the comfortable bedrooms are all individually and exquisitely decorated. It feels exactly like a private house, and it's easy to see why the famous, from D.H. Lawrence to Greta Garbo and her lover Leopold Stokowsky, have taken refuge here.

When we visited the Villa Cimbrone, we felt that all it lacked was its own restaurant. We have just heard that it is planning to open one, which should be a great addition to this lovely place. It will mean that guests won't have to make the 10-minute walk into town for dinner every night, and simply relish having the gardens all to themselves once the daytime visitors have left.

~

NEARBY Monastero di Santa Chiara; Convento di San Francesco.
LOCATION in Villa Cimbrone gardens, 10 minutes' walk from town centre; public car park in town (luggage service)
FOOD breakfast, lunch, dinner
PRICE €€€€
ROOMS 19; 15 double and twin, one single, 2 suites, all with bath or shower; all rooms have phone, TV, air conditioning, minibar, hairdrier, safe
FACILITIES sitting room, breakfast room, dining room, terrace, garden, tennis
CREDIT CARDS AE, MC, V
DISABLED access difficult **PETS** not accepted **CLOSED** Nov to Apr
MANAGER Giorgio Vuilleumier

CAMPANIA

VILLA MARIA
~ TOWN VILLA ~

Via Santa Chiara 2, 84010 Ravello , Salerno
TEL 089 857255 **FAX** 089 857071
E-MAIL villamaria@villamaria.it **WEBSITE** www.villamaria.it

SIT IN THE SUNSHINE AT one of the tables in the Villa Maria's lovely garden restaurant, sip chilled white wine, eat perfectly cooked pasta and enjoy the glorious vista of mountains sweeping down to a glittering sea. This is an understandably popular place. Inside, a charming medley of potted palms, busts, piano, inlaid furniture and silver arranged on wooden shelves lends the old villa a distinctly Edwardian feel. Up the marble staircase and through heavy wooden doors, the bedrooms strike the same note, with vaulted ceilings and solid furniture. Though almost double the price of a standard room, No. 3 is a cut above the rest, with its huge terrace, five sets of French windows and handsome *secretaire*. In a modern annexe there are six rooms with picture windows but little character.

Never far behind the scenes is the kindly Vincenzo Palumbo, who keeps a book of comments from his guests ('The food was superb – the best in all of Europe'), masterminds cookery courses and walking tours, and enjoys rubbing shoulders with the stars. Guests may use nearby Villa Eva's lawn (useful for kids) and the pool belonging to sister hotel, the Giordano.

A recent inspection revealed that little has changed at the Villa Maria, and the food is still 'delicious'.

~

NEARBY Convento di San Francesco; Villa Cimbrone.
LOCATION on path leading to Villa Cimbrone, 5 minutes' walk from town centre; car parking
FOOD breakfast, lunch, dinner
PRICE €€€
ROOMS 24 double and twin with bath or shower; all rooms have phone, TV, air-conditioning, minibar, hairdrier, safe
FACILITIES sitting room, breakfast room, dining room, dining terrace, garden, swimming pool **CREDIT CARDS** AE, DC, MC, V
DISABLED access difficult
PETS accepted **CLOSED** never
PROPRIETOR Vincenzo Palumbo

CAMPANIA

SANTA MARIA DI CASTELLABATE

PALAZZO BELMONTE
~ SEASIDE APARTMENTS ~

84072 Santa Maria di Castellabate, Salerno
TEL 0974 960211 **FAX** 0974 961150
E-MAIL belmonte@costacilento.it **WEBSITE** www.palazzobelmonte.com

JUST A STEP FROM THE COLOURFUL houses and brightly painted fishing boats of this attractive resort, the Palazzo Belmonte stands in complete privacy, surrounded by a large park enclosed by high stone walls. The *palazzo* has been in the Prince of Belmonte's family since it was built in the 17th century as a hunting lodge, where guests often included the kings of Italy and Spain.

The Prince still lives here in a top-floor apartment. The rest of the *palazzo* and neighbouring Edoardo's House have been converted into 20 guest suites and self-catering apartments of different sizes. Rooms are large, airy but not air conditioned, with their original features untouched. Many have vaulted ceilings; some private terraces. You can choose to overlook the walled courtyard, where the scent of jasmine perfumes the air, or the beautiful gardens and the sea. Despite the grandeur, the atmosphere is relaxed. Within the park, Villa Belmonte has 27 luxurious new air-conditioned rooms with private terraces and sea views.

A path through the garden leads to a gorgeous swimming pool, bordered by flowers, and beyond to a gate, which takes you down to the sandy gently-shelving beach, solely for guests' use and perfect for children. If you don't feel like cooking, meals are served in the Belvedere restaurant or on the terrace; breakfast and drinks at the pool bar.

~

NEARBY Cilento national park; Punta Licosa; Agropoli (15 km); Paestum (40 km).
LOCATION on the edge of town; car parking
FOOD breakfast, lunch, dinner
PRICE €€€€
ROOMS 47 double rooms, suites and apartments with bathroom or shower; all have phone, TV, hairdrier; some have air conditioning, kitchen facilities, terrace
FACILITIES restaurant, meeting rooms, terrace, garden, swimming pool, pool bar, private beach **CREDIT CARDS** MC, V
DISABLED not suitable **PETS** not accepted **CLOSED** Nov to Apr
PROPRIETOR Principe Angelo di Belmonte

CAMPANIA

SORRENTO

LA BADIA

~ OUT-OF-TOWN VILLA ~

Via Nastro Verde 8, 80067 Sorrento, Napoli
TEL 081 878 1154 **FAX** 081 8074159
E-MAIL info@hotellabadia.it **WEBSITE** www.hotellabadia.it

O N FIRST ACQUAINTANCE La Badia, simple and old-fashioned, seemed a great new find, almost too good to be true, until we discovered at dinner that it was a base for package tours and not a find at all. Nevertheless, if you can overlook the mainly British babble at mealtimes, you will find other compensations, not least the lovely hilly setting in on the outskirts of town, set amid groves of olives and oranges, with stunning views across the Bay of Sorrento. Then there is the pretty circular swimming pool, surrounded by greenery, and the several terraces, both on the roof and at ground level.

Run by the Picco family for decades (mother oversees, daughter serves, granddaughter runs around), this handsome 16thC former monastery, has changed little. There are lace curtains, bamboo blinds, Edwardian family antiques, potted plants, dark stained doors and wooden shutters. Rooms, many with lovely views, are plain and elderly but spacious, with simple bathrooms. A plant-filled courtyard separates the reception area from the bedrooms, and a door at the end of the first-floor corridor leads to a charming, little-used *loggia* overlooking the olive groves. The dinner menu is limited and the food as old-fashioned as the house (tinned fruit salad for dessert), but all in all we felt we had value for money. A recent reader loved the tranquillity and the views, but also found the food disappointing.

~

NEARBY Sorrento; Amalfi coast.
LOCATION in hills, 2 km by road outside Sorrento, 10 minutes' walk by path from town centre; ample car parking
FOOD breakfast, lunch, dinner
PRICE €
ROOMS 14 double and twin, all with shower; all rooms have phone, TV, hairdrier; some have air conditioning
FACILITIES sitting room, dining room, bar, lift, terraces, garden, swimming pool
CREDIT CARDS MC, V **DISABLED** access possible
PETS accepted **CLOSED** Nov to mid-Mar
PROPRIETOR Marisa Picco

CAMPANIA

CASTELLABATE

ALBERGO IL CASTELLO
TOWN HOTEL

Via Amendola 1, 84048
Castellabate, Salerno
TEL and **FAX** 0974 967169
E-MAIL castello@costacilento.it
WEBSITE www.hotelcastello.co.uk
FOOD breakfast; lunch and dinner
on request **PRICE** ©
CLOSED Nov to Apr
PROPRIETOR Franca Di Biasi

THE RELATIVELY UNDISCOVERED Cilento coast is dotted with sandy beaches and picturesque resorts. Perched above one of these, Santa Maria, is the medieval hill town of Castellabate and this friendly 17thC *albergo*, recommended to us by a reader. Bedrooms are fresh and simple: all white walls and linen, majolica-tiled floors and period furniture. Some have their own terrace or balcony with views over the Cilento national park. A breakfast of fresh croissants, homemade jam and buffalo mozzarella straight from the farm is served on the main terrace under the shade of a giant fig tree. Equally delicious lunches and dinners can be provided. The welcoming owner and staff quickly made our reader feel part of the family.

ISCHIA

IL MONASTERO
CONVERTED MONASTERY

Castello Aragonese 3, Ischia
Ponte, 80070 Ischia , Napoli
TEL 081 992435
FAX 081 991849 **E-MAIL**
ilmonastero @castelloaragonese.it
WEBSITE www.castelloaragonese.it
FOOD breakfast, dinner
PRICE ©©
CLOSED mid-Oct to Easter
PROPRIETOR Nicola Mattera

ISCHIA PONTE GETS ITS NAME from the low bridge to the precipitous islet on top of which stands the island's original settlement, known collectively as the Castello, although it consists of several buildings. One of these is an old monastery, run as a simple but captivating *pensione* with an amiable *padrone*. Paintings hang on the plain walls of the hallway and the neat little sitting room. Bedrooms, white with blue tiles, are the former monks' cells and correspondingly simple; some are reached from the spacious terrace, which gives a breathtaking view of the town and the island. Recent improvements mean that every bedroom now has its own shower or bathroom, half board is no longer obligatory, and simple snacks are served.

CAMPANIA

BELLEVUE SYRENE
SEAFRONT HOTEL

*Piazza della Vittoria 5,80067
Sorrento, Napoli*
TEL 081 87810241604 **FAX** 081
8783963 **E-MAIL** info@bellevue.it
WEBSITE www.bellevue.it
FOOD breakfast, light or packed
lunch, dinner **PRICE** €€€
CLOSED never
PROPRIETOR Giovanni Russo

BUILT AS A COUNT'S SUMMER RETREAT in 1750 in a magnificent clifftop position, this *grande dame* hotel opened in 1820, and has been carefully
restored over the years. Well-proportioned reception rooms, corridors and
bedrooms, painted in restful shades of yellow, are brought to life with
attractive frescoes, *trompe l'oeil*, and fabrics ranging from brocades and
Regency stripes to zebra prints. Public rooms are furnished with fine
European antiques; the smart majolica-tiled bedrooms with wrought iron
and marble. The airy dining room is staffed by an army of impeccable waiters and features a menu of robust, mainly local specialities. But our latest
reporters encountered too many large groups here for their taste.

LORELEY ET LONDRES
TOWN HOTEL

*Via Califano 2, 80067 Sorrento,
Napoli*

TEL 081 8073187
FAX 081 5329001
FOOD breakfast, lunch, dinner
PRICE €
CLOSED mid-Nov to Easter
PROPRIETOR Giuseppina Ercolano

ACOMPLETE DUMP. Tatty, scruffy and seedy are just some of the adjectives
that come to mind to describe the present-day condition of this once-
dignified hotel. Why include it? If rock-bottom budget is what you require,
and if you are a connoisseur of quirky time warps, then you may well for-
give the shortcomings, at least for a night. The splendidly atmospheric
façade and old sepia photographs in the lobby attest to its former status
as a favoured stop-off on the Grand Tour, and it still has a few attractive
old pieces of furniture, a (very) faded charm and an air of lingering regret.
Bedrooms and service are absolutely basic, with prices to match. Ask for a
'room with a view'; some have a tiny balcony giving on to the sea.

THE HEEL AND TOE

AREA INTRODUCTION

HOTELS IN THE HEEL AND TOE

To SAY THAT CHARMING SMALL HOTELS in the heel and toe of Italy are diffi-cult to find is a wild understatement. It would be nearer the truth to say that they don't exist. Much of the landscape is stony and barren, with imposing mountains, and a rugged, inhospitable western coastline. The exception is the area around the little resort of Maratea, where you will find two of our hotels. Most of our other recommendations are on the Strait of Otranto coast along the outside of Italy's heel. Here you will find almost deserted beaches, punctuated by small communities, and an interi-or that becomes more mountainous the further you go. The hotels which appear in the following pages are the best there are, but some alternative recommendations may be helpful, particularly in the heel.

The **San Nicola** (tel 080 3105199), a smart, 30-roomed hotel in the heart of Altamura, is one possibility, as is the **Villa Cenci in Cisternino** (tel 080 4448208), with some accommodation in *trulli* (ancient stone dwellings), a stylish restaurant and pleasant gardens and pool. In the *trul-li* capital Alberobello, the **Dei Trulli** (tel 080 4323555) also offers enthusi-asts the irresistable opportunity to stay in one of these curious little stone bungalows, set here among pines and neat flower beds. If you want to make it right to the southern tip of the heel, you could aim for the **Terminal** (tel 0833 758242), a well-run seaside holiday hotel at Marina di Léuca.

For travellers in the 'toe' heading south with time to spare, the SS18 makes a slow-paced alternative to the A3 motorway, sticking to the east-ern coast south of Lagonegro where the motorway takes a long detour inland. There are a few places further south than Maratea that are worth bearing in mind. At Diamante is the Mediterranean-style **Ferretti** (tel 0985 81428), with terraces overlooking the sea and a highly reputed restaurant. The 65-room **Grand Hotel San Michele** (tel 0982 91012) at Cetraro is rather more swish – a well-restored old house in an attractive informal garden on cliffs above the beach.

The main tourist attraction of the toe, however, is on the other side of the A3 – the magnificently wild landscape of the Sila mountains east of Cosenza and north of Catanzaro. Each of these towns has a handful of acceptable hotels. South of Catanzaro at Stilo is the charming **San Giorgio** (tel 0964 775047), a 17thC village house, once a cardinal's palace, whose terrace garden affords splendid views.

THE HEEL AND TOE

MARATEA

LOCANDA DELLE DONNE MONACHE
∽ VILLAGE HOTEL ∽

Via Carlo Mazzei 4, 85046 Maratea, Potenza
TEL 0973 877487 **FAX** 0973 877687
E-MAIL locanda@mondomaratea.it **WEBSITE** www.mondomaratea.it

FOR YEARS, MARATEA WAS one of the most unspoiled seaside villages on Italy's west coast, its pink and white houses clustered on low cliffs above the harbour and its old quarter crammed with interesting buildings, including two medieval churches. In the last decade or so new hotels have been built and restaurants opened, but its essential character remains intact, and this *locanda* is an example of how past and present can be successfully combined. Originally an old monastery, it has been transformed into an elegant contemporary hotel.

The flamboyance of the entrance hall gives way to cool modern *chic* in the bedrooms, each slightly different, but all comfortable with tiled floors and smart Italian-designed furniture and lighting. White drapes hang at the windows, while patterned, red-striped ticking or coloured drapes encircle wrought-iron canopy beds.

Jasmine, bougainvillea and lemon trees grow in the lovely peaceful garden at the front which contains a fair-sized swimming pool with a terrace and plenty of sunbeds. The beach is also conveniently close by. The *locanda* has been bought by a company, which owns two other hotels in the area, and will organize various sporting activities, such as scuba diving courses, rafting and pony trekking, as well as local excursions for guests.

∽

NEARBY Monte San Biagio; Lagonegro (20 km); Rivello (20 km).
LOCATION in village; car parking
FOOD breakfast, lunch, dinner
PRICE €€€
ROOMS 29 double and twin, suites, all with bath; all rooms have phone, TV, air conditioning, minibar, hairdrier
FACILITIES sitting room, piano bar, restaurant, garden, swimming pool, private beach **CREDIT CARDS** AE, DC, MC, V
DISABLED access difficult **PETS** accepted
CLOSED never
MANAGER Gabriella Labanchi

THE HEEL AND TOE

MARATEA

VILLA CHETA ELITE

~ LAKESIDE HOTEL ~

Via Nazionale, 85041 Acquafredda di Maratea, Potenza
TEL 0973 878134 **FAX** 0973 878135
E-MAIL villacheta@labnet.it **WEBSITE** www.costadimaratea.com/villacheta

THE REMOTE AND MOUNTAINOUS region of Basilicata does not possess much coastline. But the tiny stretch of shore on the west side, where a corniche cuts through wild and beautiful cliffs, is one of the most spectacular parts of Italy's deep south. Villa Cheta Elite is set high up on this precipitous coastline, with splendid views. If the villa enjoyed no other distinction, its position would be enough to attract many travellers to the south. But this gracious art nouveau building has other attractions.

The villa is a pleasure to behold: a confection of ochre and cream stucco, decorated with ornate mouldings that would look at home in a grand Edwardian living room. It lies among lush, flowery terraces, one of which is set out with café-style chairs and smartly-laid dining tables. Inside, lace tablecloths, chintz sofas, carefully-chosen period pieces and abundant pictures create the feel of a private house.

The beaches in the area are small, but the waters are clear, and reached in only a few minutes from the villa. The Aquadros are relaxed and charming hosts, who take great care over every aspect of their hotel, including the food, which is highly regarded, and Stefania has even introduced yoga lessons for her guests.

~

NEARBY Maratea (8 km); Lagonegro (20 km).
LOCATION 1.5 km S of Acquafredda; car parking
FOOD breakfast, lunch, dinner
PRICE €€€
ROOMS 23 double and twin with shower; all rooms have phone, air conditioning
FACILITIES dining room, TV/reading room, bar, terrace, garden
CREDIT CARDS AE, DC, MC, V
DISABLED access possible
PETS small ones accepted
CLOSED never
PROPRIETOR Stefania Aqadro

THE HEEL AND TOE

MATERA

SASSI

~ TOWN BED-AND-BREAKFAST ~

Via San Giovanni Vecchio 89, 75100 Matera
TEL 0835 331009 **FAX** 0835 333733
E-MAIL hotelsassi@virgilio.it **WEBSITE** www.hotelsassi.it

IN THIS CITY OF CAVES (*sassi*), a Unesco world heritage site, where the inhabitants lived as troglodytes for centuries (the last were evicted as recently as the 1960s), it is appropriate to stay at this unique bed-and-breakfast, where many of the bedrooms are hewn out of the tufa, their floors, walls and ceilings all gently undulating. In a peaceful pedestrian-only part of the ancient city, it occupies a labyrinthine 18thC building, with spectacular views over the Sasso Barisano to the Romanesque cathedral from its terraces and balconies.

Committed owner, Raffaele Cristallo has recently refurbished the Sassi, keeping simplicity as the keynote. Plain wooden tables and rush-seated 'peasant' chairs furnish both breakfast room and bedrooms, each one of which is different, modestly comfortable and full of character. The excavated rooms are naturally cool and only need their air conditioning on the hottest of days. Staff are charming and friendly. There is a no smoking policy.

As the hotel doesn't have its own parking, there's a short walk (with your luggage) from the nearest public car park. If you have time, try to see the exhibition, telling the story of Matera's cave dwellings, in the Ridola Museum on Via Ridola.

~

NEARBY Strada Panoramica dei Sassi (in town); Bari (65 km); Lago di San Giuliano (12 km).
LOCATION in centre of old town, just N of Via Fiorentini; public car park nearby
FOOD breakfast
PRICE €
ROOMS 20 double and twin, single and suites, all with bath or shower; all rooms have phone, TV, air conditioning, minibar, hairdrier
FACILITIES breakfast room, bar, meeting hall, terrace **CREDIT CARDS** AE, DC, MC, V
DISABLED access difficult **PETS** not accepted
CLOSED never
PROPRIETOR Raffaele Cristallo

THE HEEL AND TOE

MONOPOLI

IL MELOGRANO
~ COUNTRY VILLA ~

Contrada Torricella 345, 70043 Monópoli Bari
TEL 080 6909030 **FAX** 080 747908
E-MAIL melograno@melograno.com **WEBSITE** www.melograno.com

SOPHISTICATED ROOMS, filled with fine antiques, paintings, fabrics and oriental carpets, give us a clue to the profession of the man who master-
minded the transformation of this 16thC fortified farmhouse, used by the
Guerra family as a holiday home, to a luxurious small hotel. Until the mid-
1980s Camillo Guerra was an antiques dealer, and his special, personal
touch is evident everywhere. The elegant reception rooms are housed in
the main building. But for the individually-furnished bedrooms, he built a
clutch of white Moorish houses around a *piazza*, overlooking orange and
olive groves, lemon and pomegranate trees (the name 'melograno' means
'pomegranate').

Dinner, a Mediterranean feast, is usually *al fresco* on a canopy-covered
veranda beside a wonderfully gnarled old olive tree. Breakfast is served
beside the outdoor pool, bordered by prickly pear, almond and citrus
trees, whose fruit is the basis for the juice and jams on the table.

If relaxing by the pool or on the private beach begins to pall, there is
plenty to see in the area, including Frederick II's Swabian castles and the
mysterious *trulli* of Alberobello.

~

NEARBY ruins of Egnazia; Castellana caves; Alberobello (19 km).
LOCATION 3 km from Monópoli towards Alberobello; car parking
FOOD breakfast, lunch, dinner
PRICE €€€€€
ROOMS 37; 33 double and twin, 4 suites, all with bath; all rooms have phone, TV,
air conditioning, minibar, hairdrier, safe
FACILITIES sitting rooms, dining room, bar, health centre, indoor and outdoor
swimming pools, garden, tennis, private beach, helipad
CREDIT CARDS AE, DC, MC, V
DISABLED access possible
PETS not accepted
CLOSED never
PROPRIETORS Guerra family

THE HEEL AND TOE

SAVELLETRI DI FASANO

MASSERIA SAN DOMENICO

∽ FARMHOUSE HOTEL ∽

Litoranea 379, 72010 Savelletri di Fasano, Brindisi
TEL 080 4827769 **FAX** 080 4827978
E-MAIL masseriasandomenico@puglianet.it **WEBSITE** www.imasseria.com

ON ONE OF THE SPRAWLING agricultural estates with a fortified farmhouse at its centre that crop up all over Puglia, this *masseria* has its origins in the 14th century when the knights of Malta used it as a watchtower against the Turks. Set in 60 acres of orchards and olive groves, its metamorphosis into an impressive hotel was completed in 1996. The architecture is typically Moorish – pristine white walls, turrets and arched windows and doorways – with fitting decoration inside, where details like curvy wrought-iron bedheads and fabrics in vibrant colours or floral designs bring the rooms to life. The marble-floored bedrooms are attractively and individually furnished and equipped with large modern bathrooms.

Although the hotel is only 200 m from the sea, the huge salt-water swimming pool might have even greater appeal. Skilfully built, with no straight lines, so that it looks like a huge natural rock pool, it is surrounded by gnarled old olive trees. Drinks and meals are served here at the pool bar and barbecue grill, while in the dining room seafood is one of the specialities in a range of delicious regional dishes.

It's little surprise that this peaceful hideaway with its understated luxury has been embraced by the glitterati, who – like Sven Goran Eriksson – come here for a total escape and some serious pampering.

∽

NEARBY Castellana Caves; Fasano (7 km).
LOCATION 2 km S of Savelletri on SS379 to Torrecane; car parking
FOOD breakfast, lunch, dinner; room service
PRICE €€€€
ROOMS 35 double and twin with bath; all rooms have phone, TV, air conditioning, minibar, hairdrier
FACILITIES sitting room, dining room, gym, spa, terrace, garden, swimming pool, pool bar, tennis, golf, private beach
CREDIT CARDS AE, DC, MC, V
DISABLED access difficult **PETS** accepted **CLOSED** Jan
MANAGER Antonio Polesel

THE HEEL AND TOE

LECCE

CONVENTO DI SANTA MARIA DI CONSTANTINOPOLI
CONVERTED CONVENT B&B

Via Convento, 73030 Marittima di Diso, Lecce

TEL 07736362328
FOOD breakfast, lunch; dinner on request
PRICE €€-€€€
CLOSED never
PROPRIETORS Lord and Lady McAlpine

THIS 14THC CONVENT IS THE wonderland Puglia home fo former Tory grandee Alistair McAlpine and his wife Athena. Intoxicatingly atmospheric, the air is alive with music, the beds are Indian four-posters, and the McAlps' vast and eclectic collection ranges from Aboriginal art to Waziri fabrics. There are no phones or TV's in the rooms; instead you'll find 14 tons of books (seriously), a fresh water swimming pool in a garden filled with lavender, and sumptuous meals laid out on the kitchen table. When darkness descends ceremonial candles are lit in the cloisters. One guest wrote in the visitors' book 'it makes the Cipriani look like a transport caff'.

PARGHELIA

BAIA PARAELIOS
RESORT VILLAGE

Fornaci, 88035 Parghelia , Catanzaro

TEL 0963 600300 **FAX** 0963 600074
E-MAIL info@baiaparaelios.com
WEBSITE www.baiaparaelios.it
FOOD breakfast, lunch, dinner
PRICE €€€€
CLOSED Oct to Apr
MANAGER Adolfo Salabe

OVERLOOKING A PICTURE-POSTCARD BAY of white sand washed by a turquoise sea, Baia Paraelios is not so much a hotel as an upmarket holiday camp with accommodation in 83 small bungalows sprawled across a wooded hillside. Each has a private terrace, a view of its own, one or two bedrooms and a sitting room in mellow colours. Communal areas are equally stylish. Prints add colour to plain walls; tiled floors and a scattering of plants bask in a cosy glow from artful lighting. There is a relaxing sitting room, open-air bar and terrace dining room beside the sea. Three swimming pools (one salt-water), flood-lit tennis courts, mini-golf, bowling, windsurfing, canoeing and child-minding make this a choice for families.

THE ISLANDS

HOTELS IN THE ISLANDS

SICILY, THE LARGEST AND MOST POPULOUS island in the Mediterranean, has an extraordinary mix of sightseeing interest: spectacular scenery, ancient Greek ruins, medieval towns, splendid Baroque architecture, busy street markets, wonderful food and wine and even an active volcano. It enjoys a balmy climate and its tourist season runs from Easter through until October although July and August are particularly crowded. Taormina is the main resort and is well represented by hotels on the following pages. We have yet to find a hotel in the sprawling, chaotic city of Palermo that is 'charming' and 'small', but the **Grand Hotel Villa Igea** (tel 091 543744), set in gorgeous gardens on the edge of the sea, is a possibility if you are into old-world splendour at a price. Or there is the ornate **Grand Hotel et des Palmes** (tel 091 602 8111). We have a new entry in Siracusa (**the Gutkowski**) and another in the shadow of Etna, near Catania (**L'Olmo**). Our third new entry is in the Baroque town of Modica.

If you plan a more peaceful holiday, you might do best to choose one of the Aeolian (or Lipari) islands. We have one entry on Panarea, **the Raya**, while on Lipari itself we suggest **Villa Diana** (tel 090 9811403), **Villa Meligunis** (tel 090 9812426), **Giardino sul Mare** (tel 090 9811004) and **the Oriente** (tel 090 9811493). On the neighbouring island of Salina, try a clifftop hotel, **Punta Scario** (tel 090 9844139), or a restaurant-with-rooms, **L'Ariana** (tel 090 9809075). Off the north-west coast of Sicily near Trapani are the much quieter Egadi Islands, famous for their tuna fishing and canneries; we can recommend a simple but pleasant hotel on Favignana, **the Aegusa** (tel 092 922430).

Although about the same size as Sicily, Sardinia is completely different: its population is sparse; there are few major sightseeing attractions and no very large towns or resorts; and there are few crowds, even in the most developed area for tourists, the Costa Smeralda – which is where most of our recommendations are located. Development is gradually spreading along the coastline from there in both directions. On the north coast, the **Shardana** (tel 0789 754031) and the **Li Nibbari** (tel 0789 754453), both at Santa Teresa Gallura, are possibilities.

On the east coast, the **Hotel l'Oasi** (tel 0784 93111) at Dorgali is a well-equipped *pensione* set on a hill overlooking the sea, amidst gardens and pinewoods. But if you really want to get away from it all, two small islands just off the south-west coast of Sardinia may appeal: Sant' Antioco – try **La Rosa dei Venti** (tel 3476 364566), a justly popular bed-and-breakfast – and the Isola San Pietro – try the **Hieracon** (tel 0781 854028) on the waterfront at Carloforte.

PANAREA

SAN PIETRO

RAYA

~ SEASIDE HOTEL ~

Isole Eolie o Lipari, San Pietro, 98050 Isola Panarea, Messina
TEL 090 983013 **FAX** 090 983103
E-MAIL info@hotelraya.it **WEBSITE** www.hotelraya.it

THIS UNIQUE, STYLISH HOTEL was the creation of Myriam Beltrami and Paolo Tilche, who came to the alluring, car-less little island of Panarea in the 1960s, were enthralled and never left. The Raya consists of a cascade of pink and white bungalows, linked by arches and whitewashed steps, tumbling down the hillside through a Mediterranean garden to the sea. At every level bougainvillea-shaded terraces – for dining, sunbathing or attached to bedrooms – look out to the uninhabited Lipari islands with the threatening vision of the volcano, Strómboli, in the distance.

Inside all is cool and white – from the tiled floors to the sofas and chairs – a fitting background for the dramatic pieces of ethnic art from Polynesia, Africa and Asia that Myriam collects and loves to display. She sells similar pieces in her boutique (next door). Also predominately white, some of the bedrooms have a slightly dated feel, with Indian bedspreads and rush ceilings.

Choose between a continental breakfast in the small bar or on your terrace; or brunch in the airy dining room. In the evening, this room is lit by oil lamps on tables, which in summer are set out on the panoramic terrace. No young children.

~

NEARBY Strómboli; Salina; Sicily.
LOCATION 400 m from port on hillside; hydrofoil from Naples, Milazzo, Reggio Calabria, Palermo, Messina
FOOD breakfast, brunch, dinner
PRICE €€€€€
ROOMS 36 double and twin, duplex, all with shower; all rooms have phone, air conditioning, minibar, hairdrier
FACILITIES sitting areas, bar/breakfast room, dining room, disco, terraces, garden
CREDIT CARDS AE, DC, MC, V
DISABLED access difficult **PETS** accepted
CLOSED mid-Oct to mid-Apr
PROPRIETOR Myriam Beltrami

SARDINIA

ALGHERO

VILLA LAS TRONAS
~ SEASIDE HOTEL ~

Lungomare Valencia 1, 07041 Alghero, Sassari
TEL 079 981818 **FAX** 079 981044
E-MAIL info@hvlta.com **WEBSITE** www.hvlt.com

THIS CASTELLATED, 19THC FOLLY lords it over its own bare, rocky promonto-ry, and it stands aloof from the blocks of flats that otherwise character-ize this unattractive part of modern Alghero. The interior – all marble floors and ornate chandeliers – is as grand as you might expect of some-where that was a holiday retreat for Italian royalty until the 1940s. Yet the unstuffy and businesslike staff ensure it is not intimidatingly formal.

Antiques abound, including in the luxurious bedrooms, which feature brass or sleigh beds and grand canopies, along with swanky marble bath-rooms. Those billed as having garden views in reality overlook Alghero's apartment blocks. You pay extra to open the shutters on a view across the bay to the awesome cliff of Capo Caccia; priciest sea-facing rooms come with balconies. Rooms were totally revamped in 2000.

There are no beaches in this part of Alghero, but the hotel has a pool, and many guests swim off the rocks and from an old dockyard.

When we inspected, breakfast was dire. For food, you may be better off making the five-minute stroll along the seaside promenade into the magi-cal backstreets of old Alghero, where you'll find a wide choice of cafés and restaurants. Bicycles are provided free.

~

NEARBY Maria Pia, the best nearby beach, is 4 km north.
LOCATION in modern Alghero, 800 m S of old Alghero; with car parking
FOOD breakfast, lunch, dinner
PRICE €€€€
ROOMS 25; 20 double and 5 suites with bath; all rooms have phone, TV, air conditioning, minibar, hairdrier
FACILITIES sitting room, dining room, bar, sea-water swimming pool, gym, bicycles
CREDIT CARDS AE, DC, MC, V
DISABLED not suitable
PETS accepted
CLOSED never
MANAGER Maria Teresa Masia

SARDINIA

OLIENA

SU GOLOGONE
~ COUNTRY HOTEL ~

08025 Oliena, Nuoro
TEL 0784 287512 **FAX** 0784 287668
E-MAIL gologone@tin.it **WEBSITE** sugologone.it

THE BARBAGIA IS A MOUNTAINOUS inland region where the land-scape is wild and spectacular. The hotel is a low-lying white villa, covered in creepers, surrounded by flowing shrubs and set in a landscape of rural splendour: wooded ravines, fields of olives, pinewoods and the craggy peaks of the Supramonte mountains. It feels isolated, and it is; but the Su Gologone is far from undiscovered. Once, only a few adventurous foreign travellers found their way here; now, they come for the peace, or indeed for the food alone, which is typically Sard: cuts of local meats, roast lamb and the speciality of roast suckling pig – you can watch it being cooked on a spit in front of a huge fireplace. The wines are produced in the local vineyards. The dining room spreads in all directions – into the vine-clad courtyard, the terrace and other rooms, all in suitably rustic style. The bedrooms are light and simple, again in rustic style, in keeping with the surroundings. Walls are whitewashed, floors are tiled and there are lovely views. Despite its size, the Su Gologone still feels small and friendly, and, in most respects, still typically Sard.

~

NEARBY Gennargentu mountains; Monte Ortobene (21 km).
LOCATION 8 km NE of Oliena, in remote mountain setting, with private car parking
FOOD breakfast, lunch, dinner
PRICE €€
ROOMS 65; 53 double and twin, 8 suites, 4 family rooms, all with bath; all rooms have phone, TV, air conditioning, minibar, hairdrier
FACILITIES 5 dining rooms, 2 bars, meeting rooms, gym, health centre, swimming pool, tennis, mini-golf, bicycles, Land Rover and motorbikes for excursions
CREDIT CARDS AE, MC, V
DISABLED no special facilities
PETS accepted
CLOSED Nov to Feb, except Christmas
PROPRIETOR Giuseppe Palimodde

SARDINIA

PALAU

CAPO D'ORSO
～ SEASIDE HOTEL ～

Loc. Cala Capra, 07020 Palau
TEL 0789 702000 **FAX** 0789 702009

THIS CIVILIZED YET UNPRETENTIOUS waterside hotel stands in marked contrast to the flashy establishments on the nearby Costa Smeralda. It's a place for slow-paced, laid-back, water and beach-oriented holidays. Basking in mesmerising views of the verdant yet rocky coastline and offshore islands, its secluded setting – the nearest centre, the humdrum port of Palau, is a 10-minute drive away – could hardly be prettier. For chilling out, choose between two picturesque, sheltered slips of sand, a lovely amoeba-shaped pool and, in what amount to the focus of the hotel, thoroughly romantic drinks and dining terraces shaded by olive trees and tamarisks. The food is praised; breakfasts come in the form of buffets, and there is also a lunchtime pizzeria. The hotel is not suitable for anyone who finds steps difficult.

The simple bedrooms, in low-rise blocks, are lifted by cheerful paintings and the fact that all face the sea and have a balcony or terrace. Suites suit families: the sitting room, connected to a bedroom by a sliding door, has a sofa bed.

If boredom sets in, the hotel can arrange diving and riding. Boat trips from its jetty visit Maddalena and Caprera, and the fleshpots of the Costa Smeralda's Porto Cervo.

～

NEARBY Maddalena and Caprera islands; Costa Smeralda.
LOCATION 6 km E of Palau, car parking
FOOD breakfast, lunch, dinner
PRICE €€€€ (3-7 night miniumum)
ROOMS 70 double, family and suites, all with shower; all rooms have phone, TV, air conditioning, minibar, hairdrier, balcony or terrace
FACILITIES sitting room, 2 restaurants, bar, swimming pool, tennis, boat trips, watersports **CREDIT CARDS** AE, DC, MC, V
DISABLED not suitable **PETS** accepted
CLOSED Oct to May
MANAGER Signor Cagliero

SARDINIA

PORTO CERVO

CALA DI VOLPE
~ SEASIDE HOTEL ~

07020 Porto Cervo, Costa Smeralda, Sassari
TEL 0789 976111 **FAX** 0789 976617 **E-MAIL** caladivolpe@luxurycollection.com
WEBSITE ww.luxurycollection.com/caladivolpe

APPROACHED FROM THE FRONT, Cala di Volpe has the slightly forbidding exterior of a Moorish fortification, with towers, crenellations and turrets. Viewed from the sea, however, the hotel resembles a simple fishing village, where clusters of little houses painted in shades of ochre and amber are softened by arches and porticoes – a magical sight when lit up at night. Simplicity of style is carried through into the interior: niches, painted stairways and modern stained glass insets in the hallways; plain bedrooms (some with *trompe l'oeil* embellishments), with terraces or gardens overlooking the sea. Overall, the effect of wooden beams, bamboo, terracotta floors, and orange, yellow and brown colours, offset by cool white, creates an air of Sardinian rustic chic.

The super-rich turn up by boat and moor their vessels in the small marina. If you don't have a boat, don't worry: a free hotel launch leaves half hourly for a private beach – a little paradise, complete with sunloungers, towels and crystal clear water. Or it's just a short stroll away along a wooded track.

Beware the veneer of simplicity at Cala di Volpe: it belies discreet, understated luxury. Your credit card needs to be in good working order.

~

NEARBY Porto Cervo (8 km); Olbia (25 km).
LOCATION S of Porto Cervo, Costa Smeralda; car parking
FOOD breakfast, lunch, dinner; room service; half-board only
PRICE €€€€€
ROOMS 121; 100 double, 9 single, 12 suites, all with bath; Presidential suite has private pool; all rooms have phone, TV, air conditioning, minibar, hairdrier
FACILITIES restaurant, bar, swimming pool, terrace, garden, beach, private harbour, jetty, water-skiing, 9-hole putting green, tennis, bike hire, boat hire, fitness centre
CREDIT CARDS AE, DC, MC, V
DISABLED not suitable **PETS** not accepted
CLOSED late Oct to early Apr
MANAGER Marco Milocco

SARDINIA

PORTO CERVO

CERVO

~ SEASIDE HOTEL ~

07020 Porto Cervo, Costa Smeralda, Sassari
TEL 0789 931111 **FAX** 0789 931613
E-MAIL res064_cervo@sheraton.com **WEBSITE** www.sheraton.com/cervo

A STONE'S THROW from the old quay, this Mediterranean-style hotel over-looks the *piazzetta* right in the heart of Porto Cervo – an almost too perfect resort village, crammed with designer shops and smart restaurants. It is part of the Costa Smeralda development, started in the late fifties by a consortium led by the Aga Khan.

Within the hotel it is refreshingly airy and simple. There are textured white walls, terracotta floors, plain, bright fabrics and wooden furniture. Ceilings are low and windows are arched. Despite the fact that the Cervo has a purpose-built conference centre a short distance away and some-times hosts large groups, the terraces and shaded dining areas are small in scale and intimate. There are several restaurants to choose from: the Grill specializes in Italian cuisine and has splendid views over the marina; Il Pescatore serves fish and seafood; Il Pomodoro is informal and rustic.

For sports enthusiasts, a short walk over a little wooden bridge leads to the sports complex where tennis, squash, a fully-equipped gym and jogging track are available. Sun worshippers and sea bathers will appreciate the free boat service (between May and September) that whisks them away to a secluded beach.

~

NEARBY Olbia (30 km); Costa Smeralda coastline; boat trips.
LOCATION in middle of Porto Cervo; car parking
FOOD breakfast, lunch, dinner
PRICE €€€€€
ROOMS 108 all with bath and shower; 6 suites with private pool; all with air conditioning, minibar, satellite TV
FACILITIES 5 restaurants, bars, 3 swimming pools, sports centre and golf nearby
CREDIT CARDS AE, DC, MC, V
DISABLED not suitable
PETS not accepted
CLOSED never
MANAGER Franco Mulas

SARDINIA

PORTO CERVO

PITRIZZA
~ RESORT VILLAGE ~

07020 Porto Cervo, Costa Smeralda, Sassari
TEL 0789 930111 **FAX** 0789 930611
E-MAIL pitrizza@luxurycollection.com **WEBSITE** www.starwood.com/hotelpitrizza

THE SMART PLAYGROUND of the Costa Smeralda is liberally endowed with luxury hotels, but there is one that stands out from the rest: the Pitrizza. What distinguishes it (apart from its small size) is its exclusive, intimate, club-like atmosphere. No shops, disco or ritzy touches here. Small private villas are scattered discreetly among the rocks and flowering gardens, overlooking a private beach. Rooms are furnished throughout with immaculate taste, some of them amazingly simple. The style is predominantly rustic, with white stucco walls, beams and locally crafted furniture and fabrics. Each villa has four to six rooms, and most have a private terrace, garden or patio. The core of the hotel is the club house, with a small sitting room, bar, restaurant and spacious terrace where you can sit, enjoying the company of other guests or simply watching the sunset. A path leads down to the golden sands of a small beach and a private jetty where you can moor your yacht. Equally desirable is the sea-water pool, which has been carved out of the rocky shoreline.

There is of course a hitch to the Pitrizza. The rooms here are among the most expensive on the entire Italian coastline.

~

NEARBY Beaches of the Costa Smeralda; Maddalena archipelago.
LOCATION 4 km from Porto Cervo, at Liscia di Vacca; ample car parking
FOOD breakfast, lunch, dinner; room service
PRICE €€€€€
ROOMS 51; 38 double and twin, 13 suites, all with bath; all rooms have phone, TV, air conditioning, minibar, hairdrier
FACILITIES dining room, bar, terrace, fitness centre, sea-water swimming pool, beach, water-skiing, boat hire, windsurfing, private mooring
CREDIT CARDS AE, DC, MC, V
DISABLED no special facilities
PETS not accepted
CLOSED late Oct to early May
MANAGER Pierangelo Tondina

Sardinia

ROMAZZINO
~ SEASIDE HOTEL ~

07020 Porto Cervo, Costa Smeralda, Sassari
TEL 0789 977111 **FAX** 0789 77618
E-MAIL romazzino@luxurycollection.com **WEBSITE** www.starwood.com/romazzino

THOUGH FABULOUSLY STYLISH and expensive, the Romazzino is a little less exclusive and pricey than its smaller sister, the Pitrizza (see page 311). It's a better choice if a beach is important in your plans, since the whitewashed, terracotta-roofed complex presides over one of the biggest on the Costa Smeralda (as well as an enormous pool). Families in particular should be more at home here.

Make no mistake, however: this is still one of Europe's most luxurious beach hotels. The interior has the airiness and understated elegance of a giant Moorish-cum-Mediterranean mansion. For example, whimsical, painted ceramics adorn the walls of the sitting room, while gay colour schemes complement soothing Sardinian fabrics in the tasteful bedrooms.

A veritable army of staff panders to your every need. At dinner, it's hard to know whether to be more impressed by the creative Franco-Italian cuisine, or the zealously attentive, multilingual service. Although the Romazzino exceeds our normal room limit by a considerable margin, we continue to include it because it has the feel of a much smaller place.

~

NEARBY Hotel Cala di Volpe, a jaw-dropping faux-Medieval castle.
LOCATION 11 km from Porto Cervo; car parking
FOOD breakfast, lunch, dinner; room service
PRICE €€€€€
ROOMS 94; 78 double and twin, 16 suites, all with bath; all rooms have phone, TV, air conditioning, minibar, hairdrier
FACILITIES sitting room, 2 restaurants, bar, terrace, swimming pool, tennis, watersports
CREDIT CARDS AE, DC, MC, V
DISABLED access difficult
PETS not accepted
CLOSED mid-Feb to mid-May
MANAGER Milton Sgarbi

SARDINIA

SANTA MARGHERITA DI PULA

IS MORUS
~ SEASIDE HOTEL ~

09010 Santa Margherita di Pula, Pula
TEL 070 921171 **FAX** 070 921596
E-MAIL ismorusrelais@tin.it **WEBSITE** www.ismorus.it

IS MORUS IS ONE OF SEVERAL upmarket and isolated hotels along a strip of flat coastline dotted with holiday homes and greenhouses, and backed by parched, rocky hills.

Secluded within a garden of oleanders and a pine and eucalyptus wood, pantiled and whitewashed Is Morus is a Mediterranean rendition of a smart country-house hotel. In keeping with the fairly formal service, an understated elegance pervades the place, both in the cool, light sitting rooms that are interconnected by arches and furnished with squashy modern soft furnishings, and in bedrooms that are almost minimalist in style. Some of these are in the main building (avoid those without a sea view or balcony), others in villas sprinkled through the wood, with two or three bedrooms per villa.

The sandy beach isn't one of Sardinia's best (it can be weedy), but it is yards from the main building, private and immaculately maintained, and the swimming pool is large and inviting.

This is a civilized and peaceful corner of Sardinia, bereft of bright lights or of even anything amounting to a resort.

~

NEARBY The sand-dune beaches at Chia; the Punic and Roman ruins at Nora.
LOCATION on the coast S of Pula; car parking
FOOD breakfast, lunch, dinner; room service; half-board obligatory
PRICE €€€€
ROOMS 85 double and twin, single and suites, all with bath or shower; all rooms have phone, TV, air conditioning, minibar, hairdrier
FACILITIES sitting room, restaurant; bar, terrace, swimming pool, tennis, watersports
CREDIT CARDS AE, DC, MC, V
DISABLED no special facilities
PETS accepted
CLOSED Nov to Easter
MANAGER Maurizio Maffei

SICILY

L'OLMO
~ COUNTRY VILLA ~

Via Olmo 16, 95010 Carruba, Catania
TEL 095 964920 **FAX** 095 964729
EMAIL info@lolmo.it

IMMERSED IN THE FAMILY'S LEMON GROVE between Mount Etna and the sea, L'Olmo is the home of Andrea, Marchese di San Giuliano, and his wife Marina who have recently converted part of their property into guest accomodation; it lies within easy reach of Taormina, Catania and Siracusa.

The bedrooms are divided between the main 'casale' and another pretty adjacent building. A private house party atmosphere prevails and, indeed, is encouraged; it's the sort of place that would lend itself very well to being taken over by a group of friends. The houses are filled with family antiques and pictures, but while quite grand, the atmosphere is not at all stuffy. There are plenty of books and magazines to read and open fires burn in cooler weather. Bedroms are large and airy with good fitted wardrobes and big, well-equipped bathrooms.

The large pool is equipped with smart red and white striped sun beds while the beautiful gardens, filled with bougainvilla, jasmine and antique roses, provide plenty of shaded spots for relaxing with a book; views are of Etna in one direction and the sea in the other. Activities can be organised on request such as expeditions to view Etna's craters, fishing trips, cooking courses, water skiing and sailing.

~

NEARBY Etna; Taormina (20 km); Catania (20 km).
LOCATION exit the A18 motorway at Giarre; ask the hotel for detailed instructions from there. In own extensive grounds with ample car parking
FOOD breakfast
PRICE €€; mimimum stay three nights
ROOMS 8 doubles, all with bath or shower; all rooms have hairdrier; phone and TV on request
FACILITIES sitting rooms, dining room, terraces, garden, pool
CREDIT CARDS not accepted
DISABLED no special facilities but ground floor rooms **PETS** not accepted
CLOSED never
PROPRIETOR Andrea and Marina di San Giuliano

SICILY

ERICE

MODERNO
∼ TOWN HOTEL ∼

Via Vittorio Emanuele 63, 91016 Erice, Trapani
TEL 0923 869300 **FAX** 0923 869139
EMAIL modernoh@tin.it **WEBSITE** www.hotelmodernoerice.it

ERICE IS AN ENCHANTING medieval town, encircled by high walls and suspended 2,500 feet above Trapani. It makes a good base for a couple of days and most tourists leave in the evening making way for a rather eerie atmosphere often enhanced by swirling fog. The family-run Moderno is situated at the top of the narrow main street (park in the public parking near Porta Trapani and walk up to the hotel); it occupies a 19th century building, but as the name suggests, it is decorated in modern style, although 'modern' in this case means rather dated 70s décor mixed with traditional Sicilian elements. There are fresh flowers, pictures, ornaments and bright, locally-woven rugs everywhere and public rooms are simply furnished with groups of chairs, sofas and tables. Bedrooms (about half of which are housed in a nearby annexe) are simple and fresh with white-washed walls and tiled floors; some are furnished with antiques while others have modern pine or bamboo pieces.

The restaurant enjoys a good reputation for its traditional Sicilian fare, and the roof terrace provides spectacular views of the tiled roofs of Erice and beyond. A recent visitor was enthusiastic about the Moderno; 'it has not lost its individual touch'.

∼

NEARBY Greek temple and theatre at Segesta; Trapani (15 km); Egadi islands.
LOCATION in town centre; public car parking nearby
FOOD breakfast, lunch, dinner
PRICE €€
ROOMS 41; 33 doubles and 8 singles, all with bath or shower; all rooms have phone, TV, air conditioning, minibar, hairdrier
FACILITIES sitting areas, dining room, bar, roof terrace, lift
CREDIT CARDS AE, DC, MC, V
DISABLED no special facilities
PETS accepted
CLOSED never
PROPRIETOR Giuseppe Catalano

SICILY

GANGI

TENUTA GANGIVECCHIO
~ COUNTRY GUESTHOUSE ~

Contrada di Gangivecchio, 90024 Gangi, Palermo
TEL and **FAX** 0921 689191
EMAIL paolotornabene@interfree.it **WEBSITE** www.tenutagangivecchio.com

IF YOU WANT PEACE AND SECLUSION, then look no further than this converted 13thC monastery, reached after a long drive through the beautiful Madonie region. The home of the Tornabene family for generations, the monastery lies at the bottom of a steep valley, hidden behind tall wooden doors that open to reveal a magnificent courtyard and magical buildings. First came a restaurant in the monastery itself whose reputation for marvellous Sunday lunches soon spread far and wide; the restaurant and its reputation are still thriving. Some years later, the stables were converted into guest accomodation, now run by Paolo Tornabene. If you expected to be sleeping in the monastery, you will be disappointed, but the good-sized, simple rooms with their red-tiled floors, country antiques and pretty bedspreads are not without rustic appeal. Recently a suite has been added in the monastery building itself. The guest wing has its own dining room looking on to the garden where imaginative variations on typical Sicilian dishes using mainly home grown ingredients are served. There is no choice on the menus, so warn the 'laconic' Si. Tornabene in advance of any individual requirements. Our reporter found that the Tenuta was, in many ways, 'a very special place' and offered excellent value for money.

NEARBY Gangi (6 km); Madonie region.
LOCATION 130 km SE of Palermo. Exit the A19 autostrada at Tre Monzelli, follow the SS120 to Petralia and then Gangi. Just after the town sign for Gangi, turn right and follow signs for Tenuta Gangivecchio; the Tenuta is after 5 km on the right; car parking
FOOD breakfast, lunch, dinner
PRICE €
ROOMS 10, 9 double and triple with shower and 1 suite with bath; all rooms have phone
FACILITIES dining room, restaurant, sitting rooms, swimming pool, table tennis, mountain bikes, horse riding
CREDIT CARDS AE, MC, V **DISABLED** not suitable **PETS** not accepted **CLOSED** July
PROPRIETOR Paolo Tornabene

SICILY

RAGUSA

EREMO DELLA GIUBLIANA
~ COUNTRY HOTEL ~

Contrada Giubiliana, S.P. per Marina di Ragusa, 97100 Ragusa
TEL 0932 669119 **FAX** 0932 623891
EMAIL info@eremodellagiubiliana.it **WEBSITE** www.eremodellagiubiliana.it

IF YOU ARE TOURING BY CAR, this small, elegant hotel is well worth a detour. Alternatively, you can fly to the hotel's private airfield, from where you can also take sightseeing trips as far away as Malta or Tunisia.

The setting - far away from major roads in a pastoral landscape of rolling farmland cut by white lanes and stone walls where the dominant sound is birdsong - is idyllic. The hotel has been the home of the Nifosì family since the 18th century. Built as a fortified convent in the 15th century, it was later used by the Knights of the Order of St John on their way to Malta. In converting the convent, Signor Nifosì, an architect, has made every effort to preserve the building's original structure, retaining the original pitch and limestone floors and transforming the monks' cells into comfortable and stylish bedrooms with modern bathrooms. A recent addition is a delightful little walled garden filled with exotic Mediterranean trees and shrubs; there is small pool and bar - bliss in the summer heat.

Food is important at the Eremo; the restaurant serves unpretentious dishes from the Sicilian highlands using home grown organic produce and accompanied by a fine selection of local wines.

~

NEARBY Ragusa (7 km); private beach (8 km).
LOCATION signposted off the road from Ragusa to Marina di Ragusa; ample car parking
FOOD breakfast, lunch, dinner
PRICE €€€
ROOMS 13; 10 double, 3 suites and 5 self-catering cottages, all with bath or shower; all rooms have phone, TV, hairdrier
FACILITIES sitting room, dining room, terrace, garden, swimming pool, mountain bikes, shuttle to Ragusa and the beach
CREDIT CARDS AE, DC, MC, V
DISABLED one adapted room **PETS** accepted
CLOSED never
PROPRIETOR Salvatore Mancini Nifosi

SICILY THE ISLANDS

SIRACUSA

GUTKOWSKI

~ CITY GUESTHOUSE ~

Lungomare Vittorini 26, 96100 Siracusa
TEL 0931 465861 **Fax** 0931 480505
E-MAIL info@guthotel.it **WEBSITE** www.guthotel.it

THE THRIVING METROPOLIS of Magna Grecia, Siracusa was one of the most important cities in the Western world for over a thousand years. The spiritual heart of the city still lies in the island of Ortigia, today joined to the mainland by two bridges. Occupying an old fisherman's house overlooking the sea on the northeast corner of the island, the delightful Gutkowski makes a great base for exploring and is a refreshing change from sometimes heavy-handed traditional Sicilian style. It is painted sea blue (the only blue building on the island) with white trim around the tall windows; inside, the same summer colours prevail and all is fresh, clean and airy. Downstaris, the small breakfast room has a pretty tiled floor while a fire burns in the sitting room in cool weather. Reports praise the 'fabulous' breakfast which features home made almond granita in summer plus all sorts of home made jams, preserves and cakes served on fine china. The bedrooms are quite spartan yet stylish and comfortable. Again, natural colours dominate enhanced by the sun filtering through filmy white curtains; the five at the front of the house have small balconies overlooking the sea. Eleven rooms in a nearby (more modern) annexe have recently been added.

~

NEARBY sights of Ortigia; ginnasio Romano.
LOCATION on north east part of island; on road with limited parking
FOOD breakfast
PRICE €
ROOMS 25; 3 singles, 19 doubles and twins, 3 triples, all with bath or shower; all rooms have phone, TV, air conditioning, minibar, hairdrier (some)
FACILITIES sitting room, breakfast room, small terrace
CREDIT CARDS AE, DC, MC, V
DISABLED 2 adapted rooms
PETS accepted
CLOSED never
PROPRIETORS Paola Pretsch

SICILY

SIRACUSA

LIMONETO
~ COUNTRY GUESTHOUSE ~

Via del Platano 3, 96100 Siracusa
TEL 0931 717352 **FAX** 0931 717728
E-MAIL limoneto@tin.it **WEBSITE** www.emmeti.it/limoneto

IF YOU WANT TO VISIT the fascinating city of Siracusa but stay in the countryside, we can recommend this simple agriturismo. Run by the Norcia family, Limoneto is an organic farm producing citrus fruits, vegetables, olive oil and wine. The solid, white-painted main house is set among orange and lemon groves; the scent from the citrus blossoms in spring is quite intoxicating.

The welcome here is very Southern Italian; warm and genuine with guests being treated as part of the family. Some of the bedrooms are in the main house while others are in a renovated barn; some are large enough for a family. Though modern rather than characterful, they are 'comfortable fresh and spotlessly clean'. The main focus of any stay at the Limoneto, however, is definitely the food which, judging by reports, is fabulous; 'the best we had'. Adelina Norcia's no-choice Sicilian menus change daily and feature much of what is grown on the farm. Finish off with a glass of ice-cold home-brewed limoncello.

We would welcome more reports about this hotel; although we have included it for some years now (urged by reader's recommendations), we have not yet managed a personal visit. But we like the sound of it very much.

NEARBY Siracusa (9 km); Noto (25 km).
LOCATION 9 km W of Siracusa, off route 14 to Palazzolo, in own grounds; with car parking
FOOD breakfast, lunch, dinner
PRICE €
ROOMS 8; 2 double, 3 triple and 3 family rooms all with shower or bath; all rooms have phone
FACILITIES sitting room, dining room, terrace, garden
CREDIT CARDS not accepted
DISABLED no special facilities **PETS** accepted
CLOSED never
PROPRIETORS Norcia family

SICILY

TAORMINA

VILLA BELVEDERE
~ SEASIDE VILLA ~

Via Bagnoli Croce 79, 98039 Taormina, Messina
Tel 0942 23791 **Fax** 0942 625830
E-MAIL info@villabelvedere.it **WEBSITE** www.villabelvedere.it

THE BELVEDERE IS A REFRESHINGLY unpretentious, discreet and welcoming hotel, one of the first to be built in Taormina (in 1902). It has been in the Pécaut family ever since, and subsequent generations have managed to make their changes without altering the inherent charm of the place, Currently in charge are brother and sister Silena and Christian and their mother, all helpful and friendly.

As you would expect from its name, the Belvedere's greatest asset is its position. Close to the centre of town, near the public garden, it commands a spectacular panorama of the bay and the slopes of Etna to the south. Flowery gardens lead down to a small, delightful swimming pool where the setting and the poolside bar (serving light meals and Sicilian regional dishes) tempt guests to linger all day and postpone the more serious business of sightseeing. Arrangements can also be made to take guests to and from local beaches.

There is no proper dining room, but plenty of choice amongst restaurants in Taormina. And the hotel does have two prettily furnished sitting rooms, and a sunny breakfast room. All in all a sound choice for a reasonably priced family hotel, warmly endorsed by a recent reporter who also mentioned the 'slick valet parking (parking is at a premium in the town)' and the 'clean bright bedrooms with stunning views from the balconies'.

~

NEARBY Greek theatre; Corso Umberto, public gardens.
LOCATION next to the Belvedere of the Via Roma, close to public gardens and old town; with car parking
FOOD breakfast, light lunch
PRICE €€
ROOMS 52, 50 doubles and 2 garden suites, all with bath or shower; all rooms have phone, satellite TV, air conditioning, safe, hairdrier
FACILITIES 2 sitting areas, 2 bars, breakfast room, TV room, terrace, garden, swimming pool, poolside snack bar **CREDIT CARDS** MC, V **DISABLED** no special facilities **PETS** accepted **CLOSED** mid-Mar **PROPRIETORS** The Pécaut family

SICILY

TAORMINA

VILLA DUCALE
~ HILLTOP VILLA ~

Via Leonardo da Vinci 60, 98039 Taormina , Messina
TEL 0942 28153 **FAX** 0942 28710
E-MAIL villaducale@tao.it **WEBSITE** www.hotelvilladucale.it

I**T'S HARD TO FAULT** VILLA DUCALE. Originally a coaching inn, it was convert-ed into a patrician home at the turn of the century by the great-grandfa-ther of the present owner, Andrea Quartucci. In 1993, he and his wife opened the house to guests and their new venture was an instant success. Why? Because of the wonderful terrace, the feel of a family home, the unexpected, special touches and the friendliness of the staff.

No two rooms are alike (try for one with a private terrace), but they all have fine linen on the beds, billowing curtains and terrazzo floors, painted furniture and pretty bedheads; in one junior suite is the painted bed, inlaid with mother-of-pearl, of Andrea's grandparents. Many walls are dec-orated with *trompe l'oeil* or with fruit, a symbol of richness in Sicily.

Perhaps the real quality of Villa Ducale comes through best at break-fast, served until 11.30 am. You won't easily forget sitting on the broad bal-cony, the table before you laden with fruit, local cheeses, specially baked bread and Sicilian iced cakes, with its amazing view across the town, the bay and Mount Etna. Sipping a drink there at sunset is pretty romantic, too. A recent ecstatic report from a reader only confirms our enthusiasm.

~

NEARBY Greek theatre; Corso Umberto; excursions to Etna.
LOCATION above town centre, on road to Castelmola; limited car parking
FOOD breakfast, light snacks
PRICE €€€
ROOMS 18; 13 double and twin, 5 suites, all with bath; all rooms have phone, TV, air conditioning, minibar, hairdrier
FACILITIES sitting room, library, bar, breakfast room, terrace, hot tub, free shuttle to beaches
CREDIT CARDS AE, DC, MC, V
DISABLED access difficult
PETS accepted
CLOSED early Dec–mid Feb
PROPRIETORS Dr Andrea and Rosaria Quartucci

SICILY

VILLA PARADISO
~ SEASIDE HOTEL ~

Via Roma 2, 98039 Taormina , Messina
TEL 0942 23921 **FAX** 0942 625800
E-MAIL hotelparadiso@tao.it **WEBSITE** www.hotelvillaparadisotaormina.com

NEXT TO THE PUBLIC GARDENS and close to the heart of historic Taormina, the Villa Paradiso also has the advantage of a glorious panorama along the coast and across to the hazy cone of Etna. The only drawback to the location is that it is on a main road, which means some noise for back rooms and major problems with parking in high season.

The hotel is a well-maintained white building, and the public rooms have all the style and atmosphere of a private villa: white arches, patterned carpets on tiled floors, stylish sofas and an imaginative collection of prints, paintings and watercolours. The restaurant makes the most of the views, and the food is distinctly above average. Every bedroom has a balcony, and inevitably the most sought-after are those at the front with sea views. The majority are larger than you would expect from a *pensione;* some have attractive painted furniture. You can reach the beaches by cable car or – more conveniently – the hotel minibus, which takes you to the Paradise Beach Club in Letojanni (free facilities for guests from end of May till the end of October).

~

NEARBY Greek theatre, Corso Umberto and public gardens; excursions to Etna.
LOCATION on SE edge of town; small public car park next door, paying garage nearby
FOOD breakfast, dinner
PRICE €
ROOMS 38; 25 double and twin, 13 junior suites, all with bath; all rooms have phone, TV, air conditioning, hairdrier
FACILITIES 2 sitting rooms, dining room, bar, terrace
CREDIT CARDS AE, DC, MC, V
DISABLED access possible
PETS accepted
CLOSED never
PROPRIETOR Salvatore Martorana

SARDINIA/SICILY

FORESTERIA BAGLIO DELLA LUNA
COUNTRY VILLA

Contrada Maddalusa, 92100 Agrigento

TEL 0922 511061 **FAX** 0922 598802
EMAIL info@bagliodellaluna.com
WEBSITE www.bagliodellaluna.com
FOOD breakfast, lunch, dinner
PRICE €€ **CLOSED** never
PROPRIETOR Ignazio Altieri

SITUATED AT ONE end of Agrigento's Valle dei Templi, this useful hotel occupies a Baglio dating from the 13th century and dominated by a sturdy square tower. Recent restoration has rendered the interior a little characterless, but the public rooms, contained in the tower, are furnished in traditional Sicilian style as are the bedrooms. The banal suites are over-priced for what they are while standards are unpretentiously decorated with floral prints and coloured ceramic floor tiles; bathrooms are fairly basic. Creative renditions of Sicilian and regional Italian dishes are offered in the restaurant; in summer, meals are served on a terrace overlooking the temples.

DON DIEGO
RESORT HOTEL

Porto San Paolo, Costa Dorata, 07020 Vaccileddi, Sassari

TEL 0789 40006/4007
FAX 0789 40026
EMAIL hoteldondiego@tiscali.it
WEBSITE hoteldondiego.com
FOOD breakfast, lunch, dinner
PRICE €€€€€
CLOSED Oct to Apr
MANAGER Luigi Mennella

DESPITE A READER'S REPORT criticizing the pool and beach for being dirty, the Don Diego keeps its place in these pages on account of its sheer charm. It stands in a secluded position south of Olbia on the Costa Dorata, a quieter stretch of coastline than the Costa Smeralda, with many coves and beaches. The hotel, of typical Sardinian design, consists of airy, comfortable and stylish single-storey cottages scattered amongst the *macchia* and pine trees. Double bedrooms are located further away from the main building than the junior suites, which enjoy sea views (though they may be obscured by vegetation). From the lovely curving sea-water swimming pool there are views across to the islands of Molara and, close by, Tavolara.

SICILY

ERICE

ELIMO
TOWN HOTEL

*Via Vittorio Emanuele 75, 91016
Erice, Trapani*

TEL and **FAX** 0923 869377
EMAIL elimoh@comeg.it
WEBSITE www.charmerlax.com
FOOD breakfast, lunch, dinner
PRICE €€
CLOSED never
PROPRIETORS Tilotta family

SITUATED IN THE SAME STREET as
the Moderno (see page 315) the Elimo makes an excellent alternative.
One of our reporters described it as 'a happy mixture of traditional and
modern, with attractive public rooms, individual bedrooms, a rooftop terrace and a pretty courtyard'. A more recent visitor endorses this view. The
Elimo is a simple, straightforward hotel with no pretensions – but well
run. Public rooms consist of a combined lobby, bar and small sitting area
with a homely feel, and a dining room where fairly plain dishes are served
(breakfast is basic). Bedrooms are clean, modern and simple, not too
small, with functional but acceptable bathrooms. Some have views over
the roof to the sea beyond.

MODICA

L'ORANGERIE
TOWN GUEST HOUSE

*Vico de Naro 5, 97015 Modica,
Ragusa*

TEL 347 0674698
EMAIL info@lorangerie.it
WEBSITE www.lorangerie.it
FOOD breakfast
PRICE €
CLOSED never
PROPRIETORS Dott. Guglielmo
Antonio Cartia

AMONG THE FADED Baroque splendour of Modica bassa and housed in an
elegant 19th century palazzo is the delightful Orangerie. Elegant,
stylish simplicity are the watch words here; the 3 self-catering apartments and four double rooms all have hard wood floors and strong
colours on the walls. They are sparingly but comfortably furnished with
fine antique or déco pieces; several have painted ceilings. Some rooms
have a pretty, flower-filled terrace while others look over a garden filled
with lemon trees. Breakfast is served in the old-fashioned kitchen
around a big table. For dinner, try the imaginative food at the Fattoria
delle Torri just around the corner.

SICILY

SIRACUSA

GRAND HOTEL
LUXURY TOWN HOTEL

Viale Mazzini 12, 96100 Siracusa

TEL 0931 464600 **FAX** 0931 464611
EMAIL info@grandhotelss.it
WEBSITE www.grandhotelss.it
FOOD breakfast, lunch, dinner;
room service
PRICE €€€
CLOSED never
MANAGER Signor Bambara

SITUATED IN THE OLD PART of Siracusa on the island of Ortigia, the Grand Hotel is a splendid example of a luxurious, but not exorbitant, Mediterranean hotel. You are greeted by a cool and elegant reception area with circular marble stairs and bronze sculpture. Other public rooms are clad in marble, stained glass, and crystal, mixing modern art and furnishings with antiques. Bedrooms, are luxurious and thoughtfully equipped. There is a bar in the old pale stone-walled cistern and a sophisticated roof garden restaurant, with magnificent views of the Grand Harbour and seafront. It may not be charming and small, but the Grand makes a good base in the centre of Siracusa.

VALDERICE

BAGLIO SANTACROCE
COUNTRY HOTEL

91019 Valderice, Trapani

TEL 0923 891111
FAX 0923 891192
EMAIL baglio-santacroce@ibero.it
WEBSITE www.bagliosantacroce.it
FOOD breakfast, lunch, dinner
PRICE €€
CLOSED never
PROPRIETORS Cusenza family

LOCATED IN THE ERICE FOOTHILLS, on the outskirts of Valderice, this is a family-owned and run hotel set in a predominantly stone farmhouse dating back to 1636. With its central courtyard, thick bare stone walls (in both bedrooms and bathrooms), terracotta tiled floors and beamed ceilings, the hotel has a rustic, countrified feel – except for the annexe bar and dining room. Our original inspector liked this hotel, at least the old part, but recent guests have been disappointed by the plumbing. Breakfast is standard hotel fare, but the dinners, especially the fish, are above average. There is a small swimming pool, with superb views to the Gulf of Cornino and Mount Cofano, and the gardens are very peaceful.

Hotel Names

In this index, hotels are arranged in order of the first distinctive part of their names. Very common prefixes such as 'Hotel', 'Albergo', 'Il', 'La', 'Dei' and 'Delle' are omitted. More descriptive words such as 'Casa', 'Castello', 'Locanda' and 'Villa' are included.

HOTEL NAMES

HOTEL NAMES

Hotel Names

HOTEL LOCATIONS

In this index, hotels are arranged in order of the names of the cities, towns or villages they are in or near. Hotels located in a very small village may be indexed under a larger place nearby. An index by hotel name precedes this one.

Hotel Locations

HOTEL LOCATIONS

Hotel Locations

SPECIAL OFFERS

Buy your *Charming Small Hotel Guide* by post directly from the publisher and you'll get a worthwhile discount. *

Titles available:	Retail price	Discount price
Austria	£10.99	£9.50
Britain	£12.99	£11.50
France	£11.99	£10.50
France: Bed & Breakfast	£10.99	£9.50
Germany	£11.99	£10.50
Greece	£10.99	£9.50
Ireland	£9.99	£8.50
Italy	£11.99	£10.50
Mallorca, Menorca & Ibiza	£9.99	£8.50
Southern France	£10.99	£9.50
Spain	£11.99	£10.50
Switzerland	£9.99	£8.50
USA: New England	£10.99	£9.50
Venice and North-East Italy	£10.99	£9.50

Please send your order to:

Book Sales,

Duncan Petersen Publishing Ltd,

31 Ceylon Road, London W14 OPY

enclosing: 1) the title you require and number of copies

2) your name and address

3) your cheque made out to:

Duncan Petersen Publishing Ltd

*Offer applies to this edition and to UK only.

Visit charmingsmallhotels.co.uk
Our website has expanded enormously since
its launch and continues to grow. It's the
best research tool on the web for our kind of
hotel.

Exchange rates
As we went to press, $1 bought 1.25 euros and
£1 bought 1.47 euros